T H E
ODYSSEY
A New Verse Translation

IN NORTON PAPERBACK EDITIONS

The Illiad, a shortened version, translated and edited by I. A. Richards
The Odyssey, a new verse translation by Albert Cook
The Odyssey, a new verse translation by Albert Cook (Norton Critical Edition,
    with backgrounds, sources, and criticism)
The Homeric Hymns, translated by Thelma Sargent

HOMER ✠✠✠ THE
ODYSSEY

A NEW VERSE TRANSLATION BY

Albert Cook

W · W · NORTON & COMPANY

New York · London

W. W. Norton & Company, Inc., 500 Fifth Avenue, New York, N.Y. 10110
W. W. Norton & Company Ltd., 10 Coptic Street, London, WC1A 1PU

ISBN 0-393-00744-8

9 0

To my sons David, Daniel, and Jonathan,
joyful companions of our odyssey

CONTENTS

PREFACE

To HEAR AND RE-CREATE the sound and sense of his original is always the task of the translator, whether of the impressionist or the literalist camp. Except when the sense of the original is tied up in lost or unsurfaceable data (the jokes of Aristophanes), or when the sound is so elaborately structured as to be wholly inimitable (*The Divine Comedy*, or possibly any case of regular rhyme), there is no reason why the literalist cannot aspire to as full a re-creation as the impressionist—and therefore to a fuller one, since he has the advantage of confining himself to bringing over as much of the designative sense as possible. Of course he too misses by a considerable margin; and of course he faces any translator's problem of catching the flow of overtones and sequences of sense—and of sound.

For both sound and sense, the Homeric line is a unit, and this literal translation seeks as its major goal to preserve that crucial unit in its integrity while trying to catch something of Homer's flow. A line with a syllabic base (almost always in the range of twelve to seventeen syllables) is one possible option for an equivalent to the Homeric hexameter.

For sense, the heavily formulaic character of Homer recommends that one render words, lines, and phrases as nearly identically as possible. This conviction suggests that one should not opt for a variety in translating *kalos* ("fine," "beautiful," "lovely," "pretty," "fair," and so on) but choose one and stick to it most of the time. I chose "lovely." The English words "ocean" and "sea" must do duty for more than two Homeric words; and the translator is forced, if he would utilize both, to overlook the fact that the proper name "Ocean" in Homer designates something special. Distinguishing *Okeanos* by a slightly Anglicized proper name "Oceanos" [1] and rendering *pontos* as "ocean"

1. My middle-of-the-road position on spelling Greek names results in a mixture between Latin norm for English and true Greek transliteration. In this way I have tried to combine the familiarity of the Latin usage

seems preferable to calling it "sea" along with *hals* and *thalassa*, or to picking a metaphoric archaism like "the deep."

For *demos*, there are implications of a geographical "region," one sufficiently more restricted than a French *pays* for us to render the word "district." Sometimes the area is primarily meant, and "land" is the closest term; and sometimes the inhabitants, the "people," are primarily indicated. In this case I have settled for "district" as a normative use, and the other three when their emphases seemed the primary ones. English convention could be ignored in some cases. If *glaukopis* probably means "bright-eyed," [2] we can ignore the English tradition of rendering it "gray-eyed." And the same with the more hallowed "wine-dark," a rendering based on a specious phenomenological inference. There is no color word in the Greek.

The choices are not always easy of course. An obscure attribution of Hermes, *Argeiphontes*, presents three choices: "slayer of Argos," "the one who appears swiftly," or the opaque expression itself, *Argeiphontes*. On the hunch that the expression would not have sounded opaque to the normal reader of Homer in antiquity, I have followed the inclination of much contemporary opinion toward the first rendering.

Or again, in simple grammar, we get *theos*, masculine, "god," and *thea*, feminine, "goddess." What do we do with *theos*, with or (more usually) without feminine adjective when it is applied to a goddess? The distinction between *thea* and *theos*, confined almost exclusively to Homer, is an elusive one not to be accounted for wholly by metrical convenience. Unless the translator is prepared to identify *thea* and *theos* as "goddess," he is forced to strengthen the common-gender tinge of "god" and use that one word for the one word *theos*, masculine or feminine. "God" does sound a little odd when applied to a female immortal; *theos* is rare enough in the feminine to have struck an ancient reader as comparably odd.

The literalist provides the reader, or at least the student, with

---

with the Hellenic flavor of a Greekish new-spelling. Hitting between *Oceanus*, or merely *Ocean*, on the Latin side, and *Okeanos* on the Greek, I have produced *Oceanos*, a case I am less happy with than I am with *Telemachos* for the young man who has been known for centuries in English as *Telemachus*. But I believe the principle of combination (producing usually a Latin-like base and a Greek-like termination) is fairly consistent.

2. Manu Leumann, *Homerische Wörter* (Basel, 1950), pp. 148-152.

the comfortable assurance that for the vast designative tapestry of the original a pink thread may sometimes do duty for a red one, or a blurred one for a blurred one—but never a blue one for a red one, and never a polychrome burst for a single color of the original. The impressionist, on the other hand, for all the rationales he can muster, can never free himself of the charge leveled by T. S. Eliot at Gilbert Murray (who translates rather more literally than most of the impressionists now active): "So here are two striking phrases which we owe to Mr. Murray; It is he who has sapped our soul and shattered the cup of all life for Euripides. . . . Professor Murray has simply interposed between Euripides and ourselves a barrier more impenetrable than the Greek language."

Any rendering builds a wall. One can only hope to build a translucent one. We always need masonry, but also bricks that are translucent to begin with.

ALBERT COOK

ACKNOWLEDGMENTS

FEW PEOPLE who prepare a translation can have had as much astute help as I. Especially am I indebted to Edwin Dolin, William Chase Greene, Flora Levin, and Joseph Russo, each of whom read the entire work with close attention to the Greek. From each of them I have adopted scores of suggestions (not to mention corrections). Many others have provided equally valuable comment for smaller portions of the manuscript, among them John Finley, James Hutton, and Bernard Knox. My research assistant for 1965–66, Stephen Rodefer, also provided many suggestions for improved phrasing, in addition to carrying through technical details of preparing the manuscript, and Mark Riley compiled the Glossary.

Of the several typists who worked for me at various stages, I am particularly grateful to Cathy Freeman and Virginia White.

My Fulbright grant to Austria in 1960–61, although a teaching appointment, provided me with extra time to finish an early draft. And my work on later versions was furthered by the liberality with which the State University of New York allowed me research time while administering the English Department from 1963-66. Finally, I am grateful for having been able to refine my last draft in the stimulating leisure of a Fellowship at the Center for Advanced Study in the Behavioral Sciences.

THE
ODYSSEY
A New Verse Translation

I

Tell me, Muse, about the man of many turns, who many
Ways wandered when he had sacked Troy's holy citadel;
He saw the cities of many men, and he knew their thought;
On the ocean he suffered many pains within his heart,
Striving for his life and his companions' return.   5
But he did not save his companions, though he wanted to:
They lost their own lives because of their recklessness.
The fools, they devoured the cattle of Hyperion,
The Sun, and he took away the day of their return.
Begin the tale somewhere for us also, goddess, daughter of Zeus.[1] 10
Then all the others, as many as escaped sheer destruction,
Were at home, having fled both the war and the sea.
Yet he alone, longing for his wife and for a return,
Was held back in a hollowed cave by the queenly nymph
    Calypso,[2]
The divine goddess, who was eager for him to be her husband.   15
But when in the circling seasons the year came around,
The gods spun the thread for him to return to his home,
To Ithaca; and he did not escape struggle there either,
Even among his dear ones. All the gods pitied him,
Except Poseidon,[3] who contended unremittingly   20
With godlike Odysseus, till the man reached his own land.
But the god had gone to the far-off Ethiopians—
The Ethiopians, remotest of men, divided asunder,
Some where Hyperion sets, and some where he rises.
He was taking part in the sacrifice of bulls and rams,   25
And enjoyed being present at a feast there. The others
Were gathered together in the halls of Olympian Zeus.

1. I.e., the muse of epic poetry. Zeus, the son of Cronos, was king of the
gods and specifically the god of the sky and of weather.
2. Daughter of Atlas.
3. Son of Cronos and brother of Zeus; god of the sea, especially hostile
toward Odysseus.

The father of men and gods began to speak among them.
In his heart he was remembering excellent Aigisthos [4]
30 Whom Agamemnon's son, far-famed Orestes,[5] had slain.
Thinking of that man, he made his speech to the immortals:
"Well now, how indeed mortal men do blame the gods!
They say it is from us evils come, yet they themselves
By their own recklessness have pains beyond their lot.
35 So this Aigisthos married beyond his lot the lawful
Wife of the son of Atreus, and killed him on his return;
Knowing he would be destroyed, since we told him beforehand:
We had sent sharp-eyed Hermes, the slayer of Argos,[6]
To tell him not to kill the man and not to woo his wife,
Or payment would come through Orestes, descendant of
40   Atreus,
As soon as he came of age and longed for his own land.
So Hermes told him; but, though of good mind himself, he
    did not
Change Aigisthos' mind. And now he has paid for it all."
Then the bright-eyed goddess Athene [7] answered him:
45 "Our father, son of Cronos,[8] highest of all rulers,
As for that man, he surely lies in a fitting death.
May anyone else also perish who would do such deeds.
But the heart within me is torn over skillful Odysseus,
The hard-fated man, who long suffers griefs far from his dear
    ones
50 On a flood-circled island where the navel of the sea is.
The island is wooded, a goddess there has her dwelling,
The daughter of destruction-minded Atlas,[9] who knows
The depths of the whole sea, and holds up by himself
The enormous pillars that hold apart earth and heaven.
55 His daughter has kept back the wretched and grieving man,
And perpetually, with tender and wheedling speeches,

4. Cousin of Agamemnon and lover of Clytemnestra; after Agamemnon's
murder he became king of Mycenae.
5. Agamemnon was leader of the Greeks at Troy; killed by Clytemnestra
on his return home; Orestes killed Clytemnestra and Aigisthos to avenge
his father's murder.
6. Hermes was son of Zeus; messenger of the gods and guide of the dead.
The obscure compound *Argeiphontes* could also mean "appear rapidly" or
"appear brightly."
7. Goddess of reason and the arts and special patron of Odysseus.
8. One of the older gods; the father of Zeus, Poseidon, Hera, Hades.
9. The supporter of the pillars of heaven.

She charms him to forget Ithaca. Odysseus, however,
Wanting to catch sight even of smoke leaping up
From his land, is longing to die. But your own heart
Does not turn toward it, Olympian one. Did Odysseus   60
Not please you in broad Troy by the ships of the Argives
When he made sacrifice? Why, then, are you so angry at him,
   Zeus?"
In answer to her, cloud-gathering Zeus spoke out:
"My child, what sort of word has got past the bar of your teeth?
How could I at any time forget godlike Odysseus,   65
Who stands out among mortals for thought, and for the
   sacrifices
He has given the immortal gods who possess broad heaven?
But Poseidon, who girdles the earth, remains obstinately
Enraged about the Cyclops whom he blinded in the eye,
Godlike Polyphemos, who possesses the greatest strength   70
Of all the Cyclopes.[1] The nymph Thoosa gave him birth,
The daughter of Phorcys,[2] ruler over the barren sea,
In hollow caves, after she had lain with Poseidon.
For that, to be sure, earth-shaking Poseidon has not
Killed Odysseus but does make him wander far from his
   homeland.   75
Well, come now, let all of us here carefully devise
His return, so he may arrive; and Poseidon will slacken
His rage, for counter to all the immortals he cannot
Carry on strife alone against the will of the gods."
Then the bright-eyed goddess Athene answered him: 80
"Our father, son of Cronos, highest of all rulers,
If this course is now really dear to the blessed gods,
That many-minded Odysseus return to his own home,
Then let us urge on the runner Hermes, slayer of Argos,
To the island of Ogygia,[3] in order that with all speed   85
He may tell the fair-braided nymph an unerring plan
For the return of stout-hearted Odysseus, so he may go back.
And I myself will go to Ithaca, so that I the better
May urge his son on and place a strength in his mind

1. A lawless race of giants met by Odysseus.
2. A lesser sea divinity.
3. The legendary island home of Calypso.

⁹⁰ To call the long-haired Achaians [4] into an assembly
And to speak out to all the suitors, who are always slaying
His throngs of sheep, and his shamble-footed, crumple-horned
     cattle.
I shall send him on to Sparta, and also to sandy Pylos,
To learn of his dear father's return, if he may hear somehow,
⁹⁵ And so a noble renown among men may belong to him."
When she had said this, she bound under her feet the lovely
     sandals,
The ambrosial golden ones that bear her either over water
Or over the limitless land swift as blasts of the wind.
She grasped the valiant spear, pointed with sharp bronze,
Ponderous, big, and stout, with which she daunts the ranks
¹⁰⁰   of men,
Of heroes at whom she is angry, the daughter of a mighty father,
She went down in a rush from the summits of Olympos
     and stood
In the district of Ithaca before Odysseus' gates
At the courtyard threshold. In her fist she held the bronze spear,
¹⁰⁵ Likening herself to a stranger, the Taphian leader Mentes.
She came upon the bold suitors. They at the moment
Were delighting their hearts with a diceboard before the doors,
Seated on the skins of oxen they had killed themselves.
Heralds attended on them, and capable servants also;
¹¹⁰ Some of these were mixing wine and water in bowls.
Others were cleaning off the tables with porous sponges,
And setting them, and dividing up the meat in many pieces.
Godlike Telemachos was by far the first to see her,
For he sat among the suitors, crushed in his own heart,
¹¹⁵ Seeing his noble father in his mind, if from somewhere
He would come and make those suitors scatter through the
     halls,
So that he himself might have honor and command his own
     goods.
Thinking this over while seated with the suitors, he sighted
     Athene.
He went straight to the gate, and he resented in his heart
¹²⁰ That the stranger stood so long at the door. Standing near her
He took her right hand and received the bronze spear;

---

4. A collective appellation of the Greeks besieging Troy.

Speaking out to her, he uttered wingèd words:
"Greetings, stranger, you shall be welcomed among us. And
     when
You have eaten dinner, you will tell what it is you need."
When he had said that, he led on, and Pallas [5] Athene followed.   125
And when they had got inside of the lofty house,
He stood the spear he was carrying against the long pillar
Inside the well-polished spearcase, where many other
Spears of stout-hearted Odysseus were also standing.
He led her on and seated her in an armchair, spreading
     linen beneath,   130
Lovely and skillfully wrought. A stool was under her feet.
He placed a broidered seat alongside, apart from the others,
The suitors, lest the stranger might be disturbed at the uproar
When mingling with the insolent, and lose appetite for dinner,
And so he might ask her of the father who had gone away.   135
A handmaid poured water from a pitcher she was carrying,
A lovely golden one, over into a silver basin,
For washing the hands; she set up a polished table alongside.
A respected housekeeper served bread she was carrying,
Laying out many dishes, gracious with the provisions.   140
A carver lifted up and set out trenchers of meats
Of all sorts, and set out gold goblets alongside for them.
A herald served them attentively, pouring out the wine.
The bold suitors came in. And then they themselves
Sat down one after another in seats and in armchairs.   145
Heralds were pouring water for them over their hands.
And serving maids were heaping bread up on trays.
Young men were filling bowls up to the brim for drinking,
They stretched forth their hands to the food that was spread
     out ready.
But when the suitors had taken their fill of food and drink,   150
Other matters came to their minds for attention:
Singing and dancing, which are the graces of a banquet.
Into Phemios' [6] hands a herald placed a lyre
Of supreme beauty; he sang for the suitors under compulsion.
Playing his instrument, he struck up a lovely song.   155
Telemachos, however, addressed bright-eyed Athene,
Holding his head close so that the others might not hear:

5. An epithet of Athene.
6. Son of Terpis ("Pleasure") and bard at Odysseus' palace.

"Dear stranger, will you resent it if I say something?
These men are concerned with this, the lyre and singing,
160 At their ease, since they devour scot-free another man's living,
A man whose white bones somewhere are rotting in the rain,
Lying on a shore, or a wave tumbles them in the sea.
If they ever see that man returning to Ithaca,
They will all pray to be nimbler on their feet
165 Rather than to be richer in clothing and in gold.
As it is, an evil fate has killed him, surely; there is
No comfort for us even if some one of the men on earth
Says he will come. The day of his return is lost.
But come now, tell me this, and explain truthfully:
170 What men are you from? Where are your city and parents?
On what sort of ship did you come? How did the sailors
Bring you to Ithaca? What men did they claim to be?
For I do not think you could have got here at all on foot.
Tell me this exactly, so that I may well know
175 Whether you come on a first visit or are a friend
Of my father's, since many other men come to our home,
And since he was himself well acquainted among men."
Then the bright-eyed goddess Athene addressed him:
"All right, then, I will tell you this quite truthfully.
180 I declare I am Mentes, son of skillful Anchialos,
And I rule over the Taphians, who are fond of rowing.
Just now I have come this way by ship, with companions,
Sailing on the wine-faced sea to men of alien tongue,
To Temese for bronze, and I carry glittering iron.
185 My vessel stands here by the fields far off from the city,
In the harbor of Reithron, below wooded Neion.
We declare we are guest friends of one another through our
     fathers
Originally; if you will, go and ask Laertes,[7]
The old warrior, who they say no longer comes
190 To the city, but suffers griefs off by himself on his field,
With an old servant woman, who serves him food and drink
Whenever a weariness overcomes his limbs
As he creeps along the knoll of the vine-bearing garden.
But I have come now because they said the man really was in
     the district,

7. Father of Odysseus and former king of Ithaca.

Your father. But him have the gods hindered on his journey.   195
The godly Odysseus has not yet died on the earth,
But he is still alive somewhere, held back on the broad ocean
On a flood-circled island, and troublesome men hold him,
Savages, who somehow keep him back against his will.
Well, I will now tell you a prophecy, how the immortals   200
Cast it in my heart, and how I think it will end,
Though I am not a prophet, and have no clear skill with
     birds.[8]
Not much longer now, surely, will he be away
From his dear fatherland; not even if iron bands hold him.
He will devise how to return, since he has many resources.   205
But come now, tell me this, and explain it truthfully,
If, big as you are, you are really the son of Odysseus himself.
You resemble him strangely in your head and your fine eyes,
Since we had contact quite often with one another
Before he embarked for Troy, where the other noblest   210
Men of the Argives were headed in their hollow ships.
Since then I have not seen Odysseus, nor has he seen me."
Then the sound-minded Telemachos answered her:
"All right, stranger, I shall speak quite truthfully.
My mother calls me the son of the man. But I myself   215
Do not know. No one has ever been certain of his father.
Ah, would that I were the fortunate son of some man
Whom old age came upon with all his possessions!
As it is, he has been the most ill-fated of mortal men,
The man they say I was born of, since you ask me this."   220
And then the bright-eyed goddess Athene addressed him:
"The gods have not set it down that your race hereafter
Be nameless, since Penelope bore such a man as you.
But come, tell me this, and explain it truthfully,
What feast, what gathering is this? What is your need here?   225
A banquet or a marriage? The guests have brought no share to it.
How overweening they seem to be, how presumptuous
To be feasting in the hall! A man with any sense
Who came on these shameful things would be angry to see
     them."
Then the sound-minded Telemachos answered her: 230

8. An augur would make divinations based on the behavior of birds, as
in Book 2, lines 146-60, and elsewhere.

"Stranger, since you ask me this and inquire about it,
This house was once supposed to be wealthy and blameless,
So long as that very man was still here in the district.
Now the gods have wished otherwise and decreed misfortune;
235 They have made that person vanish more completely than all
Men. No, I would not grieve this way if he had died,
If with his companions he had gone under in the land of the
　　Trojans,
Or in the arms of his friends, after he had wound up the war.
Then all the Achaians would have made him a funeral mound,
240 And he would have won great glory for his son, too, hereafter;
As it is, the storm winds have snatched him off without glory.
He is gone, vanished and unperceived, and has left me
Pains and laments. Yet I no longer moan and grieve for that man
Only, since the gods have fashioned other evil cares for me.
245 All of the noblemen who rule over the islands,
Dulichion and Samê and also wooded Zakynthos,
And all those who are masters in craggy Ithaca,
Are paying court to my mother and wearing down my home.
She neither refuses the hateful marriage nor can she
250 Make an end of it. But they are wasting my home away
As they devour it. Soon they will tear me to pieces myself."
Pallas Athene was greatly disturbed and spoke out to him:
"Ah well, you do need Odysseus who is gone away
Very much indeed, to lay hand to these shameless suitors.
255 Would that he came now to the outer doors of the house
And stood there with a helmet and a shield and two spears,
And were the sort of man he was when I first saw him
In our very own home drinking and taking his pleasure,
As he went from Ephyre, leaving Ilos the son of Mermeros.
260 Odysseus had traveled there upon a rapid ship
Seeking after a man-killing drug, so that he might
Smear bronze-tipped arrows with it, but the man did not
Give it, since he dreaded the ever-living gods.
But my father gave it to him; he loved him terribly.
265 As that sort of man might Odysseus contend with the suitors!
They would all be swift in their doom and bitter in marriage.
Well, all these matters lie in the laps of the gods,
Whether he will return and pay them off or not,
In his own halls. So I bid you to consider
270 In what way you may drive the suitors out of the hall.

Come now, pay attention and take note of my words:
Tomorrow call the Achaian warriors to assembly;
Make a declaration to all. Let the gods witness it.
Order the suitors to disperse to their own affairs.
And your mother, if her spirit urges her to marry,   275
Let her go back to the hall of her father who is great in power.
They will prepare a wedding and set in array
The many gifts that ought to go with a dear daughter.
For yourself, I strongly advise you, if you will listen,
To fit out the ship that is best with twenty oarsmen   280
And go in search of your father who has been gone so long,
On the chance some mortal may tell you of him, or you hear
    from Zeus
The voice that best of all brings report to men.
First go to Pylos and question the godly Nestor.[9]
From there go on to Sparta and blond Menelaos,[1]   285
Who has come back the last of the bronze-clad Achaians.
If you do hear your father is alive and will return,
Though worn down, you might bear out yet another year.
But if you hear that he is dead and exists no more,
Return home then to your own dear fatherland,   290
Heap up a monument for him, and perform the many
Rites that are fitting, and give your mother to a husband.
When you have accomplished all this and brought it to pass,
Then you may consider in your heart and in your mind
How you may slaughter the suitors in your halls,   295
Either by cunning or openly. There is really no need
To indulge in childishness. You are not that age.
Or have you not heard how much glory godly Orestes seized
Among all men when he killed his father's murderer,
The cunning Aigisthos, who killed his renowned father?   300
You too, my dear friend, since I see you are handsome and
    great;
Be brave, so that a man born in the future would praise you.
Well, by now I should be going down to my swift ship
And the companions who are impatiently awaiting me.
Be concerned yourself. Pay attention to my words."   305
Then the sound-minded Telemachos answered her:

9. The aged king of Pylos and chief adviser for the Greeks at Troy.
1. Brother of Agamemnon and husband of Helen; co-commander of the
Greeks at Troy.

"Stranger, you have spoken these friendly words wisely
Like a father to his son, and I shall never forget them.
Come now, wait a while, though you are eager for the journey,
310 So that once you are bathed, delighted in your own heart,
You may board your ship rejoicing in spirit, with a gift,
An honorable and lovely one that will be a keepsake
From me, of the kind that fond guest friends give each other."
Then the bright-eyed goddess Athene answered him:
315 "Do not hold me back now, longing as I am for the journey.
Whatever gift your own heart bids to you give me,
Give it to me to carry home when I return again.
And pick a lovely one. It will be worth the exchange to you."
Having spoken so, bright-eyed Athene went off.
320 She flew upward like a bird. Into his spirit
She had put strength and courage. She put him in mind
Of his father more than before. When he thought it over,
He was amazed in his spirit; he thought she was a god.
And at once the godlike mortal went toward the suitors.
325 A renowned singer was singing to them. They were sitting
In silence listening. He sang of the baleful return
Of the Achaians from Troy that Pallas Athene laid on them.
The daughter of Icarios, prudent Penelope,
From her upper chamber hearkened to the divine song.
330 She descended the lofty stairway from her dwelling,
Not alone, but two servants followed along with her.
And when the godly woman had come to the suitors,
She stood by the pillar of the stoutly fashioned roof,
Holding the glistening headbands before her cheeks.
335 A devoted servant maid stood near her on either side.
Then, weeping, she addressed the godlike singer:
"Phemios, you know many other ravishments for mortals,
The deeds of men and of gods that singers glorify.
Sing one of these as you sit among them. And let the men
340 Drink wine in silence. But stop singing this baleful song
Which forever wears away my own heart in my breast,
Since an unforgettable grief affects me heavily.
I long for a person so dear, remembering always
That man whose glory is wide through Greece and middle
    Argos."
345 Then the sound-minded Telemachos answered her:
"Mother, for what reason do you begrudge the trusty singer's

Giving pleasure with whatever his thought rouses in him? Singers
Are not guilty; I suppose Zeus is guilty, who gives
To bread-earning men, to each one as he wishes.
It is no wrong for this man to sing about the evil fate   350
Of the Danaans.[2] Men acclaim that song the most
Which has come round newest of all to those who hear it,
Let your mind and spirit resign you to listening.
Odysseus is not alone to have lost his day of return
In Troy. Many other mortals perished there also.   355
Well, come into the house, and apply yourself to work,
To the loom and the distaff, and give orders to your servants
To set at the work. This talk will concern all the men,
But me especially. For the power in the house is mine."
She was amazed at him, and back into the house she went.   360
The sound-minded speech of her son she took to heart.
She entered the upper chamber with her serving women,
And then wept for Odysseus, her dear husband, until
Bright-eyed Athene cast sweet sleep upon her eyelids.
The suitors were making a din through the shadowy halls.   365
They all gave voice to the prayer of lying in her bed.
Sound-minded Telemachos began speaking to them:
"Suitors of my mother, with your excessive insolence,
Let us now take our pleasure and dine. And let there be
No noise, since it is lovely to listen to a singer   370
Of the kind this one is, who resembles the gods in his voice.
And at dawn tomorrow let us all go and take our seats
In council, so that I may tell you something outright;
Get out of the halls and partake of other dinners,
Eating your own goods, visiting each other's homes.   375
And if it seems better and preferable to you
To consume one man's livelihood scot-free,
Waste on. But I shall call on the eternal gods for help,
So that Zeus may grant there to be acts of retribution,
And then scot-free within this house you may die."   380
So he said, and they all set their teeth on their lips
And wondered at Telemachos that he spoke so courageously.
Antinoos,[3] the son of Eupeithes, addressed him first:

2. The Greeks (Achaians) collectively; seen as descendants of a mythical king, Danaos.
3. The ringleader and most insolent of Penelope's suitors.

"Well, Telemachos, the gods themselves must be teaching you
385 To be presumptuous and speak courageously.
May the son of Cronos over sea-circled Ithaca
Not make you king, your paternal right by birth."
Sound-minded Telemachos addressed him in answer:
"Antinoos, even if you are offended at what I say,
390 Still I would wish this very thing done if Zeus were to give it.
Would you call this the worst thing to happen among men?
It would not be bad at all to be king. There comes at once
An opulent home for the man, and he is himself more honored.
Yes, there are also other kings of the Achaians,
395 Many in sea-circled Ithaca, young ones and old ones.
And one of them shall have this, since godly Odysseus is dead.
But as for me, I shall be lord over our household,
And over the servants whom godly Odysseus won for me."
Eurymachos, son of Polybos, addressed him in answer:
400 "Telemachos, all this lies in the laps of the gods,
Who of the Achaians shall rule in sea-circled Ithaca.
May you have your own possessions and be lord in your own
home.
May a man never come, while Ithaca is inhabited,
Who would tear your possessions away from you by force.
405 But I want to ask you, my brave man, about this stranger.
Where did the man come from, and what country did he claim
To be from? Where are his birthplace and his father's land?
Does he bring some message that your father is coming home?
Or did he come here seeking some personal need of his own?
410 He started up so, and went at once, nor did he wait
For us to find him out. Yet his face did not look like a
coward's."
Then sound-minded Telemachos addressed him in answer:
"Eurymachos, surely my father's return has been lost.
I put no trust in a message, wherever it comes from,
415 And I give no heed to any divination my mother
Might ask of a diviner, calling him to the hall.
The stranger is a guest friend of my father's from Taphos.
He declares he is Mentes, son of skillful Anchialos,
And he rules over the Taphians, who are fond of rowing."
420 So Telemachos said, but in his mind knew the immortal god.
The men turned then to dancing and delightful song
And took their pleasure, and waited for evening to come.

As they took their pleasure black evening came upon them.
Then they went away, each to his own home to sleep.
But Telemachos, where his bedroom was, built aloft   425
In the very lovely courtyard in a place with a view all around,
Went to bed pondering many things in his mind.
Eurycleia went in with him and carried the flaming torches,
The devoted daughter of Ops, Peisenor's son.
Laertes bought her once as one of his possessions   430
When she was still in her first youth; he gave twenty cattle for
    her,
And honored her the same as the devoted wife in the halls.
But he had never lain with her, for he feared his wife's wrath.
Going with him, she carried the flaming torches. She loved him
Most of all the servants, and had tended him as a child.   435
She opened up the doors of the stoutly fashioned bedroom.
He sat down on the bed and took off his soft tunic
And put it in the hands of the shrewd-minded old woman.
She folded up the tunic, put it in smooth order
And hung it on a peg beside the jointed bed.   440
Then she went out of the bedroom, drew the door shut with a
    ring
Of silver, and drew the bolt full length by its thong.
There all night long, wrapped up in the sheepskin,
He pondered in his mind the course that Athene had shown.

II

And when the early-born, rosy-fingered dawn appeared,
The dear son of Odysseus rose up out of his bed,
Put on his clothes, and set the sharp sword round his shoulder,
Bound the lovely sandals beneath his shining feet
5 And went on out of the bedroom, like a god to look at.
At once he ordered the heralds with their piercing voices
To summon the long-haired Achaians to an assembly.
The heralds made summons, and they gathered together quickly.
And when they were gathered and had come together
10 He went to the assembly and held his bronze spear in his fist—
Not alone, but the swift-footed dogs went along with him.
Moreover, Athene shed a divine grace around him.
The people all marveled at him as he was coming up.
He sat down in his father's seat, and the old men gave way.
15 Then the hero Aigyptios began to speak among them,
A man bent with age who knew numberless things.
He too had a dear son, who went with godlike Odysseus
In the hollow ships to Ilion[1] that abounds in horses,
The spearman Antiphos. But the savage Cyclops killed him
20 In his hollowed cave, and prepared him as his final meal.
Three other sons he had; one fell in with the suitors,
Eurynomos; and two stayed always on their father's lands.
But still he remembered the other one, in grief and sorrow.
For him he wept as he spoke and addressed the assembly:
25 "Listen to me now, Ithacans, in what I say.
Our assembly has not once met or sat in session
From the time godly Odysseus went off in the hollow ships.
And now who has called it together? And to which of the young men
Or of those who are older, has there come so great a need?
30 Has he heard some message about an army coming on

1. Another name for Troy.

That he might plainly tell us, since he was the first to hear it?
Does he declare and announce some other public matter?
Noble he seems to me, well favored. For him may Zeus
Bring about whatever good thing he desires in his mind."
So he said, and Odysseus' dear son was glad for his statement. 35
Nor did he stay seated longer but he felt a desire to speak.
He stood up in the midst of the assembly. The herald Peisenor,
Who was full of sound advice, put the scepter in his hand.
Then he began to speak, first addressing the old man:
"Old sir, this man is not far, you yourself shall soon know it, 40
He who gathered the people: it is I. The pain comes most to me.
I heard no message about an army coming on
That I might plainly tell you, since I was the first to hear it;
I declare and announce no other public matter
But my own need, that an evil has befallen my home,   45
And a double one: I lost my noble father, who ruled as king
Over all of you here once, and was mild as a father.
And now there is a much greater evil too, that will soon
Fully tear my whole house apart and destroy all my living.
Suitors are assailing my mother against her will,   50
The dear sons of the men who are the noblest in this place.
They shudder to make a trip to the house of her father
Icarios, so he might set his daughter's dowry himself,
And give her to the man she wants, him who pleases her most.
But they cluster to our house day after day.   55
Slaughtering oxen and sheep and fat goats,
They carry on their revels and drink the sparkling wine
Wantonly. Many things are wasted. And there is no man
Of the kind Odysseus was, to ward off harm from the house.
Nor are we at all the kind to ward it off. Even hereafter   60
We shall be pitiable and not have acquired strength.
I would ward it off myself, if I had the power.
Unendurable deeds have been done; in no pretty way
Has my house been destroyed. Be indignant yourselves!
Be ashamed toward the other men of our neighborhood   65
Who live around us. Fear, too, the wrath of the gods,
Lest, aghast at all the evil deeds, they work some change.
I beseech you, both by Olympian Zeus, and by Themis,[2]
Who disbands and also convokes the assemblies of men,

2. Goddess of Just Order.

70 Leave off, my friends; and let me wear away alone
In my woeful grief, unless my noble father Odysseus
Was ever hostile to the well-greaved [3] Achaians and did them
   harm;
For this you pay me back, are hostile and do me harm
By urging these men on. It would be better for me
75 If you were to devour my property and my herd yourselves;
If you were to eat them, there might be some recompense.
In that case we should carry the story around the town,
Demanding back our goods, till they were all given back.
As it is, you are heaping incurable pains on my heart."
So he spoke, in anger. He threw the scepter down on the
80   ground,
Bursting out in tears. And pity gripped all the people.
Then all the others there were silent. No one could bear
To reply to Telemachos with severe words;
Antinoos alone addressed him in reply:
"High-talking Telemachos, unchecked in your anger, what is
85   this
You say to shame us? You would like to fix blame on us!
The Achaian suitors are not guilty toward you.
No, it is your dear mother, who knows advantages well.
It is the third year already, and will soon be a fourth,
90 Since she has slighted the spirit in the Achaians' hearts.
She gives hope to all, and she promises every man,
Sending out messages. But her thought wishes otherwise.
And she has devised in her mind this other deceit.
She set a great loom in the halls and on it she wove
95 A large and delicate fabric. She told us at once:
'Young men, my suitors, since godly Odysseus is dead,
Wait, though you are eager for this marriage of mine, till I
   finish
This robe, so that the yarn will not waste in vain,
The burial sheet of warrior Laertes for the time
100 The ruinous fate of long-sorrowful death seizes him,
Lest one of the Achaian women in the district blame me
If he who had won so much lie without covering!'
So she said, and the bold heart was persuaded within us,
Then every day she kept weaving on the great loom.
105 And in the nights she undid it when she had the torches set up.

3. A greave is a stiff protector worn on the lower leg.

So three years she has fooled the Achaians and persuaded them.
But when the fourth year came and the seasons came on,
Right then one of the women, who perceived it clearly, told it,
And we happened upon her undoing the shining fabric.
So she has finished it, though unwilling and under duress.   110
The suitors answer you this way in order that for yourself
You may know it in your heart; that all the Achaians may know
    it.
Send your mother away; command her to marry
Whatever man her father bids and who pleases her.
But if she incites the sons of the Achaians much longer,   115
Attending in her heart to the gifts Athene gave her
Beyond others, skill at beautiful tasks, a noble mind,
And wiles, such as we have heard of none of the women
Of old, the fair-braided Achaians who existed before,
Tyro and Alcmene and Mycene of the lovely crown [4]—   120
No one of them had ideas the like of Penelope's.
Yet in this she has not had a propitious idea,
Because truly they will devour your living and your possessions
As long as she keeps this purpose that the gods
Have now placed in her heart. For herself she makes great
    renown,   125
But for you, the longing for a plentiful livelihood.
We are not going first to our lands or anywhere else
Till she marries whichever of the Achaians she wishes."
Then sound-minded Telemachos addressed him in answer:
"Antinoos, in no way can I force her who bore and raised me   130
Out of the house against her will, while elsewhere on earth
My father is alive or dead. It would be a bad thing to pay
Icarios a large fine if I sent my mother off on my own.
From her father I should then suffer ills, and a god would give
Others, when my mother had invoked the dread Erinyes,[5]   135
As she went away from the house. The resentment of men
Would be upon me. So I shall never utter such a word.
And if your own spirit can feel the resentment,
Get out of the halls, partake of other dinners,
Eating your own goods, visiting each others' homes.   140

4. Tyro, bride of Poseidon, grandmother of Nestor and Jason; Alcmene,
mother of Heracles; Mycene, daughter of the river Inachos and patroness
of Mycenae.
5. Goddesses who fulfill curses and avenge crimes.

But if this seems better and preferable to you,
To use up one man's livelihood scot-free,
Waste on. But I shall call on the eternal gods for help,
So that Zeus may grant there to be acts of retribution,
145 And then scot-free within this house you may die."
So Telemachos spoke, and broad-seeing Zeus sent him
Two eagles from above from the crest of the mountain flying.
They for a time flew down along with the blasts of the wind,
Stretching their wings out close to one another.
150 But when they came to the midst of the many-voiced assembly,
Then they whirled about and beat their wings rapidly.
They went to the heads of all and destruction was in their look,
As they tore each other's cheeks and throats on both sides
     with their claws.
Then they sped off on the right, past the men's homes and city.
They were amazed at the birds when they saw them with their
155   own eyes.
They turned over in their hearts what was going to happen.
Then the old warrior Halitherses addressed them,
The son of Nestor. He alone excelled those of his age
For knowing about birds and explaining the auspices.
160 Well disposed toward them, he spoke out and addressed them:
"Listen to me now, Ithacans, in what I say.
I declare this especially to make it known to the suitors.
A great trouble for them is gathering force. Odysseus
Will not long be far from his dear ones. In fact already, perhaps,
165 He is nearby, breeding murder and fate for these men,
All of them. And it will also be ill for many of the rest
Of us who inhabit sunny Ithaca. Yet far beforehand
Let us consider how we may stop them. Let the men
Stop themselves. And surely this is better for them.
170 Not as a novice do I prophesy, but as one who knows,
And I say everything has come to pass for that man,
As I explained to him when the Argives went off
To Ilion, and with them went many-minded Odysseus.
I said he would suffer many ills, lose all his friends,
175 And then unknown to all in the twentieth year
He would get home. Now all these things are indeed coming
     to pass."
Eurymachos, son of Polybos, addressed him in answer:
"Old man, go on now and prophesy to your children,

Go on home, lest they suffer some ill afterward.
I am much better at prophesying about this than you.   180
And there are many birds that wander beneath the beams
Of the sun, and not all are in accord with fate. Odysseus
Has perished far off, and would that you too had perished
Along with him. You would not say so much in augury,
Nor would you so incite the angered Telemachos,   185
Expecting a gift for your house, if he provide one.
I will tell you this right out. And it will come to pass:
If, when you know so many ancient matters, you prevail
Over a younger man, and with your speeches urge him to rage;
First, this will be very tormenting to the man himself,   190
And he will be able to do absolutely nothing about it.
But on you, old man, we shall set a charge you will grieve
In your heart to pay off. It will be a hard pain for you.
I shall advise Telemachos myself in the presence of all:
Let him bid his mother go back to her father's house.   195
They will work out a marriage and array many bridal gifts,
As many as should go along with a dear daughter.
Before then I do not think the sons of the Achaians will cease
From the wearisome suit, since we fear no one anyway—
No, not Telemachos, however full of speeches he is,   200
And we do not give heed, old man, to the augury you tell,
Which is unfulfilled; and you are still the more hated.
Moreover, the goods shall be vilely eaten, and their equal
Shall never exist,[6] so long as she herself puts the Achaians off
About her marriage. But we are waiting day after day   205
And compete over her excellence, and we do not go
Among the other women it is fit for each of us to marry."
Then sound-minded Telemachos addressed him in answer,
"Eurymachos, and all the rest of you noble suitors,
I will not implore you about this or speak out any more.   210
Already the gods know this, and all the Achaians.
But come, give me a fast ship and twenty companions
Who can complete a journey with me, thither and back.
I am going to Sparta and also to sandy Pylos
To learn of the return of my father, who is gone so long,   215
On the chance some mortal may tell of him, or I hear from
   Zeus

6. Obscure in Greek. It means, probably, that there will be no equal
recompense for them.

The voice that most of all brings report to men.
If I do hear my father is living and will return,
Then, though worn down, I could bear out yet another year.
220 But if I hear that he is dead and exists no more,
I will then return to my own dear fatherland,
Heap up a monument for him and perform the many
Rites that are fitting, and give my mother to a husband."
When he had said just this, he sat down. There stood up
among them
225 Mentor, who was a companion of excellent Odysseus;
When he went on the ships he turned over his whole home to
him,
To obey the old man [7] and steadfastly to protect all.
Well disposed to them, he spoke out and addressed them:
"Listen to me now, Ithacans, in what I say.
230 Let no scepter-bearing king be deliberately
Kind and mild any longer, or keep his mind on the right,
But may he be perpetually harsh and act unjustly,
Since there is no one who remembers the godly Odysseus
Of the people he ruled; and he was mild as a father.
235 No, I do not make objection about the bold suitors
That they do violent deeds, with evil weaving of thought,
For they stake their own heads when they devour violently
The home of Odysseus, who, they say, will return no more.
But now I blame the rest of the people, for the way you all
240 Sit in silence, that you do not address these few suitors
With speeches, and restrain them, being yourselves so many."
Leocritos, son of Euenor, addressed him in answer:
"Stubborn Mentor, crazed in your mind, what is this you say
Urging them to put us down? But it is disastrous
245 To fight over a banquet, and with men greater in number.
Yes, even if Ithacan Odysseus himself were to come
Upon the noble suitors banqueting in his house
And plan in his heart to drive them out of the hall,
His wife, though she longed for it much, would not rejoice
250 At his coming, but he would meet his wretched fate right there,
If he fought against many. You have not spoken properly.
But come, let the people disperse, each one to his tasks;
Mentor and Halitherses will hasten the man on his way.

7. Probably Laertes, though some take it as meaning that the household
shall obey Mentor.

They have been his father's companions from the beginning.
And yet I believe he will stay a long time in Ithaca   255
And listen for the news, but will never complete this journey."
So he spoke, and he dismissed the assembly quickly.
And they did disperse, each one to his own dwelling.
But the suitors went into the dwelling of godly Odysseus.
Telemachos went off apart to the sands of the sea,   260
Washed his hands in gray salt water, and prayed to Athene:
"Hear me, you who yesterday came as a god to our house
And bade me to go in a ship onto the murky sea
To learn of the return of my father who is gone so long,
But the Achaians delay over all these things,   265
And the wickedly presumptuous suitors most of all."
So he spoke in prayer. Athene came close to him,
Likening herself to Mentor in form and in voice.
And speaking out to him, she uttered wingèd words:
"Telemachos, hereafter you will not be a coward or senseless.   270
If there is really instilled in you the good might of your father
And you are as he was to achieve both word and deed,
Then the journey will not be fruitless or unachieved.
But if you are not the offspring of him and Penelope,
Then I have no hope that you will achieve what you wish.   275
Few indeed are the sons who are equal to their fathers;
Most are worse, but few are better than their fathers.
But since you will not be a coward hereafter or senseless,
And the shrewdness of Odysseus has not quite forsaken you,
There is hope in that case you will bring these deeds to pass.   280
Therefore let the plan and the thought of the suitors go,
Mad as they are, since they are neither thoughtful nor just.
They do not know at all about the death and black fate
That is really near them, to destroy them all on a single day.
The journey you desire will not be distant for long.   285
Since I am for you the companion I was for your father,
I will get a fast ship ready for you and come with you myself.
But go on back to your house and talk with the suitors,
Lay up provisions and fit everything in containers;
Wine in jugs, and barley, the marrow of men,   290
In close-sewn skins. And I myself will soon gather
Willing companions around the district. There are
Many ships in sea-circled Ithaca, new and old.
I myself will look them over and see which is best for you.

295 We will soon get it ready and send it on the broad ocean."
So spoke Athene, the daughter of Zeus. Telemachos
Did not tarry long when he heard the voice of the god.
He went on to his home, troubled in his own heart,
And he did indeed find the bold suitors in the halls,
300 Flaying goats and singeing fat hogs in the courtyard.
Antinoos with a laugh went straight to Telemachos,
Took his hand, and spoke right out directly to him:
"High-talking Telemachos, unchecked in your anger,
Give heed in your breast to no other evil word or deed,
305 But do eat for my sake, and drink, just as before.
The Achaians will accomplish for you all these things,
A ship and chosen rowers, so you may get swiftly
To hallowed Pylos for word about your illustrious father."
Then sound-minded Telemachos addressed him in answer:
310 "Antinoos, there is no way I could dine in silence
With you, insolent men, and enjoy myself securely.
Or is it not enough, you suitors, that beforehand you wasted
Many noble possessions of mine while I was still a child?
And now that I am big and learn about the story,
315 Hearing it from others, and the spirit does wax within me,
I shall try some way to fling evil fates upon you,
Either by going to Pylos or here in this very district.
I am going, and the journey I speak of will not be fruitless—
As a passenger, for I have the disposal of neither
Ship nor rowers; that, I suppose, is the way it seemed better
320 　to you."
He spoke and drew his hand from Antinoos' hand
Lightly. The suitors busied themselves through the house with
　　dinner.
They spoke in mockery and made abusive speeches,
And this is what one of the overbearing young men would say:
325 "Well, Telemachos is devising slaughter for us.
He will bring some defenders either from sandy Pylos
Or even from Sparta, since he wants to so terribly,
Or else he wishes to go to Ephyre, the fertile land,
In order that he may get a life-killing drug there,
330 Put it in a bowl, and do away with us all."
And then another of the overbearing young men would say
"Who knows but that he too, going in the hollow ship

Far from his dear ones, will die wandering like Odysseus?
That way he would increase our labor even more!
For we would divide up all the possessions; the house, moreover, 335
We would give to his mother to have, and to whoever weds
    her."
So they spoke. He entered his father's high-roofed chamber,
A broad one, where gold and bronze lay piled up,
Clothing in coffers and abundance of fragrant oil,
And in it were large jars of aged, sweet-tasting wine   340
Standing, which contained an unmixed godly drink,
Set in a row beside the wall, if ever Odysseus
Should homeward return, though he had suffered many pains.
Bolt-fitted planks were upon it, stoutly fashioned,
Double doors, and a housekeeper by night and by day   345
Held it, who guarded all in her resourcefulness of mind,
Eurycleia, daughter of Ops, Peisenor's son.
Then Telemachos spoke to her and called her to the chamber:
"Good mother, come draw wine off for me into jars with handles,
Sweet wine, except for the most savory that you keep,   350
Thinking of that ill-fated man, in case he comes from some-
    where,
Zeus-born Odysseus, and wards off destiny and death.
Fill up twelve of them, and fit them all with lids,
And pour barley for me into well-stitched leather bags.
Let there be twenty measures of mill-crushed barley flakes. 355
Keep this to yourself. Let it all be readied together.
I shall take it away in the evening myself at the time
When my mother enters the upper room and thinks of rest.
I am going to Sparta and also to sandy Pylos
To learn of my dear father's return, if I may hear somehow." 360
So he spoke, and his dear nurse Eurycleia cried out,
And while she was sobbing she uttered wingèd words:
"How, dear child, does this thought come to be in your mind?
And where do you wish to go upon the broad earth,
Being a belovèd only child? Zeus-born Odysseus has died   365
Far from his fatherland in a country of strangers.
From the moment you are gone they will devise evils against
    you,
How by deceit you may die. Then they will divide all this
    themselves.
No, remain here among your own. There is no need

370 For you to wander and suffer ills on the barren ocean."
Then sound-minded Telemachos addressed her in answer:
"Take cheer, nurse; this plan is not without a god.
But swear you will tell nothing of this to my dear mother
Before the eleventh or the twelfth day has come,
375 Unless she misses me and hears that I am gone off,
So that she might not weep and injure her lovely skin."
So he spoke; and the old woman swore by the gods she would
        not,
A great oath; and then when she swore and completed the oath,
Right away she drew off wine for him in the jars with handles
380 And poured barley for him into well-stitched leather bags.
Telemachos went to the house and joined the suitors.
Then the bright-eyed goddess Athene had another thought.
Likening herself to Telemachos, she went all through the city.
She stood beside each mortal man and she uttered a speech
385 And bade them to gather at evening by the swift ship.
And then she asked Noemon, glorious son of Phronios,
For his swift ship. And he granted it graciously.
The sun went down and all the ways were shadowed.
Then she had the swift ship dragged to the sea. And in it
390 She put all the tackle that well-timbered ships carry.
She moored it at the verge of the bay. His noble companions
Were gathered together. The goddess urged each one on.
Then the bright-eyed goddess Athene had another thought.
And she went on to the halls of godlike Odysseus.
395 There she diffused sweet slumber down on the suitors,
And confused them as they drank. The goblets fell from their
        hands.
They rose up to go sleep through the city. And not long
Did they sit, when once slumber fell on their eyelids.
Then the bright-eyed goddess Athene spoke to Telemachos,
400 Calling him out of the well-situated halls,
Likening herself to Mentor in form and in voice:
"Telemachos, already your well-greaved companions
Are seated at the oars awaiting your urging.
Let us go, so that we may not long delay from the journey."
405 So did Pallas Athene speak, and she led on
Speedily. He went along in the god's footsteps.
But when they had got down to the ship and the sea,
They found the long-haired companions there on the sand.

And Telemachos addressed them in his holy might:
"Over here, friends. Let us load on provisions. Already   410
All are gathered in the chamber. My mother has not found out,
Nor the other serving maids. One alone has heard the tale."
So he spoke, and led them, and they went along with him.
When they had brought everything to the well-timbered ship,
They stowed it away as Odysseus' dear son ordered them.   415
Telemachos then boarded the ship, but Athene went first
And sat down in the stern of the ship. Close beside her
Telemachos sat. They let the stern cables loose,
And themselves boarded and sat down at the oarlocks.
Bright-eyed Athene sent them a driving breeze,   420
A driving West Wind roaring on the wine-faced sea.
Telemachos, as he urged his companions on, told them
To grasp the tackle. And they hearkened to his urging.
They stood a fir-wood mast in the hollow mast-block;
They raised it up, and with forestays they made it fast.   425
Then they hauled up the white sails with well-plaited oxhide
     ropes.
A wind swelled the midsail, and the purple wave
About the stem sounded loud as the ship went on.
She ran into the wave, accomplishing her course.
When they had tied down the tackle on the swift black ship,   430
They set up mixing bowls filled to the brim with wine,
And poured libations to the deathless, ever-living gods,
And of all especially to the bright-eyed daughter of Zeus.
All night the ship pierced her course, and at morning too.

III

The sun rose up, leaving the beautiful water,
Into the bronze-covered heaven, to shine for immortals
And also for mortal men upon the grain-giving earth.
They came to Pylos, the well-established city
5 Of Neleus.[1] On the sands of the sea those men were sacrificing
Bulls all of black to the earth-shaker with blue locks.
There were nine groups, and in each one five hundred men
· Were sitting. And for each group they put forward nine bulls.
While these were eating the entrails and burning the thighs to
    the god,
10 The others sailed straight in, furling into place the sails
Of the balanced ship; they pulled her up, and got out them-
    selves.
Telemachos got out of the ship, and Athene went ahead.
The bright-eyed goddess Athene addressed him first:
"Telemachos, there is no longer the least need for you to be
    modest,
15 For just this did you sail on the ocean to learn about your father,
Where the earth has hidden him and what fate he has met.
But come now, go straight to Nestor, breaker of horses.
We will see what advice he has hidden in his breast.
Entreat him yourself to speak unerringly.
20 He will not speak falsely. For he is very sound of mind."
Then sound-minded Telemachos addressed her in answer:
"Mentor, how then shall I go? How shall I approach him?
For in quick responses I have no experience.
Modesty becomes a young man addressing an elder."
25 Then the bright-eyed goddess Athene spoke to him:
"Telemachos, some thoughts you will have in your mind,
And a god will suggest others. For I do not think
You were born and raised without the favor of the gods."

1. Founder of Pylos; son of Poseidon and father of Nestor.

So did Pallas Athene speak, and she led the way
Speedily. He went along in the god's footsteps.   30
They came to the conclave and sessions of the men of Pylos,
Where Nestor sat with his sons, and about him companions
Prepared a feast, roasting some meat and skewering the rest.
When these men saw the strangers, they all came over in a body
And hailed them with gestures and asked them to sit down.   35
First Peisistratos, Nestor's son, came near,
Took the hands of both men and sat them down at the feast
In soft fleeces upon the sands of the salt sea,
Beside his brother Thrasymedes and his father.
He gave them shares of the entrails and poured out wine   40
In a golden goblet. Pledging her, he addressed
Pallas Athene, daughter of aegis-bearing [2] Zeus.
"Say a prayer now, stranger, to Lord Poseidon,
Whose feast you have come upon in arriving hither.
But when you have poured a libation and prayed, which is
    fitting,   45
Then give this man also a cup of honey-sweet wine
To pour a libation, since I believe he too says prayers
To the immortals. All men have need of the gods.
But he is younger, and equal in age to myself.
Therefore I will first give you the gold cup of libation."   50
When he had said this, he put the cup of sweet wine in her
    hand.
Athene was pleased at the sound-minded, judicious man
Because he had given her first the gold cup of libation.
At once she said many things in prayer to Lord Poseidon:
"Listen, Poseidon, you who girdle the earth. Bear no grudge   55
Against us as we are praying to bring these deeds to pass.
First of all, grant renown to Nestor and his sons.
And then give the others, all the men of Pylos together,
A pleasing recompense for their illustrious hecatomb.[3]
Grant that Telemachos and I may go back, when we have done 60
That which we came here in the swift black ship to do."
So she prayed then. But she herself brought it all to pass.
She gave Telemachos the lovely two-handled cup.
The dear son of Odysseus prayed in the same way.

2. The aegis was a weapon, or later a breastplate, carried only by Zeus and
Athene.
3. Sacrifice of a hundred oxen.

When the others had roasted the outer pieces of meat and
65   unskewered them,
They divided the portions and dined on the hearty feast.
But when they had taken their fill of food and drink,
Nestor, the Gerenian horseman, began speaking to them:
"Now is the best time to inquire, and to ask
70 Strangers who they are, after they have enjoyed food.
Strangers, who are you? Whence have you sailed the watery
        ways?
For some sort of gain, or do you wander at hazard
The way pirates do who wander over the sea,
Risking their lives, bearing evil to foreigners?"
75 Then sound-minded Telemachos addressed him in answer,
Taking courage, for Athene herself had put in his mind
Courage to ask him about the father who had gone away,
And so that a noble renown among men might belong to him:
"Nestor, son of Neleus, great pride of the Achaians,
80 You ask where we are from. And I will inform you.
We have come from Ithaca, which is under Mount Neion.
It is a private affair, not a public one, that I speak of.
I seek widespread report of my father, if somehow I may hear,
Of the stout-hearted, godly Odysseus, who once, they say,
85 Sacked the city of the Trojans, fighting at your side.
Of all the other men who waged war on the Trojans,
We have heard where each one perished by a woeful death.
But the son of Cronos made that man's death not to be heard
        of.
No one is able to say clearly just where he perished,
90 Whether on the mainland he went under to hostile men
Or on the open sea in Amphitrite's [4] waves.
So I now embrace your knees to ask if you are willing
To tell about that man's woeful death, if you saw it
With your own eyes, perhaps, or heard the tale from another
95 Wanderer. For excessive sorrow did his mother bear him!
Sweeten nothing out of pity or respect for me,
But tell me straight out how you encountered the sight.
I beseech you, if ever my father noble Odysseus
Promised you any word or deed and carried it out
100 In the Trojans' land, where you Achaians suffered troubles;

4. A sea goddess, here identified with the sea itself.

Recall that for me now and tell me unerringly."
Then Nestor, the Gerenian horseman, answered him:
"Ah friend, since you have reminded me of the woe we suffered
In that land, we sons of the Achaians, unchecked in our anger;
How much, both in the ships upon the murky sea,   105
Wandering for booty wherever Achilles led,
And how much, too, we fought around the great city
Of Lord Priam! [5] There at that time all the best were slain!
There lies warlike Ajax, there lies Achilles,[6]
There Patroclos,[7] a counselor equal in weight to the gods: 110
There lies my dear son, at once mighty and excellent,
Antilochos, outstanding as a runner and as a fighter.
Many other ills we endured besides these. Who
Of mortal men could ever recount all of them?
Not if you stayed five years, no, not six, could you ask   115
To the end of the ills the godly Achaians endured there.
Before that you would tire and return to your fatherland.
Nine years we busied ourselves weaving ills for them
By all sorts of wiles. The son of Cronos barely brought it to pass.
And no one there ever wanted to be compared to him openly   120
For craftiness, since godly Odysseus far surpassed
In all sorts of wiles—your father, if it is true
You are that man's offspring. Awe holds me to look upon you.
Yes, indeed, your speech is like his. You would not think
A man so young could speak in such a likely way.   125
There the whole time I myself and godly Odysseus
Never once spoke diversely in assembly or in council,
But holding one spirit in mind and in prudent counsel,
We advised the Argives how it should come out by far the best.
And when we had sacked the lofty city of Priam   130
And gone off in the ships, and a god had scattered the Achaians,
Then Zeus plotted out in his mind a woeful return
For the Argives, since they were not all prudent or just.
Therefore many of them encountered an evil fate
Because of the destructive wrath of the bright-eyed daughter   135
Of a strong father, who set strife on the two sons of Atreus.
The two of them called all the Achaians to a council,

5. The aged king of Troy killed by the Greeks.
6. Ajax was son of Telamon, second to Achilles in prowess; Achilles, captain
of the Myrmidons and the greatest hero of the Greeks at Troy.
7. The closest friend of Achilles; his death inspired Achilles to return to
battle.

Rashly, in no orderly way, at the sun's setting,
And the sons of the Achaians came, weighed down with wine.
140 They told the story of why they had gathered the people.
Then Menelaos commanded all the Achaians
To take thought of a return on the broad back of the sea.
But that did not please Agamemnon at all, for he wanted
To hold back the people and to offer sacred hecatombs
145 So as to appease the dreadful rage of Athene.
The fool, he did not know she was not to be persuaded.
The mind of the ever-living gods is not quickly turned.
And so they stood there and replied to each other
With harsh speeches. And the well-greaved Achaians rose up
150 With a wondrous noise. The plan pleased them diversely.
We spent the night turning over harsh thoughts in our minds
Against one another. For Zeus was shaping an evil woe.
At dawn some of us dragged the ships to the bright salt water;
We put our possessions and the deep-girdled women in.
155 But half of the people held back, staying on behind
With Atreus' son Agamemnon, shepherd of the people.
The other half embarked and went on. Swiftly indeed
They sailed, and a god smoothed out the great-gulfed ocean.
When we came to Tenedos we sacrificed to the gods,
160 Wanting to go home. But Zeus intended no return yet,
Cruel, as he stirred up evil strife for the second time.
Some turned their bobbing ships around and went their way,
Those about skillful devious-minded Lord Odysseus;
And they again favored Agamemnon, son of Atreus.
165 But I, with the massed ships that were following me,
Kept fleeing, since I knew the god was intending evil.
The warlike son of Tydeus fled and aroused his companions.
Blond Menelaos came along with us later on.
He found us in Lesbos thinking over the long voyage,
170 Whether we should take our way above rugged Chios
By the island of Psyra, keeping that on our left,
Or should go below Chios along by windy Mimas.
We besought the god to make a portent appear, and he did
Show us one and ordered us to cleave the middle sea
75 To Euboia, so we might soonest flee from under misfortune.
A sharp breeze rose up and blew. Our ships swiftly
Ran over the fish-laden courses. During the night
They put in at Geraistos. We dedicated the thighs

Of many bulls to Poseidon, when we had measured the great sea.
It was the fourth day when the companions of Diomede,[8]   180
Tydeus' horse-taming son, moored their balanced ships in
    Argos.
As for me, I held toward Pylos. Never did the breeze
Lull, from the very first time the god set it on to blow.
So I arrived, dear child, with no news. I know nothing
About them, which Achaians were saved, and which perished. 185
As much as I could learn sitting in my own halls,
You shall find out, as is right. I will not conceal it from you.
They say the spear-wielding Myrmidons [9] came safely,
Whose leader was the famous son of great-hearted Achilles,
And safely came Philoctetes, Poeas' glorious son.   190
Idomeneus [1] led all his companions to Crete,
Who escaped from the war. The ocean deprived him of none.
You have heard about the son of Atreus, though you live far
    away—
How he arrived, how Aigisthos plotted his woeful death.
Ah, but that man did pay for it terribly.   195
And how good it is for a man to leave behind when he dies
A son, since that son avenged his father's murderer,
The cunning Aigisthos, who killed his renowned father!
You too, my dear friend, since I see you are handsome and
    great;
Be brave, so that a man born in the future would praise you."   200
Then sound-minded Telemachos addressed him in answer:
"Nestor, son of Neleus, great glory of the Achaians,
Yes, that man avenged himself well. And the Achaians
Will bring him wide renown and a song for men to come.
Would that the gods might invest me with so great a power,   205
To take vengeance on the suitors for their painful transgression,
Men who in their pride devise reckless deeds against me.
But the gods have not spun the thread of so great a bliss
For my father and me. Now it must be endured, all the same."
Nestor, the Gerenian horseman, then answered him: 210
"Dear friend, since you have mentioned this and spoken of it
    to me,
They do say that there are many suitors for your mother

8. Ruler of Argos; a major Greek hero at Troy.
9. Followers of Achilles.
1. The grandson of Minos and king in Crete.

Who are devising evils in your halls against your will.
Tell me, are you willingly subjected? Or do the people
215 Despise you in the district, yielding to the voice of a god?
Who knows if he may come some day and punish their violence,
Either himself alone or all the Achaians together?
For if only the bright-eyed Athene did wish to favor you
The way she cared once for glorious Odysseus,
220 In the Trojans' land where we Achaians suffered troubles—
I never saw the gods so openly showing favor
The way Pallas Athene stood openly by that man—
If she did wish to favor you and care in her heart that way,
Then some of those men would surely forget the marriage."
225 Then sound-minded Telemachos addressed him in answer:
"Old man, I think this word will never be fulfilled.
You have said a great deal. Wonder holds me. Not for my hope
Would this happen, not even if the gods wished it to."
Then the bright-eyed goddess Athene spoke to him:
"Telemachos, what sort of word has got past the bar of your
230   teeth?
A god may easily if he wish save a man, even from afar.
I should rather myself be distressed with many pains
And travel homeward to see the day of my return
Than to arrive and perish at my hearth, as Agamemnon
235 Was killed by the guile of Aigisthos and his own wife.
Yet not even the gods can ward off from a man they love
The death that is common to all at whatever time
The ruinous fate of long-sorrowful death seizes him."
Then sound-minded Telemachos addressed her in answer:
240 "Mentor, let us speak of this no more, though we care for him.
There is no longer a real return for that man. Already
The immortal gods have devised for him death and black fate.
But now I want to ask and inquire about another story
From Nestor, since he knows justice and prudence beyond
        others.
245 For they say he has three times ruled the generations of men.
Like an immortal he strikes me to look upon.
O Nestor, son of Neleus, do utter the truth:
How did Atreus' son, broad-ruling Agamemnon, die?
Where was Menelaos? What sort of destruction did cunning
250 Aigisthos plot for him, when he killed a far better man?
Or was it not in Achaian Argos, but did he wander

Somewhere else among men, and the other took courage and
  murdered?"
Then Nestor, the Gerenian horseman, answered him,
"All right, my child, I shall tell you all of the truth.
Surely you may think for yourself how this would have happened ₂₅₅
If Atreus' son, blond Menelaos, arriving from Troy,
Had come upon Aigisthos still alive in the halls.
They would not have spread a heap of earth over him when he
  died.
But the dogs and also the birds would have devoured him
As he lay on a plain far from the city. And none   ₂₆₀
Of the Achaian women would have wept, for he devised a huge
  deed.
While we stayed there bringing many combats to an end,
He, secure in a nook of horse-nourishing Argos,
Enchanted Agamemnon's wife with many words.
Actually, she at first rejected the sorry act,   ₂₆₅
Godly Clytemnestra, since she practiced good sense.
And there was a singer with her, too, whom the son of Atreus
When he went off to Troy had strongly ordered to guard his
  wife.
But when the fate of the gods bound her to be overcome,
Then Aigisthos brought the singer to a desert island   ₂₇₀
And left the man to become a prey and a spoil for birds.
And a willing man led to his house a willing woman.
He burned many thighs on the holy altars of the gods
And set up many ornaments of woven work and gold,
Having achieved a huge deed he had never hoped in his heart. ₂₇₅
Now we sailed on together as he went from Troy,
The son of Atreus and I, knowing each what pleased the other.
When we reached holy Sunion, headland of Athens,
There Phoebos Apollo [2] slew the pilot of Menelaos,
Visiting him with his soothing shafts while the man   ₂₈₀
Was holding in his hands the rudder of the coursing ship,
Phrontis, Onetor's son, who surpassed the tribes of men
In piloting a ship wherever the storm winds rushed.
So he was held back there, though pressing on for the journey,
Till he should bury his companion and perform due rites.   ₂₈₅
But when he had gone again upon the wine-faced sea
In the hollow ships and, as he sped along, had reached

2. Son of Zeus and brother of Artemis; the god of sun and light.

Maleia, the sheer mountain, broad-seeing Zeus devised
A hateful journey and poured on a blast of shrill winds
290 And monstrous swollen waves as big as mountains.
He separated the ships there and brought some of them near
    Crete
Where the Cydonians dwelt by the streams of the Iardanos.
A certain smooth rock stands there sheer to the sea
At the extreme point of Gortyn in the murky ocean,
Where the south wind pushes a great wave up against the left
295   peak
To Phaistos and a small stone holds back a great wave.
Some ships did get there, and the men barely escaped
    destruction,
But the waves shattered the ships upon the reefs.
Yet the wind and the water carried and brought five
300 Of the dark blue-prowed ships right on up to Egypt.
So he gathered there a great deal of provisions and gold
And wandered with his ships among men of alien tongue.
Meanwhile Aigisthos plotted these woeful things at home.
For seven years he ruled Mycenae,[3] the rich in gold
When he had killed Atreus' son, and the people were subdued
305   under him.
In the eighth year, an evil for him, godly Orestes
Came back from Athens and killed his father's murderer,
The cunning Aigisthos, who had killed his renowned father.
When he had killed him, he gave the Argives a funeral feast
310 Both for his hateful mother and for cowardly Aigisthos.
That day Menelaos, good at the war cry, came to him bringing
Many possessions, as great a burden as his ships could bear.
As for you, too, my friend, do not wander long from your home
And leave behind in your home the possessions and the men
315 Presumptuous as they are, lest they divide and devour
All your possessions, and you have gone on a fruitless journey.
But I exhort you and urge you to proceed on
To Menelaos. For he has come recently from elsewhere,
From men from whom no one would expect in his heart
320 To return, whom storm winds had once led astray
Into a sea so great that not even the birds
Could get through in a year, it is so great and dire.
But go on now with your ship and your companions.

3. The chief city of Homeric Greece and residence of Agamemnon.

If you wish to go by land, a chariot and horses are here;
My own sons are here also, who will be your guides   325
To godly Lacedemon, where blond Menelaos lives.
Beseech him yourself that he may speak unerringly.
He will not speak falsely. For he is very sound of mind."
So he said. The sun went down and darkness came on.
Then the bright-eyed goddess Athene spoke to them.   330
"Old sir, indeed you have told all this properly.
Come now, cut up tongues for offering and mix wine,
So when we have poured a libation to Poseidon and the other
Immortals, we may think of sleep. It is the hour for it.
Light is already gone under the dusk. Nor does it seem right   335
To sit a long time at the gods' feast, but to go on."
So spoke Zeus's daughter, and they hearkened to her voice.
Heralds poured out water for them over their hands.
Young men were filling bowls up to the brim with drink;
And served round to all, putting the first drops in the cups.   340
They cast the tongues on the fire and did libation standing.
But when they had poured libation and drunk as much
As the spirit moved, Athene and godlike Telemachos
Both then wanted to go on to the hollow ship.
Nestor restrained them and addressed them with a speech: 345
"May Zeus and the other immortal gods prevent
Your going away from my house to the swift ship
As from someone wholly without raiment, or destitute,
Who does not have coverlets and many rugs in his house
Either for himself or for his guests to sleep in softly.   350
But there are coverlets and lovely rugs at my disposal.
Not indeed will the dear son of this man Odysseus
Lie down on his ship's deck so long as I am alive
And so long as children are left to me in the halls
To entertain guests, whoever comes to my house."   355
Then the bright-eyed goddess Athene answered him:
"Dear old sir, you have said this well: It does seem right
That Telemachos obey you, as it is much better thus.
But now he will go along with you here, so he may sleep
In your halls. I myself will go to the black ship   360
So I may cheer our companions and tell them the details.
I declare I am the only older man among them,
The others follow along in friendship, younger men,
All the same age as great-hearted Telemachos.

365 There may I lay myself down in the hollow black ship
Right now. But at dawn to the great-hearted Kaucones
I am going, where a debt is owed me, not a recent one,
Or a small one. And since this man has come to your house,
Send him off with a chariot and your son. Give him the horses
370 That are nimblest at running and the best in strength."
When she had said this, bright-eyed Athene went off,
Likening herself to a sea eagle. Wonder seized all the Achaians.
The old man was amazed when he saw it with his eyes,
He took Telemachos' hand and spoke right out directly:
375 "My friend, I do not suppose you would be craven and cowardly
If the gods so accompany a young man like you as guides.
This is no other of those who holds the halls of Olympos
Than the daughter of Zeus, the glorious Tritogeneia.[4]
Among the Argives she honored your noble father too.
380 Come, mistress, be gracious and grant me a noble renown
For myself and my children and my respected wife.
I shall sacrifice to you a yearling heifer of broad brow,
Untamed, that a man has never led under the yoke.
I will sacrifice her, and deck her horns with gold."
385 So he spoke in prayer, and Pallas Athene heard him.
Nestor, the Gerenian horseman, led them on,
His sons and his sons-in-law, to his beautiful home;
But when they arrived at the famous home of the ruler,
They sat down one after another in seats and in armchairs.
390 As they came, the old man mixed up for them a bowl
Of wine, sweet to drink, that in the eleventh year
The serving maid had opened and untied the seal string from.
The old man mixed it in a bowl. As he poured libation
He prayed much to Athene, daughter of aegis-bearing Zeus.
395 But when they had poured libation and drunk their fill,
They went to lie down to sleep, each in his own house.
But there Nestor, the Gerenian horseman, bedded down
Telemachos, the dear son of godly Odysseus,
In the jointed bed under the resounding portico.
400 Beside him was Peisistratos of the good ash spear, chief of men,
Who of the children in his halls was still unmarried.
But he himself slept in a nook of the lofty house,
And his lady wife prepared him a bed and a resting place.
And when the early-born, rosy-fingered dawn appeared,

4. A name of Athene referring obscurely to her birth.

Nestor, the Gerenian horseman, rose up out of his bed.   405
He went out and sat himself down on the polished stones
That belonged to him out in front of his lofty portals,
White ones, glistening with oil. Upon them of old
Neleus used to sit, an adviser equal in weight to the gods,
But already he had succumbed to his fate and gone to Hades.[5]   410
Then Gerenian Nestor, bulwark of the Achaians, sat there,
Bearing the scepter. His sons were gathered round in a group
As they came from their bedrooms, Echephron and Stratios,
Perseus and Aretos and the godlike Thrasymedes.
And then sixth among them came the hero Peisistratos.   415
They led godly Telemachos in and sat him at their side.
The Gerenian horseman Nestor began to speak among them:
"Dear children, fulfill my wish very speedily,
So that first of the gods I may propitiate Athene,
Who came in clear form to the lavish feast of the god.   420
Come now, let one man go to the plain for an heifer,
So it come with all speed, and the herd of the oxen drive her.
Let one of you, going to great-hearted Telemachos'
Black ship, lead all his companions, and leave just two.
Let one of them summon the goldsmith Laerkes to come   425
Hither, so he may gild the heifer's horns round with gold,
And all you others stay here in a group. Tell the maids
Within to prepare a feast through the famous halls.
Bring seats and logs for the place, and shining water."
So he said, and they all got busy. The heifer came   430
From the plain, and there came from the swift, balanced ship
The companions of great-hearted Telemachos. The smith came
Carrying bronze implements in his hands, the tools of the trade,
An anvil and a hammer and well-made fire tongs
With which he worked gold. And Athene came to take part   435
In the sacrifice. The old charioteer Nestor gave gold,
And then the other gilded it round and decked the heifer's
   horns,
So that the goddess would be pleased to see the decoration.
Stratios and godly Echephron led the heifer by the horns.
Aretos came from the chamber carrying water for washing   440
In a flower-chased vessel. He held barley grains in a basket
In his other hand. And Thrasymedes, the steady in battle,

5. That is, to the ruler of the underworld. In Homer, Hades is a person,
not a place.

Stood by, holding in his hand a sharp ax to strike the heifer.
Perseus held the blood-bowl. The old charioteer Nestor led off
445 By washing his hands and sprinkling barley. As he started,
He prayed much to Athene, throwing hairs of its head in the
        fire.
And when they had prayed and tossed the barley offering on,
At once Nestor's son, high-spirited Thrasymedes,
Stood close and struck it. The ax slit the tendons
Of the neck. The heifer's strength was loosed; the women
450   shrieked,
His daughters and daughter-in-law and the respected wife
Of Nestor, Eurydice, eldest of Clymenos' daughters.
At that point they lifted it up from the wide-traveled earth
And held it. Peisistratos, chief of the men, cut its throat.
455 When black blood flowed from it and the spirit left the bones,
They quickly dismembered it and at once cut up
The whole thighs duly and covered them over with fat,
Making a double fold, and put the raw meat thereon.
The old man burned it on split wood. He poured sparkling wine
Over that. The young men beside him held the five-pronged
460   forks
In their hands. When the thighs were burned and they had
        eaten of the entrails,
They cut up the rest in small pieces and pierced it on spits,
And they roasted it, holding the sharp-pointed spits in their
        hands.
Meanwhile, the lovely Polykaste, youngest daughter
465 Of Nestor, the son of Neleus, washed Telemachos.
And when she had washed him and anointed him richly with oil,
She put a lovely mantle on him and a tunic.
And he left the bathtub in body like the immortals;
He went and sat down by Nestor, shepherd of the people.
470 When they had roasted the outer flesh and pulled it off,
They sat feasting. Noble men did watchful service
Pouring out the wine into the golden goblets.
But when they had taken their fill of food and drink,
Nestor, the Gerenian horseman, began speaking to them:
"Come my sons, bring the lovely-haired horses, and yoke them
475   up
To the chariot for Telemachos, so he may speed on his way."
So he said, and they listened to him right away and obeyed.

Nimbly they yoked swift horses to the chariot,
And the woman who kept them put in food and wine
And cooked meat, such as kings eat who are nourished by Zeus. 480
Telemachos got into the beautiful chariot.
Nestor's son, Peisistratos, chief of the men, along with him
Got into the chariot and took the reins in his hands.
He whipped to start up. Not against their will the pair flew
To the plain, and they left the sheer citadel of Pylos.   485
All day they shook the yoke, holding it up on either side.
The sun went down and all the ways were shadowed.
They arrived at Pherai and to the home of Diocles,
Son of Ortilochos, whom Alpheus [6] sired as his son.
There they slept the night, and he gave them the fare of a guest. 490
But when the early-born, rosy-fingered dawn appeared,
They yoked up the horses and mounted the inlaid chariot.
And they drove out of the forecourt and the resounding portico.
He whipped to start up. Not against their will the pair flew.
They reached the wheat-bearing plain. From then on they strove 495
To finish their journey. So the swift horses bore onward.
The sun went down and all the ways were shadowed.

6. A river god.

IV

They came to hollow Lacedemon, full of ravines,
And drove on to the halls of glorious Menelaos.
They found him holding a wedding feast with his many clans-
men
For a son and an excellent daughter in his own house.
5 He was sending the girl to the son of rank-breaking Achilles.
He had betrothed her first in Troy and had nodded
For her to be given; the gods were fulfilling the marriage.
He was then sending her off with horses and chariots
To the famous city of the Myrmidons, whom the man ruled,
And he was bringing the daughter of Alektor from Sparta for
10 his son,
The dearly beloved, valiant Megapenthes, born to him
From a slave girl; the gods no longer granted childbirth to Helen
When she had once given birth to her charming daughter
Hermione, who had the form of golden Aphrodite.
15 So they banqueted under the great high-roofed hall,
The neighbors and clansmen of glorious Menelaos,
Enjoying themselves. Among them a divine singer sang
And played on the lyre. And a pair of tumblers about them
Started off at the song and whirled about in their midst.
20 Then the two of them stood in the gateway of the house,
The hero Telemachos and the illustrious son of Nestor,
They and their horses. The lord Eteoneus came forth
And saw them, the capable servant of glorious Menelaos.
He went through the halls to tell the shepherd of the people,
25 And he stood close to him and uttered wingèd words;
"Menelaos, nourished by Zeus, some strangers are here,
Two men, and they resemble the race of mighty Zeus.
Tell me, shall we unharness their swift horses for them
Or send them to reach another who will befriend them?"
30 Greatly disturbed, blond Menelaos spoke to him:
"Eteoneus, son of Boethoüs, you were never a fool

Before. But now you mouth foolishness like a child.
We ourselves, indeed, ate many guest offerings
Of other men as we came here, even if in the future
Zeus were to make woe cease. But unhitch the horses   35
Of the strangers. Go bring them forward to be entertained."
So he said, and the man passed quickly through the hall and
    called
Other capable servants to follow along with him.
They unhitched the sweating horses from under the yoke
And they haltered them in the mangers for horses.   40
They threw in emmer grains, and they mixed white barley in,
And leaned the chariot against the resplendent walls.
Then they led the men to the godly house. When they saw
The hall of the Zeus-nourished king, they wondered at it.
There was a gleam like that of the sun or of the moon   45
Beneath the high-roofed hall of glorious Menelaos.
But when they had taken their joy of looking with their eyes,
They went out and got washed in the well-polished bathtubs.
And when the maidservants had washed them and rubbed them
    with oil,
They put woolen cloaks around them and also tunics,   50
And they sat on armchairs beside Menelaos, son of Atreus.
A handmaid poured water from a pitcher she was carrying,
A lovely golden one, over into a silver basin,
For washing the hands. She set up a polished table alongside.
A respected housekeeper served bread she was carrying,   55
Laying out many dishes, gracious with the provisions.
A carver lifted up and set out trenchers of meats
Of all sorts, and set out gold goblets alongside for them.
Making a sign to the two men, blond Menelaos addressed them:
"Take some of the food and enjoy yourselves; and when   60
You have partaken of dinner, we shall ask what men
You may be. The race of your parents is not lost in you;
But you are of the race of men who are scepter-bearing kings,
Nourished by Zeus, since mean men would not produce sons
    like these."
So he spoke, and he took in his hands and set before them   65
The fat roast ox-back he had been given as an honor himself.
They stretched forth their hands to the food that was spread out
    ready.
But when they had taken their fill of food and drink,

Then Telemachos spoke out to the son of Nestor,
70 Holding his head close so that the others might not hear:
"Son of Nestor, you who have delighted my heart,
Notice the flash of bronze through the echoing halls,
Of gold and of amber, of silver and of ivory;
The court of Olympian Zeus must be like this inside,
75 So many wonders are here. Awe holds me when I look at them."
Blond Menelaos was aware of him as he spoke.
He addressed his voice to them and uttered wingèd words:
"Dear children, surely no mortal may contend with Zeus.
Immortal are his dwelling and his possessions.
80 But of men few if any could contend with me
In possessions. Yes, I suffered much and wandered much
When I brought them in the ships and arrived in the eighth
    year.
I wandered to Cyprus, to Phoenicia, and to the Egyptians;
I reached the Ethiopians, the Sidonians, and the Erembi,
85 And Libya, where the lambs are born sprouting horns at once.
The sheep give birth three times within a complete year.
No lord there, and also no shepherd, is at all lacking
In cheese and in meats, and not in sweet milk either;
But the flocks always furnish abundant milk for suckling.
90 I wandered thereabouts getting a great livelihood
While another man killed my brother unawares,
Secretly, through the cunning of his accursèd wife.
So it is not in delight that I rule over these possessions.
You will have heard about this from your fathers, whoever
95 They may be, since I suffered much, and ruined a home,
A good habitation, containing many noble things.
Would I might dwell in my halls with just a third share
Of those things, and the men were safe who perished then
In broad Troy, far away from horse-nourishing Argos!
100 But nevertheless I frequently sit in our halls
Mourning and grieving over all of them; sometimes
I please my mind with lamentation and sometimes
I cease from it. For quick is the glut of cold lamentation.
I do not, though I am grieved, mourn for them all so much
105 As I do for one man, who makes food and sleep hateful to me
When I think of him, since none of the Achaians suffered as
    much
As Odysseus suffered and bore. For him there were destined

To be troubles, and for me a perpetually ceaseless grief
Over him, since he has long been gone, and we do not know
If he lives or is dead. I suppose they are mourning him now,   110
The old Laertes and constant Penelope,
And Telemachos, whom he left as a newborn child in his
    house."
So he spoke, and roused in him a longing to mourn his father.
A tear fell on the ground from his eyelids as he heard of his
    father,
And he held the purple mantle up before his eyes   115
With both of his hands. Menelaos perceived him
And turned it over in his mind and in his heart
Whether he should allow him to mention his father himself
Or should first inquire and test him in the details.
While he pondered these matters in his mind and in his heart, 120
Helen[1] came out of the high-roofed fragrant bedroom,
She who resembled Artemis[2] of the golden shafts.
Adreste went with her and set up a well-made couch for her,
And Alcippé carried in a rug of soft wool.
Phylo carried a silver basket that Alcandré   125
Had given her, the wife of Polybos, who dwelt
In Egyptian Thebes, where the most goods are stored in the
    houses.
He gave two bathtubs of silver to Menelaos
And a pair of cauldrons and ten talents of gold.
His wife on her own presented the loveliest gifts to Helen;   130
She gave her a gold distaff, a basket with wheels underneath
Made of silver, and the rims of it were finished with gold.
The servant Phylo brought it in and set it out before her,
Stuffed with artfully arranged thread, and on it
There lay a distaff holding dark violet wool.   135
She sat in the chair; a footstool was beneath for her feet.
Right away she asked her husband in words for the details:
"Menelaos, nourished by Zeus, do we know who these people
Who have come to our home claim to be among men?
Shall I dissemble or speak the truth? My heart bids me to.   140
I think I have never yet seen anyone so like him,
A man or a woman; wonder holds me as I see this man,
For the way he looks like great-hearted Odysseus' son

1. Wife of Menelaos; carried off by Paris to Troy.
2. Daughter of Zeus and sister of Apollo.

Telemachos, whom he left as a newborn child in his house.
145 He did so when you Achaians, because of my bitch-faced self,
Went up under Troy intending a strenuous war."
And blond Menelaos addressed her in answer:
"My wife, I also now think it is just as you suppose.
His feet are the same as that man's, his hands are the same,
150 And the glances of his eyes, and his head, and the hair upon it.
Yes, just now I was remembering about Odysseus
And telling how much that man suffered in his grief
For my sake, and he shed quick tears from under his eyebrows,
Holding up the purple mantle in front of his eyes."
155 Peisistratos, son of Nestor, addressed him in answer:
"Son of Atreus, Zeus-nourished Menelaos , chief of the people,
This is really the son of the man, as you say.
But he is prudent; and in his heart he is ashamed
To come so the first time and make a show of bold talk
160 Before you, in whose voice we both delight as in a god's.
Now, the Gerenian horseman Nestor sent me out
To go along with him as a guide. He longed to see you,
So that you might provide him with something, a word or a
    deed.
The son of a father who is gone away has many pains
165 Within his halls, if there be no other helpers for him,
As now for Telemachos he is gone away, and there are
No others in the district who might ward off misery."
And blond Menelaos addressed him in answer:
"Well now, he comes to my house as the son of a man indeed
170 Very dear to me, one who suffered many trials for my sake,
And I thought when he came I would befriend him above all
Of the Argives, if broad-seeing Olympian Zeus had granted
A return for us both in our swift ships over the sea.
I would have settled him in a city in Argos and made a house,
175 Bringing him from Ithaca with his goods and his son
And all of his people, when I had sacked one city
Of those settled nearby that are ruled over by me.
When they were here we would often have mingled. Nothing
    else
Could have parted us two in our friendship and delight,
180 At least till the black cloud of death had veiled us about.
But the god himself must somehow have been jealous
To have made that wretched man alone fail to return."

So he said, and roused desire for lamentation in them all.
The Argive Helen wept, she who was born of Zeus,
And Telemachos wept, and Menelaos too, son of Atreus;   185
Nor did the son of Nestor keep his eyes without tears,
For in his heart he remembered excellent Antilochos,
Whom the glorious son of the brilliant Dawn had slain.
As he called that man to mind, he uttered wingèd words:
"Son of Atreus, old Nestor used to declare you to be   190
Sound-minded above mortals when we in his halls
Called you to mind and asked one another about you,
And now, if it may be, listen to me; I for my part
Do not enjoy mourning at dinner. And besides,
The early-born dawn will be here. I do not at all blame   195
Weeping for any mortal who dies and meets his fate.
This indeed is the sole honor for sorrowful mortals,
To cut the hair for them and let a tear fall from our cheeks.
Yes, my brother is dead, too, by no means the worst
Of the Argives. You probably knew him; I for my part   200
Never met him or saw him. They say Antilochos
Was better than others in fighting and in speed of running."
Then blond Menelaos addressed him in answer:
"My friend, you have said as much as a sound-minded man
Would say and perform, even one who was born before you.   205
You are the son of a great father, to speak so sound-mindedly.
Easily known is the seed of a man for whom the son of Cronos
Weaves the thread of wealth when he marries and when he is
    born,
Such as he has now steadily given Nestor all his days;
So the man himself may grow sleekly old in his halls,   210
And his sons may be wise and may excel with spears;
But let us cease the lamentation that was made before,
And let us once more think about dinner; let them pour
Water on our hands. There will be stories after dawn
For Telemachos and me to talk out with one another."   215
So he said, and Asphalion poured water over their hands,
The capable servant of glorious Menelaos.
And they stretched forth their hands to the food that was spread
    out ready.
Then Helen, who was born of Zeus, had another thought.
Right away she dropped a drug in the wine they were drinking,   220
A soothing pain-killer, that made one forget all his ills,

And whoever swallowed it down when it was mixed in the bowl
Would not shed a tear down his cheeks the whole day long,
Not if his mother and his father were both to die,
225 Not if right in front of him his brother or his dear son
Were slaughtered with a sword, and he see it with his own eyes.
Drugs of such devices did the daughter of Zeus have,
Good ones, which Polydamna gave her, wife of Thon,
From Egypt, where the grain-giving earth bears the most drugs,
230 Many of them good in mixture, and many harmful;
And each man is a physician, knowledgeable beyond
All men. For they are truly of the race of Paieon.[3]
But when she had put it in and called for wine to be poured,
She answered with a speech and spoke out once again:
235 "Zeus-nourished Menelaos, son of Atreus, and you men too,
Who are children of noble men—well, Zeus as a god gives
Good and evil now to one man and now to another;
For he can do all things. But come, sit and dine now in the hall,
And enjoy the tales. I shall tell an appropriate one.
240 Now I shall not be able to tell or enumerate all
Of the many trials there were for stout-hearted Odysseus;
But what a deed this one was the mighty man did and dared
In the land of the Trojans where you Achaians suffered troubles:
When he had submitted himself to disfiguring blows,
245 He threw a poor covering over his shoulders, and in the likeness
Of a servant he entered the enemy's broad-streeted city.
He likened himself in his concealment to another mortal,
To a beggar, he who by the Achaians' ships was nothing like
    that.
In that guise he entered the city of the Trojans. They all
250 Overlooked him. I alone recognized him as he was.
And I questioned him. He eluded me cunningly.
But when I was washing him and rubbing him with oil,
And had put garments on him and sworn a mighty oath
That I would not reveal Odysseus to the Trojans before
255 He should make his way back to the huts and the swift ships,
Then he told me the entire purpose of the Achaians.
Many of the Trojans he killed with the long-edged sword,
And went back to the Argives, and brought much information;
Then the other Trojan women lamented loudly. My heart,
    though,

3. A legendary physician of the gods; later, Apollo.

Rejoiced, since already the heart within me was turned   260
To go back home, and I bemoaned the madness Aphrodite
Gave me when she led me there far from my own fatherland,
Abandoning my daughter, my bedchamber, and my husband,
Who was lacking in nothing, either of mind or of form."
The blond Menelaos addressed her in answer: 265
"Yes, indeed, my wife, you have said all this properly.
Already I have learned the purpose and the thought of many
Men, of heroes, and I have traveled to many lands,
But never yet did I see with my own eyes such a man
As stout-minded Odysseus was, in his own heart,   270
Nor such a deed as that mighty man did and dared
In the polished horse, where all the noblest of us Argives
Sat inside bearing murder and destiny for the Trojans;
And then you came there. Some god must have beckoned you,
One of those who wished to bring glory to the Trojans;   275
Yes, and Deiphobos,[4] like a god, followed you as you went.
Three times you walked round the hollow decoy, handling it,
And called out the best of the Danaans, naming them by name,
Making your voice like that of the wives of all the Argives.
I and the son of Tydeus and godlike Odysseus,   280
As we sat in their midst, heard you as you shouted.
And the two of us were eager to make a start,
Either to get outside or to reply at once from within.
But Odysseus held us back and restrained us, though we wanted
     to.
Then all the other sons of the Achaians were silent   285
And Antilochos alone wished to give you answer
With a speech. But Odysseus steadily pressed the man's mouth
With his powerful hands, and he saved all the Achaians.
He held him until Pallas Athene led you away."
Then sound-minded Telemachos addressed him in answer: 290
"Menelaos, Zeus-nourished son of Atreus, chief of the people,
The more painful it is! This did not ward off his sad death
Nor would have, if the heart had been of iron within him.
But come, send us off to bed, so that right away
We may take the pleasure of lying down under sweet sleep."   295
So he said, and Argive Helen called to the serving maids
To put bedsteads down in the colonnade and to throw on
Lovely purple rugs, and to spread blankets above them,

4. Son of Priam and Hecuba; a prominent Trojan warrior.

And to put down woolen mantles on top of all that.
300 They went out of the hall bearing each a torch in her hand
And covered the bedsteads. And a herald led the strangers out.
So they went to sleep right there in the forecourt of the house,
The hero Telemachos and the illustrious son of Nestor.
The son of Atreus slept in a nook of the lofty house,
And by him lay Helen of the long gown, a goddess among
305   women.
And when the early-born, rosy-fingered dawn appeared,
Menelaos, good at the war cry, rose up out of his bed,
Put on his clothes, set the sharp sword round his shoulder,
Bound the lovely sandals beneath his shining feet,
310 And went on out of the bedroom like a god to look at.
He sat by Telemachos, and spoke out to him directly:
"Hero Telemachos, what need brought you hither
To godly Lacedemon, upon the broad back of the sea,
A public one or your own? Tell me this unerringly."
315 Sound-minded Telemachos addressed him in answer:
"Menelaos, Zeus-nourished son of Atreus, chief of the people,
I came to see if you might tell me some news of my father.
My house is being eaten up, my fertile lands are ruined,
My home is full of enemy men who perpetually slay
My throngs of sheep and my shamble-footed, crumple-horned
320   cattle,
Suitors of my mother, who possess presumptuous pride.
So now I embrace your knees to ask if you are willing
To tell me about that man's woeful death, if you saw it
With your own eyes, perhaps, or heard the tale from another
325 Wanderer. For excessive sorrow did his mother bear him!
Sweeten nothing out of pity or respect for me,
But tell me straight out how you encountered the sight,
I beseech you, if ever my father, noble Odysseus,
Promised you any word or deed and carried it out
330 In the Trojan's land where you Achaians suffered troubles,
Remember that for me now, and tell me unerringly."
Greatly disturbed, blond Menelaos spoke to him:
"Well now, they who are themselves without courage
Have wished to lie down in the bed of a stouthearted man!
335 As when a deer in the thicket of a mighty lion
Has put her newborn milk-sucking fawn to sleep,
And goes questing over the spurs and the grassy gorges

For grazing, and just then he comes into his own lair
And upon the two of them brings a wretched fate;
So upon these men will Odysseus bring a wretched fate.   340
Father Zeus and Athene and Apollo, I wish
He might be as he once was in well-established Lesbos,
When he stood up and wrestled in a fight with Philomelides,
Threw him down mightily, and all the Achaians rejoiced—
As that sort of man might Odysseus contend with the suitors.   345
They would all be swift in their doom and bitter in marriage.
As for what you ask and beseech me about, I myself
Will say nothing at all off the point, nor will I deceive.
But what the unerring old man of the sea told me,
Not a word of that shall I hide from you or conceal.   350
The gods were still holding me in Egypt, though I was striving
To return here, as I had not sacrificed full hecatombs for them.
The gods have always wished their injunctions to be kept in
   mind.
Well, there is a certain island in the much-surging ocean,
Over before the Nile, and they call it Pharos,   355
Just so far away as a hollow ship in a day
Could reach it, with a shrill breeze blowing on behind.
There is a well-sheltered harbor in it, from which men launch
Balanced ships on the ocean, when they have drawn black water
   on board.
There the gods held me twenty days. No breezes ever   360
Came blowing upon the sea, the ones that become
Escorts for ships over the broad back of the sea.
And all the food would have been spent, and the men's
   strength,
If one of the gods had not felt sorry for me and pitied me,
The daughter of mighty Proteus, old man of the sea,   365
Eidothëe; her heart I aroused especially,
When she met me walking alone apart from my companions,
For they were always roaming around the island fishing
With bent fishhooks, and hunger wore on their stomachs.
She stood close to me, spoke, and uttered a speech: 370
'Are you a fool, stranger? Are you too slack of mind?
Do you willingly let go and enjoy suffering pain?
So long a time are you held back on the island and cannot
Find a way out, and the heart dwindles in your companions.'
So she said, and I addressed her in answer: 375

'I shall tell you right out, whatever goddess you are,
That I do not hold back at all willingly, but I must have
Trespassed against the immortals who possess broad heaven.
But you tell me now yourself—the gods know all—
380 Which of the immortals constrains and binds me from my way;
And tell about my return, how I may go on the fish-laden
    ocean?'
So I said; she, the divine goddess, answered at once:
'All right, stranger, I shall speak out truthfully.
A certain unerring old man of the sea comes here,
385 The immortal Egyptian, Proteus, who knows
The depths of the whole sea, a subject to Poseidon.
They say he is my own father and sired me.
If somehow you could hide in an ambush and catch him,
He will tell you your course and the measures of your way,
390 About a return, how you may go on the fish-laden ocean,
And he may tell you, too, if you wish, you who are nourished by
    Zeus,
Whatever good and evil has been done in your halls
While you have been gone on the long and burdensome jour-
    ney.'
So did she speak, and I addressed her in answer:
395 'Show me now yourself the ambush for the divine old man,
Lest somehow he see me or learn of me first and escape,
As it is hard for a god to be subdued by a mortal man.'
So I said, and she, the divine goddess, answered at once:
'All right, I shall speak straight out to you truthfully.
400 At the time when the sun strides the middle of heaven,
Then the unerring old man of the sea comes from the sea
Under the blowing West Wind, hidden in a black ripple;
And when he gets out he sleeps down inside the hollow caves.
Around him the foot-swimming seals of the lovely sea's daughter
405 Sleep in a flock, when they have risen out of the hoary sea,
Exhaling a bitter smell of the sea that has many depths;
There I will lead you myself when the dawn appears
And will lay you down in due order. Make a good choice
Of three companions who are your best in the well-timbered
    ships,
410 And I shall tell you all the cunning of this old man.
At first he will number the seals and go over them,
But when he has counted them by fives and looked at them all,

He will lie in their midst like a shepherd amid flocks of sheep.
And when you first see him lying down to rest,
At that very moment give heed to your strength and might.   415
Hold him struggling there, though he be violent to escape.
He will try it by becoming all the many creatures
That move on the earth; and then water, and divinely kindled
    fire.
But hold him firmly yourselves and constrain him the more.
When at last he questions you with a speech as himself   420
And is the way he was when you saw him resting,
Then, hero, hold back your strength and release the old man,
And ask him which one of the gods oppresses you,
And about a return, how you may go on the fish-laden ocean.'
When she had said this, she vanished into the ocean's surging
    waves.   425
But I went to the ships where they were standing on the sands.
The heart within me brooded about much as I went.
But when I arrived at the ship and at the sea,
And had prepared dinner, and ambrosial night came on,
Then did we lie down to sleep by the surf of the sea.   430
And when the early-born, rosy-fingered dawn appeared,
I went on along the strand of the wide-pathed sea,
Supplicating the gods very much. And I brought along
Three companions whom I most trusted for every course.
Meanwhile she had gone down under the broad bosom of the
    sea   435
And she took four skins of the seals out of the ocean;
All of them were new-flayed. And she planned a trick on her
    father.
When she had scooped out beds in the sands of the sea,
She sat waiting. We came up very close to her.
She bedded us down in a row and threw a skin over each;   440
There the ambush would have been most dreadful. The dire
    smell
Of the sea-nourished seals oppressed us dreadfully,
For who would lie down to sleep with a monster of the sea?
But she saved us herself and thought up a great remedy;
She brought and put under each one's nostrils, ambrosia   445
That has a sweet aroma, and it destroyed the smell of seal,
And we waited with enduring heart the whole morning.
The seals came up in a flock from the sea. Then in a row

They lay down to sleep along the surf of the sea.
450 At full light the old man came from the sea and found his seals
Well nourished; he went over them all and counted their
        number,
And us he numbered first among the seals, nor did it occur
To his heart that there was a trick. Then he lay down himself.
But we rushed on him with a shout and threw our hands
455 Around him. The old man did not forget his wily skill.
First of all he became a lion with a mighty beard,
And then a serpent, and a panther, and a great boar.
Then he became watery water, and a lofty-leaved tree.
But we held on firmly with an enduring heart,
460 And when the old man of cunning skill was exhausted,
He spoke out to me and questioned me with a speech:
'Which of the gods, son of Atreus, has devised plots for you
That you catch me in ambush against my will? What do you
        need?'
So he spoke, and I for my part addressed him in answer:
465 'You know, old man—why do you say this and put me off?—
How long I am held back on this island and can find
No way out, and the heart is dwindling within me.
But you yourself tell me now—the gods know all—
Which of the immortals constrains me and binds me from my
        way,
470 And my return, how I may go on the fish-laden ocean?'
So I said, and right away he addressed me in answer:
'Surely before embarking you ought to have made fair sacrifices
To Zeus and the other gods, so that you may very soon
Reach your fatherland, sailing on the wine-faced sea.
475 For it will not be your lot to see your friends and to reach
Your well-established home and your own fatherland
Until you come once again to the waters of the Nile,
The Zeus-fallen [5] river, and there perform sacred hecatombs
To the immortal gods who possess broad heaven.
480 Then the gods will give you the journey you desire.'
So he said, but my own heart was shattered within me,
Because he ordered me back onto the murky ocean,
To go to the Nile, a long and burdensome journey.
Yet this is what I answered, addressing him with a speech:

5. This probably means "rain-fed," since it is "Zeus" who "rains" in
ancient Greece.

'So shall I perform it, old man, just as you direct me.   485
But come now, tell me this, and speak out truthfully:
Did all the Achaians arrive safe and sound with their ships,
Those whom Nestor and I left when we went from Troy,
Or did any of them perish on his ship by a harsh death?
Or in the arms of his friends, after he had wound up the war?'   490
So I said, and he straightway addressed me in answer:
'Son of Atreus, why do you ask me all this? There is no need
For you to know it or learn my thoughts. And I say that you
Will not long be tearless when you have found it all out.
Many of them were overcome, and many are left.   495
But two leaders alone of the bronze-clad Achaians
Died on the return. As for the battle, you were there yourself.
A single man, perhaps still alive, is held back on the broad
    ocean.
Ajax [6] was overcome in the midst of his long-oared ships.
Poseidon at first brought him up close to Gyrai,   500
The great headlands, and rescued him out of the sea.
And he would have escaped his fate, though hated by Athene,
If he had not thrown out a bold word and lost his senses.
He said he had escaped the sea's great gulf against the god's will,
And Poseidon heard him as he uttered his great boast;   505
Straightway then he took his trident in his muscular hands,
Struck the headland of Gyrai, and split some of it off;
One part stayed on the spot; the fragment fell in the ocean,
The one Ajax was perched on when he lost his senses,
And it carried him down to the boundless wave-breaking ocean. 510
So he perished there, when he had drunk the salty water.
Your brother, though, escaped the fates and eluded them
In his hollow ships. And the queenly Hera [7] saved him.
But just at the time when he was set to arrive at the sheer
Mountain of Malea, a tempest snatched him up   515
And carried him heavily groaning on the fish-laden ocean,
To the verge of the land where the halls of Thyestes were
Beforehand, but now Thyestes' son Aigisthos lived there.
And when from that place, too, a safe return appeared,
The gods turned the breeze back again and sent him homeward. 520
Rejoicing, he set foot on the soil of his fatherland,

6. This is the "second" Ajax, son of Oileus, not the better-known son
of Telamon.
7. Queen of the gods; wife and sister of Zeus.

And he kept kissing the fatherland as he touched it. Many warm
　　tears
Poured from his eyes when in gladness he saw his land.
But a watchman saw him from a watch point, whom cunning
525　Aigisthos had led and stationed there, and promised a reward,
Two talents of gold, and he watched there for a year
Lest the man should slip by him and recall his impetuous might.
He went through the halls to tell the shepherd of the people.
Right away Aigisthos thought up a crafty design.
530　He picked out the twenty best men in the district and set
An ambush, and bid them make dinner on the other side.
And he went to call Agamemnon, shepherd of the people,
With horses and chariot, planning his horrid plans.
He led him in unaware of his destruction,
535　And after feasting him, slew him, as one kills an ox at the crib.
None of the comrades was left who followed the son of Atreus,
And none of Aigisthos' but they were killed in the halls.'
So he said, but my own heart was shattered within me.
And I wept as I sat on the sand, and wished in my heart
540　Not to live any longer and see the light of the sun.
But when I had enough of weeping and groveling,
Then the unerring old man of the sea addressed me:
'Son of Atreus, do not weep any more so persistently
And so long, since we shall find no result from that,
545　But try to arrive as soon as you can at your fatherland.
You may find the man alive, or Orestes will have gone ahead
And killed him, and you may come upon his funeral.'
So he said, and the heart within me and the bold spirit
Were warmed again in my breast, even though I was grieved.
550　And speaking out to him, I uttered wingèd words:
'These men I know of. But tell me about the third man,
The one who was held back upon the broad sea, still alive,
Or he is dead. Though I am grieved, I want to hear of him.'
So I said, and right away he addressed me in answer:
555　'That is the son of Laertes, whose home is in Ithaca,
I saw him on an island shedding a swelling tear
In the halls of the nymph Calypso, who by compulsion
Is holding him back, and he cannot reach his fatherland,
For he has no ships there with oars, and no companions
560　Who might convey him over the broad back of the sea.
And for you it is not decreed, Zeus-nourished Menelaos,

In horse-pasturing Argos to die and to meet your fate.
But the immortals will send you to the Elysian plain
And the end of the earth, where blond Rhadamanthys [8] is,
And where the easiest living exists for men.   565
No snow is there, not much winter, and never rain,
But instead clearly blowing breezes of the West Wind
Does Oceanos [9] always send on to put a fresh breath in men,
Because you have Helen and are for them a son-in-law of Zeus.'
When he had said this, he went down under the wave-breaking
    ocean.   570
But I went to the ships with my godlike companions,
And the heart within me was troubled as I went.
But when we arrived at the ships and at the sea
And had prepared a dinner and ambrosial night came on,
Then did we lie down to sleep by the surf of the sea.   575
And when the early-born, rosy-fingered dawn appeared,
First of all we dragged our ships to the godly sea
And set up masts and sails upon the balanced ships,
Then we ourselves boarded and sat down at the oarlocks.
Seated in a row, we beat the hoary sea with our oars.   580
Back at the Egyptian Nile, the Zeus-fallen river,
I beached the ships and sacrificed complete hecatombs.
When I had calmed down the wrath of the ever-living gods
I set up a mound for Agamemnon so his fame would be
    unquenched.
When I completed this, I left. The immortals gave me   585
A breeze, and they sent me quickly to my dear fatherland—
But come, stay on for the time being here in my halls,
Until the eleventh day comes, and also the twelfth.
Then I will send you off well; I will give you glorious gifts,
Three horses and a well-polished chariot. And then   590
I will give you a lovely libation cup, so you may pour
To the immortal gods, remembering me all your days."
Then sound-minded Telemachos addressed him in answer:
"Son of Atreus, do not hold me back here a long time.
I myself would surely stay sitting here with you   595
For a year, and no longing for home or parents would take me;
So terribly pleased am I to be listening to your words
And stories. Already my companions in hollowed Pylos

8. A judge over the dead.
9. The mythical ocean encircling the earth.

Are worrying, and you have held me back here for some time.
600 As for the gift you would give me, let it be a keepsake.
I will not bring horses to Ithaca, but I shall leave them here
As an adornment for yourself. You rule a broad plain
And in it there is much clover and galingale,
Wheat in it, and emmer grain, and broad-growing white barley.
605 In Ithaca there are no broad courses or any meadow;
It has pasture for goats and is pleasanter than a horse pasture.
But none of the islands that lie by the sea has good meadows
Or a place for driving horses, and Ithaca surpasses them all."
So he said, and Menalaos, good at the war cry, smiled.
610 He caressed him with one hand, and spoke out to him directly:
"You are of good blood, dear child, to judge by what you say,
And so I will exchange these for you, since I can.
Of the gifts that lie stored as keepsakes in my house,
I shall give you the one that is loveliest and of highest worth.
615 I shall give you a well-fashioned mixing bowl. It is all
Of silver, and its rim is finished round with gold,
The work of Hephaistos. The hero Phaidimos gave it,
King of the Sidonians, when his house took me in
As I had returned that far. I would like to give it to you."
620 And so they said such things to one another,
While the dinner guests went to the halls of the godly king.
They drove in sheep and brought in wine that is good for men,
And their wives with beautiful shawls sent them bread.
So they were busying themselves about dinner in the halls.
625 Meanwhile the suitors out in front of the hall of Odysseus
Were amusing themselves by throwing weights and javelins
On the leveled terrace, as before, in their insolence.
Antinoos sat by, and the godlike Eurymachos,
Leaders of the suitors, who for excellence were far the best.
630 Noemon, the son of Phronios, came close to them
And addressed Antinoos, questioning him with a speech:
"Antinoos, do we or do we not know in our minds
When Telemachos is coming back from sandy Pylos?
He has gone off in my ship. A need for it has arisen
635 To cross over to Elis of the broad dancing-place
Where I have twelve brood mares, and suckling mules, tough
    workers,
That are untrained; one of these I would drive and tame."

So he said. They were amazed at heart. They did not think
He had gone to Nelean Pylos, but was somewhere there
Around in the fields with the sheep or with the swineherd.   640
Then Antinoos, son of Eupeithes, addressed him:
"Tell me unerringly when he went away and what
Young men went with him. Were they the chosen of Ithaca
Or his own slaves and hirelings? He could have done this too.
Tell me this exactly, so that I may know it well,   645
Did he take the black ship by force from you against your will,
Or did you give it willingly when he begged you with a speech?"
Noemon, son of Phronios, addressed him in answer:
"I gave it to him willingly. What would another man do
When a man of such a kind had cares in his heart   650
And requested it? It would be hard to refuse the gift.
The young men who are best in the district, next to us,
Went with him. And I noticed Mentor boarding as leader,
Or a god who in every way resembled him.
And I wonder at this; I saw godlike Mentor here   655
Yesterday morning. Yet he was gone then in the ship to Pylos."
When he had said this, he went off to the halls of his father.
And in both of them the bold spirit was amazed.
They sat the suitors down together and stopped their contests.
Antinoos, son of Eupeithes, spoke out to them,   660
Troubled. For his heart, black all round, was greatly filled
With rage. And his eyes resembled a shining fire:
"Well now, this voyage is a great deed carried out very boldly
By Telemachos. We thought he would not carry it out.
In spite of us all, he went off, the young child, just like that,   665
When he had dragged down the ship and chosen the best in the
     district.
He will begin to be a trouble even more. Yet may Zeus
Destroy his power before he gains the measure of manhood.
But come now, give me a swift ship and twenty companions,
So that I may lie in ambush and watch for him as he comes   670
In the channel between Ithaca and rugged Samos,
That this voyage for his father may be a grievous one."
So he said, and they all spoke out and assented.
They stood up at once then and went to the house of Odysseus,
Nor was Penelope for a long time unaware   675
Of the plots that the suitors were pondering in their hearts:

Medon, the herald, told her, who had listened to their plans
When he was outside the courtyard; they were weaving their de-
    ceit within.
He went through the halls to announce it to Penelope,
And Penelope addressed him as he stepped down on the thresh-
680   old:
"Herald, why did the noble suitors send you out?
To bid the maidservants of the godly Odysseus
To cease from their labors and fix a dinner for them?
May they never go wooing or come together elsewhere;
685 May they dine here now for the last and final time.
You who often gather and consume a large living,
The wealth of skilled Telemachos, did you not hear
From your fathers long ago, when you were children,
The sort of man Odysseus was among your parents?
690 He never performed or said anything unjust
In the district—this is the way of godly kings,
Who might despise one mortal and love another—
But he never acted recklessly against any man.
Now your own hearts and your disgraceful deeds
695 Are clear. There are no thanks afterward for deeds well done."
Then Medon, sound-minded in knowledge, addressed her:
"Well, my queen, may this be your greatest misfortune.
But the suitors are devising another one greater by far
And more disastrous. May the son of Cronos not bring it to
    pass!
700 They are eager to murder Telemachos with the sharp sword
As he comes homeward. He went off to hear of his father
To divine Pylos, and also to godly Lacedemon."
So he said; right there her knees and her own heart went slack.
Speechlessness seized her for a long time. Her two eyes
705 Were filled with tears, and her resonant voice was held back.
She answered him at last with a speech and addressed him:
"Herald, why did my son go away? There was no need
At all to embark in the swift-faring ships, that are
Horses of the sea for men and cross over much water.
710 Was it so that not even his name might be left among men?"
Then Medon, sound-minded in knowledge, answered her:
"I do not know whether some god incited him
Or his own spirit roused him to go to Pylos to learn
If his father will return or has met his fate."

When he had said this, he went into the house of Odysseus.   715
But heartbreaking anguish poured over her. No longer
Could she bear sitting on a chair, and many were in the house.
But she sat down on the threshold of the richly adorned bed-
    room,
Lamenting piteously, and the serving maids moaned about her,
All the many that were in the halls, young and old.   720
When she had moaned heavily, Penelope spoke out to them:
"Hear me, my friends. For Olympian Zeus has given me pain
Beyond all the women who were born and raised in my time;
Beforehand I lost a noble lion-hearted husband,
Who excelled in all the virtues among the Danaans,   725
A noble man whose glory is wide through Greece and middle
    Argos.
And now storms have snatched away my beloved son
Unnoticed from the halls; nor did I hear of his rushing off.
Cruel ones—why did each of you at least not put it in her mind
To wake me out of bed, when you clearly knew in your heart   730
The time he was going down to the hollow black ship?
If I had found out he was considering the voyage,
Then, though eager for voyage, he would surely have stayed
    here,
Or else he would have left me in the halls a dead woman.
But let someone speedily call the old man Dolios,   735
My servant, whom my father gave me before I came here,
Who tends my garden with its many trees; so he shall right
    away
Sit down beside Laertes and explain all this to him;
If somehow that man may weave some plan in his mind
And may go out and complain to the people about these men   740
Who wish to destroy his stock and that of godly Odysseus."
Then the beloved nurse Eurycleia addressed her:
"Dear bride, you may slay me with the pitiless sword,
Or leave me in the house. I will not hide the story from you.
I knew all this. I provided all that he ordered,   745
Bread and sweet wine. He put me under a great oath
Not to tell you until either the twelfth day should come,
Or you should miss him yourself and hear of his rushing off,
So you might not weep and injure your lovely skin.
But do take a bath and put clean clothes on your skin.   750
Then ascend to the upper chamber with the serving women

And pray to Athene, daughter of aegis-bearing Zeus,
For she can save him in that case, even from death.
Do not trouble the troubled old man. I do not think
755 The offspring of Arkesios' son is entirely hated
By the blessed gods; there may yet be someone to own
The high-roofed dwelling and the rich fields far away."
So she said, and soothed the other's weeping: she held her eyes
    from weeping.
She did take a bath and put clean clothes on her skin,
760 Ascended to the upper chamber with the serving women,
Put barley for sprinkling in a basket, and prayed to Athene.
"Hear me, unwearying child of aegis-bearing Zeus,
If ever in his halls Odysseus of many devices
Burned the fat thighs of an ox or a sheep for you,
765 Remember them now for me and save my dear son.
Ward the suitors off in their evil presumption."
She wailed as she said this. And the goddess heard her prayer.
The suitors were making a din through the shadowy halls,
And this is what one of the overbearing young men would say:
770 "Yes, indeed, the much-wooed queen is planning a wedding
For us, and does not know that murder is prepared for her son."
So one would say, and they did not know how it was prepared.
And Antinoos spoke out to them and addressed them:
"You fools, keep away from all insolent speeches
775 Entirely, lest someone announce them inside as well.
But come, let us stand up, and accomplish in silence
The very plan that suited the minds of all of us."
When he had said this, he selected the twenty men that were
    best
And they went on down to the swift ship and the strand of the
    sea.
780 First of all they dragged the ship into a depth of salt water,
Then set up a mast and sails upon the black ship.
They fitted the oars into the straps made of leather
All in order—and then stretched out the white sails.
Proud-spirited servants carried equipment on for them.
785 High in flowing water they moored her, and got out themselves.
There they took dinner and waited for evening to come.
The prudent Penelope there in her upper chamber
Lay without eating, not partaking of food or drink,
Pondering whether her excellent son might escape death,

Or would go under to the presumptuous suitors.   790
As much as a lion deliberates in a crowd of men,
Fearing when they draw the stealthy circle about him;
So much did she ponder, and balmy sleep came upon her.
She sank back, and slept, and her limbs were all slackened.
Then the bright-eyed goddess Athene had another thought.   795
She made an image and likened it in form to a woman,
To Iphthime, daughter of great-hearted Icarios
That Eumelos, whose house of dwelling was in Pherai, married.
She sent her to the halls of the godly Odysseus,
So that she could make the grieving and wailing Penelope   800
Cease from her tearful wailing and lamentation.
She went into the bedroom by the thong of the bolt,
Stood over her head, and addressed a speech to her:
"Are you asleep, Penelope, sorrowing in your own heart?
No, the gods who live without care do not allow you   805
To mourn or to grieve, since your son is still set
To return. For he is in no way sinful before the gods."
And then the prudent Penelope answered her,
Slumbering very sweetly within the gates of dreams:
"My kinswoman, why have you come here? Never before   810
Did you visit, since the halls you dwell in are far, far away.
Do you bid me to desist from sorrow and from pains,
The many that beset me in my mind and in my heart?
Beforehand I lost a noble, lion-hearted husband,
A noble man whose glory is wide through Greece and middle
    Argos.   815
Who excelled in all the virtues among the Danaans,
And now my dear son has gone off in a hollow ship,
A foolish child who has no good knowledge of toils or of
    councils,
And I am more grieved about him than about the other.
I tremble for him and fear lest he suffer something   820
In the land of those he has gone to, or on the ocean,
For there are many hostile men who contrive against him,
Wanting to kill him before he reaches his fatherland."
The shadowy image answered and addressed her:
"Take courage; do not fear excessively in your mind.   825
Such is she who goes as his guide, she whom other men
Have prayed to stand by them, and she has the power,
Pallas Athene. She takes pity on your lamenting

And has sent me forth now to say these things to you."
830 Then the prudent Penelope spoke forth to her:
"If indeed you are a god, and have heard the voice of a god,
Come tell me also about that sorrowful man,
Whether he still lives somehow and sees the light of the sun,
Or has already died and is in the halls of Hades."
835 The shadowy image answered her and addressed her:
"About that man I shall not tell you in full detail
Whether he is dead or alive. It is bad to utter windy things."
When it had said this, it slipped through the bolt of the
   doorpost
Into the blasts of the wind. The daughter of Icarios
840 Rose up out of sleep. And her own heart was gladdened,
So clear had the dream rushed upon her in the gloom of the
   night.
The suitors had boarded and were sailing on the watery ways,
Devising in their minds sheer murder for Telemachos.
There is a rocky island in the middle of the sea,
845 Halfway between Ithaca and rugged Samos,
Asteris, not large. Its harbors have coves for ships,
On both sides. There the Achaians lay waiting in ambush.

V

Dawn, out of her bed, from beside the noble Tithonos,[1]
Rose up to bring light to immortals and to mortals.
The gods took their seats in assembly. And in their midst
Was high-thundering Zeus, who has the greatest might.
Athene spoke to them, reminding them of the many cares   5
Of Odysseus. His being in the nymph's home concerned her.
"Father Zeus, and you other blessed, ever-living gods,
Let no scepter-bearing king be deliberately
Kind and mild any longer, or keep his mind on the right,
But may he be perpetually harsh and act unjustly;   10
Since there is no one who remembers the godly Odysseus
Of the people he ruled; and he was mild as a father.
He is staying on an island suffering strong pains
In the halls of the nymph Calypso, who by compulsion
Is holding him back, and he cannot reach his fatherland,   15
For he has no ships there with oars and no companions
Who might convey him over the broad back of the sea.
And now they are striving to kill his beloved son
As he comes homeward. He went off to hear of his father,
To divine Pylos, and also to godly Lacedemon."   20
And cloud-gathering Zeus addressed her in answer:
"My child, what sort of word has got past the bar of your teeth?
Why did you not think out this idea by yourself,
That Odysseus might indeed take vengeance on them when he
     came?
Guide Telemachos yourself, skillfully; you can do it,   25
So that he may arrive unscathed at his fatherland,
And so the suitors may go in their ship back where they came
     from."
He said that, and addressed in turn his dear son Hermes:
"Hermes—for in other matters you are my messenger—

1. The mortal husband of Dawn, granted immortality but not perpetual
youth.

30 Tell the nymph of the fair braids my unerring plan,
   A return for stout-hearted Odysseus, how he may go back
   Without an escort of gods or one of mortal men.
   Yes, and he, on a strongly-bound raft, suffering troubles,
   Will arrive at rich-loamed Scheria on the twentieth day,
35 To the land of the Phaeacians, who are close kin to the gods,
   And they will honor him most heartily as a god.
   They will send him in a ship to his dear fatherland
   When they have given him bronze and gold and sufficient
       clothing,
   Much more than Odysseus would ever have taken from Troy
40 If he had come safe and sound and got his share of the booty.
   And so it is his lot to see his dear ones and arrive
   At his high-roofed home and his own fatherland."
   So he said, and the runner, slayer of Argos, did not disobey.
   At once, then, he bound beneath his feet the lovely sandals,
45 The ambrosial golden ones that carry him over water
   Or the limitless land, swift as the blasts of the wind.
   And he took the wand with which he entrances the eyes
   Of those men he wishes, and wakes up others who are sleeping.
   The strong god, slayer of Argos, flew on with that in his hands.
50 He passed Pieria, and fell from the air on the ocean,
   Then he hastened upon the wave as a sea gull does
   That over the terrible gulfs of the barren sea
   Dips its rapid wings, while catching fish, in the brine.
   Like one of these, Hermes bore himself over many waves.
55 But when he arrived at the island that was far away,
   He stepped from the violetlike ocean onto the dry land,
   And went on till he came to the great cave wherein the nymph
   Of the fair braids was dwelling. He came upon her within.
   On the hearth a big fire was burning, and the smell from afar
60 Of cedar and easy-split citron was exhaled through the island
   As it blazed. She within, singing in a lovely voice,
   Moved to and fro at the loom and wove with a gold shuttle.
   Wood was growing in abundance around the cave,
   Alder and black poplar and fine-scented cypress,
65 Where the birds with their long wings went to sleep,
   Horned owls and hawks and, with their long tongues,
   Salt water crows, who are busy with things of the sea.
   And right on the spot round the hollow cave had been drawn
   A trained vine in bloom that was blossoming with clusters.

Four springs one after another flowed with white water   70
All close together; one turned one way, one another.
All around soft meadows of violet and wild parsley
Were blooming. And even an immortal who might come there
Would wonder to look and be delighted in his mind.
As he stood there, the Runner, the slayer of Argos, wondered,   75
But when he had wondered in his heart at it all,
He went right away into the broad cave. As she faced him,
Calypso, the divine goddess, did not fail to know him by sight,
For the gods never fail to know one another,
The immortals, not even one who lives in a far-off home.   80
And he did not come upon the great-hearted Odysseus within;
The man was weeping, seated on the beach where he had been
     before,
Shattering his heart with tears and laments and groans.
He was looking out on the barren sea, shedding tears.
But Calypso, the divine goddess, questioned Hermes,   85
When she had seated him upon a bright, glistening chair.
"Hermes of the golden wand, my respected friend,
Why have you come to me? You have not come often before.
Say what you have in mind. My spirit bids me to do it
If I am able to do it and if it can be done;   90
But follow me, so I may entertain you as a guest."
When she had said this, the goddess set a table alongside
Full of ambrosia, and she mixed up ruddy nectar.
Then the Runner, the slayer of Argos, ate and drank.
When he had dined and satisfied his heart with food,   95
He spoke out and addressed her in answer with a speech:
"You, a goddess, ask me, a god, why I come. And I
Will tell you the story unerringly, since you ask me.
Zeus ordered me to come here against my own will.
Who would willingly cross so much indescribable   100
Salt water? There is no city of mortals nearby
Who offer sacrifices and choice hecatombs to the gods.
But in no way is it possible for another god
To slip by or frustrate the purpose of aegis-bearing Zeus.
He says you have with you the wretchedest man of all   105
Those men who were fighting around the city of Priam
For nine years; and in the tenth year sacked the city
And went home. But on the return they sinned against Athene,
Who roused up against them an ill wind and great waves.

110 Then all the others, his noble companions, perished.
But the wind and the water carried and brought him here.
Zeus now orders you to send him off as fast as you can.
For it is not right he should waste here far from his dear ones.
No, his fate is still to see his dear ones and come
115 To his high-roofed home and his own fatherland."
So he said, and Calypso, the divine goddess, went cold;
And she spoke out to him and uttered wingèd words:
"You are cruel, you gods, jealous above all others,
Who begrudge it to goddesses when they sleep with men
120 Openly, if one wants to make a man her dear husband.
So when the rosy-fingered Dawn chose Orion,
You gods, who live at ease, begrudged him to her
Till the chaste golden-throned Artemis in Ortygia
Came upon him and slew him with her soothing shafts.
125 And so when fair-braided Demeter yielded in her heart
To Iasion,[2] and lay with him in love and in bed
In a thrice-plowed fallow, it did not take Zeus long
To find out; he slew him, hurling a dazzling thunderbolt.
So now you gods begrudge me a mortal man's being with me.
130 I myself saved him as he was bestriding his keel
All alone, when Zeus with a dazzling thunderbolt
Crushed his swift ship, and sank it in the middle of the
       wine-faced sea.
Then all the others, his noble companions, perished.
But the wind and the water carried and brought him here.
135 I have loved him and nourished him and I have declared to him
I would make him immortal and ageless all his days.
But in no way is it possible for another god
To slip by or frustrate the purpose of aegis-bearing Zeus.
Let him go, if that god commands him and drives him
140 Out on the barren ocean. I myself will send him nowhere,
For I have no ships here with oars, and no companions
Who might convey him over the broad back of the sea.
But I shall advise him graciously, and shall conceal nothing,
So that he may arrive unscathed at his fatherland."
145 And then the Runner, the slayer of Argos, spoke to her:
"Send him off this way now, and respect the wrath of Zeus,

2. Probably an early cult figure, an agricultural god who may have been
united with Demeter, the grain goddess, in a primitive rite on a plowed
field (as suggested in these lines).

So that afterward he will not be enraged and hold it against
    you."
When he had said this, the strong slayer of Argos departed,
And the queenly nymph went to great-hearted Odysseus,
Since she had indeed given ear to the message of Zeus.   150
She found him seated on the shore. His eyes never
Were dry of tears, but his sweet life was flowing away
As he mourned for a return, since the nymph no longer pleased
    him.
But he slept the nights with her by necessity
In the hollow cave, an unwilling man with a willing woman.   155
During the days, sitting up on the rocks and on the beaches,
Shattering his heart with tears and laments and groans,
He kept looking over the barren ocean, shedding tears.
The divine goddess stood close to him and addressed him:
"Ill-fated man, do not mourn here longer beside me, do not let 160
Your life waste away, for I shall now graciously send you off.
But come, cut long pieces of wood and fit them with a bronze
    ax
For a wide raft. And fashion half-decks upon it
High up, so that it may bear you over the murky sea.
And in it I shall put food and water and ruddy wine   165
That are satisfying and will check your hunger.
I shall dress you in clothes and send a breeze behind you,
So that you may arrive unscathed at your fatherland,
If the gods are willing, who possess broad heaven,
Who are more powerful than I at planning and achieving."   170
So she said, and godly Odysseus, who had borne much, went
    cold,
And he spoke out to her and uttered wingèd words:
"You devise this, goddess, for some other reason, not to get me
    there,
And you bid me to traverse in a raft the great gulf of the sea,
Terrible and disastrous, which not even balanced ships,   175
In their swift course, may cross, exulting in the breeze of Zeus.
I would not for my part board the raft against your will
Unless you will put up with swearing me a great oath, goddess,
That you will not plot some other bad trouble against me."
So he said, and the divine goddess Calypso smiled,   180
She caressed him with one hand, and spoke out to him directly:
"Ah, you are a real rogue, skilled in tricks that are not futile,

To have conceived and uttered a speech of this sort.
May the earth and broad heaven above witness this oath,
185 And the flowing water of Styx,[3] which is the greatest
And most dreadful oath there is for the blessed gods:
I will not plot any other bad trouble against you,
But I am thinking and considering the very things
I would plan for myself should an equal need come upon me.
190 Yes, and this is my fitting intention. The heart
In my breast is not of iron, but a pitying one."
When she had said this, the divine goddess led the way
Nimbly. And he went along in the footsteps of the god.
The god and the man arrived at the hollow cave
195 And he sat down there on the chair out of which Hermes
Had risen up. The nymph set out every sort of dish
To eat and drink, of the kind that mortal men eat.
She herself sat down facing the godly Odysseus,
And handmaids placed ambrosia before her and nectar.
They stretched forth their hands to the food that was spread out
200   ready,
And when they had taken their pleasure of eating and drinking
Calypso, the divine goddess, began a speech to him:
"Zeus-born son of Laertes, much-contriving Odysseus,
Do you really want to go home to your dear fatherland
205 Right at once, now? Well, even so, luck be with you!
If you knew in your mind how many sorrows it is
Your fate to fulfill before reaching your fatherland,
Then you would stay right here with me and keep this home
And you would be immortal, even though you would desire
210 To see your wife, whom you long for always every day.
I declare I am not a bit inferior to that woman
In form or in shape, since it is not at all seemly
For mortals to contend with immortals in looks and in form."
Odysseus of many devices addressed her in answer:
215 "Lady goddess, be not angry at me this way. I myself know
All this, that beside you the prudent Penelope
Seen face to face is less striking in form and size.
For she is a mortal and you are immortal and ageless.
Yet even so I am wishing and longing all my days
220 To go home and to see the day of my return.
And if one of the gods wrecks me on the wine-faced sea,

3. River of the Underworld by which the gods swore oaths.

I shall bear it in my breast, with a long-grieving heart.
For I have suffered much already and endured much,
On the waves and in war; and let this be added to those."
So he said, and the sun went down, and darkness came on.   225
The two of them went into a nook of the hollow cave
And took pleasure of love, abiding with one another.
And when the early-born, rosy-fingered dawn appeared,
Then Odysseus at once put on his cloak and his tunic,
And the nymph herself put on a great shining mantle   230
Finely made and pleasing, and a lovely gold sash
Around her waist, and a veil upon her head above.
Then she took thought about sending great-hearted Odysseus
     away;
She gave him a great ax fitted to the palms,
A bronze one, sharpened at both ends; upon it there was   235
A beautiful olive wood handle, well fitted in place.
Then she gave him a well-polished adz and led the way
To the verge of the island where tall trees were growing,
Alder and poplar, and fir that was tall to the heavens,
Dry for a long time, well seasoned, that would float lightly for
     him.   240
And when she had shown him where the tall trees were growing,
Calypso, the divine goddess, went back to her home.
But he cut beams, and the work went quickly for him.
He felled twenty in all and hewed them with the bronze ax,
Planed them skillfully, and set a straight line upon them.   245
Meanwhile, the divine goddess Calypso brought along augers,
And he then bored them all and fitted them to one another.
Then he made it fast with pegs and with fastenings;
And just the way a man who is a well-skilled craftsman
Rounds off the hull of a broad ship for carrying freight,   250
The same measure did Odysseus make for his own broad raft.
He made it by setting deck planks on and fitting them
To the close-set ribs. And he finished it off with long gunwales.
Then he made a mast and a yardarm fitted to it.
He made a rudder, too, so that he might steer straight.   255
And he plaited it all through with wicker osiers
To be a bulwark against the wave. And he set much wood upon
     it.
Meanwhile the divine goddess brought along a piece of cloth
For making sails, and he fashioned those well too.

260 Upon it he tied braces and halyards and tackle and sheets,
And with levers he dragged it down to the godly sea.
It was the fourth day, and he had finished everything.
On the fifth day the divine Calypso sent him from the island
After she had clothed him in fragrant garments and bathed him.
265 The goddess put on board for him a skin of dark wine,
And another, a big one of water, and food, too,
In a bag. And she put many satisfying morsels in for him.
And then she sent on a soothing and gentle breeze.
Delighted at the breeze, godly Odysseus stretched his sails
270 And he steered on with the rudder skillfully
As he sat. Nor did sleep fall upon his eyelids
While he watched the Pleiades and late-setting Boötes,
And the Bear, which they call, too, by the name of the Wagon,
Which turns in one place and also points at Orion,
275 And alone has no share in the washings of Oceanos.
The divine goddess Calypso bade him to keep that star
Upon his left hand, as he fared over the sea.
He sailed seventeen days, faring on the sea,
And on the eighteenth there appeared the shadowy mountains
280 Of the land of the Phaeacians where it was nearest him.
It seemed to be just like a shield on the murky sea.
But the earth-shaking ruler, coming back from the Ethiopians,
Saw him from afar, from the mountains of the Solumoi;
He was seen sailing the ocean. The god in his heart
285 Got very angry. He shook his head and addressed his spirit:
"Well, the gods have now made quite a different plan
About Odysseus, while I was with the Ethiopians;
He is near the Phaeacians' land, where it is his lot
To escape the great bound of woe which has come upon him.
290 And I think I will still drive him into quite enough evil."
When he had said this, he gathered clouds and troubled the
    ocean,
Grasping the trident in his hands. He stirred up whole storms
Of all the winds and covered earth and ocean alike
With clouds. And night rose up from the heavens.
The East Wind fell down, and the South Wind and the hard-
295 blowing West Wind,
And the North Wind that makes clear skies, rolling a great
    wave.
Then Odysseus' knees and his own heart went slack;

He was distressed, and he spoke to his own great-hearted spirit:
"Ah, wretched as I am, what will happen at last to me now?
I fear that the goddess spoke all unerringly   300
When she said I would have a fill of pains on the ocean
Before reaching my fatherland. It has all come to pass,
With such large clouds has Zeus crowned heaven about
And has disturbed the ocean; and storms are rushing on
Of all the winds. Now my sheer destruction is sure.   305
Thrice and four times blessed are the Danaans who perished
In broad Troy then, doing the pleasure of the sons of Atreus.
Would that I myself had died and had met my fate
On that day when numbers of the Trojans did hurl
Bronze-tipped spears at me over the dead son of Peleus: 310
I would have gotten my rites; the Achaians would have spread
    my glory.
But now I am fated to get caught in a miserable death."
A great wave dashed on him as he said that, pushing
Fearfully from its peak, and it spun the raft about.
He himself fell far from the raft. The rudder   315
Shot out of his hands. A fearful storm of intermingled
Winds came up and broke the mast in the middle.
The sail and the yardarm fell into the ocean.
It put him under the water a long time, and he could not
Quickly rise up from the rush of the great wave,   320
For the clothes weighed him down that divine Calypso gave
    him.
At last he did come up, and spat out of his mouth
The bitter brine that flowed plenteously off his head.
Nor did he forget the raft, though he was wearied.
But as he rushed into the waves he caught hold of it   325
And sat in the middle, shunning the end of death.
A great wave carried it here and there along the current.
As when the North Wind at harvest time carries thistles
Over the plain, but they hold close to one another,
So the winds carried it here and there over the sea.   330
Sometimes the South Wind threw it to the North Wind to carry
And sometimes the East Wind yielded it to the South Wind for
    pursuit.
But Cadmos' daughter saw him, Ino [4] of the lovely ankles,

4. She leaped into the sea to save her son, and was made a goddess; her
father, Cadmos, was founder of Thebes.

Leucothea, who earlier had a mortal voice
335 And now in the sea swells gets honor from the gods.
She took pity on Odysseus as he was driven about in his pains.
Like a shearwater she rose in flight from the sea,
Perched on the raft, and addressed a speech to him:
"Ill-fated man, why is the earth-shaker Poseidon
340 So strikingly angry that he spawns you these many ills?
He will not wear you down, however he may desire it.
But do as follows: you do not seem foolish to me:
Take off these clothes and leave the raft for the winds
To carry; and swim with your hands, and strive for reaching
345 The Phaeacians' land, where it is your fate to escape.
And here now, stretch this veil out across your chest.
It is immortal. Have no fear of suffering or dying,
But when you have touched the mainland with your hands,
Untie it again and throw it into the wine-faced sea,
350 Far from the mainland, and turn yourself the other way."
When she had said this, the goddess gave him the veil.
She plunged back herself into the surging waves of the ocean
Like a shearwater. And a black wave covered her.
Godly Odysseus, who had borne much, meditated;
355 And he spoke, grieving, to his own great-hearted spirit:
"Alas for me, I fear one of the immortals is weaving
A snare for me, to have bade me get off the raft;
I shall not yet obey her, since I saw with my own eyes
The land far off where she said was a refuge for me.
360 But this I shall do, and it seems to be best to me.
So long as the beams are fitted to their fastenings,
I will stay here and hold out while I suffer pain.
But when a wave does shake my raft into pieces,
I shall swim, since there is nothing better to think of."
365 While he pondered these things in his mind and in his heart,
Earth-shaker Poseidon stirred up a great wave,
A terrible disastrous one, overarching; it dashed him.
As when a blustering wind shakes up a heap
Of dry husks, and scatters them in all directions,
370 So it scattered the raft's long beams. And Odysseus
Bestrode one spar as if he were riding a horse.
He took off the clothes that divine Calypso gave him,
And he stretched the veil right away beneath his chest.
He fell headlong down in the sea, spreading out his hands

And striving to swim. The lord who disturbs the earth saw him; 375
He shook his head and spoke out to his own spirit;
"So wander now on the ocean, after suffering many ills,
Until you may mingle with men who are nourished by Zeus.
Yet I do not expect you will find fault with your misfortune."
When he had said this, he whipped up his lovely-maned horses [5] 380
And arrived at Aigai, where his renowned dwelling is.
But Athene, daughter of Zeus, had another thought.
She bound up the courses of all the other winds
And bade them die down and all go to sleep.
She stirred up a rapid North Wind and broke waves before it 385
Till Zeus-born Odysseus could mingle with the Phaeacians,
Who love rowing, when he had warded off destinies and death.
Then for two nights and two days upon the thick wave
He wandered, and his heart many times saw destruction ahead.
But when fair-braided Dawn finished the third day, 390
Then at that point the wind died down and there was
A windless calm, and he sighted land nearby,
Scanning sharply, as he raised himself from the great wave.
As when it appears delightful to sons if their father
Lives, who lies in sickness and undergoes strong pains, 395
Long wasting away, and some dread god has assailed him,
Whom now the gods have delightfully freed from misfortune;
So delightful did land and forest appear to Odysseus.
Vigorously he swam to set foot on the mainland.
But when he was as far off as a shout may carry, 400
And had heard against the reefs the noise of the sea—
For the great wave was dashing upon the dry mainland.
Fearfully spraying, it covered all with saltwater foam;
For there were indeed no secure harbors for ships, or channels,
But headlands there were, jutting out, and reefs and cliffs; 405
Then Odysseus' knees and his own heart went slack,
And, grieving, he addressed his own great-hearted spirit:
"Alas, that Zeus has granted me to see unhoped-for land
And I have come to the end of cleaving this gulf,
And no way of escape appears from the hoary sea. 410
But offshore there are sharp reefs, and the wave about them
Moans as it surges, and the rock runs on up smooth.
The sea is deep close in, and there is no way
To stand with both feet and to escape misfortune,

5. Poseidon is fabled to ride a horse chariot through the waves.

415 For a great wave perhaps may snatch me as I am getting out
And hurl me on rough rock, and my trying would be in vain.
But if I can swim along still further and can find
Spits of land jutting out and harbors of the sea,
Then I fear that a storm will seize me back again
420 And bear me heavily groaning onto the fish-laden ocean,
Or some god may drive a great monster on me from the sea,
Of the kind that in numbers the renowned Amphitrite [6] feeds;
For I know how angry the renowned earth-shaker is at me."
He pondered these matters in his mind and in his heart
425 Till a great wave bore him up on the rugged shore.
There his skin would all have been stripped off and his bones
broken
If the bright-eyed goddess Athene had not put a thought in his
mind;
He caught at the rock with both hands as he dashed upon it,
And held onto it moaning, till a great wave came along.
430 And he avoided it so, but it struck him again with its backwash,
And dashed on him and threw him far into the ocean.
As when an octopus is pulled out of its den,
Numerous pebbles are caught in its suckers,
So against the rocks the skin from his stout hands
435 Was stripped off. And the great wave covered him over.
Then surely wretched Odysseus would have died in excess of
fate
If bright-eyed Athene had not given him presence of mind.
Getting up out of the wave that spewed on the mainland,
He swam along it outside, looking for land, if he might happen
440 On spits of land jutting out and harbors of the sea.
But when as he swam on he came up to the mouth
Of a fair-flowing river, there the best place seemed to him to be.
It was bare of rocks, and it had a shelter from the wind.
He perceived it flowing and prayed to it in his heart.
445 "Hear me Lord,[7] whoever you are; I approach you with many
Prayers, fleeing the rebukes of Poseidon out of the ocean.
A man should be respected even by the immortal gods
When anyone approaches, wandering, as now I,
Who have suffered much, approach your knees and your flowing.
450 Have pity, Lord. I declare I am a suppliant to you."

6. A goddess of the sea.
7. The rivers are gods in Homer.

So he said. At once the river stopped flowing and held the wave.
It made a calm in front of him and rescued him
At the issue of the river. Then he bent both his knees
And his stout hands. For his own heart was downed by salt
 water.
All his skin was swollen, and much seawater oozed   455
From his mouth and his nostrils. Breathless and voiceless
He lay with slight strength, and dread fatigue came upon him.
But when he caught his breath and the spirit in his mind
Awakened, he unbound the god's veil from himself
And he let it go into the sea-mingling river.   460
A great wave bore it back down the stream. Ino quickly
Took it in her own hands. He slipped out of the river,
Lay down on a rush bed, and kissed the grain-giving earth.
Then, grieving, he spoke to his own great-hearted spirit:
"Ah, what do I suffer; what will happen to me at last?   465
If I watch through the troublesome night beside the river,
I fear that the evil frost and gentle dew together
May subdue my winded spirit in its slight strength,
For a cold breeze blows from the river just before dawn.
But if I ascend the slope to the shadowy wood   470
And go to sleep in the thick bushes; even if fatigue
And cold let go of me and sweet sleep does come upon me,
I fear I may become a spoil and a prey to wild beasts."
So, as he thought, this seemed to him to be better.
He went on into the wood; he found it near the water   475
In the clearing around, and came upon two bushes growing
From the same place, one of wild olive, one of tame.
Nor did the moist force of the blowing winds breathe through
 them,
And the shining sun never struck them with its beams,
Nor did rain ever reach through to them, so thick   480
Did they grow over and under each other. Odysseus
Went in beneath them. He quickly gathered a broad bed
With his own hands. Leaf-shedding had been quite plentiful,
Enough to give shelter for two or three men
In the winter season, even if it were especially hard.   485
Godly Odysseus, who had borne much, rejoiced to see it.
He lay down in the middle, heaping the fallen leaves over him,
As a man may cover a torch with black embers
At the edge of a field, where no neighbors may be by,

490 And save the fire's seed, so he need not light it from elsewhere.
So Odysseus covered himself with leaves. Athene
Shed sleep on his eyes, so it might release him quite soon
From toilsome fatigue, and she covered his eyelids over.

VI

And so godly Odysseus, who had suffered much, slept there,
Worn out with fatigue and sleepiness. Yet Athene
Went on to the district and city of the Phaeacians,
Who at one time dwelt in Hyperia of the broad dancing-place,
Close to the Cyclopes, presumptuous men   5
Who used to injure them, and were more powerful in strength.
Then godlike Nausithoos [1] rose up and led them off
And settled them in Scheria, far from bread-earning men.
He set a wall around the city, built houses,
Made temples to the gods, and divided up the fields.   10
But already he had succumbed to his fate and gone to Hades.
Alcinoos ruled at the time, who had his thoughts from the gods.
The bright-eyed goddess Athene went to his home,
Devising a return for great-hearted Odysseus.
She entered the highly wrought bedroom where there was
    sleeping   15
A girl like the immortals in shape and in form,
Nausicaa,[2] daughter of great-hearted Alcinoos,
And beside her two servants, who had beauty from the Graces,
On either side of the door posts. The bright doors were shut.
She rushed to the girl's bed like a blast of the wind,   20
Stood over her head and spoke a word to her,
Likening herself to the daughter of Dymas, famous for ships,
Who was the girl's own age and delighted her heart.
In the likeness of her, bright-eyed Athene spoke out:
"Nausicaa, how did your mother have such a careless child?   25
Your shining garments are lying uncared for,
And your wedding is near, when you yourself will need
Lovely clothes to put on, and to give to the men who will lead
    you;
Through them does a noble reputation arise

1. The colonizer of Scheria; son of Poseidon.
2. Daughter of Alcinoos and Arete.

30 Among men, and a father and queenly mother rejoice.
But let us go washing as soon as dawn appears.
I will follow as a helper so you may array yourself
Very soon, since you will not be a maiden much longer.
Already in the land the best men of all the Phaeacians,
35 Where your own family is too, are wooing you.
But come, and urge your illustrious father at dawn
To harness up mules and a wagon to carry you
And the girdles and the gowns and the shining mantles.
It is much better for you to go that way yourself
40 Than by foot. For the place of washing is far from the city."
When she had said this, the bright-eyed Athene went off
To Olympos, where they say the gods' seat is forever
Secure. It is not shaken with winds and is never wet
With rain, nor does snow fall there, but a cloudless clarity
45 Spreads far upon it, and a white gleam runs over it.
In that place the blessed gods enjoy themselves day after day.
The bright-eyed one went off there when she had prompted the
        girl.
And right away the fair-throned Dawn came and awakened
The fair-gowned Nausicaa. At once she wondered at her dream,
50 And went through the halls to announce it to her parents,
Her dear father and mother. She found them within.
Her mother sat at the hearth with her serving women
Turning sea purple yarn on the distaff. She came on her father
At the door as he was going with his illustrious kings
55 To council, where the noble Phaeacians were summoning him.
She stood very close to her dear father and addressed him:
"Papa dear, won't you have a chariot harnessed for me,
A high one with good wheels, so I may take the splendid clothes
And wash them at the river, the ones I have lying dirty?
60 Yes, and it is fitting for you to be with the chief men
And hold council, wearing clothes on your skin that are clean.
And five dear sons have been born to you in the halls,
Two of them are married; three are blooming youths
Who are always wanting to wear freshly washed garments
65 To go dancing; all these cares are on my mind."
So she said. But she was ashamed to speak of lusty marriage
To her dear father. He saw all, and replied with a word:
"I do not begrudge you mules or anything else, child—
Come, the servants will harness you a chariot,

A high one, with good wheels, fitted with a hood."   70
When he had said this, he ordered the servants, and they
    obeyed.
Outside they set up a well-running wagon for mules.
They brought up mules and yoked them to the chariot.
The girl brought the shining garments from the bedroom
And she put them upon the well-polished chariot.   75
Her mother put all sorts of satisfying food
In a chest, and put in dainties, and poured wine
In a goatskin bag. Her daughter got up on the chariot.
And she gave her moist olive oil in a golden flask
So she and her serving women might anoint themselves.   80
And she took hold of the whip and the glistening reins
And whipped them to go; there was clatter of the two mules.
They drew it strenuously and bore the clothes and the girl,
Not alone: along with her other serving women went also.
And when they came to the beautiful stream of the river   85
Where there were plentiful places to wash and much
Lovely water flowed forth to clean what had got very dirty,
There they unharnessed the mules from the chariot
And shooed them out along the eddying river
To graze on honey-sweet field-grass. From the chariot   90
They took the clothes in their hands, carried them to the black
    water,
And trod them in pits, swiftly vying with one another.
But when they had washed and cleaned all the dirty clothes,
They spread them in a row on the strand where especially
The ocean washed pebbles up along the shore.   95
They bathed and anointed themselves richly with olive oil.
Then they had their dinner along the banks of the river
And waited for the clothes to dry in the gleam of the sun.
When she herself and the serving maids had enjoyed the food,
They played with a ball, having taken off their shawls.   100
White-armed Nausicaa began the sport with them.
Just as arrow-shooting Artemis goes along mountains,
Along the lofty Taygetos or Erimanthos,
Delighting in the boars and in the swift deer;
And field-haunting nymphs, daughters of aegis-bearing Zeus,   105
Play with her, and Leto [3] rejoices in her mind;
She holds her head and her forehead higher than all

3. Mother of Apollo and Artemis.

And is easily outstanding, but all are lovely:
So the unwed girl stood out among her serving maids.
110 But when she was ready to go back home again
And had hitched up the mules and folded the lovely clothes,
Then the bright-eyed goddess Athene had another thought:
Odysseus would wake up, he would see the fair-faced girl,
And she would conduct him to the city of the Phaeacians.
115 Then the princess threw the ball to a serving maid;
She missed the maid and shot it into a deep eddy.
They gave a long shout. And godly Odysseus woke up.
He sat there and deliberated in his mind and heart:
"Ah me, to what land of mortals have I come this time?
120 Are these men proud and savage and without justice,
Or are they friendly to strangers and have a god-fearing mind?
How the sound of girls' voices has surrounded me,
Of nymphs, who hold the lofty peaks of mountains,
And the sources of rivers and the grassy meadows!
125 Or am I somewhere near men who are of clear speech?
Well, come, I shall make a trial myself and see."
When he had said this, godly Odysseus came from under the
    bushes.
From the thick wood he broke off in his stout hand a branch
With leaves, that it might cover the skin round a man's loins,
130 And he went like a mountain-bred lion, who, relying
On his strength, goes rained on and blown on, but his eyes
    within
Are burning, and he chases after oxen or sheep
Or after the wild deer, and his belly bids him
To try for sheep and to go into their thick fold—
135 So was Odysseus about to mingle with the fair-braided girls,
Although he was naked. For need had come upon him.
Frightfully begrimed with brine did he appear to them.
One ran one way, one another, on the jutting shores.
The daughter of Alcinoos alone stayed; Athene
140 Had put courage in her mind and taken fear from her limbs.
She stood in one place, facing him. Odysseus wondered
Whether he should grasp the fair-faced girl's knees in prayer
Or supplicate her where he was at a distance, with soothing
    words,
To show him the city and also to give him clothes.
145 As he thought it over, it seemed better to him

To supplicate her at a distance with soothing words,
Lest if he grasped her knees the girl's mind be angered.
Right at once he made a soothing and wily speech:
"I am at your knees, mistress. Are you some god or a mortal?
If you are one of the gods who possess broad heaven,   150
I myself would liken you in look and size and form
Most closely to Artemis, the daughter of great Zeus.
And if you are one of the mortals who dwells on the land,
Three times blessed are your father and your queenly mother,
And three times blessed your kinsmen. Surely their hearts   155
Must be warmed forever with happiness on your account,
Beholding so fine a flower stepping into the dance.
Blessed above all others within his heart is the man
Who, laden down with bride-gifts, may lead you home.
Never before have I seen with my eyes such a person,   160
Either man or woman. Awe holds me as I look.
On Delos [4] once by the altar of Apollo I caught sight
Of such a one, the sapling of a date palm coming up.
For I went there also, and a large company followed me
On that journey whereon evil cares lay in store for me.   165
When I saw that, I was stunned in spirit a long time, lady,
Since such a shaft never rose from the ground; the same way
That I wonder at you, and am stunned, and dreadfully fear
To touch your knees. And a difficult sorrow comes on me.
Yesterday, on the twentieth day, I fled the wine-faced ocean.   170
All during that time did the waves and rapid storms carry me
From the island of Ogygia. Now a god has cast me here
To suffer some evil in this place. I do not think
It will stop, but the gods will perform many things yet first.
Do have pity, mistress. As one who has endured many evils   175
I come to you first. I know not one of the others,
Of the men who possess this city and this land.
Point the town out to me. Give me a rag to throw on,
If perhaps when you come here you had some wrapper for the
     clothing.
May the gods grant you as much as you wish in your mind.   180
May they provide you a husband and also a home,
And noble sympathy. Nothing is better or higher than that,
When a man and wife have a home who are sympathetic
In their thoughts. It gives many pains to their enemies

4. A small island sacred to Apollo.

185 And joys to their friends. And they know it best themselves."
Then white-armed Nausicaa spoke to him in answer:
"Stranger, since you seem like a man neither evil nor senseless,
And Olympian Zeus himself controls prosperity for men,
For the noble and the evil, as he wishes for each,
190 So perhaps he gave you this, and still you have to bear it.
And now, since you have come to our city and our land,
You will not want for clothing, or for anything else
That befits a long-suffering suppliant who encounters us.
I will show you the town and tell you the name of the people.
195 The Phaeacians possess this city and this land.
I am the daughter of great-hearted Alcinoos,
On whom the strength and might of the Phaeacians depend."
So she said, and she called out to her fair-braided servants,
"Come here to me, servants. Where do you flee when you see a
     man?
200 Surely you don't think him to be one of our enemies?
There is no man so vigorous and no mortal born
Who would come to the land of the Phaeacian men
Bringing hostility. For they are very dear to the gods.
And we dwell far away in the much-surging ocean,
205 The remotest of men. And no other mortal has congress with us.
Now this man, a wretched wanderer, has come here,
Whom we must look after, for all strangers and beggars
Are in the care of Zeus, and a gift, even small, is friendly.
Come, maidens, give food and drink to the stranger.
210 Wash him in the river where there is shelter against the wind."
So she said, and they stood and urged one another,
And they took Odysseus down to a shelter, as Nausicaa,
Daughter of great-hearted Alcinoos, had ordered.
They put down a mantle and a tunic and clothes for him,
215 And gave him liquid olive oil in a golden flask,
And bade him to wash himself in the streams of the river.
Then godly Odysseus addressed the servant maids:
"Maidens, stand off where you are, so that I myself
May wash the brine from my shoulders and with olive oil
220 May anoint me all over. Oil has been long from my skin;
I do not want to wash in front of you. I am ashamed
To come out naked in the midst of fair-braided girls."
So he said, and they went apart and spoke to the girl.
But Odysseus in the river washed off of his skin

The brine that he had on his back and his broad shoulders,   225
And he wiped from his head the scurf of barren salt water.
When he had fully washed and had rubbed himself richly,
He put on the clothes that the unwed girl had provided,
And Athene, she who was born from Zeus, made him
Bigger to look at and stouter, and on his head   230
Made his hair flow in curls, like the hyacinth flower.
As when some man overlays gold upon silver,
A skilled man whom Hephaistos [5] and Pallas Athene have taught
Art of all kinds, and he turns out graceful handiwork;
So she poured grace upon his head and his shoulders.   235
Then he sat off apart, when he had gone along the beach of the
     sea,
Gleaming with beauty and graces. And the girl marveled.
And then she spoke out to her fair-braided serving maids:
"Listen to me, white-armed servants, in what I say.
Not against the will of all the gods who hold Olympos   240
Does this man mix with the Phaeacians, who are equal to gods.
Beforehand he appeared to me to be unseemly,
And now he seems like the gods who possess broad heaven.
Would that a man of this sort might be called my husband
And be dwelling here, and it might please him to stay   245
In this place. But, maidens, give the stranger food and drink."
So she said, and they listened closely and obeyed her.
They set out before Odysseus food and drink.
Godly Odysseus, who had suffered much, ate and drank
Greedily, for he had been a long time without eating.   250
But white-armed Nausicaa had another thought.
She folded up the clothes, put them on the lovely chariot,
Harnessed the stout-hooved mules, got in herself,
And urged Odysseus on, speaking out to him directly:
"Rise up now, stranger, to go to the city, so I may   255
Convey you to my skillful father's home, where I think
You may get to know all the noblest of the Phaeacians.
Well, this is what you should do—you do not seem to me to be
     foolish.
As long as we are passing the fields and the farms of men,
Come speedily along with the serving maids behind the mules   260
And the chariot. And I myself shall lead the way.
But when we walk into the city—about it there is a high

5. Son of Zeus and husband of Aphrodite; god of fire and the forge.

Tower wall, and there is a lovely harbor on either side of the city
And a narrow entrance, and bobbing ships from the voyage
265 Are pulled in there—it is a slip for one and all.
There is the assembly place, round a fine temple to Poseidon,
Fashioned from deep-bedded stones that have been quarried.
And there they take care of the tackle of the black ships,
Cables and sails, and they sharpen oars off to a point.
270 For the Phaeacians the bow and the quiver are of no concern,
But sails and the oars of ships and the balanced ships;
Delighting in these, they traverse the hoary sea.
I shun an unseemly repute among them, lest one
Rebuke me hereafter. For there are presumptuous men in the
        district,
275 And this is what some meaner one, if he met us, might say:
'Who is this great and handsome stranger that follows
Nausicaa? Where did she find him? He will be her husband.
She must have brought him off his own ship wandering
From distant men, since there are not any near at hand;
280 Or else some much-invoked god has come at her prayer,
Descending from the sky and will have her all her days.
Better so, if she went herself and found a husband
From elsewhere. For she despises these men in the district,
The Phaeacians, though many men who are noble woo her.'
285 So they will say. And these reproaches will come against me.
I myself would blame anyone else who should do such things,
Who against the will of her dear ones, a father and mother still
        alive,
Should mingle with men before coming to open marriage.
Stranger, understand quickly what I say, so you may
290 Very soon get an escort and a return from my father.
Near the road you will find a shining grove of Athene,
One of poplars; a spring flows in it, a meadow is about it.
There is my father's preserve and his fruitful vineyard,
The same distance from the city that a shout would carry.
295 Sit there a while and wait till the time that we
Come to the town and arrive at the house of my father.
But when you consider that we have arrived at the house,
Then go to the city of the Phaeacians and ask
For the house of my father, great-hearted Alcinoos.
300 It is easy to recognize; even a foolish child
Could lead you. There is none of the Phaeacians' houses

Made to resemble the home of Alcinoos,
Who is a hero. But when the house and courtyard enclose you,
Go very swiftly through the hall until you reach
My mother. She sits at the hearth in the fire's gleam,   305
And turns sea purple yarn on the distaff, a wonder to see,
Propped against a pillar. And serving maids sit behind her.
And there the chair of my father is propped up against hers,
Where, seated like an immortal, he drinks his wine.
Pass him by and throw your hands around the knees   310
Of my mother, so you may speedily rejoice and see
The day of your return, even if you are from very far away.
And if that woman thinks kindly of you in her heart,
Then there is hope for you of seeing your dear ones and reaching
Your well-established home and your own fatherland."   315
When she had said this, she lashed with her shiny whip
At the mules, and they quickly left the streams of the river.
They ran along well and nimbly bent their legs.
She managed the reins so that the servants and Odysseus
Might follow on foot. And she skillfully applied the lash.   320
The sun went down and they came to the famous grove
Sacred to Athene, and there godly Odysseus sat down.
Then at once he prayed to the daughter of great Zeus:
"Hear me, unwearied one, child of aegis-bearing Zeus,
Hear me now, since you did not hear me before   325
When I was smitten and the famous earth-shaker smote me.
Grant that I come to the Phaeacians as a pitied man and a
    friend."
So he said in prayer; and Pallas Athene heard him,
But she did not yet appear to him face to face. For she feared
Her father's brother. He was contending vehemently   330
With godlike Odysseus till the man reached his own land.

VII

And so godly Odysseus, who had suffered much, prayed there
While the strength of the two mules bore the girl toward the
 town.
And when she had arrived at her father's famous house
She halted them in the gateway, and her brothers were standing
5 About her like immortals; they unhitched the mules
From the chariot and carried the clothing on inside.
She herself went to her bedroom. An old woman of Apeire
Was kindling a fire for her, the chambermaid Eurymedousa,
Whom once the bobbing ships took away from Apeire,
10 And they chose her as a prize for Alcinoos because he ruled
All the Phaeacians. The people obeyed him like a god.
She waited on white-armed Nausicaa in the halls,
And kindled the fire for her, and set out her dinner within.
And then Odysseus got up to go to the city. Athene,
15 With kind thoughts for Odysseus, shed a thick mist about him,
Lest some great-hearted Phaeacian should confront him,
Taunt him with a speech, and ask him who he might be.
But when he was ready to enter the charming city,
Then the bright-eyed goddess Athene confronted him.
20 Likenening herself to a virginal young girl with a pitcher,
She stood in front of him, and godly Odysseus asked:
"My child, would you lead me to the home of Alcinoos,
The man who is the ruler over these people?
For I have come here as a long-suffering stranger
25 From afar, from a distant land; so I know no one
Of the men who possess this city and its fields."
Then the bright-eyed goddess Athene addressed him:
"Yes, father stranger, I will show you the home
You ask of, since it lies close to my blameless father's.
30 But come very silently and I shall lead the way.
Do not catch any man's eye or question anyone.
Those here do not easily endure strange men,

And they do not befriend or welcome one coming from
    elsewhere.
Putting their confidence in the swift and speedy ships,
They traverse the great gulf, since the earth-shaker gave it to
    them,   35
And their ships are as swift as any wing or thought."
When she had said this, Pallas Athene conducted him
Speedily; he went along in the footsteps of the goddess.
But the Phaeacians, famous for ships, did not perceive him
As he went through the town among them, for fair-braided
    Athene,   40
The dreadful goddess, did not allow it; she shed
A divine fog about him, with kind thoughts in her heart.
Odysseus wondered at the harbors and the balanced ships,
The meeting places of the heroes themselves, and the walls,
Long and lofty, fitted with stakes, a wonder to behold.   45
When they came to the illustrious house of the king,
The bright-eyed goddess Athene began to speak among them:
"Father stranger, this is the house that you requested me
To point out to you. You will find kings nourished by Zeus
Eating dinner there. Go in and do not be frightened   50
In your heart. A man who is bold in all his deeds
Thrives better, even when he comes from somewhere else.
You will first come upon the mistress in the halls.
Arete [1] is the name she is called, and her ancestors
Are the same ones who begot King Alcinoos.   55
First Nausithoos was born of earth-shaker Poseidon
And of Periboea, the best for her form, among women,
The youngest daughter of great--hearted Eurymedon,
Who ruled as king over the high-spirited Giants.
But he destroyed his reckless people, and was himself destroyed. 60
Then Poseidon lay with the girl and fathered a son,
Great-spirited Nausithoos, who ruled the Phaeacians.
Nausithoos begat Rhexenor and Alcinoos.
Apollo of the silver bow slew the first while still sonless
And a bridegroom in the hall: he left one sole daughter,   65
Arete. And her did Alcinoos make his wife.
He honored her as no other woman on earth is honored,
Of all women who now have a household under men.
So she was highly honored in heart, and she still is,

1. Queen of the Phaeacians; wife of Alcinoos and mother of Nausicaa.

70 By her beloved children and by Alcinoos himself
And by the people who look on her as on a god
And welcome her with speeches as she goes through the town.
Nor is she herself at all lacking in any noble thought.
She dissolves disputes for those of whom she thinks well, even
for men.
75 And if that woman has kind thoughts for you in her heart,
There is hope for you of seeing your dear ones and reaching
Your lofty-roofed house and your own fatherland."
When she had said this, bright-eyed Athene went away
Over the barren ocean, and left charming Scheria;
80 She arrived at Marathon, and at Athens with its broad streets,
And entered the stout house of Erechtheus. Meanwhile
Odysseus
Went to the famous house of Alcinoos. His heart
Pondered much as he stood there before reaching the bronze
threshold.
There was a gleam like that of the sun or of the moon
85 Beneath the high-roofed hall of great-hearted Alcinoos.
Bronze walls were run round it on every side to the corner
From the threshold, and there was a frieze of dark blue about it.
Golden portals shut up the stout home within,
And silver door posts were set upon the bronze threshold,
90 And a silver lintel above, and a golden handle.
And on either side there were gold and silver dogs
That Hephaistos with his skillful faculties had formed
To watch over the house of great-hearted Alcinoos;
They were immortal, and ageless for all their days.
Inside, armchairs had been propped round the wall here and
95   there
To the corner from the threshold in unbroken line. And cloths
Were strewn there, fine and well-woven, the work of women.
And there the leaders of the Phaeacians were seated
When they ate and drank. They possessed unfailing abundance.
100 And there were golden youths on well-built pedestals
That stood there holding in their hands flaming torches
Illuminating the nights for the diners through the halls.
And there were fifty serving maids through the hall, women
Who grind up in a mill grain of an apple hue,
105 And who do weaving on looms and turn the distaff
Seated, the way the leaves of the tall poplar turn;

And from the close-woven linen the moist oil drops off.
As the Phaeacians are knowing beyond all other men
To drive a swift ship in the ocean, so their women
Are skilled in weaving. Athene has endowed them highly   110
With skill in beautiful tasks and with noble minds.
Outside the courtyard is a great garden before the portals,
One of four measures. A fence runs round it on both sides.
And in that place tall blossoming trees are growing,
Pears, and pomegranates, apple trees with shining fruit,   115
And sweet fig trees and blossoming olive trees.
Of these the fruit never perishes and never leaves off
In winter or summertime, all the year round. But always
A blowing West Wind makes some grow and ripens others.
Pear matures upon pear, apple upon apple,   120
Grape cluster on grape cluster, and fig on fig,
And there is rooted a vineyard that bears much fruit,
One part of which, light-parched in a level place,
Dries in the sun, and others they harvest at vintage.
Still others they tread. First there are the unripe grapes   125
Shedding flowers, and others are darkening underneath.
Well-ordered vegetable beds in the last row there
Grow things of all kinds and shine green in unceasing
    abundance.
And in it are two springs: one through the whole garden
Is dispersed, and the other rises by the courtyard threshold   130
Before the lofty house, whence the townspeople draw water.
Such were the gods' glorious gifts to Alcinoos' house.
As he stood there, godly Odysseus, who had endured much,
    marveled.
And when he had marveled in his heart at everything,
He went speedily over the threshold into the hall.   135
He found the leaders and counselors of the Phaeacians pouring
Libations to the far-sighted god, the slayer of Argos.
They poured him the last cup whenever they remembered sleep.
But godly Odysseus, who had endured much, went through the
    hall,
Clad in the large mist that Athene had shed about him,   140
Until he reached Arete and King Alcinoos.
Odysseus threw his hands about the knees of Arete,
And then the divine mist poured away from him.
They grew silent through the hall when they saw the man

145 And wondered to behold him. Odysseus pleaded with her:
"Arete, daughter of Phrexenor, who was equal to a god,
I, who have suffered much, fall at your knees and your husband's
And all those dining here: may the gods grant them to live
With blessings; and may each one turn his possessions over
150 To his children in his halls, and any prize the people have given.
But call up an escort for me to reach my fatherland
Soon, as I have long suffered woes apart from my dear ones."
When he had said this, he sat down on the hearth in the ashes
By the fire. And they all became silent in stillness.
155 After a pause the old hero Echeneus spoke out,
A man who was oldest by birth of the Phaeacian men,
Who excelled in speaking and knew many ancient things.
In good will he spoke out to them and addressed them:
"Alcinoos, this does not seem to be very good,
160 To let a stranger sit on the ground by the hearth in the ashes.
Those here are holding back and waiting for your word.
Come now, have the stranger stand up, and sit him down
In a chair studded with silver; give your herald bidding
To mix up more wine so we may pour a libation
165 To bolt-hurling Zeus, who protects pious suppliants.
Let a housekeeper give the stranger dinner from what is within."
When Alcinoos in his sacred strength had heard this,
He took the hand of skillful, various-minded Odysseus,
Raised him from the hearth, and seated him on a shining chair.
170 He had his son stand up, the manly Laodamas,
Who sat nearest to him and whom he loved especially.
And a handmaid poured water from a pitcher she was carrying,
A lovely golden one, over into a silver basin,
For washing the hands; she set up a polished table alongside.
175 A respected servant served bread she was carrying,
Laying out many dishes, gracious with the provisions.
Godly Odysseus, who had suffered much, ate and drank,
Then Alcinoos in his might spoke out to the herald:
"Pontonoos, mix up a bowl and serve out the wine
180 To all through the hall so we may pour a libation
To bolt-hurling Zeus, who protects pious suppliants."
So he said, and Pontonoos mixed the mind-honeying wine
And distributed the first drops into the cups of all.
When they had poured and drunk as much as the spirit wished,
185 Alcinoos spoke out to them and addressed them:

"Hear me, leaders and counselors of the Phaeacians,
So I may say what the spirit in my breast bids me to.
Now that you have dined, go home and go to bed,
And at dawn when we have beckoned more of the elders,
Let us welcome the stranger in the halls and offer   190
Fine sacrifices to the gods; then let us take thought
For a convoy, so this stranger without pain or distress
Under our convoy may arrive at his fatherland,
And speedily rejoice, even if he is from very far away.
May he undergo no evil or suffering in mid-passage   195
Before coming upon his land; but then he will suffer
Whatever his fate and the grave Spinners [2] have spun for him
With his birth thread at the time when his mother bore him.
And if he has come down as one of the immortals from heaven,
Then it is something else that the gods are contriving in this.   200
Always before have the gods appeared to us plainly
Whenever we have offered the famous hecatombs,
And they dined along with us seated where we are;
Even if some wayfarer meets them when he is alone
They conceal it not at all, since we are close to them,   205
As are the Cyclopes and the wild tribes of the Giants."
Odysseus of many devices spoke to him in answer:
"Alcinoos, concern yourself with something else. As for me,
I am not like the immortals who possess broad heaven,
Either in body or form, but am like mortal men.   210
Whomever you may know among men who have borne
The most woe, I would equal myself to them in griefs,
And indeed I myself might tell of still further ills
Of the great number I have endured at the will of the gods.
But permit me to eat dinner, burdened as I am with cares,   215
For there is nothing at all more shameless than the hateful belly
Which bids a man to remember it by compulsion,
Even one who is much worn down and has sorrow in his mind,
As I now have sorrow in my mind. It perpetually
Bids me to eat and drink and makes me forget   220
All I have undergone, and commands me to fill up.
But arouse yourselves at the appearance of dawn
And bring me, wretched as I am, to my fatherland.
Indeed I have suffered much. May my life abandon me

2. Often identified with the three Fates—Clotho, Lachesis, and Atropos
—who have in charge the "thread" of a man's life.

Once I have seen my goods, my servants, and my great high
225 house."
So he said, and they all assented and gave orders
To guide the stranger off, since he had spoken properly.
When they had poured and drunk as much as the spirit wished,
They went on off to sleep, each one to his own house.
230 But godly Odysseus was left behind in the hall.
And with him Arete and Alcinoos, godly in form,
Were sitting. Servants put the dishes of the meal in order.
Arete of the white arms began to speak among them.
She recognized the mantle, tunic, and clothes when she saw
     them,
235 Lovely ones, that she made herself with her serving women.
And she spoke out to him and uttered wingèd words:
"Stranger, I should first like to ask you a question myself:
Who are you? What men are you from? Who gave you these
     clothes?
Did you not say you got here wandering on the ocean?"
240 Odysseus of many wiles addressed her in answer:
"It is difficult, queen, to speak out in full detail
About troubles, when the celestial gods have given me so many.
But this I will tell you that you ask and question me of.
A certain island, Ogygia, lies far off in the sea,
245 Where the daughter of Atlas dwells, wily Calypso
Of the fair braids, a dread goddess. With her no one
Has intercourse, either of gods or of mortal men.
But some god led me to her hearth, wretched as I am,
All alone, when Zeus with a dazzling thunderbolt
Crushed my swift ship, and sank it in the middle of the wine-
250 faced sea.
Then all the others, my noble companions, perished,
But I alone took in my hands the keel of the bobbing ship
And was carried nine days. And on the tenth black night
The gods brought me near the island Ogygia, where Calypso
255 Of the fair braids dwells, dread goddess. She took me in
And kindly befriended me, nourished me, and said
She would make me immortal and ageless all my days,
But she did not persuade the heart within my breast.
I waited there steadily seven years. And always I moistened
260 With my tears the ambrosial clothes that Calypso gave me.
But when the eighth year in its cycle came around,

Then she urged me and bid me to go away,
Because of a message from Zeus, or else her mind had changed.
She sent me on a strongly-bound raft, gave me much
Bread and sweet wine, clothed me in ambrosial garments,   265
And then she sent on a soothing and gentle breeze.
Seventeen days, faring upon the ocean, I sailed,
And on the eighteenth there appeared the shadowy mountains
Of your land. And my own heart was delighted in me,
Ill-fated as I was. And yet I was to have still more to do   270
With the great distress earth-shaker Poseidon raised against me.
He stirred up winds and hindered me from the voyage
And he raised an indescribable sea so the wave did not
Allow me, heavily groaning, to be borne on the raft.
Then a tempest scattered it, and I myself   275
Cleft this gulf as I swam on through, until the wind
And water carried me and brought me near your land.
Then the wave as I tried to get out would have driven me on
     land,
Throwing me against great rocks and a joyless place,
But I withdrew and swam the other way until I came   280
To the river, where the best place seemed to me to be,
Smooth of rocks, and where there was shelter from the wind.
I fell out struggling for life, and ambrosial night
Came on. Back away from the Zeus-fallen river
I stepped out and went to sleep in the bushes and heaped   285
Leaves about me. A god poured down boundless sleep.
There in the leaves, wearied in my own heart I slept
All the night long, and till dawn and the middle day,
And the sun declined, and then sweet sleep let me free.
Then I noticed your daughter's serving maids playing   290
On the strand. She herself was among them, like the goddesses.
I begged her, and she did not fail of such noble intent,
As one would not expect a young person he encountered
To demonstrate. For the very young are always thoughtless.
She gave me sufficient food and sparkling wine   295
And had me washed in the river and gave me these clothes.
This is the truth I have told you, though I am distressed."
Then Alcinoos spoke out and answered him:
"Stranger, of this at least my daughter did not properly
Take thought, in that she did not lead you to our house,   300
With her serving women. For you besought her first."

Odysseus of many wiles addressed him in answer:
"Do not, hero, reproach your blameless daughter for my sake.
She bade me to follow along with the serving women,
305 But I did not want to, as I was afraid and ashamed
Lest somehow your heart be offended at seeing me.
Very suspicious are we tribes of men on the earth."
Then Alcinoos spoke out and answered him:
"Stranger, my own heart in my breast is not such
310 As to rage easily. Everything proper is best.
Would that by father Zeus, Athene, and Apollo,
Being such as you are, and of a mind like my own,
You might have my daughter and be called my son-in-law,
And stay here. I would give you a home and property
315 If you willingly stayed. No Phaeacian would hold you back
Against your will. May that not be pleasing to father Zeus.
I appoint your convoy for a day, so you may know it well,
That is, tomorrow. Then you may lie overcome in sleep.
And they will row on a calm sea until you arrive
320 At fatherland, home, and whatever is dear to you,
Even if it is very much farther off than Euboea,
Which those of our people say to be farthest off
Who saw it when they brought blond Rhadamanthys
To go and see Tityos, the son of Gaia.
325 They went there and accomplished it without difficulty
On the same day, and completed the voyage back home.
You too shall know in your own mind how much the best
Our ships and our youths are who toss up the sea with their
    oars."
So he said, and godly Odysseus, who had borne much, rejoiced.
330 He said a prayer then, and spoke right out directly:
"Father Zeus, may Alcinoos bring to pass all
That he has said; may his fame be unquenchable
On the grain-giving earth; may I reach my fatherland."
So they addressed such speeches to one another.
335 And white-armed Arete bade her serving women
To put bedsteads down in the colonnade, and to throw on
Lovely purple rugs, and to spread blankets above them
And to put down woolen mantles on top of all that.
They went from the hall with torches in their hands.
340 And when they had spread down the thick bed busily,
They stood beside Odysseus and urged him with speeches:

"Come rise up, stranger, the bed is made for you."
So they said. It seemed welcome to him to lie down.
So godly Odysseus, who had endured much, slept there
In the jointed bed under the resounding portico.   345
Alcinoos slept in a nook of the lofty house;
His lady wife beside him prepared a bed and a resting place.

VIII

And when the early-born, rosy-fingered dawn appeared,
Alcinoos rose up out of bed in his sacred strength.
And Odysseus, the Zeus-born sacker of cities, rose up.
Alcinoos in his sacred strength led them to the assembly place
5 Of the Phaeacians, which was made for them beside the ships.
When they got there they sat down on the polished stones
Close together. Pallas Athene went on through the town,
Likening herself to a herald of skillful Alcinoos,
Devising a return for the great-hearted Odysseus.
10 And she said something to each man, standing beside him:
"Come hither, leaders and counselors of the Phaeacians;
Go to the assembly, so you may learn about the stranger
Who has recently come to skillful Alcinoos' house,
Having wandered the ocean, like the immortals in form."
When she had said this, she aroused the strength and the heart
15   of each.
Speedily the assembly and its seats filled up with men
As they gathered. And many marveled to behold
The skillful son of Laertes. On his behalf Athene
Shed a divine grace over his head and his shoulders,
20 And she made him loftier and stouter to behold,
So that he might become cherished by all the Phaeacians,
And fearful, and respected, and might carry out many
Of the contests in which the Phaeacians tested Odysseus.
But when they were gathered and had come together,
25 Alcinoos spoke out to them and addressed them:
"Hear me, leaders and counselors of the Phaeacians,
That I may say what the spirit in my breast bids me to.
This stranger—I know not who he is—reached my house,
From the men of the dawn or of the evening,[1] wandering.
30 He urges a convoy and beseeches that it be assured,
And let us ourselves, as before, speed on a convoy,

1. That is, of East and West.

For never did anyone else who came to my halls
Wait here and long lament for the sake of a convoy.
Come then, let us drag a black ship on its first voyage
To the godly sea, and let two and fifty young men   35
Be picked through the land of those who are far the best up to
    now.
And when you have fastened the oars well in the oarlocks,
All of you get out of it. Then come to my house and partake
Of a hasty meal. I shall make good provision for all.
This I command the young men. And as for you others, 40
You scepter-bearing kings, come to my lovely home,
So that we may entertain the stranger in the halls.
Let no one refuse. Summon the godlike singer
Demodocos.[2] The gods have granted him to please beyond
    others
With whatever kind of song his spirit urges him to sing." 45
When he had said this, he led on, and the scepter-bearing kings
Followed along. A herald brought in the godly singer.
The two and fifty young men were selected
And went, as he bade them, to the strand of the barren sea.
But when they got down to the ship and to the sea   50
They dragged the black ship into a depth of salt water
And set up a mast and sails upon the black ship.
Then they fitted the oars into the straps made of leather
All in order and then stretched out the white sails.
Then they anchored her high in flowing water, and then 55
They entered the great house of skillful Alcinoos.
The porticoes and courts and rooms were filled with the men
As they gathered. There were many, both old and young.
And among them Alcinoos sacrificed twelve sheep,
Eight shining-tusked sows and two shamble-footed heifers.   60
They flayed them and prepared them and made a delightful
    banquet.
Then a herald came near, leading the trusty singer
Whom the Muse loved dearly and gave both good and ill.
She blinded him in the eyes but gave him a sweet song.
Pontonoos set out a silver-studded armchair for him   65
In the midst of the banqueters, propping it on a tall pillar.
The herald hung his clear-toned lyre from a peg
There above his head and showed him how to take it

2. The blind bard of the Phaeacians.

In his hands. He put a basket and lovely table alongside
70 And a cup of wine for when the spirit should bid him to drink.
They stretched forth their hands to the food that was spread out
    ready,
And when they had taken their fill of food and drink
The Muse bade the singer to sing famous deeds of men
From the lay whose fame had by then reached broad heaven,
75 The quarrel of Odysseus and Achilles, son of Peleus,
How once they wrangled at an abundant feast of the gods
With terrible words, but the lord of men, Agamemnon,
Was pleased in his mind that the best Achaians were wrangling.
For so Phoebos Apollo had told him by an oracle
80 In divine Pytho [3] where he had gone over the stone threshold
Seeking an oracle. For then the beginning of trouble was rolling
On the Trojans and Danaans through the plans of great Zeus.
This did the far-famed singer sing. But Odysseus
Took his great purple mantle in his stout hands,
85 Pulled it over his head, and concealed his handsome face;
He was ashamed before the Phaeacians for shedding tears
    under his eyebrows.
And whenever the godlike singer paused in his singing,
He lifted the mantle over his head and wiped the tears,
Took a two-handled cup, and poured libation to the gods.
90 But whenever he started again and the Phaeacian nobles
Urged him on to sing, since they were pleased with his stories,
Odysseus again covered his head over and moaned.
Now, as he shed tears, he escaped the notice of all the others.
But Alcinoos alone took note of him and perceived him,
95 While seated near him, and heard him as he deeply groaned.
At once he addressed the Phaeacians, who are fond of rowing:
"Listen, leaders and counselors of the Phaeacians,
Now we have sated our spirits with a well-shared feast
And the lyre, the consort of an abundant banquet;
100 Now let us go out and make trial in all sorts
Of contests, so that the stranger may tell his friends
When he returns home how much we surpass others
In boxing and wrestling, in jumping and also in running."
When he had said this, he led, and they followed along.
105 The herald hung the clear-toned lyre up on its peg,
Took Demodocos' hand, and led him from the hall.

3. The oracle of Apollo at Delphi.

He led him along the same path that the other
Phaeacian nobles took to witness at the contests.
They went to the assembly, and a large crowd followed along,
Myriads. And many young noblemen stood up.   110
Acroneus rose up, Ocyalos and Elatreus,[4]
Nauteus and Prymneus and Anchialos and Eretmeus,
Ponteus and Proireus, Thoon and Anabesineus,
And Amphialos, son of Polyneus, son of Tecton,
And Euryalos too, the equal of man-slaying Ares,[5]   115
Naubolos' son, who was best in form and in body
Of all the Phaeacians, after excellent Laodamas.
And the three sons of excellent Alcinoos stood up,
Laodamas and Halios and godlike Clytoneus.
And first they made a trial at a running race.   120
And their running was strained from the turning post on, and
   all
Flew speedily together, raising dust on the plain.
The best of them at running was excellent Clytoneus.
By as much as the range of two mules in a fallow field
He ran ahead and reached the crowd, and they were left behind. 125
Then they made a trial of painful wrestling.
And in that Euryalos surpassed all the best.
In jumping, Amphialos was most outstanding of all.
And Elatreus was by far the best of all with the weight.
In boxing it was Laodamas, Alcinoos' good son.   130
And when they had all delighted their minds with the contests,
Laodamas, the son of Alcinoos, addressed them:
"Come, friends, let us ask the stranger if there is any contest
That he knows and is skilled in. He is not bad in form,
In his thighs and in his calves and both hands above them, 135
And his neck is stout, and his strength great, nor does he lack
His prime; but he is broken down by many evils.
I think for my part there is nothing worse than the sea
To shatter a man, even though he be very strong."
Then Euryalos answered him and addressed him: 140
"Laodamas, indeed you have said this properly.
Go challenge him now yourself and say what you said."
And when the good son of Alcinoos heard that,

---

4. These are all names formed on marine terms: Ship-top, Swift-sea,
Rower, etc.
5. Son of Zeus; the god of war.

He went and stood in the middle and addressed Odysseus:
145 "Father stranger, come here too, and try the contests,
If you have ever learned any—you seem to know about contests.
Yes, there is no greater glory for a man as long as he lives
Than what he achieves by his feet or by his hands.
Come now, have a try; scatter the cares from your heart.
150 Your journey is not far off, and already the ship
Is drawn down for you, and the companions are ready."
Odysseus of many wiles addressed him in answer:
"Laodamas, why do you taunt me in calling me to this?
Troubles are more in my mind than contests are.
155 As a man who has endured much before and suffered much,
I am now sitting in your assembly, seeking
A return, beseeching your king and all the people."
Euryalos answered and rebuked him to his face:
"No, stranger, I would not say you were like a man skilled
160 In contests of the many sorts that exist among men,
But are like one who is used to a ship with many oarlocks,
A leader of sailors who are also merchantmen
With his mind on a load, an overseer of cargoes
And of gain got by greed. You do not resemble an athlete."
165 Odysseus of many wiles answered, glowering at him:
"You have spoken not well, stranger; you are like a fool,
And so the gods do not grant delightful gifts
To all men, in shape or in mind or in speaking.
One man is rather insignificant in look;
170 But a god crowns his speech with grace, and men behold him
And are pleased. And he speaks without faltering,
With soothing deference, and he stands out in the gathering.
And they look upon him like a god as he goes through the city.
And another man will be like the immortals in look,
175 But there is no gracefulness to crown his speech;
And so you are striking in look, and not even a god
Could make you otherwise. But you are of futile mind.
You have aroused the spirit inside my own breast,
As you spoke unbecomingly. I am not unskilled in contests,
180 As you have said, but I think I was among the first
So long as I relied on my vigor and my hands.
But now I am held in pains and misfortune. I have suffered much,

Passing through the wars of men and the troublesome waves.
But even though I have felt many ills, I will try the contests,
For your speech gnaws my heart. What you say urges me on." 185
So he said. Springing up with cloak and all, he took a weight,
A broad one, not by a trifle larger and stouter
Than the ones the Phaeacians threw among themselves.
He whirled it around and shot it from his stout hand.
The stone whirred, and the Phaeacians, who have long oars,   190
Men famous for ships, crouched down upon the ground
At the stone's rush. It flew past the marks of all,
Speeding quickly from his hand. Athene set the distance,
Likened in body to a man; she spoke out directly:
"Even a blind man, stranger, could make out this mark   195
By feeling it, since it is not mingled at all with the throng,
But is first by far. Take heart, at least for this contest.
None of the Phaeacians will reach or exceed this mark."
So she said, and godly Odysseus, who had borne much, rejoiced,
Pleased to behold a helpful companion in the game.   200
Then he addressed the Phaeacians in a lighter spirit:
"Reach this mark now, young men. I believe someone else
May soon hereafter hurl an equal distance, or greater.
Of all the rest, come and try what your heart and spirit
Bid you to try—since you have got me highly angered—   205
In boxing or wrestling or running—I say nothing against it—
Any of the Phaeacians except Laodamas himself,
For he is my host. And who could contend with a friend?
That man would be indeed a senseless and worthless person
Who should bring competition in contests upon his host 210
In a foreign land. He would cut all short for himself.
But of the others I do not refuse or slight a one.
I should like to know them and try them out face to face.
I am not bad in any of the many kinds of games among men.
I know well how to handle a well-polished bow;   215
I would be first, shooting in a crowd, to hit my man
Among the enemy, even if many companions
Were standing close to me and shooting at people.
Philoctetes alone surpassed me with the bow
In the land of the Trojans when we Achaians were shooting.   220
But I say I am far more outstanding than any
Of the mortals who now eat bread upon the earth.

I should not want to contend with men of earlier times,
Either with Heracles or Oichalian Eurytos,[6]
225 Who contended even with immortals in archery.
For that, great Eurytos died quickly; old age did not
Come on him in his halls, for Apollo got angry
And killed him because he challenged him to shoot.
I shoot farther with a spear than anyone else with an arrow.
230 In running alone do I fear that some Phaeacians
Might surpass me. I was very disgracefully overcome
In the numerous waves, since there was no lasting
Provision on my ship. Therefore my knees are slackened."
So he said, and the others were silent in stillness.
235 Alcinoos alone addressed him in answer:
"Stranger, you have said this to us not ungracefully,
But you would like to show the excellence that belongs to you,
Angry that this man has stood up to you in the games
And blamed you, as no man would reproach your excellence
240 Who knew in his mind how to speak sensibly.
But come now, give heed to my word, so you may tell it
To another hero when you are in your halls
Dining beside your wife and your own children,
And remember our excellence in such deeds as Zeus
245 Bestows on us steadily since the time of our fathers.
We are not blameless in boxing or in wrestling,
But we do run nimbly in races and are best in ships.
Feasting is dear to us always, the lyre, and dances,
Changes of clothes and hot baths, and the bed.
250 But you who are the best dancers of the Phaeacians, come
And frolic, so the stranger may report to his friends,
When he returns home, how much we surpass others
In seamanship and running and dancing and in song.
Let someone go at once and bring for Demodocos
255 The clear-toned lyre which is lying somewhere in our halls."
So said the godlike Alcinoos, and a herald rose
To bring the hollow lyre from the home of the king.
The umpires appointed for the district stood up,
Nine in all, who attended well to details of the games.
260 They smoothed a dancing place and broadened a lovely ring;

6. A legendary archer, slain by Apollo in a contest; Heracles was the most
famous of Greek legendary heroes, noted especially for his performance
of twelve nigh-impossible labors.

The herald came near, carrying the clear-toned lyre
For Demodocos. He went to the middle then. Young men
In their first youth stood round him, skillful in the dancing,
And beat the godly floor with their feet. Odysseus
Gazed at their flashing feet and wondered in his heart.   265
Then playing the lyre, the man struck up a beautiful song
Of the love of Ares and fine-crowned Aphrodite,[7]
How they first had lain together in the home of Hephaistos,
Secretly. He gave her many gifts and shamed the marriage bed
Of her lord Hephaistos. A messenger came at once to him,   270
Helios,[8] who perceived them lying together in love.
Hephaistos, when he heard the spirit-hurting story,
Went into his bronze works plotting evil in his mind
And put a great anvil on the anvil block, and hammered bonds
Unbreakable and indissoluble, that would hold them there fast.   275
And when in his anger he had fashioned a snare for Ares,
He went into his bedroom where his own precious bedstead
    stood
He spread bonds all around the bedposts in a circle
And he spread many out from the rafters up above,
Subtle as spider web, that no one would ever see,   280
Even of the blessed gods, so well for deceit did he make them.
And when he had put the whole snare around in the bedding,
He made as if to go to Lemnos, the well-built citadel
That is the dearest by far to him of all the lands.
Nor did Ares of the golden rein keep a blind watch   285
When he saw the famed craftsman Hephaistos going off.
He went to the home of the highly renowned Hephaistos,
Craving for the love of Cytherea [9] with the fine crown.
She had recently come from her father, the mighty son
Of Cronos, and had sat down. And he went into the house,   290
Took her hand, and spoke right out directly to her:
"Come, darling, let us enjoy the couch and the bed ourselves.
Hephaistos is no longer in the district. Already
He is gone off to Lemnos among the wild-speaking Sintians."
So he said. It struck her as delightful to go to bed.   295
The two of them went to sleep in the bed clothes. And the
    bonds

7. Daughter of Zeus; the goddess of love.
8. The sun god.
9. Another name for Aphrodite; from Cythera, an island where a shrine
to her was located.

Fashioned by various-minded Hephaistos were spread about
  them,
So they could not move or raise their limbs at all.
And then they knew it when they could no longer escape.
300 The far-famed double cripple came up close to them;
He had turned back again before reaching the land of Lemnos,
As the Sun had kept watch for him and told him the story.
He went into his home, troubled in his own heart.
He stood in the doorway, and a wild anger seized him.
305 Terribly he shouted and cried out to the gods:
"Father Zeus and you other blessed ever-living gods,
Come see deeds to laugh at that are not to be endured,
How Aphrodite, the daughter of Zeus, dishonors me always,
Lame as I am, and loves the destructive Ares
310 Because he is handsome and nimble of foot, while I
Was born feeble. I know no other cause of that
Than my two parents; would that they had never had me!
But you shall see how the two of them have gone into my bed
And are making love there. It grieves me to see it.
But I suppose they would not like to be that way a moment
315   more,
Though they love one another much. Nor will they soon
Want to sleep, but the snare and the bond will constrain them
To the point where our father gives me back all the bride gifts
I paid to him for the sake of the bitch-faced maiden,
320 Since his daughter is lovely, but does not restrain her heart."
So he said, and the gods gathered in the bronze-floored hall.
Poseidon came, who girdles the earth, and Hermes,
The helper; the far-darting Lord Apollo came.
Of the feminine goddesses each stayed home out of shame.
325 The gods, givers of good things, stood in the doorways.
Unquenchable laughter rose up among the blessed gods
To see the devices of many-minded Hephaistos.
This is what one of them would say as he looked to his neigh-
  bor:
"Evil deeds do not win. The slow man finds out the swift,
330 As even now Hephaistos, who is slow and a cripple,
With his devices caught Ares, swiftest of the gods
Who possess Olympos. He owes the adulterer's fine."
This was the sort of thing they said to one another.
The son of Zeus, Lord Apollo, addressed Hermes:

"Hermes, son of Zeus, runner and giver of good things,   335
How would you like to be constrained in strong bonds
And sleep in a bed alongside golden Aphrodite?"
Then the Runner, the slayer of Argos, answered him:
"Far-darting Lord Apollo, I wish that might come about!
Three times as many endless bonds might hold me fast   340
And all you gods and all the goddesses might look at me,
But I should be sleeping alongside golden Aphrodite."
So he said, and laughter arose among the immortal gods.
Laughter did not touch Poseidon; he kept imploring
Hephaistos, renowned for his works, to release Ares;   345
And he spoke out to him and uttered wingèd words:
"Release him, and I will promise for him what you ask:
He will pay all that is proper among the immortal gods."
Then the widely renowned double cripple addressed him:
"Poseidon, holder of earth, do not ask me to do this.   350
The pledges of the worthless are worthless to be kept as
     pledged.
How should I constrain you before the immortal gods
If Ares should go off, avoiding the debt with the bond?"
Then the earth-shaker Poseidon spoke to him:
"Hephaistos, even if Ares gets out from under the debt   355
And goes off in flight, I shall pay it to you myself."
Then the widely renowned double cripple answered him:
"It is not seemly or right to deny your request."
When he had said this, Hephaistos in his force undid the bond.
When the two were released from the bond, strong as it was, 360
They rushed off right at once. He went away to Thrace,
And Aphrodite of the lovely smile got to Cyprus,
To Paphos, where she had a sacred grove and fragrant altar.
There the Graces washed her and anointed her with immortal
Olive oil, such as is poured on the ever-living gods;   365
And they put her in charming clothes, a wonder to see.
This was what the widely renowned singer sang. Odysseus
Was delighted in mind as he listened, and so were the others,
The Phaeacians, who have long oars, men famous for ships.
Alcinoos bade Halios and Laodamas   370
To dance alone, since no one would contend with them.
And so when they had taken a lovely ball in their hands,
A purple one that skillful Polybos had made them,
One of them threw it up to the shadowy clouds,

375 Doubling himself backward. The other rose high off the earth
And easily caught it before touching ground with his feet.
And when they had tried their skill at throwing the ball straight
   up,
The two of them danced upon the much-nourishing earth,
Rapidly changing position. The other youths beat time,
380 Standing in a ring; and a great sound of stamping arose.
Then godly Odysseus spoke to Alcinoos:
"Lordly Alcinoos, illustrious among all peoples,
You did claim that these dancers were most excellent,
And it has been shown true. Awe holds me as I look."
385 So he said, and Alcinoos in his sacred strength rejoiced.
Right away he spoke to the Phaeacians, who are fond of rowing:
"Listen, leaders and counselors of the Phaeacians,
The stranger seems to me to be very prudent.
Come now, let us give him a guest's gift, as is seemly.
390 There are in the district twelve distinguished kings,
Rulers who hold sway, and I am myself the thirteenth.
Each of you give him a well-washed mantle and tunic
And bring him a talent of precious gold. Let us at once
Bring all these together so the stranger may hold them
395 In his hands and go to dinner rejoicing in his heart.
But let Euryalos propitiate him in person
With words and a gift, since he spoke an improper speech."
So he said, and they all assented and gave the order,
And each one sent off a herald to bring the gifts.
400 Then Euryalos answered him and addressed him:
"Lordly Alcinoos, illustrious among all peoples,
I will propitiate the stranger just as you bid me,
And I shall give him this sword all of bronze, whose hilt
Is silver, and a sheath of newly sawn ivory
405 Circles it about. It is worth a great deal for him."
When he had said this, he placed a silver-studded sword in his
   hands;
And he spoke out to him and uttered wingèd words.
"Greetings, father stranger: if any terrible word
Has come out, let storms at once snatch it and carry it off.
May the gods grant that you see your wife and reach your fa-
410 therland,
Since you have long suffered troubles far from your dear ones."
Odysseus of many devices addressed him in answer:

"Kind greetings to you, friend. May the gods grant blessings to
    you,
And may there come to you henceforth no longing for this
    sword
Which you have given me, appeasing me with words."   415
So he said, and put the silver-studded sword over his shoulders.
The sun went down, and the glorious gifts for him were brought.
Noble heralds carried them to the home of Alcinoos.
The sons of excellent Alcinoos, when they had taken them,
Lay the beautiful gifts before their respected mother.   420
Alcinoos led the way for them in his sacred strength.
When they had entered, they sat down on the high armchairs,
And Alcinoos in his might spoke to Arete:
"My wife, bring a fine coffer here, the best there is,
And put a well-washed mantle and tunic in it yourself,   425
Warm the bronze cauldron round the fire for him and heat up
    water
So that when he has bathed, he may look at all the gifts,
Well arrayed, that the excellent Phaeacians have brought,
And enjoy dinner and listen to the strain of a song.
I shall present him myself with this beautiful cup   430
Of gold, so that he may remember me all his days
When he pours in his halls to Zeus and the other gods."
So he said, and Arete gave the word to her handmaids
To set a big cauldron over the fire as quickly as they could.
They stood a cauldron for bath water on a blazing fire,   435
Poured in water, took wood, and kindled it beneath.
The fire circled the cauldron's belly, and the water heated.
Meanwhile Arete brought the lovely coffer for the stranger
From the chamber, and put in it the splendid gifts,
The clothing and the gold that the Phaeacians had given.   440
She herself put in a mantle and a lovely tunic.
And she spoke out to him and uttered wingèd words:
"Look to the lid yourself, and quickly fasten the knot,
Lest someone rob you of it on your trip, at a time when
You are resting in sweet sleep as you go in the black ship."   445
When godly Odysseus, who had endured much, heard that,
He at once fitted the lid on and quickly fastened the knot,
The subtle one that queenly Circe [1] had once taught his mind.
At the same moment a housekeeper called him to go

1. An enchantress living in Aiaia; daughter of the sun.

450 To the bathtub to be washed. He saw the hot water
With gladdened heart, as he had received no such treatment
Since he had left the home of Calypso with the lovely locks.
The care he got all that while was as it would be for a god.
When the handmaids had washed him and anointed him with
        oil,
455 They threw a lovely mantle around him and a tunic,
And out of the bathtub he stepped, and he went amid the men
As they were drinking wine. Nausicaa, who had her beauty
From the gods, stood by the column of the stoutly made roof
And wondered at Odysseus as she took him in with her eyes.
460 She spoke out to him, and she uttered wingèd words:
"Farewell, stranger; and even when you are in your fatherland
May you remember me as the one you first owe the ransom of
        life."
Odysseus of many devices addressed her in answer:
"Nausicaa, daughter of great-hearted Alcinoos,
465 May Zeus, the thunderer, husband of Hera, now grant
That I go homeward and see the day of my return,
And that there, too, I may pray to you as to a god
Forever all my days. For you saved my life, maiden."
He spoke, and sat on an armchair beside King Alcinoos.
470 They were already passing out portions and mixing wine,
And a herald came near, leading the trusty singer
Demodocos, honored by the people. And he set him
In the midst of the diners, propped against a tall pillar.
Then Odysseus of many devices addressed the herald
475 When he had cut some off the back—but more was left on it—
Of a shining-tusked boar; and swelling fat was about it.
"Herald, take this portion over to Demodocos
So he may eat, and I will embrace him, grieved as I am,
For among all the men on the earth singers are sharers
480 In honor and respect, because the Muse has taught them
Poems, and she cherishes the tribe of singers."
So he said; the herald brought the meat and put it in the hands
Of the hero Demodocos. He took it and rejoiced in his heart.
They stretched forth their hands to the food that was spread out
        ready,
485 And when they had taken their fill of food and drink,
Odysseus of many devices addressed Demodocos:
"Demodocos, I give you praise above all mortal men,

Either a Muse, a child of Zeus, has taught you, or Apollo.
Very becomingly did you sing the fate of the Achaians,
All they acted and endured, all the Achaians suffered,   490
As though you had somehow been there yourself or heard one
    who was.
Come, change your subject and sing of the stratagem
Of the wooden horse Epeios made with Athene's help,
The trap that godly Odysseus once led to the citadel,
When he had filled it up with the men who sacked Ilion.   495
If you do tell me these matters in proper form,
Then at once I will proclaim among all men
How a propitious god endowed a divine singer."
So he said. Inspired by the god, he began and showed forth his
    song,
Starting from where some of the Argives on the well-timbered
    ships   500
Boarded and sailed off, when they had set fire to the huts,
And the others who were round the famous Odysseus already
Were seated in the assembly of the Trojans concealed within
    the horse,
For the Trojans themselves dragged it to their citadel.
So it stood, and they made many ill-considered speeches   505
Seated about it. Three plans there were that pleased them:
To strike through the hollow wood with the pitiless sword,
To drag it to the peak and throw it off the rocks,
Or to let the great ornament be a charm for the gods.
Even then it was destined to end in just this way.   510
Fate was, they should be destroyed, since the city enfolded
The great wooden horse, where all the best men of the Argives
Were seated, bringing death and destiny on the Trojans.
He sang how the sons of the Achaians sacked the city,
When they had poured from the horse and abandoned the
    hollow ambush;   515
He sang how one man ravaged one place and one another,
In the lofty city, and Odysseus like Ares went
To the halls of Deiphobos, with godlike Menelaos.
There he said the man dared fight his most dreadful battle
And won, that time too, through great-hearted Athene.   520
This did the renowned singer sing. And Odysseus
Melted, and a tear from under his eyelids wet his cheeks,
As a woman weeps embracing her beloved husband

Who has fallen before his own city and his own people,
525 Warding off from city and children the pitiless day,
And she sees the man dying and breathing heavily,
And falls down upon him and piercingly shrieks. The enemy
From behind strike her back and her shoulders with spears
And lead her off in bonds to have trouble and woe,
530 And her cheeks are wasted for her most wretched grief;
Just so did Odysseus shed a piteous tear under his eyebrows.
Then, as he shed tears, he escaped the notice of all the others
But Alcinoos alone took note of him and perceived him
While seated near him, and heard him as he deeply groaned.
535 At once he addressed the Phaeacians, who are fond of rowing.
"Hear me, leaders and counselors of the Phaeacians,
And let Demodocos hold off now from the sharp-toned lyre.
For he does not give everyone pleasure when he sings this.
Since we have been dining and the divine singer rose,
540 The stranger has not at all ceased his woeful lament,
For grief has very much compassed his mind about.
But come, let him hold off, so we may all alike take pleasure,
Hosts and the guest, since it is much more pleasant so.
All this has been done for the sake of our respected guest,
545 The convoy and the precious gifts we give him in friendship.
A guest and a suppliant is held equal to a brother
By a man who has even a little grasp with his wits.
And so in your cunning notions do not yourself now conceal
What I ask you about. It is better for you to speak.
550 Tell the name which your mother and father called you there,
And the others who dwell in that city and about it,
For no one among men is wholly without a name,
Neither a worthless man nor a noble, from the time he was
born;
Parents when they have children bestow them on everyone.
555 Tell me your land and your district and your city,
So that the ships that are steered by thought may convey you
there,
For there exist no pilots among the Phaeacians,
And there are no rudders at all such as other ships have,
But the ships themselves know the intentions and minds of
men.
560 They know the cities and fertile fields of all men
And very swiftly, shrouded in mist and a cloud,

They traverse the gulf of the sea. There is no fear
At all for them that they suffer harm or be lost.
But once I heard my father Nausithoos
Say this: he asserted that Poseidon bore a grudge   565
Against us, because our convoys are safe for all men.
He said a well-made ship of the Phaeacian men
Coming back sometime from an escort on the murky ocean
Would be dashed, and a great mountain would hide our city
    round.
So the old man said. And the god will either fulfill it   570
Or it will be unfulfilled, as his spirit desires.
Come tell me this, and speak out truthfully.
Where have you wandered, and what places have you reached
Among men: tell of them and their well-inhabited cities,
Those that were difficult and savage and without justice,   575
And those who were friendly to strangers and have a godfearing
    mind.
Tell also why you lament and grieve in your heart
When you hear the fate of Ilion and the Danaan Argives.
That did the gods fashion, and they spun the thread of death
For men, so that it would be a song for those to come.   580
Did some kinsman of yours perish before Ilion,
A nobleman, son-in-law, or father-in-law,
Those who are dearest, next to one's blood and family,
Or perhaps some companion of sympathetic mind,
A noble one? Since not inferior to a brother   585
Is a companion who possesses a prudent mind."

IX

Odysseus of many devices addressed him in answer:
"Lordly Alcinoos, exalted among all your people,
Indeed it is pleasant to listen to such a singer
As this one is, who resembles the gods in his voice.
5 I would say myself there is no more delightful result
Than when happiness so prevails through a whole district
And when diners seated in order through the halls
Listen to a singer, and the tables nearby are full
Of bread and meat, and the wine pourer draws wine off
10 From the bowl, carries it around, and pours it in the cups.
To my mind this seems to be the loveliest thing.
But your heart turns toward me to ask of my woeful cares,
So that I may grieve still further as I lament.
What then shall I tell you first, what tell last,
15 Since the heavenly gods bestowed many cares upon me?
Well now, I shall tell you my name first, so that you too
May know it, and then, when I have escaped the pitiless day
I may be your guest friend, though I dwell far off in my halls.
I am Odysseus, son of Laertes, who for my wiles
20 Am of note among all men, and my fame reaches heaven.
I dwell in sunny Ithaca. A mountain is on it,
Neritos, with trembling leaves, conspicuous.
Many islands lie about it quite close to one another,
Dulichion and Samê and wooded Zakynthos;
25 She herself sits low-lying, farthest out to sea
Toward dusk, and they are apart toward dawn and the sun,
Rugged but good for bringing up young men. And I
Can look upon nothing sweeter than a man's own land.
Well, Calypso, the divine goddess, kept me in one place,
30 In a hollow cave, desiring that I be her husband.
The same way in her halls would the wily Aiaian
Circe have held me back, desiring that I be her husband.
But they never persuaded the heart within my breast.

So nothing grows sweeter than a man's own fatherland
And his parents, even if he dwell in a fertile home   35
Far off in a foreign land apart from his parents.
But come, let me tell you of the much-troubled return
That Zeus put upon me when I went away from Troy.
The wind bearing me from Ilion brought me near the Cicones,[1]
To Ismaros. There I sacked the city and killed its men.   40
From the city we took the wives and many possessions
And divided them so none for my sake would lack an equal
    share.
Then I gave the order for us to take rapid flight,
But the men, great fools as they were, did not obey;
They had drunk much wine there and slain many sheep   45
Along the strand, many shamble-footed, crumple-horned cattle.
Meanwhile the Cicones went and called other Cicones
Who were their neighbors, at once more numerous and brave,
Who dwelt on the mainland, skilled in fighting with men,
From horses, and, when necessary, on foot.   50
As thick as leaves and flowers grow in their season,
They came, in early morning. Then an evil fate of Zeus was with
    us
In our dread destinies, so we might suffer many pains.
They took their stand and fought a battle by the swift ships,
And they threw bronze-tipped spears at one another.   55
So long as it was morning and the sacred day increased,
We stayed and warded them off, many as there were.
But when the sun declined to the time of ox-loosing,
Then the Cicones turned back the Achaians and routed them.
Six from each ship of my well-greaved companions   60
Perished. The rest of us escaped death and destiny.
Then we sailed on further, grieving in our hearts,
Glad to escape death, having lost our dear companions.
My bobbing ships, however, did not proceed further
Till someone had thrice called for each of our wretched com-
    panions   65
Who had died on the plain, slaughtered by the Cicones.
Cloud-gathering Zeus raised a North Wind against the ships
In an immense storm, and covered land and ocean alike
Over with clouds. And night rose up out of heaven.
The ships were borne headlong, and the force of the wind   70

1. Thracian allies of the Trojans raided by Odysseus.

Ripped the sails up into three fragments and four.
We lowered them onto the ships, fearing destruction,
And rowed the ships forward to the mainland hastily.
There for two whole nights and two days continually
75 We lay, eating our hearts with pain and fatigue alike.
But when fair-braided Dawn had brought the third day to the
full,
We set up our masts and hoisted the white sails
And took our seats. The wind and the pilots steered them,
And I would have arrived unscathed at my fatherland,
80 But as I rounded Malea a rushing wave
And a North Wind pushed me off and drove me past Cythera.
Thence for nine days I was borne by destructive winds
On the fish-laden ocean. But the tenth day I set foot
On the land of the Lotus-eaters, who eat a flowery food.
85 Then we went onto the dry land and drew off water,
And at once my companions took dinner beside the swift ships.
But when we had partaken of food and of drink,
I sent my companions forth to go and find out
Who these were of the men who eat bread on the earth.
90 I picked out two men and sent on a third as a herald.
They went off at once and mingled with the Lotus-eaters.
And the Lotus-eaters did not plot destruction
For our companions, but gave them the lotus to taste of.
Whoever among them ate the honey-sweet fruit of the lotus
95 Wished no longer to bring word back again or return,
But wanted to remain there with the Lotus-eaters
To devour the lotus and forget about a return.
Back weeping to the ships I led them, by compulsion,
Dragged them and bound them in the hollow ships under the
benches,
100 And I called all my other trusty companions
To hasten and to get on board the rapid ships,
Lest someone perchance eat the lotus and forget a return.
They got in at once and took their seats at the oarlocks.
Seated in order, they beat the hoary sea with their oars.
105 Then we sailed further on, grieving in our hearts,
To the land of the Cyclopes, an overweening
And lawless people, who, trusting in the immortal gods,
Do not sow plants with their hands and do not plow
But everything grows for them unplowed and unsown,

Wheat and barley and vines that produce a wine grape   110
Of large clusters, and a rain from Zeus makes them grow.
They have neither assemblies for holding council nor laws,
But they inhabit the crests of the lofty mountains,
In hollow caves, and each one dispenses the laws
For his children and his wives and is not concerned for the
    others.   115
A fertile island stretches there from the harbor
Of the land of the Cyclopes, not near and not far away,
A wooded one. And on it numberless wild goats flourish,
For there is no beaten path of men to keep them away.
Nor do hunters land upon it, who in the woods   120
Undergo pains and chase them over the mountain peaks.
And it is not held, either, with flocks or with plowed lands,
But it lies unsown and unplowed day after day
Bereft of men, and it nourishes bleating goats.
There are no vermilion-prowed ships for the Cyclopes,   125
As there are no shipwrights among them who might work
At good-timbered ships to accomplish it all for them
So they may visit cities among men, as frequently
Men do cross the sea in ships toward one another;
And these would have worked to make the island well settled
    for them,   130
As it is not really bad, and would bear all things in season.
There are meadows in it along the banks of the hoary sea,
Soft, moist ones. And there would be fine, unwithering vines
And smooth plowing, and they would mow the deep-standing
Grain in season, as it is very rich beneath the surface.   135
There a sheltered harbor is, where there is no need of a rope
Or of throwing out anchor stones or fastening cables,
But they could put in and stay a time till the hearts
Of the sailors urged them on and breezes should be blowing.
And shining water flows down from the head of the harbor,   140
A spring under a cave. Poplars grow about it.
There we sailed on in. And some god guided us
Through the murky night. There was not light enough to see.
Dark air was deep about the ships, nor did the moon
Show forth from heaven, but it was contained in clouds.   145
There no one looked upon the island with his eyes,
And we did not behold the great waves rolling up
On the mainland, before we beached our well-timbered ships.

When the ships had been beached, we took down all the sails,
150 And got out ourselves beside the surf of the sea.
We fell asleep there and awaited the godly dawn.
And when the early-born, rosy-fingered dawn appeared,
We wondered at the island and traveled all around it.
The nymphs, daughters of aegis-bearing Zeus, roused up
155 Mountain goats, so that my companions might have dinner.
At once we took curved bows and long-socketed goat spears
Out of the ships. We divided into three groups
And went shooting. At once the god gave us satisfying game.
The men of twelve ships followed along with me. Nine goats
160 Fell the lot of each ship. They picked ten out just for me.
So then for the whole day till the setting of the sun
We sat dining on the endless meat and sweet wine,
For the red wine from the ships had not yet been exhausted,
But was still there. Each group had drawn off much in jars
165 When we sacked the holy citadel of the Cicones.
We were looking over to the land of the Cyclopes nearby,
To their smoke, to their sound and that of their sheep and goats.
But when the sun went down and the darkness came on,
We lay down to sleep beside the surf of the sea.
170 And when the early-born, rosy-fingered dawn appeared,
I called an assembly and spoke out to them all:
'Stay here now, the rest of you, my trusty companions;
But I will go myself with my ship and companions
To inquire about these men, whoever they may be,
175 Whether they are proud and savage and without justice
Or are friendly to strangers, and have a god-fearing mind.'
When I had said this, I went on the ship and called my companions
To go on board themselves and to undo the stern cables.
At once they got on and took their seats at the oarlocks;
180 Seated in order, they beat the hoary sea with their oars.
And when we had arrived at the place that was nearby,
There we saw a cave on the verge, close to the sea
High up, overhung with laurel. Many animals
Usually slept there, sheep and goats; a courtyard
185 Was built high around it out of deep-bedded stones
And tall pines and oak trees with lofty foliage.
There a monstrous man usually slept, who alone
And aloof tended the animals. He did not consort

With the others, but stayed apart and had a lawless mind.
And indeed he was formed as a monstrous wonder. He looked 190
Not like a grain-eating man but like a wooded crest
On lofty mountains that appears singled out from the others.
And then I ordered the rest of my trusty companions
To remain there beside the ship and to guard the ship.
But I myself picked out twelve of my best companions   195
To go on. Now I had a goatskin flask of black wine,
A sweet wine that Maron gave me, Euanthes' son—
The priest of Apollo, who watches over Ismaros—
Because we protected him along with his wife and son,
And reverenced him. He dwelt in the tree-filled grove   200
Of Phoebos Apollo. And he gave me glorious gifts:
He gave me seven talents of well-fashioned gold,
And he gave me a mixing bowl all of silver, and then
Into two-handled jars, twelve in all, he drew off wine
Sweet and unmixed, a godly drink, nor was any   205
Maidservant or serving man in the house aware of it,
But himself and his wife and one single housekeeper.
And whenever they drank that honey-sweet red wine,
He would fill one cup and pour it into twenty measures
Of water, and a sweet aroma came from the bowl   210
Of marvelous fragrance: to abstain then would not have been
    easy.
I filled a great skin with it and brought it, and also I put
Provisions in a bag. At once my bold spirit
Sensed that the man would approach, clad in his great strength,
The wild man who had clear in his mind neither justice nor
    laws.   215
Speedily we came to the cave and did not find him
Within. But he was tending rich flocks in a pasture.
We entered the cave and gazed at each separate thing.
Baskets were weighed down with cheeses, and the folds were
    thronged
With lambs and kids. All were divided in groups,   220
And confined; here the first born, there the middlers,
The dew-fleeced apart too. All the pails flowed with whey,
The vessels and the pans, well wrought, in which he milked
    them.
Then at first my companions besought me with speeches
To go back again, when we had picked some cheeses and then 225

When we had hastily driven the kids and lambs out of the pens
On board the swift ship, to set sail upon the salt water.
But I did not listen—that would have been far better—
So I might see the man and he give me the gifts of a guest.
But when he appeared, he was not to be joyful to my com-
230   panions.
We kindled a fire there, sacrificed, and ourselves
Also picked out some cheeses and ate, and awaited him
Seated inside, till he did come driving sheep. He carried
A stout burden of dry wood to use for his supper.
235   Throwing it down inside the cave, he made a din;
And we drew back in fear into a nook of the cave.
But into the broad cavern he drove his fat flocks,
All those that he usually milked, and he left the males
By the entrance, rams and he-goats, in the deep yard outside.
240   Then he put a great doorstone on, raising it aloft,
A mighty one. And twenty-two excellent wagons
With four wheels could not pry it up from the ground,
So great was the towering rock he set on the entrance.
He sat down and milked the sheep and the bleating goats,
245   All in due order, and set each young one to his mother;
And at once when he had curdled half the white milk,
He skimmed it off and put it up in wicker baskets,
And half of it he stood in pails so he would have it
To drink when he reached for it, to have it for supper.
250   And when he had hurried at attending to all his tasks,
He kindled a fire, and looked at us, and spoke to us:
'Strangers, who are you? Whence have you sailed the watery
       ways?
For some sort of gain, or do you wander at hazard
The way pirates do who wander over the sea
255   Risking their lives, bearing evil to foreigners?'
So he said, and our own hearts were shattered within us,
In terror at his deep voice and the monster himself.
Yet even so I answered him with a speech and addressed him
       thus:
'We are Achaians coming from Troy, driven off course
260   By all kinds of winds over the great gulf of the sea;
Wanting to go homeward, we came by other passages,
By another way. So Zeus I suppose wished to devise it.
We declare we are the men of Agamemnon, son of Atreus,

The glory of whom is now the most under heaven,
So great a city did he sack, and he destroyed many   265
People. And so we have arrived here and come up to your
    knees
To see if you may provide some guest gift or otherwise
Give a present, such as is the custom among guest friends,
Mighty one, revere the gods. We are your suppliants.
Zeus is the protector of suppliants and guest friends,   270
The god of guests, who accompanies respectful guests.'
So I said, and he answered me at once in his pitiless spirit:
'You are a fool, stranger, or have come from afar,
To bid me to be afraid or to shrink from the gods.
Cyclopes have no regard for aegis-bearing Zeus,   275
Or the blessed gods since we are mightier by far.
Nor to shrink from the hatred of Zeus would I spare
You or your companions, unless the spirit moved me.
But tell me where you have come and put your well-made
    ships,
Whether on the mainland or nearby, so I may know.'   280
So he said, testing us; I who knew much was not deceived.
I addressed him in return with guileful words:
'The earth-shaker Poseidon has shattered my ship,
Throwing it on the rocks at the borders of your land,
Driving it on the cape, but a wind bore it from the ocean.   285
And I escaped with these men from sheer destruction.'
So I said; in his pitiless spirit he answered nothing,
But he leaped up, stretched his hands to my companions,
Snatched up two together, and dashed them like whelps to the
    earth.
Their brains flowed out onto the ground and wet the earth.   290
Then he tore them limb from limb and made them his meal.
He ate like a mountain-reared lion, and did not leave off
Their entrails and their flesh and their marrowed bones.
We wailed and held our hands out to Zeus when we
Had seen the cruel deeds. Helplessness held our hearts.   295
And when the Cyclops had filled up his great belly
By eating human flesh and then drinking unmixed milk,
He lay down in the cave, stretched full length through the sheep.
And in my great-hearted spirit I made a plan myself
To go closer to him, draw the sharp sword from my thigh   300
And wound him in the chest where the midriff holds the liver,

Striking with my hand. But another spirit restrained me;
For there we too would have perished in sheer destruction,
Since from the lofty entrance we could not push away
305 The mighty rock with our hands that he had set upon it.
And so we lamented then and awaited the godly dawn.
And when the early-born, rosy-fingered dawn appeared,
He kindled a fire and milked his glorious flocks,
All in due order, and set each young one to his mother.
310 And when he had hurried at tending to all his tasks,
He again snatched two men together and made them his meal.
When he had finished, he drove the rich flock from the cave,
Taking the great doorstone off easily. And then
He put it back, as one would put the lid on a quiver.
315 With a great whistling, the Cyclops turned his fat flock
To the mountain. I was left deeply devising evil,
If I might somehow avenge me and Athene give me glory.
And this seemed to me in my heart to be the best plan.
In the fold a great club of the Cyclops was lying,
320 A green one of olive wood. He had cut it to carry
When it was dry. As we beheld it, we thought it
To be as large as the mast of a black, twenty-oared ship,
A wide freighter that traverses the great gulf:
So great was its length, so great its breadth to behold.
325 I stood by and cut off a piece the size of a cubit,
Gave it to my companions and told them to plane it;
They made it smooth, and I stood by and sharpened it to a
 point.
I took it at once and brought it to a glow in the blazing fire;
Then I hid it well, placing it under the dung
330 Which was strewn through the cave in great abundant heaps.
Then I ordered the others to cast lots for a choice
Of the one who would dare to raise the pole along with me
And bore it in his eye when sweet sleep had come upon him.
The lots fell to those I would have wished to choose myself,
335 Four men, and I picked myself as the fifth among them.
He came at evening driving the flocks with their lovely fleece.
At once he drove the fat flocks into the broad cave,
All, and did not leave any outside in the deep yard;
Either he suspected something or a god bade him so.
340 Then he put the great doorstone on, raising it aloft,

And he sat down and milked the sheep and the bleating goats,
All in due order, and set each young one to his mother.
And when he had hurried at attending to all his tasks,
He again snatched two men together and made them his meal.
Then I addressed the Cyclops, standing close to him,   345
Holding in my hands an ivy bowl of black wine:
'Here, Cyclops, drink wine, now you have eaten human flesh,
So you may see what sort of wine this is that our ship contained.
I brought it for libation to you that you might pity me
And send me home. Your rage may be borne no longer;   350
Cruel wretch, how could anyone else come to you later on
Of the number of mankind, since you have not acted properly.'
So I said. He took and drank it. He was fearfully pleased
As he drank the sweet wine, and he asked me for a second.
'Kindly grant me something more and tell me your name   355
At once now, so I may give you a guest gift to delight you.
Yes, indeed, for the Cyclopes the grain-giving land bears
Large-clustered wine grapes, and a rain of Zeus makes them
     grow,
But this is a runnel of nectar and ambrosia.'
So he said. And I gave him more of the sparkling wine.   360
Thrice I brought it and gave it, thrice he thoughtlessly drank.
And when the wine had overcome the mind of the Cyclops,
At that point I addressed him with soothing words:
'Cyclops, do you ask me my famous name? Well, I
Will tell you. Then give me the guest gift you promised.   365
Noman is my own name. Noman do they call me,
My mother and my father and all my companions.'
So I said, and he answered at once in his pitiless spirit:
'Noman I shall eat last among his companions
And the others first. This will be my guest gift to you.'   370
With that he leaned over and fell down on his back. And then
He lay with his massive neck twisted. All-subduing
Sleep seized him. Wine poured out of his gullet,
And chunks of human flesh. He belched out drunkenly.
And then I drove the pole up under a mass of ashes   375
Until it should heat. And I encouraged all my companions
With speeches, lest one of them should draw back from me in
     fear.
But just when the olive pole was ready to catch fire,

Green as it was, and was glowing dreadfully,
At that moment I came closer and took it out of the fire. My
380 companions
Stood about. And some god breathed great courage into them.
They lifted the olive pole that was sharp at its tip
And thrust it in his eye; I myself, leaning on it from above,
Twirled it around as a man would drill the wood of a ship
With an auger, and others would keep spinning with a strap
385 beneath,
Holding it at either end, and the auger keeps on going.
So we held the fire-sharpened pole in his eye
And twirled it. The blood flowed around it, hot as it was.
The fire singed his eyebrows and eyelids all around
390 From the burning eye. Its roots swelled in the fire to bursting,
As when a smith plunges a great ax or an adz
Into cold water and the tempering makes it hiss
Loudly, and just that gives the strength to the iron;
So did his eye sizzle around the olive pole.
395 He wailed a great terrible wail; the rock resounded,
And we were afraid and rushed back, while he drew
The pole out of his eye spattered with much blood;
Then he threw it from him with his hands, maddened by pain,
And let out a great roar for the Cyclopes, who dwelt
400 All around him in caves throughout the windy peaks.
When they heard the shout they trailed in from every side;
They stood around the cave and asked what bothered him:
'Polyphemos, how is it you are hurt so much as to shout so
Through the ambrosial night and to make us sleepless?
405 No mortal drives your flocks against your will, does he?
And no one is murdering you by craft or by force?'
Mighty Polyphemos addressed them from the cavern:
'Friends, Noman is murdering me by craft, not by force.'
And they answered him and addressed him with wingèd words:
410 'If no one is compelling you when you are alone,
There is no way to escape a sickness from great Zeus.
Come now and pray to our father Lord Poseidon.'
So they said and went away; and my own heart laughed
At how my name had deceived him, and my faultless device.
415 The Cyclops, though, was in pain as he groaned, and felt pangs.
Groping with his hands, he took the stone from the entrance
And sat in the entrance himself, stretching out his hands

To see if he could catch someone going outdoors with the sheep;
So foolish did he in his mind think me to be.
And I myself kept planning what way might be far the best   420
If I could find some release from death for my companions
And for myself. I wove all sorts of wiles and deceit
As for very life, since a great ill was near at hand.
This seemed to me in my heart to be the best plan:
The males of the sheep were well nourished and shaggy coated, 425
Handsome and large, with a fleece of dark violet.
These I joined fast in silence with easily twisted twigs
On which the monster Cyclops slept, lawless in his mind.
I bound them in threes, and the middle one would carry a man.
The other two went on either side, protecting my companions. 430
So three sheep bore each mortal man. As for myself,
There was a lead ram, by far the finest of all the sheep,
Whose back I grasped and lay under his shaggy belly
Curled up. And with my hand twisted in his marvelous
     wool
I held on relentlessly with an enduring heart.   435
So then, lamenting, we awaited the godly dawn.
And when the early-born, rosy-fingered dawn appeared,
At that moment he drove the male flocks to pasture,
And the females were bleating unmilked around the pens.
Their udders were swollen. And then the master, afflicted   440
By bad pains, felt over the backs of all the sheep
As they stood erect. And the fool did not perceive
How the men were bound under the breasts of the thick-fleeced
     sheep.
Last of all the lead ram of the flock went outdoors
Encumbered by his wool and by me with my rapid thoughts.   445
The mighty Polyphemos felt him over and addressed him:
'Friend ram, why of all the sheep do you move this way as
     the last
Out of the cave? You were not left behind by the sheep be-
     fore;
You were much the first to pasture on the tender flowers of
     grass
With your long strides, and you came first to the rivers' streams, 450
And you were the first to deisre to return to the fold
At evening. But now you are last of all. Ah, you long
For the eye of your master that an evil man put out

With woeful companions, overcoming his mind by wine,
455 Noman, who I say has not yet escaped destruction.
And if you could sympathize and become able to speak,
To say in what place that man is evading my rage,
Then once he were struck, his brains should be dashed through
     the cave
In all directons on the threshold. And then my heart
460 Should be relieved of the ills worthless Noman brought me.'
When he had said this, he sent the ram from him out the en-
     trance.
When I had gone a short way away from the cave and the yard,
I first got loose from the ram and then freed my companions.
Speedily we drove the long-legged sheep, rich in fat,
465 Rounding the many of them up, until we came
To the ship. We were welcome to our dear companions,
We who escaped death. The others they would have lamented,
     wailing,
But I did not allow it and nodded with my eyebrows to each
Not to weep. I ordered them to put the many sheep
470 With lovely fleece quickly on the ship and sail the salt water.
They got on board at once and took their seats at the oarlocks;
Seated in order, they beat the hoary sea with their oars.
And when I was as far off as a man's shout would carry,
I addressed the Cyclops myself with taunting speeches:
475 'Cyclops, you were not destined to eat in your hollow cave,
For your powerful might, the companions of a strengthless man.
And truly it was destined for your evil deeds to find you out,
Cruel wretch, since you did not shrink from eating the guests
In your house. Zeus and the other gods have paid you for that.'
480 So I said. Then he got the more angry in his heart.
He broke off the crest of a great mountain and threw it,
And it fell down in front of the dark blue-prowed ship,
Just short, and it missed hitting the end of the rudder.
The sea was heaved up by the rock as it descended,
485 And a great back-washing wave bore the ship at once to land,
As it swelled from the ocean, and drove it to hit the mainland.
And I took hold of a very long pole in my hands
And pushed on out. I called to urge on my companions,
Nodding with my head, to throw themselves on the oars,
490 So we could flee misfortune. Falling to it, they rowed.
When we had crossed twice as much water and were far away,

Then I would have shouted to the Cyclops, but my companions
   around me
From all sides tried to restrain me with soothing speeches:
'You wretch, why did you want to provoke the wild man,
Who, even now, when he threw his missile into the ocean,   495
Has brought the ship back to land? And we really thought we
   would die there.
And if he had heard anyone speaking or shouting out
He would have broken our brains and our ship timbers
Casting a jagged piece of sparkling rock. So powerfully does he
   throw!'
So they said, but they did not sway my great-hearted spirit.   500
But in my angry spirit I answered him back:
'Cyclops, if someone among mortal men should inquire
Of you about the unseemly blindness in your eye,
Say that Odysseus, sacker of cities, blinded it,
The son of Laertes, whose home is in Ithaca.'   505
So I said. He moaned and answered me with a tale:
'Well then, the decrees uttered of old have come upon me.
Once there was a prophet here, a man fine and great,
Telemos, Eurymos' son, who excelled in prophecy,
And grew old prophesying among the Cyclopes,   510
Who said all these things in the future would come to pass,
That I would be deprived of my sight at Odysseus' hands.
But I always expected some mortal great and handsome
To arrive in this place decked out in great strength.
And now, a man small and worthless and feeble   515
Has blinded my eye when he overcame me with wine.
Come here now, Odysseus, so I may present you with gifts,
And urge the famed earth-shaker to give you an escort,
For I am his son, and he declares he is my father.
He himself, if he wishes, will heal me. No one else   520
Can do it, of the blessed gods or of mortal men.'
So he said, and I myself addressed him in answer:
'Would I might as surely be able to make you devoid
Of breath and life and send you to the hall of Hades,
As I am sure not even the earth-shaker will heal your eye.'   525
So I said, and then he prayed to Lord Poseidon,
Stretching his hand up to the heaven filled with stars:
'Hear me, earth-girdling Poseidon of the dark-blue locks,
If truly I am yours, and you declare you are my father,

530 Grant that the city-sacker Odysseus not go homeward,
The son of Laertes whose home is in Ithaca.
But if it is his fate to see his dear ones and arrive
At his well-established home and his fatherland,
May he come late and ill, having lost all his companions,
535 On someone else's ship, and find troubles at home.'
So he said in prayer. The god with the dark-blue locks heard
     him.
And then once more he lifted up a far bigger stone.
Whirling it, he shot it and thrust it with boundless strength
And threw it down behind the dark blue-prowed ship,
540 Just short, and it missed hitting the end of the rudder.
The sea was heaved up by the rock as it descended.
A wave bore the ship forward and drove it to hit land.
And when we arrived at the island, where the other
Well-timbered ships were waiting, gathered, and our
     companions
545 Sat lamenting all around, forever awaiting us;
As we came there, we beached our ship upon the sand
And got out ourselves beside the surf of the sea.
Taking the flocks of Cyclops out of the hollow ship,
We divided them so none would lack an equal share for my
     sake.
550 But my well-greaved companions chose the ram especially
For me alone, when the flocks were divided. On the strand
We slew it and burned the thighs to black-clouded Zeus,
The son of Cronos, who rules all. But he received not the rites;
Instead he kept on plotting how all the well-timbered ships
555 And the companions faithful to me might be destroyed.
So then the whole day till the setting of the sun
We sat dining on endless meat and sweet wine.
But when the sun went down and darkness came on,
We lay down to sleep beside the surf of the sea.
560 And when the early-born, rosy-fingered dawn appeared,
I myself called to my companions and bade them
To go on board themselves and to undo the stern cables;
At once they got on and took their seats at the oarlocks.
Seated in order, they beat the hoary sea with their oars.
565 Then we sailed further on, grieving in our hearts,
Glad to escape death, having lost our dear companions.

X

"Then we came to the island of Aeolia, where dwelt
Aeolos,[1] Hippotas' son, who is dear to the immortal gods,
On a floating island. All about it there was
An unbreakable bronze wall, and up it the stone ran smooth.
And there are twelve children of his living in his halls;   5
Six of them are daughters and six are blooming sons.
So he gave the daughters to the sons to be their wives.
They always take their meals with their dear father
And devoted mother. Numberless dishes lie ready for them;
The redolent house resounds all round with the flute   10
In the day, and at night beside their respected wives
They sleep in blankets and upon their jointed bedsteads.
And so we came to their city and their lovely halls.
A whole month he befriended me and asked in detail
About Ilion, the Argives' ships, and the Achaians' return,   15
And I told him everything in its due order.
But when I inquired about the way and asked him
To send us, he did not refuse, and he made a conveyance.
He gave me the skin of a nine-year-old ox he had flayed,
And in it he had bound the courses of the blustering winds.   20
For the son of Cronos had made him steward of the winds,
So he could make the one he wished rise up or subside.
He bound it in the hollow ship with a shining cord
Of silver, so it would not blow at all, not a little.
Then he set a breeze of the West Wind blowing for me   25
That would carry the ship and the men onward. He was not
Destined to complete it. We were lost by our own foolishness.
Nine days we sailed alike by night and by day;
On the tenth the soil of our fatherland already appeared,
And we were close enough to see men tending the fire.   30
Then sweet sleep came upon me in my weariness,
For I always saw to the ship's sheet, and did not give it

1. Lord of the winds.

To another companion, so we might reach the fatherland
   quicker.
But my companions addressed one another with speeches
35 And said that I was bringing gold and silver home
As gifts from Aeolos, the great-hearted son of Hippotas.
This is what one, looking at his closest neighbor, would say:
'Well now, how beloved and honored this man is
Among all those men at whose city and land he arrives.
40 He is bringing much fine treasure out of Troy
As booty. And we, who have accomplished the same journey,
Are going homeward, all of us, with empty hands.
Now Aeolos has given him these things as a favor
In friendship. Come, let us see quickly what they are,
45 How much there is of gold and silver in the skin.'
So they said, and evil advice won my companions over.
They undid the skin, and the winds all rushed out.
At once a storm seized them and bore them onto the ocean,
Far away from our fatherland, weeping. And I,
50 As I awoke, wondered in my own blameless heart
Whether I should drop from the ship and perish in the ocean
Or endure silently and stay among the living still.
But I endured and waited, and lay with head covered
In my ship. The ships were borne in a bad storm of wind
55 Back to the island Aeolia, and my companions groaned.
Then we went onto the dry land and drew off water,
And at once my companions took dinner beside the swift ships.
But when we had partaken of food and of drink,
I took a herald and a companion along with me
60 To the famous halls of Aeolos. And I found him
Having a meal along with his wife and his children.
When we came to the hall we sat beside the columns
On the threshold. They wondered in their hearts, and asked
   right out:
'How have you come, Odysseus? What evil god has attacked
   you?
65 We did send you off kindly, so that you might reach
Fatherland and home and whatever is dear to you.'
So they said, and I spoke out, grieved in my heart:
'My evil companions ruined me; and besides them, a wretched
Sleep. But give relief, friends. You have the power.'
70 So I said, addressing them with gentle words.
But they grew silent. The father answered with a speech:

'Go quickly from the island, most shameful of living men.
It is not lawful for me to help or to send on his course
Any man who is despised by the blessed gods.
Go, since you came to this place despised by the gods.'   75
When he had said this, he sent me deeply groaning from his
    halls.
Then we sailed further on, grieving in our hearts.
The spirit of the men was worn down by the rowing, painful
Through our folly, since conveyance appeared no more.
Six days did we sail alike by night and by day.   80
And on the seventh we came to Lamos' sheer citadel,
Lestrygonian [2] Telepylos, where a shepherd driving in the flock
May call to a shepherd, and the one driving out answers.
And there a sleepless man could have earned double pay
For tending cattle and for pasturing bright sheep,   85
For the courses of the day and night are close together.
There, when we came to the famous harbor, about which a rock
Is set towering on both sides without a break,
And crags jutting out against one another
Are projecting at its mouth, and the entrance is slight,   90
There all the others brought their bobbing ships on inside.
The ships were tied up inside the hollow harbor
Close to one another, for no wave rose in it,
Either great or small, but there was a white calm all around.
But I myself alone brought my black ship outside   95
There on the verge and tied the cables to a rock.
I got up and stood on a rugged point of outlook.
There nothing that was done by oxen or man appeared,
But we saw a lone smoke column rising from the land.
Then I sent my companions to go and find out   100
Who these were of the men who eat bread on the earth.
I picked out two men and sent a third as a herald.
They went off, going by a smooth path where wagons
Brought wood down to the town from the high mountain.
And they happened on a girl getting water before the city,   105
The goodly daughter of Lestrygonian Antiphates.[3]
She was going down to Artacia, a spring with a lovely stream.
From there they carried water on to the city.
Standing beside her, they spoke out to her and asked

2. The Lestrygonians were a tribe of savage giants whose king was Lamos.
3. A king of the Lestrygonians.

110 Who the king of these men was and over whom he ruled.
    She at once pointed out the high-roofed house of her father.
    When they entered the glorious hall, they found his wife
    As big as the crest of a mountain, and they loathed her.
    Right away she called renowned Antiphates from assembly,
115 Her husband, who planned a woeful destruction for the men.
    Snatching one companion at once, he made a meal of him.
    The other two rushed in flight and came to the ships.
    But he sent a shout through the town. They heard it, the
        mighty
    Lestrygonians, and ran out from all directions,
120 Thousands of them, like giants and not like men.
    From the cliffs they threw boulders the size of a man's load.
    And at once an evil din rose up among the ships
    Of men being destroyed and ships being crushed together.
    Spearing the men like fish, they bore off their gruesome meal.
125 While they were destroying the men in the very deep harbor,
    I myself drew my sharp sword from along my thigh
    And with it cut the cable of the dark blue-prowed ship.
    At once I called and urged my companions on
    To throw themselves on the oars so we could flee misfortune.
130 They all strained together, in fear of destruction.
    To my joy my own ship escaped from the overhanging rocks
    Onto the ocean. But the others were lost there all together.
    From there we sailed further on, grieving in our hearts,
    Glad to escape death, having lost our dear companions.
135 We came to the island of Aiaia. There did dwell
    Fair-braided Circe, dread god with a singing voice,
    The blood sister of destructive-minded Aietes.[4]
    They were both descended from the sun who gives light to
        mortals,
    And from their mother Perse, whom Oceanos had for a child.
140 There we put in silently to land on the shore with the ship
    Into a sheltered harbor, and some god guided us.
    When we had got out there, for two days and two nights
    We lay still, eating our hearts with pain and fatigue alike.
    But when fair-braided Dawn had brought the third day to the
        full,
145 I myself took hold of my spear and my sharp sword
    And went up speedily from the ship to a place of lookout,

    4. King of Colchis; father of Medea.

To look for the works of mortals or to hear their sound.
I went up onto the rugged lookout and stood there,
And smoke appeared to me from the wide-traveled earth
In the halls of Circe through dense thickets and a wood.   150
Then I deliberated in my mind and my heart
About going and finding out, since I had seen the lurid smoke.
As I thought about it, it seemed to be better so:
First to go to the swift ship and the strand of the sea
To give my companions a meal, then send to inquire.   155
But when on my way I got close to the bobbing ship,
Some one of the gods pitied me, as I was alone,
And he sent me in my very path a great stag
With high horns who was going down from the wood grove
To the river to drink. For the strength of the sun gripped him.   160
As he was coming out, I hit him along the spine
In the middle of his back. The bronze spear went right through
   him.
He fell with a cry in the dust and his spirit flew off.
I put my foot on him and drew out the bronze spear
From his wound. Then I laid it there along the ground   165
And left it. Thereupon I pulled up brushwood and twigs;
I twined a rope of a fathom in length, well twisted
From both ends, and tied the feet of the vast creature,
Carried it across my back, and went to the black ship
Leaning on my spear, since I could not carry it on one shoulder   170
With my other hand, for the animal was very large.
I threw it down before the ship, roused my companions,
Stood by each man, and spoke to him with soothing words:
'My friends, though we are grieving, we shall not yet go down
To the halls of Hades before the fated day arrives.   175
Come now, while there is food and drink in the swift ship,
Let us take thought of food and not waste away in hunger.'
So I said, and they swiftly hearkened to my words.
Uncovering their heads by the strand of the barren sea,
They gazed at the stag, for the animal was very large.   180
And when they had taken their joy of looking with their eyes,
They washed their hands and prepared a glorious feast,
And so the whole day till the setting of the sun
We sat dining on endless meat and on sweet wine.
And when the sun went down and the darkness came on,   185
We lay down to sleep beside the surf of the sea.

And when the early-born, rosy-fingered dawn appeared,
I called an assembly and spoke out to them all:
'Hear my speech, my companions, though you have suffered ills;
190 My friends, we do not know where dusk is, or dawn,
Nor where the sun that gives light to mortals sets under earth
Nor where it rises. Let us consider quickly
If there is any plan left. I do not think there is.
When I went up to the rugged lookout I saw
195 An island that an endless sea girds all around.
The island itself is low lying. I saw with my own eyes
A smoke in the middle through dense thickets and woods.'
So I said, and the heart of each man was shattered
To remember the deeds of Lestrygonian Antiphates
200 And of Cyclops, great-hearted in strength, the eater of men.
So they wailed piercingly, and they shed swelling tears,
And yet no result came from their lamentation.
But I numbered all my well-greaved companions
Into two groups and appointed a leader for each.
205 I led one of them, godlike Eurylochos [5] the other.
Quickly we shook the lots in a bronze-fitted helmet.
The lot of great-hearted Eurylochos leaped out.
He went off, and along with him went twenty-two companions,
Lamenting. And they left us grieving behind them.
210 In the glen they found the hall of Circe, constructed
Out of polished stone in a place with a view all around.
About her were wolves of the mountains and also lions
That she had charmed herself when she gave them evil drugs.
Nor did these creatures rush upon the men, but instead
They reared up on them and fawned over them with their long
215 tails.
As when dogs fawn about their master when he comes
From dinner, and he always brings blandishments for their
     temper,
So did the wolves with powerful claws and the lions
Fawn about them. They were afraid when they saw the dread
     creatures.
220 So they stood in the forecourt of the fair-braided goddess
And they heard Circe singing in a lovely voice within
As she went to and fro at a great immortal web, such as are

5. The chief companion of Odysseus.

The works of goddesses, fine woven, pleasing, and bright.
Then Polites, chief of the men, began speaking to them:
He was dearest to me of my companions, and the most devoted. 225
'My friends, some woman within, as she tends a great web,
Sings beautifully, and the whole ground echoes about;
A god or a woman; well, let us quickly call out.'
So he said to them, and they did call out, shouting.
At once she opened the shining doors and came out   230
And called. They all went with her in their ignorance.
Eurylochos hung back, thinking it to be a trick.
She led them in and sat them in seats and in armchairs.
She mixed for them cheese and barley and green honey
With Pramnian wine. And she stirred into the food   235
Woeful drugs that make one forget his fatherland wholly.
But when she had given it and they had drunk, she at once
Struck them with her wand and shut them up into sties.
They had the heads of swine and the voice and the hair
And the body, but the mind was steady as before.   240
So they were penned in, weeping, and to them Circe
Threw two kinds of acorns and the fruit of the cornel tree
To eat, such as swine who sleep on the ground always eat.
Eurylochos came back at once to the swift black ship
To tell the news of his companions and their harsh fate.   245
He was not able to speak a word, though he wanted to,
Struck in his heart with a great grief; and his eyes
Were filled with tears, and his heart brooded on weeping.
And when all had questioned him and were amazed,
He recounted the ruin of our other companions: 250
'We went, as you bid, through the thicket, noble Odysseus,
And in the glen we found lovely halls constructed
Of polished stones in a place with a view all around.
There a woman tending a great web sang clearly,
A god or a woman. They called out to her, shouting.   255
At once she opened the shining doors and came out
And called. They all went with her in their ignorance.
But I hung back myself, thinking it to be a trick.
They all vanished together. Nor did one of them
Appear. And I sat for a long time and kept watching.'   260
So he said. And I threw my silver-studded sword
On my shoulders, a big bronze one, and a bow about me,

I ordered him to lead me back by the same path.
But he clutched my knees with both of his hands and begged
   me;
265 And lamenting to me, he uttered wingèd words:
'You whom Zeus nourished, do not lead me there against my
   will;
Leave me here. I think you will not come back or lead back
Any of your companions. No, let us quickly flee
With these men, for we may still avoid the fatal day.'
270 So he said, and, answering him, I addressed him:
'All right, Eurylochos, you stay here in this place,
Eating and drinking by the hollow black ship.
But I will go myself; strong necessity is on me.'
When I had said this, I went up from the ship and the sea.
275 And when I was about to go through the sacred glen
To come to the great house of Circe of the many drugs,
Hermes of the golden wand came across my path
As I was going to the house, resembling a young man
With his first beard, at the most pleasing time of youth.
280 He took my hand and spoke right out directly to me:
'Where are you going, alone through the hills, hapless man,
Ignorant of the place? These companions of yours are confined
In Circe's house as swine, and keep to their dense lairs.
Are you going there to free them? I do not think
285 You will return yourself, but will stay where the others are.
Well, I will release you from evil and rescue you.
Here, take this excellent drug to the halls of Circe
And enter; so it may ward off from your head the evil day.
I shall tell you all of Circe's pernicious wiles.
290 She will make you a mixture and drop drugs into the food.
But she will not be able to charm you so. The excellent drug
I shall give you will not permit it. I will tell you the details.
At the moment when Circe hits you with her very long wand,
Draw your sharp sword at once from along your thigh
295 And rush upon Circe as if intending to kill her.
She will be afraid of you and ask you to go to bed.
And from that point on do not refuse the bed of the god,
So she may free your companions and guide you yourself.
But order her to swear a great oath by the blessed gods
300 That she plot no other bad trouble against your person,

Lest when you are naked she make you unmanly and a
    coward.'
When he had said this, the god, the slayer of Argos, gave me
    the drug
He had plucked out of the earth, and showed me its nature.
It was black at the root, but its flower was like milk.
The gods call it moly. It is difficult to dig   305
For mortal men. But gods are able to do all things.
Then Hermes went away toward tall Olympos
Along the wooded island. And to the halls of Circe
I proceeded. My heart was greatly disturbed as I went.
I stood in the courtyard of the goddess with the lovely hair.   310
As I stood there I shouted, and the goddess heard my voice.
She came out right away and opened the shining doors
And called. I followed her, grieving in my heart.
She led me in and seated me on a silver-studded chair,
Lovely and cleverly wrought. A footstool was beneath my feet. 315
She made me a mixture in a golden cup to drink
And put in a drug, devising evil in her heart.
When she gave it and I drank and it did not charm me,
She struck me with a wand and spoke right out directly:
'Come to the sty now. Lie down with the others, your
    companions.'   320
So she said, but I drew the sharp sword from along my thigh
And rushed on Circe as if intending to kill her,
She gave a great shout, ran up under and took my knees;
And lamenting to me, she uttered wingèd words:
'What men are you from? Where are your city and parents?   325
Wonder holds me that you drank this drug and were not
    charmed.
No other man at all has been able to bear this drug
Once he had drunk it and let it pass the bar of his teeth.
You have in your breast some mind that is not to be charmed.
Surely you are the Odysseus of many turns, who,   330
The gold-wanded slayer of Argos always told me
Would come on his way out of Troy in a swift black ship.
Well, come, put your sword in the sheath and let us now
Go up to our bed so that when we have lain together
In love and in bed we may rely on one another.'   335
So she said; and answering her, I addressed her:

'Circe, how can you request that I be mild to you,
Who in your halls have turned my companions to swine
And now with wiles on your mind you request me
340 To go into your bedroom and to enter your bed,
That when I am naked you may make me unmanly and a
    coward.
I myself do not want to enter your bed, goddess,
Unless you will put up with swearing me a great oath,
That you will not plot some other bad trouble against me.'
345 So I said, and she swore at once as I had asked her.
And when she had sworn the oath and completed it,
I went up to the bed of the beautiful Circe.
Serving maids busied themselves around her halls,
Four of them, who are servants for her in the house.
350 These women are born from the springs and from the groves,
And from the sacred rivers that flow down to the sea.
One of them threw lovely blankets upon the armchairs,
Purple ones about them, and underneath she put linen.
Another one out in front of the armchairs arranged tables
355 Of silver and set out golden baskets before them.
The third one mixed sweet mind-honeying wine
In a bowl of silver and set out golden goblets.
The fourth one carried water and lit up a large fire
Underneath a great cauldron. And the water was warmed.
360 And when the water was boiling in the gleaming bronze,
She set me in a bathtub and washed me, from the great
    cauldron pouring
Water mixed to a pleasing warmth on my head and shoulders
Till it took the spirit-destroying fatigue from my limbs.
And when she had washed and anointed me richly with oil
365 And had thrown a lovely mantle about me and a tunic,
She led me in and seated me on a silver-studded armchair,
Lovely and cleverly wrought. A footstool was beneath my feet.
A handmaid poured water from a pitcher she was carrying,
A lovely golden one over into a silver basin,
370 For washing the hands; she set up a polished table alongside.
A respected housekeeper served bread she was carrying,
Laying out many dishes, gracious with the provisions,
And bade me eat. But no pleasure was in my heart.
I sat thinking other thoughts. My heart foreboded ills.

Circe, when she perceived that I sat there and did not   375
Reach my hands to the food, and that powerful grief held me,
Came and stood nearby and uttered wingèd words:
'Why do you sit this way, Odysseus, as one with no voice,
Eating your heart out, and do not touch food or drink?
Perhaps you expect another trick. There is no need   380
To fear; I have already sworn you a powerful oath.'
So she said, and in answer to her, I addressed her:
'Circe, what man is there, if he be righteous,
Who could endure to be partaking of food and drink
Before he got his companions free and saw them with his eyes? 385
If really in good faith you bid me to eat and drink,
Free them, so my eyes may behold my trusty companions.'
So I said, and Circe walked on out through the halls
Holding a wand in her hand; she opened the gates of the sty
And drove out the men, who looked like swine nine years old. 390
They stood opposite us. She went in their midst
And with another drug she rubbed each one of them.
The hair fell off their limbs that the baleful drug
The queenly Circe gave them before had made grow there.
They became men again, younger than they were before   395
And far more handsome and larger to behold.
They recognized me, and each one grasped my hands.
The longed-for weeping came on them all. The house about
Terribly resounded, and the goddess herself felt pity.
The divine goddess stood close to me and addressed me: 400
'Zeus-born son of Laertes, much-contriving Odysseus,
Go on now to your swift ship and the strand of the sea,
And first of all, draw your ship up on the mainland,
Put your property and all your gear into caves.
Then come back yourself and bring your trusty companions.' 405
So she said. Then the bold heart was persuaded within me
And I went down to the swift ship and the beach of the sea.
There I found my trusty companions on the swift ship,
Lamenting piteously, shedding large tears.
As when calves of the fields all skip around together   410
In front of the drove of cows that are coming into the dung
    yard
When they are filled up on grass, and the pens no longer
Hold them, but they run in throngs around their mothers,

Lowing on and on, so did those men act when their eyes saw
 me:
415 They shed tears, weeping. And it seemed to their hearts
As though they had come to the fatherland and the very city
Of rugged Ithaca, where they were born and brought up.
And lamenting to me, they uttered wingèd words:
'At your return, Zeus-nourished one, we have rejoiced
420 As if we had come to Ithaca, our fatherland.
Come and tell about the ruin of our other companions.'
So they said. And I addressed them with soothing words:
'First of all, let us draw the ship up onto the mainland
And bring our possessions and all our gear into caves.
425 Then press on yourselves and follow me all together
So you may see our companions in Circe's sacred halls,
Eating and drinking; they have unfailing abundance.'
So I said, and they quickly hearkened to my words.
Eurylochos alone tried to hold back all my companions,
430 And addressing them, he uttered wingèd words:
'Ah, wretched men, where are we going? Why long for these ills,
And go down to the halls of Circe, who will make us all
Into swine or wolves or lions, so that we may guard
The great house for her, and by necessity,
435 The way the Cyclops acted when our compaions came
To his middle yard, and bold Odysseus went with them,
And they were all destroyed because of his recklessness.'
So he said, and I pondered myself in my mind
About drawing my sharp-pointed sword from my stout thigh,
440 To cut his head off and to bring it to the ground,
Though he was very close kin to me. But my companions
Restrained me on every side with soothing words:
'You who were born of Zeus, let us leave this man here
Beside the ship, if you bid it, and guard the ship,
445 And you lead the way for us to Circe's sacred halls.'
When they said this they went up from the ship and the sea.
Nor was Eurylochos left beside the hollow ship,
But he followed, for he feared my striking rebuke.
Meanwhile Circe in her halls had kindly washed the rest
450 Of our companions and anointed them richly with oil.
She threw woolen mantles and tunics about them.
And we came upon them all dining well in the halls.
When they had seen and looked at each other face to face,

They wept, lamenting, and the halls rang around.
The divine goddess stood near me and addressed me: 455
'Zeus-born son of Laertes, Odysseus of many wiles,
Raise this swelling lament no longer. I myself know
How many pains you have suffered on the fish-laden ocean
And how many wrongs hostile men did to you on land.
So come now and eat victuals and drink wine   460
Until you have taken the spirit into your breast again
As it was when you first left your fatherland
Of rugged Ithaca. Now, wasted and without spirit,
You remember hard wandering always, and your spirit has never
Been in gladness, since you have suffered very much!'   465
So she said, and the bold spirit was persuaded in us.
There day by day till the year was brought to a close
We stayed, dining on endless meat and on sweet wine.
But when the year was up and the seasons turned round
As the moons were declining, and the long days came round to
    an end,   470
Then my trusty companions called me out and said to me:
'You fool, at this time now remember your fatherland,
If it is decreed that you be saved and arrive
At your well-established home and your fatherland.'
So they said, and the bold spirit was persuaded within me.   475
So then the entire day till the setting of the sun
We stayed, dining on endless meat and on sweet wine.
But when the sun went down and the darkness came on
They lay down to sleep through the shadowy halls,
And I went up to the beautiful bed of Circe   480
And took her knees in prayer. The goddess heard my voice.
Then I spoke out to her and uttered wingèd words:
'Circe, fulfill for me the promise you made,
To send me home; the spirit is eager in me already
And in my other companions, who consume my precious heart 485
In complaining around me whenever you are absent.'
So I said, and the divine goddess at once answered:
'Zeus-born son of Laertes, Odysseus of many devices,
Do not stay any longer in my home unwillingly.
Yet you must first achieve another journey and come   490
To the halls of Hades and dread Persephone,[6]
So you may consult the soul of Theban Tiresias,

6. Daughter of Zeus and Demeter; queen of the underworld.

The blind prophet in whom there is a steadfast mind.
To him alone, even when dead, did Persephone grant
495 A mind that could understand. The others flit, shadows.'
So she said, and my own heart was shattered within me.
Seated on the bed, I lamented, nor did my heart
Wish still to live and to see the light of the sun.
500 But when I was sated with lamenting and wallowing,
I answered her and addressed her with a speech:
'O Circe, who will be my guide on this journey?
No one ever got to the place of Hades in a black ship.
So I said, and at once the divine goddess answered:
'Zeus-born son of Laertes, Odysseus of many devices,
505 Give heed to no longing for a guide upon your ship,
But set up a mast and stretch out the white sails,
And then sit down. The blast of the North Wind will carry it
      for you.
And when in your ship you have traversed Oceanos,
Where the scrubby strand and groves of Persephone are,
510 Both tall poplars and willows that lose their fruit,
Beach your ship there by deep-whirling Oceanos;
But go on yourself to the moldy hall of Hades.
There into Acheron flow Puriphlegethon
And Cocytus, which is a branch of the Styx's [7] water,
515 And a rock and a concourse of the two resounding rivers.
Then go up near there, hero, as I bid you to;
Dig a pit the size of a cubit on all sides.
Pour a libation about it for all the dead,
First of honey mixture, and then of sweet wine,
520 And the third one of water; sprinkle white barley on it.
Beseech the feeble heads of the dead with many prayers,
Saying that when you go to Ithaca you will sacrifice
Your best barren cow in your halls, heap a pyre with goods,
And consecrate apart for Tiresias alone
525 A sheep all of black that stands out among your flocks.
And when you have besought the famed tribes of the dead with
      prayers,
Sacrifice a ram and also a black female,
Bending their heads to Erebos; [8] turn the other way yourself,

7. Rivers of the Underworld. Their names mean Distress, Fire-flaming, Lament, and Hate.
8. Outer darkness for the dead.

Setting on for the streams of the river. And there many
Souls will come of the corpses of those who have died.   530
And then urge your companions on and command them
To take sheep which lie slain with the pitiless sword,
To flay them and burn them and pray to the gods,
To mighty Hades and dread Persephone.
You yourself draw your sharp sword from beside your thigh.   535
Stay put, and do not let the feeble heads of the dead
Go near the blood till you learn from Tiresias.
At once, then, leader of the people, the prophet will come,
Who will tell you the course and measures of the way
And about a return, how you may go on the fish-laden ocean.'   540
So she said, and at once the golden-throned Dawn came.
She clothed me in garments, a mantle and a tunic,
And the nymph herself put on a great shining mantle
Finely made and pleasing, and a lovely gold sash
Around her waist, and she put a veil on her head.   545
I went through the halls and urged my companions on,
Standing by each man and speaking with soothing words:
'Slumber now no longer as you lie in sound, sweet sleep,
But let us go. Queenly Circe has already informed me.'
So I said, and the bold spirit in them was persuaded.   550
But I did not lead my companions from there unscathed.
There was one very young man, Elpenor, not overly
Courageous in battle and not steadfast in his mind,
Who apart from my companions in Circe's sacred halls,
Longing for coolness, lay down drunk with wine.   555
Hearing the noise and din of his companions moving,
He rose up suddenly and wholly forgot in his mind
To go back down again by way of the long ladder.
But he fell right down off the roof. And his neck
Was broken from the joint. His soul went down to Hades.   560
Then I addressed a speech to the men as they were going:
'You think, perhaps, you are going home to your dear
Fatherland. Circe has decreed another way for us,
To the halls of Hades and dread Persephone,
So that we may consult the soul of Theban Tiresias.'   565
So I said, and their own hearts were shattered within them;
They sat on the spot lamenting and tearing their hair.
And yet no result came from their lamentation.
And when we had gone grieving to the swift ship

570 And to the strand of the sea, shedding large tears,
   Circe had meantime gone alongside the black ship
   And bound down a ram and also a black female.
   She passed by nimbly; for who could see with his eyes
   A god who did not wish it, whether going this way or that?

XI

"And when we came down to the ship and to the sea,
First of all we dragged the ship to the godly water
And set up the mast and the sails upon the black ship.
We took sheep and brought them on board, and we ourselves
Went on, grieving and pouring down swelling tears.   5
Then a driving wind full in the sails, a fine companion,
Did the fair-braided Circe, dread god with a singing voice,
Send on for us from behind the dark blue-prowed ship.
And when we had tended to the gear through the ship, piece by
    piece,
We took our seats. The wind and a pilot steered her.   10
The sails were stretched all day long as she fared on the ocean.
The sun went down and all the ways were shadowed.
She arrived at the bounds of deep-flowing Oceanos.
There is the land and city of Cimmerian men,
Who are shrouded in mist and cloud. Never does the sun   15
Look down upon them, glittering with his rays—
Never when he climbs up into the starry heaven
Or when he turns back from the heaven to the earth,
But deadly night is stretched out for hapless mortals.
Arriving there, we beached the ship and took out the flocks.   20
Then we ourselves went along the stream of Oceanos
Until we arrived at the place that Circe had said.
There Perimedes and Eurylochos held the victims.
I myself drew my sharp sword from along my thigh,
Dug a pit the size of a cubit on all sides,   25
And poured a libation about it for all the dead,
First of honey mixture, and then of sweet wine,
And the third one of water; I sprinkled white barley on it.
I besought the feeble heads of the dead for many things,
Saying that when I went to Ithaca I would sacrifice   30
My best barren cow in my halls, heap a pyre with goods,
And consecrate apart for Tiresias alone

A sheep all of black that stands out among my flocks.
And when I had besought the tribes of the dead with prayers
   and vows,
35 Then I took the sheep and cut their throats into the pit.
And the black-clouded blood poured out. And out of Erebos
The souls gathered of the corpses of those who had died,
Brides and bachelors and old men who had suffered much,
And tender maidens whose hearts were fresh in sorrow,
40 And many who had been wounded by bronze-tipped spears,
Men slain in battle wearing gore-spattered armor,
Many of whom hovered round the pit on every side
With a tremendous shout. And sallow fear seized me.
Then I urged my companions on and commanded them
45 To take the sheep which lay slain with the pitiless sword,
To flay them and burn them and then pray to the gods,
To mighty Hades and to dread Persephone.
I myself drew my sharp sword from beside my thigh
And stayed put, and did not let the feeble heads of the dead
50 Go near the blood till I could learn from Tiresias.
First came the soul of our companion Elpenor,
For he had not yet been buried beneath the wide-traveled earth;
We ourselves had left his body in the hall of Circe,
Unwept and unburied, since another labor drove us on.
55 I wept when I saw him and pitied him in my heart.
So I spoke out to him, and uttered wingèd words:
'Elpenor, how did you get here under the murky dusk?
You went faster by foot than I did with the black ship.'
So I said, and he wailed and answered me with a speech:
60 'Zeus-born son of Laertes, Odysseus of many devices,
The ill fate of some god destroyed me, and abundant wine.
When I lay down in the hall of Circe I did not think
To go back down again upon the long ladder,
But I fell straight down off the roof. And my neck
65 Was broken from the joint and my soul came down to Hades.
Now I beseech you by those left behind who are not here,
By your wife and the father who reared you when you were small,
And by Telemachos, whom you left alone in your halls,
For I know on your way from here out of the hall of Hades
70 You will stop the well-made ship at the island of Aiaia.
There at that time, lord, I ask you to remember me.
Do not go and leave me henceforth unwept and unburied

And turn not from me, lest I bring on you the wrath of the gods,
But burn me with all the armor that belongs to me
And heap a tomb for me by the strand of the hoary sea,   75
Hapless man that I am, so that those to come may learn of me.
Do this for me, and set my oar fast on the mound
With which when alive I rowed among my companions.'
So he said, and then I addressed him in answer:
'Wretched man, I shall do this for you and carry it out.'   80
Exchanging grim words this way with one another,
We sat, and on one side I held my sword over the blood.
On the other side the phantom of my companion told me much.
Then there came the soul of my mother who had died,
Anticleia,[1] daughter of great-hearted Autolycos,   85
Whom I had left alive when I went to sacred Ilion.
I wept when I saw her and pitied her in my spirit,
But though I grieved heavily, I did not let her
Get near the blood first till I could learn from Tiresias.
Then the soul of Theban Tiresias came up,   90
Holding a gold scepter; he knew me and spoke to me:
'Zeus-born son of Laertes, Odysseus of many devices,
Why, hapless man, have you left the light of the sun
And come here to see the dead and a joyless place?
But draw back from the pit and hold back your sharp sword   95
So I may drink the blood and speak to you unerringly.'
So he said. I drew back and thrust the silver-studded sword
Into the sheath. And when he had drunk the black blood,
The excellent prophet addressed me with a speech:
'You seek a honey-sweet return, noble Odysseus;   100
A god will make it disastrous for you. I do not think
You will elude the earth-shaker; against you he has laid up a
     grudge,
In his heart, enraged that you blinded his beloved son.
You may get there yet, even so, though you suffer ills;
If you are willing to check your spirit and your companions',   105
At the time when you first bring the well-made ship up close
To the isle of Thrinacria, fleeing the violet ocean,
And you find grazing there the cattle and goodly sheep
Of the Sun, who sees everything and hears everything.
If you let them go unmolested and think of your return   110
You may yet get to Ithaca, though you do suffer ills.

1. Wife of Laertes and mother of Odysseus.

If you molest them, then I prophesy destruction
For your ship and companions. And even if you escape yourself
You will return late and ill, having lost all your companions,
115 On another's ship. You will find troubles in your house,
Presumptuous men who consume your livelihood
While wooing your godlike wife and giving her bridal gifts.
But when you get there, then you will avenge the violence of
those men,
But when you have killed the suitors in your own halls,
120 Whether by guile or openly with the sharp sword,
Thereupon take a well-fitted oar and go on
Till you arrive at the place of men who do not know
The sea and eat a food that has not been mixed with salt,
And where they do not know about ships with purple cheeks,
125 Or about well-fitted oars that are the wings for ships.
I will tell you a very plain token; do not forget it:
When another wayfarer has confronted you
And says you have a winnowing fan [2] on your gleaming
shoulder,
Then set your well-fitted oar fast in the earth
130 And carry out fine sacrifices to Lord Poseidon,
A ram, a bull, and a boar, the mounter of sows.
Then go back home and sacrifice sacred hecatombs
To the immortal gods who possess broad heaven,
To all of them in order. Far from the sea will death come,
135 Ever so gently to your person and slay you
When you are worn out with sleek old age. And the people
about you
Will be happy. I tell you this unerringly.'
So he said, and then I addressed him in answer:
'Tiresias, the gods themselves have perhaps spun this thread,
140 But come tell me one thing, and speak out truthfully:
I see here the soul of my mother who has died.
She sits in silence close to the blood and does not dare
To look her son in the face or speak out to him.
Tell me, lord, how may she know me as who I am?'
145 So I said, and at once he addressed me in answer:
'Easily shall I say the word and put it in your mind.
Whomever you permit of the souls of the dead
To approach the blood closer will speak without error to you.

2. A tool for sifting grain.

The one you begrudge it to will go back away.'
When he had said this, the soul of Lord Tiresias went   150
Within the halls of Hades, after it spoke what was decreed.
I waited there steadily until my mother
Came up and drank the black-clouded blood. She knew me
At once, and, lamenting, she uttered wingèd words:
'My child, how have you come down under the murky dusk   155
While yet alive? This is dangerous for the living to see.
In between us there are great rivers and dread streams,
Oceanos first, that it is not possible to cross
On foot; one must possess a well-made ship.
Have you just got this far in wandering from Troy   160
A long time with ship and companions? Have you not yet come
To Ithaca and seen the wife within your halls?'
So she said, and then I addressed her in answer:
'Mother, need led me down to the place of Hades
To consult the soul of Theban Tiresias.   165
I have not yet come close to Achaia. I have not yet
Set foot on our land, but wander always, possessing woe,
From the very first time I followed godly Agamemnon
To Ilion with its fine horses to fight the Trojans.
But tell me one thing, and speak out truthfully: 170
What fate overcame you of long-sorrowful death?
A lengthy sickness, or did Artemis who shoots arrows
Visit you and slay you with her gentle shafts?
Tell me of the father and the son I left behind.
Is my honor still with them, or does some other man   175
Already have it, and they say I will return no more?
Tell me about the purpose and thought of my wedded wife;
Does she stay with my son and steadily guard all,
Or has the best man of the Achaians wed her already?'
So I said, and at once my queenly mother answered me: 180
'Too long that woman in her enduring spirit waits
Within your halls. And the miserable nights
And the days always waste away for her as she sheds tears.
No one else yet holds your fine honor, but Telemachos
Possesses the acres securely, and he dines   185
On well-shared feasts, whereof it befits a judge to partake.
All invite him. But your father remains in one place
In the country and does not visit the city. No bed
He has, no bedclothes and mantles and glistening blankets,

190 But he sleeps all winter where servants do in the house,
In the ashes by the fire, and he puts bad clothes on his flesh.
But when the summer comes and the blossoming autumn,
Everywhere along the knoll of the wine-bearing vineyard
His beds of fallen leaves have been strewn on the ground.
195 He lies there grieving; great sorrow grows in his mind
As he longs for your return. Hard old age has come upon him.
And so I myself have perished and have met my fate.
And the far-sighted one who shoots arrows did not
Visit me in the hall and slay me with her gentle shafts,
200 Nor did sickness come on me, such as especially
With grim wasting away takes the spirit from the limbs.
But longing for you and your counsels, noble Odysseus,
And your kindliness, reft my honey-sweet spirit away.'
So she spoke. And pondering in my mind, I wished
205 To take hold of the soul of my mother who had died.
Three times I tried and my spirit bade me to grasp her.
And three times like a shadow or a dream she flew
Out of my hands. Sharp grief grew ever greater in my heart.
So I spoke out to her and uttered wingèd words:
210 'Mother, why do you not wait as I strive to grasp you,
So that even in the place of Hades we might throw our dear
     hands
Round each other and take pleasure in cold lamentation?
Or is this some phantom that noble Persephone
Sends me, so that I may grieve and lament still more?'
215 So I said, and my queenly mother answered at once:
'Alas, my child, ill-fated beyond all mortals,
Persephone, daughter of Zeus, does not beguile you;
But this is the rule for mortals, whenever one dies.
No longer do the sinews hold the bones and the flesh,
220 But the mighty power of burning fire subdues them
When first the spirit has abandoned the white bones,
And the soul, flying off like a dream, flutters.
But be eager to go to the light as fast as you can,
And note all this to tell it to your wife hereafter.'
225 So we exchanged words with one another. Women
Came up, and noble Persephone sent them forth,
All of whom were the wives and daughters of excellent men.
They gathered in clusters around the black blood.
And I thought about how I might question each one.

This seemed to me in my heart to be the best plan: 230
To draw the long-pointed sword from beside my stout thigh
And not allow all to drink the black blood together.
They came on in succession, and each one
Announced her descent. I inquired of them all.
First I saw Tyro [3] there, who had a fine father,   235
Who claimed to be descended from blameless Salmoneus.
She said she was the wife of Cretheus, son of Aeolos;
She had fallen in love with a river, the godly Enipeus,
Which flows loveliest by far of the rivers on earth,
And she frequented the lovely streams of the Enipeus.   240
Likened to him, the earth-shaker who girdles the world
Lay beside her at the mouth of the eddying river.
The purple wave stood up around them like a mountain
Arching, and it hid the god and the mortal woman.
He loosened her virgin sash and shed sleep down upon her.   245
And when the god had completed the deed of love
He took her hand and spoke out to her directly:
'Rejoice in this love, woman, and when the year comes round
You will bear glorious children; not barren are the beds
Of the immortals. Take care of them and bring them up.   250
And now go to your home; stay quiet and do not mention it.
Behold, I am Poseidon, the shaker of the earth.'
When he had said this, he went down under the wave-
    breaking ocean.
She was pregnant and gave birth to Pelias and Neleus,[4]
Who became mighty servants of great Zeus, both of them.   255
Pelias in Iolcos of the broad dancing-place,
Dwelt rich with flocks, and the other in sandy Pylos.
And to Cretheus the queen of women bore other sons,
Aeson [5] and Pheres and Amythaon, whose delight was in horses.
After her I saw Antiope, Asopos' daughter,   260
Who declared she had lain in the embrace of Zeus
And gave birth to two sons, Amphion and Zethos,
Who first founded the seat of Thebes with the seven gates
And built its rampart, since without a rampart they could not,
Though mighty, inhabit Thebes of the broad dancing-place.   265

3. Grandmother of Jason and Nestor.
4. Pelias, Pheres, and Amythaon are uncles of Jason; Neleus, father of
Nestor.
5. Father of Jason.

And after her I saw Alcmene, Amphitryon's wife,
Who bore Heracles of steadfast boldness and a lion's heart
After she had lain in the embrace of great Zeus;
And Megara, the daughter of haughty-spirited Creon,[6]
Whom Amphitryon's son, ever unwearied in his strength, had
270   wed.
    I saw the mother of Oedipos,[7] lovely Epicaste,
Who did an enormous deed in the ignorance of her mind
And married her son. He slew his own father
And married her. The gods soon made these things known to
    men.
275 But he suffered pains in his much-beloved Thebes,
And ruled the Cadmeians through the destructive plans of the
    gods;
And she went to the place of the mighty gatekeeper Hades.
She hung up a high noose from the lofty roofbeam,
Possessed by her grief. For him she left many pains
280 Behind her, the kind a mother's Furies bring to pass.
And I saw the Beautiful Chloris,[8] whom Neleus once
Married for her beauty, and gave numberless bridal gifts.
She was the youngest daughter of Amphion, son of Iasos,
Who once ruled by force in Minyan Orchomenos.
285 She was queen over Pylos; she bore him glorious children,
Nestor, Chromios, and honored Periclymenos,
And she bore, besides, goodly Pero, a wonder to mortals,
Whom all her neighbors wooed. Nor would Neleus give her
To one who could not drive away from Phylace
290 The crumple-horned, broad-browed cattle of mighty Iphiclos,
Difficult as they were. An excellent prophet [9] alone
Undertook to drive them. The hard fate of the gods bound him,
And difficult bonds, and the cowherds of the fields.
But when the months and the days were finished out
295 Of the year coming back around, and the seasons came on,
Then mighty Iphiclos released him when he had told all
That was decreed. And a plan of Zeus was accomplished.
I saw Leda also, the wife of Tyndareus,[1]
Who bore to Tyndareus two sons of mighty mind,

6. A king of Thebes.
7. A king of Thebes; son of Laios and Epicaste (in Homer).
8. Mother of Nestor.
9. The seer Melampos, whom Iphiclos first captured and then released.
1. Father of Clytemnestra.

Horse-taming Castor and Polydeuces, who is good at boxing,   300
Both of whom the grain-giving earth holds alive.
Even beneath the earth they have honor from Zeus.
One time they live, on alternate days, and another time
They are dead. Honor equal to the gods is allotted them.
And after her I saw Iphimedeia, the wife   305
Of Aloeus, who said she had lain with Poseidon,
And she had two sons that were born short-lived,
The godlike Otos and the far-famed Ephialtes,
Who were the tallest men nourished by the grain-giving earth,
And by far the handsomest, next to famous Orion,   310
For after nine seasons these men were nine cubits
In breadth, and they were also nine fathoms in height.
They made threats to the immortals upon Olympos
That they would start the combat of an impetuous war.
They strove to put Ossa on Olympos, and to put on Ossa ,   315
Leaf-quivering Pelion, so that heaven might be scaled.
And they would have done it had they reached the measure of
     their prime;
But the son of Zeus,[2] whom fair-haired Leto bore, destroyed
Both of them, before the whiskers beneath their temples
Had flowered and their chins got thick with blossoming down. 320
I saw Phaedra and Procris and lovely Ariadne,[3]
Daughter of destruction-minded Minos, whom Theseus
Once was leading out of Crete to the knoll of sacred Athens
But did not enjoy her, for Artemis slew her beforehand
In flood-circled Dia for what Dionysos testified.   325
Maire and Clymene I saw and hateful Eriphyle,[4]
Who took precious gold in return for her own husband.
I cannot tell or mention all of the women
I saw in numbers there, wives and daughters of heroes.
Ambrosial night would wane first. Now it is time   330

2. Apollo.
3. Phaedra: daughter of the Cretan king Minos and wife of the Athenian
hero Theseus after he killed the Minotaur. Procris: daughter of Erechtheus,
king of Athens, unfaithful to a husband who accidentally killed her.
Ariadne: Phaedra's sister who, after helping Theseus out of the labyrinth
and escaping with him, was abandoned by him on the island where Artemis
killed her.
4. Maire: a nympth of Artemis, killed for breaking her vow of chastity.
Clymene: wife of a king of Minyan Orchemenos. Eriphyle: wife of Am-
phiaraos, whom she persuaded to join the siege of Thebes, where he
knew he would be killed.

For me to sleep, whether I go to my companions on the swift
   ship
Or stay here. The convoy shall be your concern, and the gods'."
So he said. And they all became silent in stillness.
They were held in rapture through the shadowy halls.
335 Then white-armed Arete began to speak among them:
"Phaeacians, how does this man appear to you to be,
In form and in size, and in his mind well-balanced within?
He is my guest, and yet each has a share in the honor.
Let us not hasten to send him off, and do not stint
340 Of gifts to a man so needy, since, by favor of the gods,
Many possessions lie stored for you in your halls."
And the old hero Echeneus spoke out among them,
Who was an elder among the Phaeacian men:
"My friends, our prudent queen has not spoken to us
345 Wide of the mark or of repute. Do as she says.
On Alcinoos here the word and the deed depend."
Then Alcinoos spoke to him and gave him an answer:
"So shall this word come about, if I be indeed
Alive and rule the Phaeacians, who are fond of rowing.
350 Let the stranger, though greatly desiring a return,
Still endure to wait till tomorrow until I complete
The entire gift. The convoy will concern all the men,
And me especially, as I have power in the land."
Odysseus of many wiles addressed him in answer:
355 "Lordly Alcinoos, exalted among all your people,
Even if you should bid me to stay here for a year
And urged on an convoy and gave glorious gifts,
I would want to do it, since it would be better by far
To reach one's dear fatherland with a fuller hand;
360 Then I would be more respected and loved by all
The men who might see me return to Ithaca."
Alcinoos gave him an answer and spoke to him:
"Odysseus, as we look on you we would not think you
To be a deceiver and cheat the way many men are
365 Whom the black earth nourishes, and are widely dispersed,
Fashioning falsehoods out of what no one could see;
There is grace in your words and your thoughts are noble.
As a singer would, you have skillfully told the tale
Of all the Argives' sad troubles and of your own.
370 But come, tell me this and speak out truthfully:

Did you see any of the godlike companions that went
Along to Ilion with you and there met a fate?
This night is prodigiously long. It is not yet time
To sleep in the hall. Do tell me your wondrous deeds.
I would hold out until the godly dawn, so long   375
As you could endure to recount your cares in the hall."
Odysseus of many wiles addressed him in answer:
"Lordly Alcinoos, exalted among all your people,
There is a time for many tales and also a time for sleep.
But if you are still longing to listen, I would not myself   380
Refuse you in this, to tell other more piteous things,
The cares of my companions who perished afterward,
Who escaped from the grievous war cry of the Trojans
But died on returning at the will of an evil woman.
Moreover when holy Persephone had scattered the souls   385
Of the womanfolk off in all directions,
The soul came of Agamemnon, son of Atreus,
Grieving; and others gathered about who had died
And had met their fate with him in the house of Aigisthos.
He recognized me at once when he had drunk the black blood.   390
He wailed piercingly and shed a swelling tear,
Stretching his hands toward me in striving to reach me.
But his strength was not still steadfast and he had no force
Such as there used to be before in his supple limbs.
I wept to see him and pitied him in my heart.   395
And speaking out to him, I uttered wingèd words:
'Glorious son of Atreus, lord of men, Agamemnon,
What fate has overcome you of long-sorrowful death?
Was it that Poseidon overcame you in your ships,
Raising up a dreadful blast of disastrous winds?   400
Or did hostile men ravage you upon the mainland
As you were cutting off cattle and the fine fleece of sheep,
Or as you were fighting over their city and their women?'
So I said, and he at once addressed me in answer:
'Zeus-born son of Laertes, Odysseus of many devices,   405
Poseidon did not overcome me in my ships,
Raising up a dreadful blast of disastrous winds.
Nor did hostile men ravage me on the mainland.
But Aigisthos fashioned for me my death and my fate.
With my cursèd wife he killed me, inviting me to his house,   410
Feasting me, the way a man slaughters an ox in a crib.

So I died a most grievous death, and my other companions
They killed without blenching, as boars with shining tusks
Are killed in the house of a rich and very powerful man
415 At a marriage or a joint feast [5] or a fruitful banquet.
You have encountered already the slaughter of many men
Slain singly, and also in a mighty combat,
But you would most have grieved in your heart to see that,
How we lay in the hall about the mixing bowls
420 And the full tables, and the whole ground swam with blood.
Most pitiful of all, I heard the voice of Priam's daughter,
Cassandra, whom wily Clytemnestra murdered
Next to me. But I reached my hands to the earth,
Then threw them as I died around the blade. The bitch-faced
    woman
425 Turned away; as I went to Hades she could not bear
To shut my eyes with her hands and close up my mouth.
So there is nothing more dreadful and shameless than a
    woman
Who would set out within her mind such deeds at these,
The sort of disgraceful deed which that woman plotted,
430 Devising murder for her wedded husband. I thought
Indeed that I would come home welcome to my children
And my servants. But she, with utter evil on her mind,
Poured shame upon herself and upon womenkind to come
Hereafter, even on one who might do good deeds.'
435 So he said, and then I addressed him in answer:
'Alas, broad-seeing Zeus has terribly hated
The descent of Atreus from the outset because of the plans
Of women. Many men perished because of Helen;
Clytemnestra made a plot against you while you were far away,
440 So I said, and he at once addressed me in answer:
'So never be mild yourself, henceforth, even to your wife.
Reveal to her no entire story that you know well,
But tell a part of it and let the rest be concealed.
But your own death, Odysseus, will not at all be from your wife.
445 Highly trustworthy and of good care in her mind
Is Icarios' daughter, the prudent Penelope.
We left her as a young bride when we went off to war
And she had an infant child at her breast, who now
Is seated, I suppose, amid the number of the men;

5. To the *eranos* each guest brought an equal share.

Blessed, for his dear father will see him when he comes,   450
And the man will embrace his father, as is right.
My wife never allowed me to fill my eyes up
With my son. She killed me beforehand, my very self.
I will tell you another thing and put it in your mind:
Hold your ship on course secretly, not openly,   455
To your fatherland. There is no longer any trust in women.
But come, tell me this and speak out truthfully:
If perhaps you men have heard of my son as still living
In Orchomenos or else in sandy Pylos
Or perhaps with Menelaos in broad Sparta.   460
For godly Orestes is not yet dead on the earth.'
So he said, and I addressed him in answer:
'Son of Atreus, why do you ask me this? I know nothing
Whether he is dead or alive. It is bad to utter windy things.'
The two of us stood there exchanging dreadful speeches   465
In that way, grieving, and shedding our swelling tears.
The soul of Achilles, son of Peleus, came up;
The soul of Patroclos and of excellent Antilochos,
And of Ajax who was the finest in body and form
Of all the Danaans, after the excellent son of Peleus.   470
The soul of the swift-footed offspring of Aeacos [6] knew me,
And in lamentation he uttered wingèd words:
'Zeus-born son of Laertes, Odysseus of many devices,
Rash man, what still greater deed will you plot in your mind?
How have you dared to come down to Hades, where the dead   475
Dwell senseless, the phantoms of mortals who are worn out?'
So he said, and I addressed him in answer:
'Achilles, son of Peleus, bravest of the Achaians,
I came in need of Tiresias, if he might tell me
Some plan whereby I might come to craggy Ithaca;   480
For I have not yet come close to Achaia, I have not yet
Set foot on my land, but have ills always. Achilles,
No man in the past or hereafter is more blessed than you.
When you were alive before, the Argives honored you
Equal to the gods. Now you greatly rule over the dead,   485
Being here as you are. So do not grieve now you are dead,
     Achilles.'
Thus I spoke, and he at once addressed me in answer:
'Noble Odysseus, do not commend death to me.

6. Grandfather of Achilles.

I would rather serve on the land of another man
490 Who had no portion and not a great livelihood
Than to rule over all the shades of those who are dead.
Come now and tell me the story of my noble son,
Did he follow to battle and become a chief or not?
Tell me about blameless Peleus, if you have heard anything;
495 Does he have honor still with the many Myrmidons,
Or do they show him no honor through Hellas and Phthia
Because old age constrains him in his hands and feet?
For I am no protector under the rays of the sun
Of the kind I was at one time when in broad Troy
500 I slew their best men, defending for the Argives.
If I could come that way just a while to my father's house,
Then I would make my might and invincible hands hateful
To any of those who compel him and force him from honor.'
So he said, and I for my part addressed him in answer:
505 'No, I have not heard anything about blameless Peleus.
But about your beloved son Neoptolemos
I shall tell you the whole truth, as you request me.
I brought him myself on my hollow, balanced ship,
Out of Scyros after the well-greaved Achaians.
510 And when we declared our proposals about the city of Troy,
He always spoke first, and he did not err in his speech.
I believe godlike Nestor and I alone did surpass him.
And when on the plain of the Trojans we Achaians fought
He would never remain in the throng or the crowd of men.
515 He ran far out front, yielding in his strength to no one.
In the dreadful combat he slaughtered numerous men.
I shall not myself mention and tell of them all,
The great host he killed, blameless among the Argives.
Yes, how he slaughtered with the sword the son of Telephos,
520 The hero Eurypylos! Many companions about him
Of the Ceteians were killed for the gifts of a woman.
He was the handsomest man I saw next to godly Memnon.
And when we, the best of the Argives, went into the horse
That Epeios had made, the whole rule was laid on me
525 Of opening and closing the door of the stout decoy.
There the other leaders and counselors of the Danaans
Wiped their tears, and the limbs of each trembled beneath him.
But that man I never saw with my eyes at all
Go pallid on his fair flesh or wipe off the tears

From his cheeks. He besought me very frequently   530
To let him go out of the horse. He kept stroking his sword's
   hilt
And his bronze-heavy spear; and he planned ills for the Trojans.
And when we had sacked the lofty city of Priam,
He went on board the ship with a noble portion and prize,
Unscathed; he had not been hit by the sharp bronze spear   535
Or wounded in close combat, such as many times
Happens in war; Ares does rage helter-skelter.'
So I said; the soul of the swift-footed son of Aeacos
Moved on with great strides through the asphodel meadow
In joy that I said his son was illustrious.   540
The other souls of the shades of those who had died
Stood there grieving, and each one asked of his cares.
Alone did the soul of Ajax, son of Telamon,
Stand off apart, angered about the victory
That I had won over him when judgment was made by the
   ships   545
About the armor of Achilles. His queenly mother had set it.
The sons of the Trojans judged it, and Pallas Athene.
Would I had not won in a contest of that kind!
For the sake of those arms the earth closed over the great head
Of Ajax, who by his form and his deeds had surpassed   550
The other Danaans, after Peleus' blameless son.
I myself spoke out to him with soothing words:
'Ajax, son of blameless Telamon, are you destined
Not to forget, even in death, your anger at me
For the cursèd armor? The gods gave it as a trouble to the
   Argives,   555
Since you died, such a bulwark of them. The Achaians
Grieved constantly for you when you perished, just as much
As for Peleus' son Achilles. There was no one else
To blame but Zeus, who terribly hated the host
Of Danaan spearsmen, and set your fate upon you.   560
But come hither, lord, so that you may hear our speech
And our story. Subdue your strength and your bold heart.'
So I said, but he answered me nothing and went with the other
Souls of the shades of the dead to Erebos.
And he would have spoken in anger, just as I to him,   565
But the spirit within my own breast desired
To see the souls of the other men who had died.

There I saw Minos, the illustrious son of Zeus,
With a golden scepter dealing out justice to the dead,
570 Seated. And they kept asking that lord about laws,
While they sat and stood in the wide-gated house of Hades.
After him I caught sight of the enormous Orion,
Driving beasts together through the asphodel meadow
That he had slaughtered himself on the lovely mountains,
575 Holding in his hands an all-bronze club, ever unbroken.
And I saw Tityos, the renowned son of Gaia,
Lying on the ground. He lay more than nine measures long.
And two vultures, perched on both sides, rent at his liver,
Plunging into the caul. He could not ward them off with his
    hands,
580 For he had dragged off Leto, the glorious mistress of Zeus,
As she came to Pytho through fair-lawned Panopeus.
And I saw Tantalos, who had difficult pains,
Standing in a lake. He was plunged up to his chin,
And pressed on in his thirst, but he could not reach to take
    a drink.
585 As often as the old man bent over striving to drink
The water disappeared, swallowed, and at his feet
Black earth appeared; and some god kept drying it up.
Trees with lofty foliage from their tops shed fruit,
Pears, pomegranates, and apples with shining fruit,
590 And sweet figs and blossoming wild olives;
And when the old man straightened to stretch his hands for
    them,
The wind kept tossing them toward the shadowy clouds.
And then I saw Sisyphos, who had difficult pains
Pushing a monstrous stone up with both of his hands.
595 And indeed he made a leaning effort with hands and feet
To push the stone up the crest. But when it was about
To go over the top, then it turned back down with its force;
The shameless stone rolled on down again to the plain.
Then he pushed it back again, exerting himself, and the sweat
600 Flowed off his limbs and dust rose up around his head.
After him I caught sight of powerful Heracles,
A phantom. For he himself with the immortal gods
Enjoys abundance and has Hebe of the fair ankles,
Child of great Zeus and of Hera with the golden sandals.
605 There was a shrieking about him of the dead as of birds

Terrified on all sides. And he like the gloomy night
Held his bare bow with an arrow on the string,
Peering dreadfully like one who is ever about to shoot.
Terrible was the sword strap circling him round the chest,
A golden belt on which wonderful things were fashioned,   610
Bears and savage boars and lions with glaring eyes,
Battles and combats and slaughters and murders of men.
May he never make or never have made any other,
The man who conceived that belt in his own skill.
He knew me at once when he saw me with his eyes,   615
And lamenting to me, he uttered wingèd words:
'Zeus-born son of Laertes, Odysseus of many devices,
Wretched man, what an evil fate you too are carrying on,
Such as I bore myself beneath the rays of the sun!
I was a child of Zeus, son of Cronos, but I had   620
Boundless woe, for I was subdued to a mortal,
Inferior by far, who put difficult tasks on me.
He sent me here once to bring the dog. He did not think
Any task would be more difficult for me than this.
But I did take the dog and lead him out of the place of Hades.   625
Hermes escorted me, and bright-eyed Athene.'
When he had said this, he went back into the hall of Hades.
But I stayed there on the spot in case anyone came
Of the heroes, men who had perished in time before,
And I still would have seen men of old whom I wished to see,   630
Theseus and Perithous,[7] glorious children of the gods,
But first numberless bands of the dead came on
With a tremendous shout, and sallow fear seized me
Lest noble Persephone send the Gorgon [8] head
Of the dread monster from the hall of Hades against me.   635
At once I went on the ship and called my companions
To board it themselves and to untie the stern cables.
They boarded it at once and sat down at the oarlocks,
And a wave of the stream bore it to the river Oceanos;
First there was rowing, and after that a fair breeze.   640

7. Proverbial friend of Theseus.
8. The dead head of a fearful monster (possibly not the same as the later Gorgon).

XII

"And when the ship had left the stream of the river
Oceanos, and reached the wave of the wide-pathed sea
And the island Aiaia, where the home and the dancing floors
Of the early-born dawn are, and the risings of the sun;
5 When we arrived there, we beached the ship on the sands
And got out ourselves beside the surf of the sea.
We fell asleep there and awaited the godly dawn.
And when the early-born, rosy-fingered dawn appeared,
I sent my companions off to the halls of Circe
10 To bring the body of Elpenor, who had died.
At once we cut logs where the shore jutted highest out,
And we buried him, lamenting and shedding a swelling tear.
When his dead body had been burned, and the gear of his
    body,
We heaped up a mound, dragged a grave marker up on it,
15 And set up his well-shaped oar on top of the mound.
We talked out the details, nor did we escape the notice
Of Circe as we came from Hades, but very swiftly
She adorned herself and came. Servants with her carried
Bread, many pieces of meat, and sparkling red wine.
20 The divine goddess took her stand in our midst and spoke:
'Rash you are, who have gone alive into the hall of Hades,
Dying twice, when other men die a single time:
Well, come, eat of the provisions and drink wine
All day long in this place, and as soon as dawn appears
25 You shall set sail. I shall show you the way and point out
All the details, lest by some troublesome complication
You be hurt and suffer pain on land or on the sea.'
So she said, and the bold heart was persuaded within us.
So then for the entire day till the setting of the sun
30 We sat there dining on the endless meat and sweet wine.
But when the sun went down and the darkness came on
The men lay down by the stern cable of the ship.

She took me by the hand aside from my dear companions,
Sat me down, lay next to me, and asked me the details,
And I told everything to her in its due order.   35
Then the queenly Circe addressed a speech to me:
'So all this has been brought to an end. Now listen
To what I tell you; a god himself shall remind you.
First you will come to the Sirens, who enchant
All men, whenever anyone comes upon them.   40
Whoever in ignorance nears them and hears the voice
Of the Sirens—for that man, his wife and infant children
Do not stand by or rejoice at his homeward return,
But the Sirens enchant him with their clear-toned song,
Seated in a meadow. About is a large heap of bones,   45
Of men rotting, and the skin is shrinking around them.
But go on past; soften honey-sweet wax and smear it
In the ears of your companions lest any of the rest
Should listen. And if you yourself desire to listen,
Let them bind you upon the swift ship hand and foot   50
Erect at the mast; and let the rope ends be made fast from it,
So that you may hear and enjoy the Sirens' song.
If you implore your companions and call on them to free you,
Then have them bind you in further fastenings.
And when your companions have got on past those women,   55
At that point I shall no longer tell you in full detail
Which one of two ways will be yours, but you yourself
Must decide in your heart. I will tell you the alternatives:
In one place there are overhanging rocks; and against them
The great wave of dark blue-eyed Amphitrite roars.   60
Those, indeed, do the blessed gods call the Wandering Rocks,
Where nothing that flies can get by, not even the timid
Doves that carry ambrosia to father Zeus.
And the sheer rock always takes away one of them,
But the Father sends another to make up the number.   65
No ship of men that arrives there ever escapes,
But sea waves and storms of destructive fire carry off
The timbers of the ships and the bodies of the men alike.
One seafaring ship alone did sail past the place,
The Argo, known to all men, as it sailed from Aietes,[1]   70
And it would swiftly have been dashed there on the great rocks
But Hera sent it past, since Jason was dear to her.

1. King of Colchis, father of Medea. The *Argo* was Jason's ship.

The other way there are two crags; one reaches to broad heaven
With its sharp peak, and a dark blue cloud surrounds it
75 That never recedes, nor ever does a clear sky
Hold the peak of it, either in summer or in autumn.
No mortal man could ever climb it or get on top,
Not even if he had twenty hands and twenty feet,
For the rock is sheer, as though polished all around,
80 And in the middle of the crag is a murky cave
Turned facing to the dusk toward Erebos, and there,
Noble Odysseus, you should steer your hollow ship.
Nor could a vigorous man shooting with a bow
From the hollow ship reach to the open cave.
85 There within dwells Scylla, who barks dreadfully,
And her voice comes as loud as that of an unweaned puppy,
But she herself is an evil monster, nor would anyone
Take pleasure to see her, not if a god should confront her.
There are twelve feet on her, all dangling in air;
90 She has six very long necks, and on each one
A terrible head, and on it three rows of teeth
Thick-set and in a cluster, and full of black death.
She is withdrawn to her middle down in the hollow cave;
She holds her heads outside of the dreadful abyss,
95 And there she fishes and reaches all around the crag
For dolphins and dogfish and whatever larger sea creature
She may catch that roaring Amphitrite feeds by the thousands.
There no sailors may ever claim to have escaped past
Unharmed with their ship. She carries off in each head
100 A mortal she has snatched up from a dark blue-prowed ship.
The second crag you will see lying lower, Odysseus,
Close to the other. And you could shoot an arrow across it.
Upon it is a large wild fig tree blooming with leaves;
There divine Charybdis sucks black water back under.
105 Three times daily she sends it up, three times sucks back
Terribly. Do not happen to be there when she sucks,
For not even the earth-shaker could save you from evil then,
But sail to the crag of Scylla very rapidly
And drive your ship on past, since it is better by far
110 To miss six companions on the ship than all at once.'
So she said, and I spoke out to her in answer:
'Come now, goddess, tell me this unerringly,
May I get away from destructive Charybdis somehow

And ward off the other, once she has despoiled my companions?'
So I said, and the divine goddess answered at once: 115
'You rash man, do the works of war concern you again
And toil? Will you not yield to the immortal gods?
She is not mortal for you, but an immortal evil,
Dreadful, oppressive, wild, and not to be fought.
And there is no defense. It is best to flee from her.   120
But if you linger and helm yourself beside the rock,
I fear that she may search and light on you again
And take away as many mortals as she has heads.
No, drive very strongly on, cry aloud for Cratais,
The mother of Scylla, who bore her as a bane for mortals.   125
Then she will stop her from reaching out a second time.
You will arrive at the isle of Thrinacria. There many
Oxen of the Sun and goodly sheep are pasturing,
Seven herds of cattle and as many lovely flocks of sheep,
Fifty in each. No offspring are born from them,   130
Nor do they ever wane. Goddesses and shepherds over them,
The fair-braided nymphs, Phaethusa and Lampetie,
Whom divine Neaira bore to Hyperion, the Sun.
When their queenly mother had borne them and raised them,
She sent them to the isle of Thrinacria to live far off,   135
To guard the sheep and crumple-horned cattle of their father.
If you let them go unmolested and think of your return,
You may get to Ithaca, though you do suffer ills.
But if you molest them, then I prophesy destruction
For your ship and companions. And even if you escape
   yourself   140
You will return late and ill, having lost all your companions.'
So she said, and at once the golden-throned Dawn came on.
The divine goddess herself returned then up the island,
But I went on to the ship and urged my companions
To go on board themselves and to undo the stern cables.   145
At once they got on and took their seats at the oarlocks.
Seated in order, they beat the hoary sea with their oars.
A driving wind full in the sails, a fine companion,
Did the fair-braided Circe, dread god with a singing voice,
Send on for us from behind the dark blue-prowed ship.   150
At once when we had tended to the gear through the ship piece
   by piece
We took our seats. The wind and a pilot steered her.

Then, grieving in my heart, I spoke to my companions:
'My friends, not one person or two alone need to know
155 The prophecies that the divine goddess Circe told me.
But I will tell them, so you may know whether we
Shall die or might avoid death and escape fate.
She ordered us first to avoid the voice of the marvelous
Sirens, and also their meadow full of flowers.
160 Me alone she ordered to hear their voice; but bind me
In hard bonds so that I may stay firm in my place
Erect at the mast. And let the rope-ends be fastened from it.
And if I implore you and call you to untie me
Then constrain me yourselves in further fastenings.'
165 So I declared, and made known the details to my companions.
Meanwhile the well-made ship arrived speedily
At the isle of the Sirens. A fair breeze drove it on.
Then at that point the wind died down, and there was
A windless calm, and some god put the waves to sleep.
170 My companions stood up and furled the sails on the ship.
They threw them in the hollow ship; then, seated at the oars,
They made the water white with the blades of smooth fir.
But I cut up a great disc of wax with the sharp sword
Into small pieces and kneaded it with my stout hands.
175 At once the wax softened when my great force had compelled it,
And the gleam of the Sun, Hyperion's lordly child.
I smeared it in all my companions' ears one by one,
And they bound me on the ship by my hands and feet
Erect on the mast and fastened rope ends from it.
180 Taking their seats, they beat the hoary sea with their oars.
But when it was as far off as a man's shout would carry,
While we pushed swiftly on, the fast-sailing ship did not get
    past
The Sirens—as it drew near, they struck up their clear-toned
    song:
'Come near, much-praised Odysseus, the Achaians' great glory;
185 Bring your ship in, so you may listen to our voice.
No one ever yet sped past this place in a black ship
Before he listened to the honey-toned voice from our mouths,
And then he went off delighted and knowing more things.
For we know all the many things that in broad Troy
190 The Argives and the Trojans suffered at the will of the gods.
We know all that comes to be on the much-nourishing earth.'

So they said, sending their lovely voice out. My heart
Desired to listen, and I told my companions to free me,
Signaling with my eyebrows. Falling to it, they rowed.
Standing up at once, Perimedes and Eurylochos   195
Bound me in further bonds and constrained me more,
And when we had got on past them and could no longer
Listen to the cry of the Sirens or their voice,
At once my trusty companions took out the wax
I had smeared in their ears and freed me from my bonds.   200
But when we had left the island, then at once
I saw smoke and a great wave and heard a noise.
As the men were afraid, the oars flew from their hands;
They all splashed down on the current. And the ship held
In place, since they could no longer drive the sharp-bladed oars
    with their hands.   205
But I went on through the ship, urging my companions
With soothing speeches, standing close to each man:
'Friends, so far we are not unacquainted with evils,
And this is really no greater evil upon us than when the
    Cyclops
Penned us in his hollow cave by his powerful force.   210
Yet even from there, through my prowess and my plan and
    thought,
We escaped, and I think perhaps we shall remember this too.
Come now, do as I tell you, let us all obey.
Beat the deep breakers of the sea with your oars,
Seated at the oarlocks, so that Zeus somehow   215
May grant that we escape and avoid this destruction.
To you, pilot, I give this command. And put it
In your heart as you tend the rudder of the hollow ship.
Keep the ship on the outside of this smoke and this wave,
And make for the crag lest the ship get away from you   220
As it rushes out there and you plunge us all into evil.'
So I said, and they obeyed my words right away.
I said no more of Scylla, the unavoidable danger,
Lest somehow in their fear over me my companions
Should cease from the rowing and crowd themselves within.   225
And then I forgot the hard injunction of Circe
When she ordered me in no way to arm myself.
I put on my famous armor, took two long spears
In my hands, and went up on the deck of the ship

230 At the prow, for from that place I expected rocky Scylla
First to be sighted, who bore me woe for my companions.
I could not discern her anywhere. My eyes were tired
As I peered everywhere out toward the murky rock.
And we sailed on through the narrow passage, lamenting.
235 There was Scylla, and on the other side godly Charybdis
Sucked back terribly the salt water of the sea.
Whenever she disgorged, like a basin in a large fire,
She seethed, all stirred up. And from overhead, foam
Fell down on both sides of the peaks of the crags,
240 And when she swallowed down the salt water of the sea
She appeared all stirred up within, and the rock roared
Terribly about, and the earth appeared underneath
In dark blue sand. Sallow fear seized the men.
We looked toward her in fear of our destruction.
245 Meanwhile Scylla snatched off of the hollow ship
Six of my companions, who were mightiest in strength.
But when I looked into the swift ship toward my companions
I saw already their hands and their feet from above
As they were lifted on high. They called to me with a cry,
250 Calling me then by name for the last time, grieving in heart.
As a fisher on a promontory with a very long rod
Throws down morsels as a lure for the little fish
And sends down into the ocean the horn of a field ox;
Then when he catches one writhing, throws it ashore;
255 So they, writhing, were raised up toward the rocks.
There at the entrance she ate them as they shrieked,
Reaching their hands toward me in their dread struggle.
That was the most piteous thing I saw with my eyes
Of all that I suffered as I sought out the paths of the sea.
260 But when we had fled the rocks and terrible Charybdis
And Scylla, we arrived at once at the blameless island
Of the god, where the beautiful broad-browed cattle were,
And the many goodly flocks of Hyperion, the Sun.
Then, while I was still on the ocean in the black ship,
265 I heard a lowing of cattle coming to the fold
And a bleating of sheep. Then there fell on my heart the speech
Of the blind prophet Theban Tiresias,
And of Aiaian Circe, who enjoined me many times
To avoid the isle of the Sun, who delights mortal men.
270 So then I addressed my companions, grieving in my heart:

'Hear my speech, though you have suffered ills, my companions,
So I may tell you the prophecies of Tiresias
And of Aiaian Circe, who enjoined me many times
To avoid the isle of the Sun, who delights mortal men.
They said a most dreadful evil would come on us there.   275
So let us drive the black ship on past that island.'
So I said, and their own hearts were shattered within them.
Eurylochos answered me at once with a hateful speech:
'You are tough, Odysseus, with your superior strength; your
     limbs
Do not get tired, but they are made all of iron for you   280
Who will not let your companions, worn out with fatigue
And sleepiness, set foot on land, where, moreover,
On the flood-circled island we might make a pleasant dinner,
But you bid us to wander as we are through the sudden night,
Carried away from the island upon the murky ocean.   285
And hard winds come up out of the night, the destroyers
Of ships. Where might one escape sheer destruction
If suddenly a storm of wind by chance came on,
Of the South Wind or the hard-blowing West Wind, that most
Tear ships to pieces beyond the will of the ruling gods?   290
No, but indeed, let us now give in to the black night.
Let us prepare dinner as we stay by the swift ship.
At dawn we shall get in and proceed on the broad ocean.'
So Eurylochos said, and my other companions agreed.
Then I knew that some god had devised evils,   295
And I spoke out to him, uttering wingèd words:
'Eurylochos, indeed you compel me, single as I am.
Come then, all of you, and swear me a mighty oath.
If we find some herd of cattle or a great flock
Of sheep, that no one in evil recklessness   300
Will slaughter any cow or sheep. But be secure
And eat the provisions that immortal Circe gave.'
So I said, and they at once swore an oath as I bid them.
And when they had sworn the oath and completed it,
They set the well-fashioned ship in a hollow harbor   305
Near sweet water. My companions got out and away
From the ship and then prepared dinner skillfully.
But when they had taken their fill of food and drink,
They then remembered and wept for our dear companions
Whom Scylla had snatched out of the hollow ship and eaten.   310

Balmy sleep came upon them as they were weeping.
When it was the third part of night and the stars had gone by,
Cloud-gathering Zeus raised a wind to blow against them
In a tremendous storm, and he covered land and ocean alike
315 Over with clouds. And night rose up out of heaven.
And when the early-born, rosy-fingered dawn appeared,
We beached the ship, dragging her into a hollow cave
Where the fair dancing-floors and the haunts of the nymphs
     were.
And then I made an assembly and addressed them a speech:
320 'My friends, since there is food and drink in the swift ship,
Let us hold off from the cattle, lest we suffer something.
These are the cattle and goodly sheep of a dreadful god,
The Sun, who sees everything and hears everything.'
So I said, and the bold spirit was persuaded in them.
325 The South Wind blew steadily a whole month; no other
Wind came up then except the East Wind and the South.
So long as they possessed grain and red wine
They held off from the cattle in their desire for life.
But when all the provisions had been used up from the ship,
330 They went out on the hunt, roving from necessity
For fish and birds, with bent hooks, for whatever came
Into their own hands. Hunger wore down their bellies.
Then I went away, up into the island so that I might pray
To the gods, for one to show me the way to return.
When I had gone through the island and got clear of my
335   companions,
I washed my hands where there was shelter from the wind,
And I prayed to all of the gods who possess Olympos.
But they poured sweet sleep on me over my eyelids.
And Eurylochos unfolded a bad plan to my companions:
340 'Hear my speech, companions, though you have suffered ills.
There are all kinds of hateful deaths for wretched mortals,
But most piteous is to die and meet one's fate by hunger.
Come then, let us drive the best of the cattle of the Sun
And sacrifice them to the immortals who hold broad heaven,
345 And if we ever get to Ithaca, our fatherland,
We shall at once build a rich temple to Hyperion,
The Sun, and put in it many noble ornaments.
But if he is at all enraged for his straight-horned cattle
And wishes to destroy the ship, and the other gods follow,

I would rather gasp once into a wave and lose my life   350
Then to be starved a long time on a desert island.'
So Eurylochos said, and the other companions agreed.
At once they drove the best of the cattle of the Sun
From nearby. For not far away from the dark blue-prowed
      ship
Did the fine crumple-horned, broad-browed cattle pasture.   355
They surrounded them and made prayers to the gods,
When they had plucked tender leaves from an oak with high
      foliage,
For they did not have white barley on the well-timbered ship.
But when they had prayed and had slaughtered and flayed
      them,
They cut out the thighs and covered them over with fat.   360
They made two folds and lay the raw flesh upon them,
Nor did they have wine to pour on the burning sacrifices,
But used water for libation and roasted all the entrails.
And when the thighs were burned and they had eaten the
      inward parts,
They cut the rest in pieces and pierced it on spits.   365
And then balmy sleep flew away from my eyelids.
I went down to the swift ship and the strand of the sea.
And when I got up close to the bobbing ship,
The sweet aroma of roasting came over to me.
Then I groaned and cried out to the immortal gods: 370
'Father Zeus, and you other blessed, ever-living gods,
To my ruin, indeed, have you lulled me in relentless sleep;
And my companions, while waiting, have devised an enormous
      deed.'
Then a messenger came swiftly to Hyperion the Sun,
Long-gowned Lampetie, to say we had killed his cattle.   375
At once he addressed the immortals, angered in his heart:
'Father Zeus, and you other blessed, ever-living gods,
Take vengeance on the companions of Laertes' son Odysseus,
Who have presumptuously killed my cattle, in which I
Took delight when I went into the starry heaven   380
And when I turned back again from heaven to earth.
If they do not pay fitting recompense for the cattle,
I will go down to the place of Hades and shine among the
      dead.'
Cloud-gathering Zeus spoke out to him in answer:

385 'O Sun, do indeed shine among the immortals
And among mortal men on the grain-giving earth.
I shall smite their swift ship soon with a gleaming bolt
Into small pieces, and burn it in the middle of the wine-faced
    ocean.'
I heard these things from Calypso of the fair hair,
390 Who said she had heard them herself from the runner Hermes.
And when I had got down to the ship and the sea,
I rebuked them one after another on the spot. Nor could we
Find any remedy. The cattle were already dead.
Then at once the gods showed forth portents to the men;
395 The skins were creeping, meat lowed upon the spits,
Both roast and raw, and there came up the voice as of cattle.
And so for six days did my trusty companions
Feast on the fine cattle of the Sun they had driven off.
But when Zeus, son of Cronos, had added the seventh day,
400 At that point the wind ceased raging in a tempest.
We boarded at once and set out upon the broad ocean,
When we had set the mast up and hoisted the white sails.
And when we had left the island behind, no other land
Appeared at all, but only heaven and the sea.
405 Then the son of Cronos halted a dark blue cloud
Over the hollow ship, and the ocean darkened beneath it.
She ran on not too long a time. For at once there came
The shrieking West Wind raging in a great tempest,
And a storm of wind broke the forestays of the mast,
410 Both of them, and the mast fell backward, and all the tackle
Was thrown into the hold. On the stern of the ship
It hit the pilot's head. And in an instant it crushed
All the bones of his head together. Like a diver
He dropped down from the deck, and the bold spirit left his
    bones.
415 Zeus at that instant thundered and threw a bolt on the ship.
It whirled all around, struck by Zeus's thunderbolt,
And was filled with brimstone. My companions fell from the
    ship,
And they resembled sea crows around the black ship
As they were borne on the waves; a god took away their return.
420 I wandered through my ship until the surge had loosed
The planks from the keel, and the wave carried it stripped.
It broke the mast off the keel, and then the backstay,

Which had been made out of oxhide, was flung up on it.
Then I bound both the keel and the mast together.
Seated on them, I was carried by the destructive winds.   425
And then the West Wind ceased raging in a tempest
And the South Wind came quickly, bearing pains for my heart,
That I should still remeasure my course to destructive
    Charybdis.
All night long I was carried, and with the rising sun
I came to the crag of Scylla and to dreadful Charybdis.   430
And she had sucked back the salty water of the sea,
But I raised myself high up against the tall wild fig tree
And held myself fastened to it like a bat. Nor anywhere
Could I plant my feet firmly or climb up on it,
For its roots held far off and its branches were high swaying,   435
Tall and great, and they shadowed Charybdis over.
I held there steadily, till she should disgorge back
The mast and keel again. I longed for them, but they came late.
At the time when a man gets up from the assembly for dinner,
One who judges many quarrels of youthful adversaries,   440
At that time did the timber appear out of Charybdis.
I let my hands and feet be brought down from above
And plunged right on in the midst of the lengthy timbers.
Seated upon them, I rowed on with my hands.
The father of men and gods no longer let Scylla   445
See me, or I would not have escaped sheer destruction.
Nine days I was borne thence, and on the tenth night
The gods brought me near the island of Ogygia, where lives
Fair-braided Calypso, dread god with a singing voice.
She befriended me and cared for me. Why tell this story?   450
Already I have told it in your house yesterday
To you and your goodly wife. It is hateful to me
To tell over again a story that has been clearly told."

XIII

So he said, and they all became hushed in silence.
They were held in rapture through the shadowy halls.
Then Alcinoos gave him an answer and spoke to him:
"Odysseus, since you have come to my bronze-based home
5 With its high roof, I think you will not be driven off course
In your return back, though you have suffered much.
And I say this in urging every man of you,
All those who in my halls are forever drinking
The sparkling wine of the elders and listening to the singer.
10 Clothes are laid up for the stranger in a polished chest,
And highly wrought gold and all sorts of other gifts
That the members of the Phaeacian council brought here.
Come now, let us give him a great cauldron and a basin,
Man by man. Then we shall collect among the people and
    get paid back.
15 It is hard for a single man to give freely for nothing."
So Alcinoos spoke, and his speech was pleasing to them.
They all went off, each to his house, to lie down to sleep.
And when the early-born, rosy-fingered dawn appeared,
They hastened to the ship and brought bronze that is a help for
    men.
20 Alcinoos in his sacred strength stored it well under the benches,
Going himself through the ship so it might not hamper
Any of the rowing crew as they sped with the oars.
They went to the home of Alcinoos and partook of dinner.
Alcinoos in his sacred strength sacrificed an ox for them
25 To black-clouded Zeus, son of Cronos, who rules all.
When they had burned the thighs, they dined on the illustrious
    feast
And enjoyed it. Among them the godly singer played,
Demodocos, who was honored by the people. But Odysseus
Turned his head many times to the resplendent sun,
30 Impatient for it to set. So eager was he to return;

As when a man longs for dinner whose wine-faced oxen
Have drawn the jointed plow on his fallow land all day:
He is glad when the light of the sun goes down on him
As he heads for dinner, and his knees fail as he goes;
So was Odysseus glad when the sun's light went down.   35
At once he addressed the Phaeacians, who are fond of rowing.
And to Alcinoos especially did he make known his speech:
"Lordly Alcinoos, exalted among all your people,
Pour a libation and send me home unharmed. Farewell to you!
What my own heart was wanting has now been brought to pass,   40
An escort and friendly gifts; and may the heavenly gods
Make them blessed for me! On my return may I find
My wife at home blameless, with my friends safe and sound.
You, though, stay here and give pleasure to your wedded wives
And to your children. May the gods grant excellence   45
Of all sorts to you, and no evil be among your people."
So he said, and they all assented and gave the order
To escort the stranger, since he had spoken properly.
Then Alcinoos in his might spoke out to a herald:
"Pontonoos, mix up a bowl and pass out wine   50
To all through the hall, so we may pray to Father Zeus,
And escort the stranger to his own fatherland."
So he said, and Pontonoos mixed the mind-honeying wine.
He passed it to all in turn. From the seats where they were
They poured libation to the blessed gods   55
Who possess broad heaven. Godly Odysseus stood up,
Placed a cup with two handles in Arete's hand,
And speaking out to her he uttered wingèd words:
"May you constantly fare well, my queen, till old age
And death come upon you, which do exist for men.   60
But I am going now. Enjoy yourself in this house,
With your children and your people and King Alcinoos."
When he had said this, godly Odysseus went over the threshold.
Alcinoos in his might sent a herald along with him
To lead him to the swift ship and the strand of the sea.   65
And Arete sent serving women along with him,
One of whom held a well-washed mantle and tunic,
Another she sent with her to bring the stout chest along,
And still another was carrying bread and red wine.
And when they had come down to the ship and the sea,   70
At once his noble escorts took those things and placed them

Inside the hollow ship, all of the food and drink.
They spread out a blanket and linen cloth for Odysseus
On the deck of the hollow ship, so he might sleep without
    waking,
75 Upon the stern. He himself boarded too and lay down
In silence. Each of them sat down at the oarlocks
In order. They loosed the cable from the pierced stone.
As soon as they leaned on the oars and flung up salt water with
    the blade,
For him there fell down upon his eyelids a balmy sleep,
80 Unwaking, most sweet, nearest in semblance to death.
As for the ship, the way four yoked stallions on a plain
All rush on together under the blows of a whip,
Leap up high, and pursue their journey rapidly;
So was her stern raised up, and behind her there surged
85 A great purple wave of the loud-roaring sea.
She ran safely and steadily, nor could the circling
Hawks, the nimblest of winged things, have kept up,
So rapidly did it run as it cut the waves of the sea
Carrying a man who had plans like those of the gods,
90 Who in time past had suffered very many pains in his heart,
Passing through the wars of men and the troublesome waves,
But at this time he slept without a tremor, forgetting what he
    had suffered.
When the brightest star rose up that most of all
Comes on to announce the light of early-born dawn,
95 At that time did the seafaring ship reach the island.
There is a certain harbor of Phorcys, the old man of the sea,
In the land of Ithaca; and there, jutting out on it,
Are two headlands broken off, sloping down to the harbor.
They give shelter against the great wave from hard-blowing
    winds
100 Outside. And inside of it well-timbered ships remain
Without a cable when they reach the measure of mooring.
At the head of the harbor is an olive with long leaves,
And close to that is a pleasant and shadowy cavern
Sacred to the nymphs who are called Naiades.
105 And in it there are mixing bowls and two-handled jars
Of stone. And the bees store up their honey in them.
There are very long stone looms in it, where the nymphs
Weave sea purple mantles, a wonder to behold,

And ever-flowing waters are there. It has two doors,
One toward the North Wind, accessible to men,   110
And the other one divine is toward the South Wind, nor may men
Approach by that one, but it is a path for immortals.
The men, who knew it beforehand, drove the ship in there;
And then she was beached on the mainland, half her whole length
As she ran in, so fast was she pushed on by the rowers' hands.   115
They got out of the well-benched ship onto dry land.
First they raised Odysseus out of the hollow ship,
The linen sheet and the glistening blanket and all;
They set him down on the sand overcome with sleep.
They lifted out the goods the noble Phaeacians had given   120
As he was going home through great-hearted Athene's help,
And then put them in a heap by the base of the olive tree,
Out of the path lest by chance some wayfaring man
Might find and despoil them before Odysseus woke up.
Then they started back homeward. Nor did the earth-shaker   125
Forget the curses he had made originally
Against godlike Odysseus. And he asked about Zeus's plan:
"Father Zeus, I myself shall no longer be honored
Among the immortal gods when mortals do not respect me,
The Phaeacians, who are of my very own descent.   130
For I just now said Odysseus would suffer many ills
Before he got home; I have never deprived him of a return
Entirely, since you promised this first and nodded agreement.
Yet these men have brought him asleep on the ocean in a swift ship,
Have set him down in Ithaca and given him prodigious gifts,   135
Bronze and gold and woven clothing aplenty,
Much more than Odysseus ever would have taken from Troy
If he had arrived unharmed with his share of booty."
Cloud-gathering Zeus addressed him in answer:
"Well now, wide-powered earth-shaker, what a speech you have made!   140
The gods do not at all insult you. It would be hard
To attack with insults the oldest and finest god—
And if some man, yielding to his strength and might,
Does not honor you, vengeance is yours forever after.
Do as you wish and as is pleasing to your own heart."   145

And then the earth-shaker Poseidon answered him:
"Black-clouded one, I would do at once as you say.
But always I respect and do deference to your heart.
And now I would like to dash the beautiful ship
150 Of the Phaeacians as it comes from escort on the murky sea,
So that henceforth they may hold back and refrain from escort
For men; and I would hide their city round with a great
    mountain."
Cloud-gathering Zeus addressed him in answer:
"Dear friend, in my heart this seems to me the best course:
155 When all the people are away from the city and catch sight
Of the ship coming on, make it into a stone near the land
Resembling the swift ship, so that all the men may be
Amazed; and hide the city round with a great mountain."
And when earth-shaker Poseidon had heard this speech,
160 He went on to Scheria where the Phaeacians dwell
And stayed there. The seafaring ship came very near,
Running on nimbly. The earth-shaker came near it,
And he turned it to stone and rooted it beneath,
Pressing it with the flat of his hand. Then he departed.
165 The Phaeacians with their long oars, men famous for ships,
For their part addressed wingèd words to one another.
This is what a man who saw it would say to his neighbor:
"Ah me, who has detained the swift ship in the ocean
As it was coming home? It has just appeared all in view."
170 So one man would say. They did not know how this was done.
Then Alcinoos spoke out to them and addressed them:
"Ah well, the prophecies have come upon me, spoken of old
By my father, who used to say Poseidon resented us
Because we are secure escorts for everyone.
175 He said a beautiful ship of the Phaeacian men
Coming back sometime from an escort on the murky ocean
Would be dashed, and a great mountain would hide our city
    round."
So the old man said. Now it has all come to pass.
But come now. Let us all observe what I shall say:
180 Give up escorting mortals when anyone comes
To our city, and let us sacrifice to Poseidon
Twelve chosen bulls so that he may take·pity
And not hide our city round with a very tall mountain."
So he said; they were afraid, and prepared the bulls.

And so the leaders and counselors of the land   185
Of the Phaeacians were praying to Lord Poseidon,
Standing round the altar. But godly Odysseus woke up
From sleeping on his fatherland soil and did not recognize it,
For he had been gone a long time. A god shed a mist round
    him,
Pallas Athene, the daughter of Zeus, so she could make him   190
Unrecognizable, and tell him the details,
Lest his wife recognize him, and his townsmen and friends,
Before the suitors had paid for all their transgressions.
And so everything appeared of a changed form to its lord;
Continuous pathways and harbors with mooring all round,   195
Towering rocks and trees that were blossoming.
He sprang up, stood still, and looked on his fatherland soil,
And then he uttered a groan and struck both his thighs
With the flat of his hands. And he made a speech, lamenting:
"Woe is me, to the land of what mortals have I come this time?   200
Are the men proud and savage and without justice
Or are they friendly to strangers and have a god-fearing mind?
Where am I carrying these many goods? Where do I myself
Wander? Would that they had stayed with the Phaeacians
In that place. But I would have come on another of the
    exalted kings   205
Who would have befriended me and sent me on my return.
As it is I do not know where to put these things. Nor can I
Leave them here, lest they become a prey to others.
Well now, the leaders and counselors of the Phaeacians
Were not wholly prudent and just when they led me off   210
To another land. They did say they would lead me
To sunny Ithaca, and they did not bring it to pass.
May the Zeus of suppliants pay them back, who watches
Over all men and punishes whoever errs.
All right, I shall number the goods and look at them   215
Lest they have taken some from me and gone on the hollow
    ship."
When he had said this, he counted the beautiful cauldrons
And the basins and the gold and the lovely woven clothes.
He missed none of them. But he bemoaned his fatherland,
Dragging himself along the strand of the loud-roaring sea   220
And grieving much. And Athene came up close to him,
Likening her body to a young man's, a feeder of sheep,

All tender, the way the children of rulers are.
She wore a well-made double-folded mantle on her shoulders
225 And had sandals under her glistening feet, a javelin in her hands.
Odysseus rejoiced to see her and came up facing her.
And speaking out to her, he uttered wingèd words:
"My friend, since you are the first one I find in this place,
Greetings. And may you not confront me with an evil mind.
230 But save these things and save me; I pray to you
As to a god, and I come up to your precious knees.
Tell me this one thing, truly, so I may know it well;
What land is this, what people? What men are native here?
Is it some sunny island, perhaps, or some shore
235 Of the rich-loamed mainland that lies sloping to the sea?"
Then the bright-eyed goddess Athene spoke to him:
"You are simple, stranger, or have come from far away
If you ask what this land is. To no great degree
Is it nameless. Very many men know which it is,
240 Both all those who are living toward dawn and the sun
And also all those who live back toward the murky dusk.
Indeed it is rough and not for driving horses,
Nor is it excessively poor, though not broad in shape.
In it is produced immense food and also wine.
245 Rain holds it perpetually and the fertile dew.
It is a good goat pasture and cow pasture. Woods
Are all over it, and it affords year-round watering places.
And so, stranger, the name Ithaca has reached even to Troy,
Which they say is far off from the Achaian land."
So she said, and godly Odysseus, who had endured much,
250   rejoiced,
Glad at his fatherland soil, that Pallas Athene,
The daughter of aegis-bearing Zeus, told him of,
And speaking out to her, he uttered wingèd words.
He did not speak the truth, but he held back his story,
255 Forever managing the very shrewd thought in his breast:
"I have heard of Ithaca even in broad Crete,
Far over the ocean. And now I have come myself
With these goods; leaving as much again to my children,
I fled, since I had killed the dear son of Idomeneus,
260 Swift-footed Ortilochos, who in broad Crete
Surpassed all bread-earning men with his swift feet,
Because he wanted to deprive me of all my booty

From Troy, for which I had suffered pains in my heart,
Passing through the wars of men and the troublesome waves,
And because I was not graciously willing to serve his father   265
In the Trojans' land, but led other men as companions.
I hit him with the bronze-tipped spear as he was coming back
From a field, lying in ambush with a companion by the path.
A very dark night held the heavens, nor did any man
Perceive us, and I took away his life unnoticed.   270
But when I had killed the man with the sharp bronze spear
I went on a ship at once and pleaded with the noble
Phoenicians, and I gave them booty to their heart's desire.
I asked them to bring me to Pylos and put me to shore,
Or close to godly Elis, where the Epeians are ruling.   275
But then the force of the wind drove them away from there,
Much against their will, for they did not want to deal falsely.
Wandering from there we arrived at this place by night.
With haste we rowed into the harbor, nor did any of us
Have dinner in mind, though we wanted much to take it;   280
But getting off the ship, we all lay down as we were.
Then sweet sleep came on me, fatigued as I was,
And they took my goods out of the hollow ship
And set them down where I was lying on the sands.
Embarking for well-inhabited Sidonia,   285
They went off, and I was left grieving in my heart."
So he said, and the bright-eyed goddess Athene smiled.
She reached her hand to him and likened her body to a woman's,
Lovely and tall and skilled in glorious tasks;
And speaking to him, she uttered wingèd words: 290
"Cunning would he be and deceitful, who could overreach you
In various wiles, and even if a god should confront you.
Versatile-minded wretch, insatiate in wiles, you would not
Cease from deceits though you are in your own land,
Or from fraudulent stories that from the ground up are dear to
    you.   295
Come, let us say no more of this, as both of us are skilled
In shrewdness, since you are by far the best of mortals
In plans and in stories, and I among all the gods
Am famed for planning and shrewdness, and you did not know
Pallas Athene, daughter of Zeus, who always stands   300
Beside you and guards you in all sorts of troubles
And made you beloved by all of the Phaeacians.

And now I have come here so I may weave a plot with you
And hide all the goods the noble Phaeacians gave you
305 When you came homeward by my plan and my thought.
And I shall tell you how many cares it is your lot to put up with
In the well-made halls. But endure them, for you must,
And do not declare to any one of them all,
Men or women, that you came here wandering. But in silence
310 Suffer many pains, submitting to the violence of men."
Odysseus of many wiles addressed her in answer:
"It is hard, goddess, for a mortal who meets you to recognize
    you,
Even one who is knowing. You liken yourself to anything.
I know this well, that you were mild to me before,
315 While we sons of the Achaians were making war in Troy,
But when we had sacked the lofty city of Priam,
And went off in ships and a god scattered the Achaians,
I did not see you then, daughter of Zeus, or discern you
Boarding my ship to ward any pain off from me.
320 But having always a heart cut asunder in my breast
I wandered until the gods freed me from evil,
Till the time when in the rich land of the Phaeacians
You cheered me with words and led me yourself to the city.
Now I embrace your knees for your father—I do not think
325 I have come to sunny Ithaca, but turn on through
Some other land. And I think you ridicule me
By saying this, so that you may deceive my mind.
Tell me truly if I have reached my dear fatherland."
And then the bright-eyed goddess Athene answered him:
330 "You have an idea like this forever in your breast.
And so I cannot forsake you when you are wretched,
Because you are polite, ready-minded, and of steadfast thought.
Gladly another man who had come in his wandering
Would push on to see his wife and children in his halls.
335 But it is not dear to you to find out or inquire
Before you may yet try your wife out; and she sits
As ever in the halls. Woeful for her always
The days and the nights waste away as she sheds tears.
I never failed to believe it myself, but in my heart
340 Knew you would return, having lost all your companions.
And yet I did not want to quarrel with Poseidon,

My father's brother, who laid up a grudge against you in his
    heart,
Enraged at you for having blinded his dear son.
Come, I will show you Ithaca's site, to convince you.
This is the harbor of Phorcys, the old man of the sea;   345
This at the harbor's head the olive with long leaves,
And close to it the charming and shadowy cavern
Sacred to the nymphs who are called Naiades.
This is the broad, high-roofed cave where you used to offer
Many acceptable hecatombs to the nymphs.   350
And that is Neriton, the mountain clothed over with woods."
When she had said this, the goddess scattered the mist;
    ground showed.
Then godly Odysseus, who had suffered much, rejoiced,
Glad at his own land, and he kissed the grain-giving soil.
At once he prayed to the nymphs, holding up his hands: 355
"Nymphs, Naiades, daughters of Zeus, I never thought
I would see you myself. And now, do take pleasure
In my kindly prayers. I shall give gifts as before,
If Zeus's daughter, driver of the spoil, graciously allows
Me to live myself and makes my dear son grow up."   360
Then the bright-eyed goddess Athene spoke to him:
"Take cheer. Do not give heed to this in your mind,
But right away now we shall place the goods in a nook
Of the marvelous cavern, so they may stay there safe for you,
And let us ourselves discuss how it may be for the best."   365
When she had said this, the goddess entered the shadowy cave,
Searching out the recesses in the cave. And Odysseus
Brought everything nearer, the gold and unyielding bronze
And the well-made clothes that the Phaeacians gave him.
Pallas Athene, the daughter of aegis-bearing Zeus,   370
Put them in well and placed a stone at the entrance.
They both sat down at the base of the holy olive tree
And talked about destruction for the presumptuous suitors.
The bright-eyed goddess Athene was the first to speak:
"Zeus-born son of Laertes, Odysseus of many devices,   375
Take thought about how you may lay hands on the shameless
    suitors
Who for three years have held sway over your hall,
Wooing your godlike wife and giving her bridal gifts.

But she always grieves in her heart for your return.
380 She gives them all hope and makes promises to each man,
Sending out messages, but her mind plans other things."
Odysseus of many devices addressed her in answer:
"Well now, I might surely have perished in my halls
By the evil fate of Agamemnon, son of Atreus,
385 If you, goddess, had not duly told me the details.
Come, devise a plan, that I may do vengeance on them.
Stand beside me yourself, putting in me such courageous might
As we had when we undid Troy's shining diadems.
And if you stood as then pressing on so beside me, bright-eyed
one,
390 I myself would do battle against three hundred men
With you, honored goddess, when you would earnestly help
me."
Then the bright-eyed goddess Athene answered him:
"Yes, I shall surely stand strongly beside you, nor shall you
miss me
When we are busy with these matters, and I think
395 Some of the suitors who devour your livelihood
Shall spatter the immense ground with their blood and brains.
Come, I shall make you unrecognizable to all mortals.
I shall shrivel the lovely flesh on your supple limbs,
Destroy the blond hair from your head, and cloak you about
400 In rags a man seeing you wear would loathe you for.
And I shall mar your eyes that were beautiful beforehand,
So that you may appear ill-favored to all the suitors,
And to your wife and your child that you left in the halls.
But first of all go on up yourself to the swineherd
405 Who is guardian of your swine, kindly disposed to you also,
And a friend to your son and the constant Penelope.
You will find him staying with the swine. They pasture
Beside the rock of the Raven and the spring Arethusa.
They eat the satisfying acorn and drink black water,
410 The things that nourish abundant fat on swine.
Stay there, remain beside him and ask him everything,
So that I may go to Sparta that is lovely in women
And summon Telemachos, your dear son, Odysseus,
Who went to Menelaos in Lacedemon of the broad dancing-
place
415 To learn tidings about you, if you were still alive."

Odysseus of many wiles addressed her in answer:
"Why did you, who know all in your mind, not tell him?
So that he too might wander and undergo pains
On the barren sea and others eat his livelihood?"
Then the bright-eyed goddess Athene answered him: 420
"As for him, do not really take him too much to heart.
I escorted him myself so he might gain noble renown
When he went there. But he has no trouble; he sits secure
In the halls of Atreus' son, and he has endless bounty.
The young men do wait in ambush for him with a black ship,   425
Wanting to kill him before he reaches his fatherland.
But I do not think that will be; sooner shall the earth contain
Some one of the suitors who devour your livelihood."
When she had said this, Athene touched him with a wand.
She shriveled the lovely flesh on his supple limbs,   430
Destroyed the blond hair on his head, and put the skin
Of an aged old man around all of his limbs.
And she marred his eyes that were beautiful beforehand.
She threw other clothing about him; a foul rag and a tunic,
Dirty and full of holes, begrimed with foul smoke,   435
And she clothed about him the great skin of a swift deer,
Bare of hair, and she gave him a staff and a sorry wallet
Thick with holes; a rope shoulder strap was on it.
When they had this plan the two of them parted. And she
Went to godly Lacedemon after the child of Odysseus.   440

XIV

Then he went over the rugged path from the harbor
Up wooded country through the heights, to where Athene
Had showed him the way to the godly swineherd, who, of all the
    servants
Godly Odysseus owned, best took care of his livelihood.
5 He found him seated in the forecourt where the courtyard
Was built up lofty in a place with a view all around,
Lovely and large, circled round, that the swineherd himself
Had built for the swine when his master had gone away,
Secretly from his mistress and the old man Laertes,
10 Out of quarried stones; and he coped it with a prickly shrub.
Outside when he had hewn off the black part of an oak
He drove in stakes, stout and close set, right through on either
    side,
And inside of the courtyard he made twelve pig sties
Close to one another, beds for the swine. In each
15 Fifty swine that sleep on the ground were shut up,
The females for breeding. And the males slept on the outside,
Fewer by far. The godlike suitors diminished those
By eating them, since the swineherd always sent
The best one out of all the well-nourished hogs.
20 Three hundred and sixty there were of them in all.
And dogs that resembled wild beasts slept always beside them,
Four of them, that the swineherd, chief of the men, had reared.
He himself was fitting sandals about his feet,
And cutting oxhide of good color. The other men
25 Were gone off in different directions with the droves of swine,
Three of them. And he had sent the fourth one off to the city
To bring a pig to the presumptuous suitors, under constraint,
So they might sacrifice it and glut their hearts on meat.
The yelping dogs sighted Odysseus suddenly
30 And ran on after him barking, and Odysseus
Sat down in cunning, and the staff fell from his hand.

And then by his own pen he would have suffered a sorry pain,
But the swineherd came up quickly on nimble feet,
Rushed in the front gate, and the leather fell from his hand.
He shouted at the dogs and scattered them this way and that   35
With showers of stones. And he addressed his master:
"Old man, in a little while the dogs would suddenly
Have torn you to pieces, and you would have heaped reproach
        on me.
To me also have the gods given other pains and griefs.
As I groan and lament over my godlike master,   40
I sit here and keep fattening swine for other men
To eat. But that man, perhaps, longing for food,
Wanders to the city and the land of alien men,
If he is indeed still alive and sees the light of the sun.
But follow me, old man, let us go to the hut, so for yourself   45
When you are satisfied in your heart with food and wine,
You may tell where you come from and how many cares you
        have endured."
When he had said this, the godly swineherd led him into the
        hut.
He brought him in and sat him down; and heaped shaggy
        brushwood
And spread on it the hide of a hairy wild goat   50
Great and shaggy, which was his own bedding. Odysseus
        rejoiced
That he had received him so. He spoke out directly:
"Stranger, may Zeus and the other gods grant you whatever
You wish the most, since you have received me kindly."
And you addressed him in answer, swineherd Eumaeos: 55
"Stranger, it would not be right for me to dishonor
A stranger, not if one worse than you came. In Zeus's care
Are all strangers and beggars. And a gift that comes from us,
Even a small one, is friendly, because the rule for servants is
        always
To be afraid when young masters hold power over them.   60
And indeed, the gods have hindered the return of the man
Who kindly befriended me and gave me possessions,
A home and a portion and a wife wooed by many,
Such things as a good-hearted master gives his servant
Who toils much for him, and a god also fosters the work,   65
As he fosters for me too this work at which I abide.

And so my master would have given me much, had he aged here.
But he is dead. Would that the whole race of Helen had died
On their knees, since she undid the knees of many men.
70 But that man went off for the honor of Agamemnon
Toward Ilion that abounds in horses to fight with the Trojans."
When he had said this he quickly bound his tunic with his belt
And went to the sties where the herds of pigs were shut up.
Then he took two, bore them off, and sacrificed them both.
75 He singed them and cut them up and pierced them on spits.
When he had roasted it all he brought it over to Odysseus,
Hot on the very spits, and sprinkled white barley on it,
And in a bowl made of ivy he mixed up honey-sweet wine;
He sat across from him and spoke out, urging him on:
80 "Eat now, stranger, the food that is furnished to servants,
Plain pork. But the suitors eat the fatling swine
And in their minds do not think of divine surveillance or pity,
For the blessed gods are not fond of cruel deeds;
No, they reward justice and the righteous deeds of men.
85 And even the hostile and unfriendly men that approach
The country of others, and Zeus gives booty to them,
When they fill up the ships and go to return home—
Even on their minds does a strong fear of the surveillance fall.
But these men know—they have heard some voice of a god—
Of that man's woeful death, and so they do not wish to pay
90   court
Justly, or to return to their own goods, but at their ease
They presumptuously devour his goods, and there is
No restraint. As many days and nights as there are from Zeus
I think they have never made one sacrifice, or two.
95 They presumptuously draw off the wine and waste it.
His living was unspeakably great. Not so much was there
For any of the heroes, not upon the black mainland
Or Ithaca itself. Not twenty mortals together
Have so much wealth. I shall tell you all about it myself.
There are twelve herds on the mainland, as many flocks of
100   sheep,
As many of swine and as many extensive droves of goats
That strangers pasture, and also his own herdsmen.
There are eleven extensive droves of goats here in all
That pasture at the verge, and good men watch over them.
105 Each one always brings them an animal every day,

Whichever of the well-nourished goats seems to be best.
I watch over these swine and protect them myself
And I make a good choice and send them the best of the
    swine."
So he said. The other gratefully ate meat and drank wine,
Reaching for it in silence. And he was sowing ill for the suitors. 110
But when he had dined and satisfied his heart with eating
The other filled a cup from which he drank himself and gave
    it to him
Full of wine. He took it and rejoiced in his spirit.
And speaking out to the other, he uttered wingèd words:
"My friend, who was it that bought you with his resources,   115
And he so very rich and so mighty as you say?
You say he was destroyed for the honor of Agamemnon.
Tell me, if I might somehow know him for the man he is.
Zeus knows, perhaps, and the other immortal gods,
If I might give news of having seen him; I have wandered
    much."   120
Then the swineherd, the chief of the men, answered him:
"Old man, no wanderer who came here bringing news of him
Could ever convince his wife and his dear son.
Yet anyway, wanderers who need entertainment
Tell lies, and they are not willing to speak the truth.   125
Whoever in wandering reaches the land of Ithaca
Comes to my mistress and utters deceptive stories.
She receives him, befriends him, and asks for the details,
And as she laments, the tears fall from her eyelids,
As is right for a woman when her husband has perished abroad. 130
And you too, old man, would quickly fashion a story
If someone gave you a mantle and a tunic and clothes.
By now the dogs and swift birds have probably
Torn the skin from his bones and the soul has left him,
Or fish have eaten him in the ocean and his bones   135
Are lying on a mainland wrapped over with much sand.
So he has perished there, and afterward many cares
Have been made for all his friends, most for me; I shall not
    again
Find another master so mild anywhere I go,
Not if I should reach my mother's and father's home again,   140
Where I was first born and they themselves brought me up.
Nor should I yet mourn them so much, though I do want

To see them with my eyes in my own fatherland.
But longing takes hold of me for Odysseus who is gone away.
145 I am in awe to speak his name, stranger, though he is not here.
For he loved me exceedingly and cared for me in his heart.
But I call him 'honored sir' even when he is far away."
Godly Odysseus, who had endured much, spoke to him then:
"My friend, since you wholly deny it, you do not still think
150 That man will come, and your heart is ever unbelieving;
I shall still say it, not just that way, but with an oath:
Odysseus shall return. Let me have reward for good news
Right away when that man arrives at his own halls;
Clothe me in a mantle and a tunic, lovely clothes.
155 Before then, though I need them much, I will take nothing.
Hateful to me as the gates of Hades is that man
Who yields to poverty and tells deceitful stories.
May Zeus now be my witness, first of the gods, and this guest
    table,
And the hearth of the blameless Odysseus, to which I have come.
160 Truly, all these things shall come to pass as I say.
Within the light of this very month will Odysseus be coming
    here:
While one moon is waning and another is on the rise
He will return home and do vengeance on anyone
Who here dishonors his wife and his glorious son."
165 And you addressed him in answer, swineherd Eumaeos:
"Old man, I shall not reward you for this good news,
Nor will Odysseus still come home. But at your ease,
Drink. Let us think of quite other things. Do not
Remind me of these matters. The heart in my breast
170 Is grieved when anyone mentions my beloved master.
Well, we will let the oath go, but may Odysseus
Come, as I wish myself, and Penelope wishes,
And the old man Laertes, and godlike Telemachos.
I mourn ceaselessly now for the son Odysseus fathered,
175 Telemachos. When the gods had reared him like a young tree,
And I thought among men he too would be not inferior
To his own dear father, wondrous in body and form,
Then one of the immortals hurt his mind, balanced within,
Or else some man. He went after hearsay about his father
180 To sacred Pylos. And the noble suitors lie in ambush
For him as he comes home so that out of Ithaca

The race of godlike Arkesios [1] might perish nameless.
Well, let us forget that man, whether he is captured
Or escapes, and the son of Cronos holds his hand over him.
But come now, old man, tell me about your own cares,   185
And tell me this really so I may know it well.
What men are you from? Where are your city and parents?
On what sort of ship did you come? How did sailors
Bring you to Ithaca? What men did they claim to be?
For I do not think you could have got here at all on foot."   190
Odysseus of many wiles addressed him in answer:
"All right, I shall tell you this quite truthfully.
And now a long time for the two of us might there be
Both food and sweet wine while we stayed within the hut
To feast in quiet while others performed the work: 195
Easily in that case even for an entire year
I would not come to an end of telling the cares of my heart,
All the many things I have suffered at the will of the gods.
I declare I am of the race of those who live in broad Crete,
The son of a wealthy man. And many other sons   200
Were both born and nourished in his hall, legitimate,
From his wife. A bought mother bore me, a concubine.
But Castor, son of Hylax, of whose race I declare I am,
Honored me as he did the sons rightfully born.
Then among the Cretans he was honored as a god in the land   205
For his prosperity and his wealth and his glorious sons.
But the fates of death came and carried him off
To the halls of Hades. His haughty-spirited sons
Divided his living up and cast lots for it.
Yet they gave me a very poor part and assigned me a dwelling.   210
I took a wife among men who had a large portion,
Because of my excellence, since I was not a good-for-nothing
Or a coward in battle. And now it has all left me.
Nevertheless I think if you look at the stubble
You can know what the grain was. For a great deal of distress
    holds me.   215
Ares and Athene gave me the courage and power
To break the ranks of men, whenever I picked for ambush
Excellent men, sowing evils for enemies;
Never did my bold spirit look forward to death
But I leapt forward by far the first and took with my sword   220

1. Grandfather of Odysseus.

Any man of the enemy who yielded to me in running.
Such was I in war. Labor was not dear to me
Or household-tending, that raises glorious children.
No, ships with good oars were always dear to me
225 And battles, and well-made javelins and arrows,
Woeful things, that for others are to be shuddered at.
But to me things are precious, I think, that a god put in my
    mind,
For one man delights in one task, one man in another.
Before the sons of the Achaians arrived at Troy
230 Nine times I had been a leader of men on swift-faring ships
Against alien men, and many things fell in my hands.
Of them, some satisfying things I chose, but got many
Afterwards by lot. At once my house increased, and then
I became respected and feared among the Cretans.
235 But when broad-seeing Zeus devised that hateful journey
Which has undone the knees from under many man,
Then they kept urging me and renowned Idomeneus
To lead them in ships to Ilion. There was no means
For us to refuse; the stern talk of the people held.
240 There for nine years we sons of the Achaians waged war.
In the tenth we sacked the city of Priam and went
Home in our ships, and a god scattered the Achaians.
But Zeus, the counselor, planned evil for my poor self.
A single month I remained delighting in my children
245 And my wedded wife and possessions. But then my heart
Ordered me to equip the ships well and embark
On a voyage to Egypt with my godlike companions.
I equipped nine ships, and my crew collected quickly.
For six days then my trusty companions dined with me
250 And I presented as victims many animals
To offer the gods and to prepare as dinner for themselves,
And on the seventh day, as we set off from broad Crete,
We sailed on in a fair, steadily blowing North Wind
Easily, as if down a stream. Nor did anyone
255 Give trouble on my ships, but we sat there unharmed
And without disease, and the wind and pilots steered them.
On the fifth day we came to the fair-flowing river of Egypt.
I beached my bobbing ships by the Egyptian river
And then I called upon my trusty companions
260 To remain there beside the ships and to guard the ships,

And I ordered spies to go up on places of lookout.
But they gave in to excess; relying on their own strength,
They sacked the beautiful fields of the Egyptians
At once and carried their women and infant children off.
They killed the men. And soon the noise reached the city.   265
They perceived the shouting, and at the appearance of dawn
Came on. The whole plain was filled with foot soldiers and
    horses
And the flash of bronze. Zeus, who hurls the thunderbolt,
Threw evil panic among my companions, nor could any
Bear to stay face to face; ills surrounded us on all sides.   270
Then they slaughtered many of us with the sharp bronze
And led some off alive to work for them under constraint.
But Zeus himself put the following idea
In my mind: I wish I had died and met my fate
There in Egypt, for trouble was still to welcome me.   275
I at once took the well-made helmet off my head and the shield
From my shoulders and threw the spear out of my hand.
Then I came up in front of the horses of the king.
I took his knees and kissed them. He pitied me and spared me.
He put me on the chariot and led me weeping to his home.   280
Very many men rushed upon me with ashwood spears,
Wanting to kill me, for they were angered highly.
But he held them off and showed awe for the wrath of Zeus,
Who protects strangers and gets highly incensed at evil deeds.
Then I stayed seven years there, and I gathered many   285
Goods among the Egyptian men, for they all gave me some.
But when the eighth year in its course came round for me,
Then a Phoenician man came, skilled in deceits,
A sharp dealer who had worked many evils among men.
He led me and induced me by his cunning till we came   290
To Phoenicia, where his own home and possessions lay.
There I stayed with him till the completion of the year.
But when the months and the days had been filled out
Of the year coming round again, and the seasons came on,
He put me on a seafaring ship to Libya   295
On the false plan that I should bring cargo with him,
But so that he might sell me there and get an immense price.
Though suspicious, I followed him onto the ship, by constraint.
The ship ran under a fair, steadily blowing North Wind
On the main above Crete. Then Zeus planned their destruction.   300

And when we had left Crete, no other point
Of land appeared, but just the heaven and the sea.
Then the son of Cronos halted a dark blue cloud
Over the hollow ship, and the ocean darkened beneath it;
305 Zeus at that instant thundered and threw a bolt on the ship.
The whole ship quivered, struck by the bolt of Zeus,
And it was filled with brimstone. All fell from the ship.
The men like sea crows all about the black ship
Were borne in the waves. A god took away their return.
310 Though I had many pains in my heart, Zeus himself
Put the enormous mast of the dark blue-prowed ship
Into my hands so I might still escape from distress.
Embracing it, I was carried in the destructive winds.
I was carried nine days, and on the tenth black night
315 A great rolling wave brought me near the Thesprotians' land,
Where the hero Pheidon, king of the Thesprotians,
Saved me without reward. His dear son came on me,
Overcome by cold and fatigue, and led me to his home,
Taking me by the hand till we reached his father's halls.
320 He clothed me about in garments, a mantle and tunic.
There I heard of Odysseus. That man said he had entertained
And befriended him as he was going to his fatherland.
And he showed me all the possessions Odysseus had gathered
Of bronze and of gold and of heavily wrought iron.
325 They would support each man in turn to the tenth generation,
So many were the treasures that lay in the lord's halls.
He said the man had gone to Dodona [2] in order to hear
The plan of Zeus from the lofty-leaved oak of the god
As to how he might return to the rich land of Ithaca,
330 Openly or in secret, as already he had been long away.
He swore to me personally, pouring libation in his house,
That a ship had been drawn down and companions were
    ready
Who would conduct him to his beloved fatherland.
But he sent me off first. For a ship happened to come
335 Of Thesprotians headed for Dulichion, rich in wheat.
And thither he bade them to convey me attentively
To King Akastos. But an evil plan for me pleased their minds.
That I should still come wholly to the woe of grief.
And when the seafaring ship had sailed a great way from land,

2. A shrine of Zeus.

At once they were contriving my day of slavery.   340
They took off my tunic, my mantle, and my clothes
And put another evil rag and tunic around me,
The torn one that you see yourself before your eyes.
At evening they reached the tilled fields of sunny Ithaca,
And there they tied me up on the well-timbered ship,   345
Tightly with a well-twisted cord. They themselves
Went off hastily to the strand of the sea and took dinner.
But the gods themselves bent the bonds back for me
Easily. I covered my head over with the rags,
Went down the smooth loading plank, and slid to my breast   350
Into the sea. Then I stroked through it with both hands,
Swimming. Very quickly I got out and away from them.
Then I came up where there was a copse of much-flowering
     wood
And lay crouched down. They were groaning greatly
As they wandered around. But it did not seem any good to
     them   355
To search further, and so they went back again
On board the hollow ship. And the gods themselves concealed
     me
Easily. They led me and brought me to the homestead
Of a man with knowledge. For it is still my fortune to live."
And you addressed him in answer, swineherd Eumaeos: 360
"Ah, wretched stranger, you have stirred my heart very much
As you tell the details of how you suffered and wandered.
But this I think is not in order, nor will you convince me
When you speak about Odysseus. Why does a man like you
     need
To lie fruitlessly? Well do I myself also know   365
Of my master's return, that he has been very much hated
By all the gods, as they did not subdue him among the Trojans
Or in the arms of his friends, after he had wound up the war.
Then all the Achaians would have made him a funeral mound,
And he would have won great glory for his son, too, hereafter.   370
As it is, the storm winds have snatched him off without glory.
But I myself live apart among the swine. Nor do I
Go to the city unless prudent Penelope happens
To urge me to come when a message comes from somewhere,
But then the men sit there and ask for the details,   375
Both those who grieve for the master who is gone so long

And those who enjoy devouring a livelihood scot free.
But for myself, I do not like to ask or inquire
Since the time an Aetolian cheated me with a story—
380 One who had killed a man and wandered far on the earth.
He came to my home and I embraced him in friendship.
He said he saw him among the Cretans with Idomeneus
Repairing his ships that storms had broken to pieces.
And he said he would come toward summer or harvest time
385 Bringing many possessions, with his godlike companions.
And you, much-grieved old man, since some god led you to me,
Do not blandish me or charm me at all with lies,
As I shall not respect and befriend you for that, but in fear
Of Zeus, the god of strangers, and pity for your person."
390 Odysseus of many wiles addressed him in answer:
"Surely you have an unbelieving spirit in your breast,
When I do not bring a man like you round by oath, or
      persuade you.
But come, let us make an agreement. Let the gods
Who hold Olympos be henceforth witnesses for both.
395 If your master does return to this very home,
You will dress me in clothes a mantle and a tunic and send me
On a trip to Dulichion, where I would like in my heart to be.
But if your master does not come as I say he will,
You may urge the servants to throw me from a great rock,
400 So any other beggar may shrink from deceiving."
The godly swineherd spoke out to him in answer:
"Stranger, there would surely be much honor and excellence
For me among men both at present and in after time
If when I led you to the hut and gave you a guest's gifts
405 I then should kill you and take your dear life away!
Then I might zealously pray to Zeus, son of Cronos!
But now is the time for dinner. May my companions soon
Be here inside, so we may make a tasty dinner in the hut."
In this way they addressed such words to one another.
Then did the swine approach, and the men who were
410   swineherds.
The men shut them up in their sties to go to sleep,
And an immense clamor arose from the pigs that were
      penned up.
Then the godly swineherd called to his companions:
"Bring the best swine, so I may slaughter it for the stranger

From far away. And we too may enjoy it, who have long   415
Had sorrow as we labored for the swine with shining tusks,
And other men do devour our hard work scot free."
When he had said this, he split wood with the pitiless bronze,
And they led in a very fat pig five years of age.
Then they stood it by the hearth, nor did the swineherd   420
Forget the immortals, for he had good understanding.
He began by cutting the hairs of the head off the shining-tusked
     boar,
Threw them into the fire, and prayed to all the gods
That many-minded Odysseus return to his own home.
He stood up and hit it with a chunk left from the oak he had
     split,   425
And the life left it. They cut its throat and singed it.
At once they divided it; the swineherd took a first part
From all the limbs and laid the raw pieces on the rich fat.
And he threw some in the fire, sprinkling on barley meal.
The rest of it they cut up small and pierced it on spits,   430
Roasted it carefully, and pulled it all off.
They put it in a mass on platters, and the swineherd
Stood up to carve it. He understood what was right.
Dividing it, he apportioned it all in seven parts.
One he gave with a prayer to the nymphs and to Hermes,   435
The son of Maia, and the others he distributed to each.
To Odysseus he did honor with the whole long back
Of the shining-tusked swine, and pleased his master's heart.
Odysseus of many wiles spoke out and addressed him:
"Eumaeos, would you might be as dear to Father Zeus   440
As you are to me, that you honor a man like me with good
     things!"
And you addressed him in answer, swineherd Eumaeos:
"Eat, marvelous stranger, and enjoy these things
That are here. A god gives one thing and lets another go
As he wishes in his heart. For he can do all things."   445
So he said, and offered the first parts to the ever-living gods.
He poured sparkling wine, put the cup in the hands of
     Odysseus,
The sacker of cities, and sat down with his own share.
Mesaulios passed bread to them, a man that the swineherd
Had got by himself alone while his master was gone,   450
Secretly from his mistress and the old man Laertes;

He bought him from the Taphians with his own resources.
They stretched forth their hands to the food that was spread
  out ready,
But when they had eaten their fill of food and drink
455 Mesaulios took the bread off, and they hurried
Away for sleep, satiated with bread and meat.
A bad night came on, dark of a moon. Zeus rained
All night, and a great watery West Wind steadily blew.
Odysseus spoke to them, testing the swineherd out,
460 If he would take off his mantle and give it to him, or urge
Another of his companions to, since he cared much for him.
"Listen now, Eumaeos, and all you other companions,
I have a boast, and will tell a story, for crazing wine
Bids it, that sets even a man of many thoughts on
465 To sing and to laugh gently, and it drives him to dance,
And he brings out a story that would be better untold.
But since I was the first to speak up, I shall not hide it:
Would that I were in my prime and my strength were steadfast
As when we prepared and led our ambush up under Troy!
470 Odysseus led, and Menelaos, son of Atreus.
I was third leader among them. They ordered it themselves.
But when we arrived before the city and the sheer wall,
We lay around the town in the thick brushwood
Among the reeds and the marsh, crouching under our armor,
475 And as the North Wind fell off, a bad night came,
A freezing one. And snow came from above like hoar frost,
Cold, and ice clustered all around on our shields.
Then the other men all had mantles and tunics.
They slept securely, covering their shoulders with their shields.
480 But I, when I went, left my mantle with my companions,
Foolishly, since I thought I would not freeze in any case.
I went along with only my shield and a shining apron.
When it was the third part of night and the stars had gone past,
I shouted out then to Odysseus, who was near at hand,
485 Nudging him with my elbow. He hearkened quickly:
'Zeus-born son of Laertes, Odysseus of many devices,
I shall not be long among the living, but the cold
Overcomes me. I have no mantle. Some god tricked me
To have just one tunic. And there is no way out any longer.'
490 So I said. And then he had this purpose in his heart,
Such a man was he for deliberation and fighting.

Speaking in a little voice, he addressed a speech to me:
'Silence now, lest someone else of the Achaians hear you.'
And he held his head on his elbow and said his speech:
'Listen, friends, a godly dream came to me in my sleep.   495
We have come too far from the ships. Would there were
    someone
To go tell Agamemnon, son of Atreus, shepherd of the people,
That he might urge on more of the men from beside the
    ships.'
So he said. Then Thoas rose up, son of Andraemon,
Hastily. And he took his purple mantle off   500
And ran off to the ships. In that man's clothing I
Lay gladly. Then Dawn of the golden throne appeared.
So would I were now in my prime and my strength steadfast!
Then might someone in the swineherds' lodge give me a
    mantle,
For two reasons: friendship and respect for a good man.   505
Now men dishonor me for the bad clothes I wear on my skin."
Then you addressed him in answer, swineherd Eumaeos:
"Old man, the story is excellent that you have told.
And no profitless word did you speak improperly.
So you shall not want for clothes or for anything else,   510
Of the things that befit a long suffering suppliant one meets—
For now. But at dawn you shall bundle your own rags on,
As there are not many mantles and changes of tunic
To put on here, just a single one for each mortal man.
But when the beloved son of Odysseus comes,   515
He himself will give you clothes, a mantle and tunic,
And will send you wherever your heart and spirit bid."
When he had said this, he rose up and made a bed for him
Near the fire. And on it he threw skins of sheep and goats.
There Odysseus lay down. He threw on him a mantle   520
Great and thick, which lay beside him as a change
To put on when any terrible storm arose.
So Odysseus slept. And beside him those young men
Were sleeping. But to lie there was not pleasing
To the swineherd, to be sleeping apart from the swine.   525
He went out to go and get ready. Odysseus was pleased
That the man took care of his livelihood when he was away.
First the man threw a sharp sword around his stout shoulders
And put on a very thick mantle that warded off wind.

530 Then he put on the fleece from a great well-nourished goat.
He grasped a sharp javelin, a defense against dogs and men,
And he went on to lie down where the shining-tusked swine
    slept
Beneath a hollow rock under shelter from the North Wind.

XV

Pallas Athene had gone to Lacedemon of the broad dancing-
    place
To remind the illustrious son of great-hearted Odysseus
About his return and to urge him to go back.
She found Telemachos and the noble son of Nestor
Lying in the forecourt of glorious Menelaos.   5
The son of Nestor was overcome with soft sleep,
But sweet sleep did not hold Telemachos. In his heart
Concern for his father kept him awake through the ambrosial
    night.
Bright-eyed Athene stood close to him and addressed him:
"Telemachos, it is no longer good to wander far from home,   10
And leave behind in your home the possessions and the men,
Presumptuous as they are, lest they divide and devour
All your possessions and you have gone on a fruitless journey.
But right away urge Menelaos who is good at the war cry,
To send you on, so you may still find your blameless mother
    at home.   15
For already her father and her kinsmen are calling on her
To marry Eurymachos. He outdoes all the other
Suitors with presents and greatly augments the bridal gifts.
Let her bear no goods from your home against your will.
You know what sort of heart there is in a woman's breast.   20
She wishes to increase the house of the man she weds;
She no longer remembers or inquires of her former
Children or of her dear wedded husband who is dead.
But you should go yourself, and turn each piece of property
Over to whichever of the maids appears best to you,   25
Till the gods reveal to you an illustrious wife.
I will say something else to you; store it in your mind.
The best of the suitors lie ready in ambush against you
In the strait between Ithaca and the rugged Samê,
Wanting to kill you before you reach your fatherland.   30

But I do not think that will be: sooner shall the earth contain
Some one of the suitors who devour your livelihood.
But keep your well-made ship far from the islands
And sail by night as well. Whoever of the immortals
35 Guards and protects you will sent a breeze behind you.
And when you arrive at the first shore of Ithaca
Send your ship on to the city, and all your companions,
But first of all go on up yourself to the swineherd
Who is guardian of your swine, and kindly disposed to you also.
40 Rest the night there. And send him on inside the city
To give the message to the prudent Penelope
That you are safe for her and have arrived from Pylos."
And when she had said this, she went off to tall Olympos.
Then he woke the son of Nestor out of his sweet sleep,
45 Nudging him with his foot, and addressed a speech to him:
"Wake, Peisistratos, son of Nestor! Lead the single-hooved
    horses,
And harness them to the chariot, so we may hurry away."
Then Peisistratos, son of Nestor, replied to him:
"Telemachos, though we press on our way, we cannot
50 Drive through the dusky night. Soon it will be dawn,
But wait till the hero, son of Atreus, spear-famed Menelaos
Has brought the gifts and put them on the chariot
And has addressed us with gentle words and sent us off.
For a guest remembers all of his days the man
55 Who has received him as a guest and shown friendliness."
So he said, and at once Dawn of the golden throne came.
Menelaos, good at the war cry, came up close to them
When he had got out of bed from beside the fair-haired Helen.
And when the beloved son of Odysseus noticed him,
60 The hero hurried and put the glistening tunic on
Over his skin and threw a great mantle on his stout shoulders.
Telemachos, beloved son of godly Odysseus,
Went outside, stood beside him, and addressed him:
"Zeus-nourished Menelaos, son of Atreus, chief of the people,
65 Send me off right away to my dear fatherland,
For already my heart is longing to return home."
Then Menelaos, good at the war cry, answered him:
"Telemachos, I shall not hold you back here a long time,
Wanting to return as you do. I would resent another
70 Who, receiving a guest, acted excessively friendly

Or excessively hostile. All things are better when in measure.
It is equally bad when a man urges a guest to go off
Unwillingly, and when he holds back one who strains to go.
One must welcome a guest who stays, send one off who wishes.
Well, wait till I have brought the lovely gifts and put them   75
On the chariot, till your eyes behold them, and I tell the
    women
To make dinner in the halls out of the abundance inside.
It is glory, splendor, and refreshment all together
For men, after dining, to go far on the unbounded earth.
If you would like to wind through Hellas and middle Argos,   80
So that I should go with you, I will yoke up horses for you;
And lead you to the cities of men. No one will send us off
The way we are, but will give us some one gift at least to carry,
Some sort of cauldron of good bronze or a basin
Or a pair of mules or a golden libation cup."   85
Sound-minded Telemachos addressed him in answer:
"Zeus-nourished Menelaos, son of Atreus, chief of the people,
I would rather go right now to our home. For I did not
Leave a guard behind for my possessions when I went.
I fear I may perish myself in seeking my godlike father   90
Or have some noble treasure perish from my halls."
And when Menelaos, good at the war cry, heard him
He at once called to his wife and his serving women
To make dinner in the halls out of the abundance inside.
Eteoneus, son of Boethoüs, came up close to him   95
When he got out of bed, as the man did not live far from him.
Menelaos, good at the war cry, told him to kindle a fire
And to roast some meat. The other heard and did not disobey.
And he himself went off to his fragrant chamber,
Not alone, but Helen went with him, and Megapenthes.   100
And when they had reached the place where the treasures lay,
The son of Atreus took out a two-handled cup
And ordered his son Megapenthes to carry a mixing bowl
Of silver. And Helen took her stand alongside the coffers,
Where there were all the embroidered robes she had made
    herself.   105
Helen, godlike among women, picked one up and brought it,
The one that was largest and loveliest in embroidery.
It shone like a star; it lay beneath all the rest.
They went on further through the house till they reached

110 Telemachos. And blond Menelaos addressed him:
"Telemachos, may Zeus, Hera's loud-thundering husband,
Fulfill for you the return you desire in your mind.
And of the gifts that lie stored as keepsakes in my house
I will give you the one that is loveliest and of highest worth.
115 I shall give you a well-fashioned mixing bowl. It is all
Of silver, and its rim is finished round with gold,
The work of Hephaistos; the hero Phaidimos gave it,
King of the Sidonians, when his house took me in
As I had returned that far. I would like to give it to you."
120 When he had said this, the hero, son of Atreus, put
The two-handled cup in his hands, and stout Megapenthes
Carried the shining mixing bowl out and set it before him,
The silver one. Helen of the fair cheeks stood alongside
With the robe in her hands; she said her speech right out:
125 "'I, too, give you a gift, dear child, this remembrance
From the hands of Helen for your own wife to wear at the
     time
Of your lovely marriage. And until then, let it lie
In the hall with your dear mother. And may you come, I pray,
Rejoicing to your well-built home and your fatherland."
When she had said this, she put it in his hands. He took it and
130   rejoiced.
The hero Peisistratos took the things and put them
In the wagon box, and he marveled in his heart at them all.
Blond-headed Menelaos led them to his house.
And they took their places in seats and in armchairs.
135 A handmaid poured water from a pitcher she was carrying,
A lovely golden one, over into a silver basin,
For washing the hands; she set up a polished table alongside.
A respected housekeeper served bread she was carrying,
Laying out many dishes, gracious with the provisions.
Near her, the son of Boethoüs carved meat and served it in
140   portions,
And the son of glorious Menelaos poured the wine.
They stretched forth their hands to the food that was laid out
     ready
But when they had taken their fill of food and drink,
Then Telemachos and the glorious son of Nestor
145 Hitched the horses up, mounted the inlaid chariot,
And drove out of the forecourt and resounding portico.

With them went blond Menelaos, the son of Atreus,
Holding in his right hand the mind-honeying wine
In a gold cup, so both might pour libation and go.
He stood before the horses and spoke with a pledging gesture: 150
"Farewell, young men. And to Nestor, shepherd of the people,
Give greetings. To me he was always mild as a father
While we sons of the Achaians waged war in Troy."
Then sound-minded Telemachos answered him:
"All this that you say, you who are nourished by Zeus,   155
We shall certainly tell that man when we arrive.
Would that thus, returning to Ithaca and finding
Odysseus at home, I might tell him how I come from you
As one who got all your friendship and also bear many noble
     treasures."
A bird flew to the right of him, as he was speaking,   160
An eagle bearing a huge, bright goose in his claws,
A tame one from the courtyard. The men and the women
Followed them shrieking. He came up close to them
And rushed off to the right before the horses. When they saw it,
They rejoiced, and the spirit was warmed in all their minds.   165
Peisistratos, son of Nestor, began speaking to them:
"Consider, Zeus-nourished Menelaos, chief of the people,
Whether a god has shown this portent to the two of us or to
     you."
So he said, and Menelaos, dear to Ares, pondered
So that he might give a proper judgment when he had thought.   170
Helen of the long gown began speaking before he could:
"Listen to me, and I shall prophesy the way the immortals
Have put it in my heart, and how I think it will end.
Just as this bird seized the goose reared in our home
When he came from the mountain where his descent and his
     birth are,   175
So Odysseus who has suffered many ills and wandered much
Will return homeward and do vengeance. Or else already
He is at home and breeds evil for all the suitors."
Then sound-minded Telemachos answered her:
"May Zeus, Hera's thundering husband, make it so.   180
And then, even there, I should pray to you as to a god."
He spoke and lashed the whip at the two horses. They swiftly
Rushed to the plain, pressing on through the city.
All day they shook the yoke, holding it up on either side.

185 The sun went down and all the ways were shadowed.
They arrived at Pherai to the home of Diocles,
Son of Ortilochos, whom Alpheus sired as his son.
There they rested at night, and he gave them the gifts of a guest.
And when the early-born, rosy-fingered dawn appeared,
190 They yoked up the horses and mounted the inlaid chariot
And drove out of the forecourt and resounding portico.
He whipped them to go, and both flew on, not unwilling.
Soon thereupon they reached the sheer citadel of Pylos.
Then Telemachos addressed the son of Nestor:
195 "Son of Nestor, will you promise me, if you can, to carry out
What I ask? We declare we are guest friends in unbroken line
Through our fathers' friendship. And we are the same age.
This trip will bring us to greater congeniality.
You who are nourished by Zeus, do not carry me on past the
     ship,
200 But leave me there, lest the old man keep me unwilling
In his house, wanting to befriend me. I must arrive quicker."
So he said, and the son of Nestor deliberated in his heart
How he might promise him this and duly carry it out.
And thus it seemed to him to be best as he thought about it.
205 He turned the horses to the swift ship and the strand of the sea
And unloaded the beautiful gifts on the ship's stern,
The clothing and the gold Menelaos had given him.
Then urging him on, he uttered wingèd words:
"Board quickly now and call all your companions,
210 Before I reach home and announce it to the old man.
For this I know well in my mind and in my heart,
How overbearing his heart is. He will not let you go,
But he would come here to invite you himself. I think
He would not go back empty handed, but still would be very
     angry."
215 When he had said this, he drove the fair-maned horses back
To the town of Pylos and rapidly reached his home.
But Telemachos urged his companions on and called them:
"Put the gear in order, my companions, on the black ship,
And let us get on board ourselves, so we may press on the
     journey."
220 So he said, and they listened to him and obeyed him.
At once they got on board and took their seats at the oarlocks.
So he busied himself, prayed, and sacrificed to Athene

At the stern of the ship. And a man came up close to him,
An alien who had killed a man and was fleeing from Argos,
A seer. He was descended from the race of Melampos   225
Who dwelt once long ago in Pylos, the mother of sheep,
A rich man who dwelt among the Pylians in a very large house.
But then he reached the country of others, fleeing from his
     fatherland
And from great-hearted Neleus, noblest man of the living,
Who held as many goods by force, till the completion   230
Of the year. The first one, meanwhile, in the halls of Phylacos
Was bound in a harsh bond, having suffered strong pains
For the daughter of Neleus and for the deep madness
That Fury, the hard-smiting goddess, had put in his mind.
Still, he fled from fate and he drove the lowing cattle   235
To Pylos from Phylace. He paid the godlike Neleus
With a wretched deed and brought the woman for his brother
To the halls. And then he went to the land of other men,
To horse-nourishing Argos. There it was fated for him
To dwell while ruling over many of the Argives.   240
Then he married a wife and set up a high-roofed house,
And had Antiphates and Mantios, mighty sons.
Antiphates fathered great-spirited Oikles;
Oikles had Amphiaraos, rouser of the people,
Whom aegis-bearing Zeus loved in his heart and Apollo   245
Loved with all affection. Still, he did not reach the threshold of
     age,
But perished in Thebes on account of gifts to a woman.
The sons born to him were Alcmaeon and Amphilochos.
And Mantios fathered Polypheides and Kleitos,
But Dawn of the golden throne seized Kleitos away   250
On account of his beauty, that he might be with the immortals,
And Apollo made high-spirited Polypheides a prophet,
By far the best of mortals, after Amphiaraos died.
He migrated to Hyperesia in anger at his father,
Where he dwelt and prophesied to all mortal men.   255
This man's son came up, whose name was Theoclymenos,
And stood close to Telemachos. He found him
Pouring a libation and praying by the swift black ship,
And speaking out to him, he uttered wingèd words:
"My friend, since I find you sacrificing in this place   260
I pray you by the burnt offerings, by the god, and then

By your own head and by the companions who follow you,
To tell me unerringly what I ask; do not hide it.
What men are you from? Where are your city and parents?"
265 Then sound-minded Telemachos answered him:
"Indeed I shall speak to you, friend, quite truthfully.
My descent is from Ithaca, my father is Odysseus,
If he ever was. He has already died by a woeful death.
So now I have taken companions and a black ship
270 And come to find out about my father who is gone so long."
And then the godly Theoclymenos spoke to him:
"I have gone from my fatherland too, having killed a man
Of my tribe. He has many kinsmen and relatives
In horse-nourishing Argos; they rule the Achaians mightily.
275 Escaping from them, I flee death and black fate,
Since it is now my lot to wander among men.
Do put me on your ship, since as a fugitive I beseech you,
So they may not kill me. I believe I am pursued."
Then sound-minded Telemachos answered him:
"Since you wish to be on the balanced ship, I shall not push you
280 off.
Come, you shall be befriended there, with what we have."
When he had said this, he took his bronze spear from him
And put it along on the deck of the bobbing ship.
And the man himself got on board the seafaring ship.
285 Then he sat him down on the stern and at his side he sat
Theoclymenos. And they loosed the stern cables.
Telemachos called to his companions and urged them
To take hold of the gear. And they hastily obeyed.
They stood a fir-wood mast in the hollow mast block;
290 They raised it up, and with forestays they made it fast.
Then they hauled up the white sails with well-plaited oxhide
    ropes.
Bright-eyed Athene sent on a driving breeze for them,
Rushing rapidly through the air so the ship might soon
Arrive as it ran over the salt water of the sea.
295 They went past the Springs and the fair-flowing Chalcis.
The sun went down and all the ways were shadowed.
She came close to Pheai drawn on by the breeze of Zeus,
And passed godly Elis, where the Epeians rule.
And then he drove it on forward to the Sharp Islands,
300 Wondering whether he should flee death or be taken.

Meanwhile, both Odysseus and the godly swineherd
Were dining in the hut. The other men dined with them.
But when they had taken their fill of food and drink
Odysseus addressed them, trying the swineherd out,
Whether he would still kindly befriend him and ask him to stay 305
There in the fold, or would urge him on to the city:
"Listen now, Eumaeos, and all you other companions,
I am longing to go off to the town at dawn
To beg, so I may not wear down you and your companions.
But advise me well and send a good guide along with me   310
Who may lead me there. I myself from necessity
Shall stray to the city to try to get a cup and a loaf.
And when I come to the dwelling of godly Odysseus,
I would like to give a message to prudent Penelope
And mingle with the presumptuous suitors, to see   315
If they who have countless dishes give me a dinner.
Right away in their midst I could do whatever service they
    wished.
I shall speak out to you; put it in your mind and hear me:
Through the favor of the runner Hermes, who provides
Grace and glory for the actions of all men,   320
No other mortal could ever rival my service
At kindling a fire and splitting up dry wood,
At carving and roasting and pouring out wine,
The sort of service humble men do for noble ones."
Greatly disturbed, you spoke to him, swineheard Eumaeos: 325
"Alas, stranger, what is this thought that has come about
In your mind? You must surely long to die on the spot
If you wish to enter the company of the suitors,
Whose presumption and might reaches iron heaven.
Not men of your sort are the servants under them,   330
But young men, clothed well in mantles and in tunics,
Perpetually sleek on their heads and fair of face,
The ones who serve them. And their well-polished tables
Are loaded down with bread and with meats and with wine.
But stay, no one is troubled at your being here,   335
Not I or any other of the companions who are with me.
But when the beloved son of Odysseus comes,
He will clothe you in garments, a mantle and a tunic,
And he will send you wherever your heart and spirit bid."
Then godlike Odysseus, who had suffered much, answered him: 340

"Eumaeos, would that you might be as dear to father Zeus
As to me, that you stop me from straying and from dire woe.
There is nothing worse for mortal man than wandering.
But for the cursed belly's sake men have evil cares,
345 Anyone that straying and trouble and pain come upon—.
Now, since you hold me back and bid me, as I am, to stay,
Come, tell me about the mother of godly Odysseus,
And the father whom he left on the threshold of old age when
   he went.
Are they perchance still living under the rays of the sun,
350 Or are they already dead and in the halls of Hades?"
Then the swineherd addressed him, a chief of the men:
"All right, stranger, I shall tell you that quite truthfully:
Laertes is still alive; he forever prays to Zeus
That the spirit may waste from his limbs in his own halls.
355 He mourns terribly for his son who is gone away
And for his wise wedded wife who, when she perished,
Brought the greatest grief on him and put him in raw old age.
She did perish for grief over her renowned son
By a miserable death, and may no one who dwells here die
360 That way who is kind to me and acts in a kindly way.
And so as long as that woman lived, even though she grieved,
I always liked to ask and inquire about her,
Because she brought me up along with long-gowned Ktimene,
Her goodly daughter, whom she bore youngest of her children.
365 I was reared along with her; she honored me little less.
But when both of us arrived at youth that is full of love,
They married her off in Samê, and they took countless gifts,
But me she clothed in a mantle and a tunic, clothes
That were very lovely, gave me sandals for my feet
And sent me off to the fields. But she loved me much in her
370   heart.
As it is, I am now deprived of these things, Yet for me
The blessed gods foster the work at which I abide.
From them have I eaten and drunk and given to respected men.
And of the mistress there is nothing pleasant to be heard,
375 Neither word nor deed, since an evil has fallen on the house,
These presumptuous men. The servants greatly miss
Speaking in their mistress' presence and hearing tidbits,
And eating and drinking, and then carrying something off
To the fields, the things that always warm servants' hearts."

Odysseus of many wiles addressed him in answer: 380
"Well, swineherd Eumaeos, what a little one you were
When you wandered far from your parents and your fatherland!
But come, tell me this, and speak quite truthfully:
Was the broad-streeted city of that people destroyed
In which your father and your queenly mother were dwelling,   385
Or while you were alone with cattle or with sheep
Did hostile men take you in ships and bring you for sale
To the home of this man, and he gave a worthy price?"
Then the swineherd addressed him, the chief of the men:
"Stranger, since you ask me and inquire of these matters,   390
Listen in silence now, and take pleasure; drink wine
While you are sitting. These nights are immense. One can sleep
And one can listen if he enjoys it. There is no need
To lie down before it is time. And much sleep is a weariness.
As for the others, let any man leave and go to sleep   395
By what the heart and the spirit bid, and when dawn appears
Let him eat and follow the swine that are the master's;
But let us two be in the hut drinking and dining,
And we shall take pleasure in one another's sad sorrows
As we recall them; for a man takes pleasure even in pains,   400
One who has suffered very much and wandered much.
And I will tell you this of which you ask and inquire.
There is a certain island called Syria, as you may have heard,
Above Ortygia where the turnings of the sun are.
It is not very populous, and yet it is good,   405
Rich in cattle and sheep, full of wine, with much grain.
Poverty never comes to the land, nor any other
Disease exists there that is sad for wretched mortals.
But when the tribes of men grow old in the city
Apollo of the silver bow comes with Artemis   410
And slays them by visiting them with his soothing shafts.
In that place are two cities. They are wholly divided asunder.
My father used to rule as the king over both of them,
Ktesios, son of Ormenos, who resembles the immortals.
There the Phoenicians came, men who are famous for ships,   415
Sharp dealers, who brought in a black ship countless trinkets.
There was a Phoenician woman in my father's house,
Lovely and tall and skilled at excellent tasks.
The very wily Phoenicians deceived her.

One lay with her first, as she was washing clothes by the hollow
420   ship,
In the bed and in affection which deceives the minds
Of womankind, even one who is good in what she does.
Then he asked her who she was and where she was from,
And she at once pointed out my father's high-roofed house.
425   'I declare I am from Sidon that is full of bronze,
And I am the daughter of Arybas, a man of overflowing wealth,
But Taphian men, pirates, snatched me away
As I was coming from the fields. They brought me here and
      sold me
To the home of this man. And he gave a worthy price.'
430   Then the man who had secretly lain with her said to her:
'Well then, would you follow along with us back to your home,
So you may see the high-roofed house of your father and mother,
And themselves? For they still exist, and are called wealthy.'
Then the woman spoke to him and answered with a speech:
435   'This too, might come about, sailors, if you are willing
To pledge me an oath and take me back home safe and sound.'
So she said, and they all swore an oath as she asked.
But when they had sworn and had completed the oath,
The woman addressed them again and answered with a speech:
440   'Keep silence, now, and let none of your company
Speak out to me as he comes upon me in the street
Or at the well, perhaps; lest someone go to the house
And tell the old man, and when he learns he bind me
In a hard binding and devise destruction against you.
But keep my words in your mind; hurry your buying for the
445   journey,
And when the ship gets filled up with the goods of life,
Let one quickly come with a message for me to the house.
For I shall bring gold, too, whatever comes to my hand.
And I would willingly give other things, too, as fare,
450   For I am rearing the son of this nobleman in his halls.
Such a clever one he is, who runs along when I go outdoors.
I might bring him into the ship, and he would gain for you
A boundless price if you brought him to alien men.'
When she had said this, she went off to the lovely home.
455   They remained there with us for an entire year
And traded to get many goods in the hollow ship.
When the hollow ship was loaded for them to go,

They sent a messenger to give the woman word.
He came, a very shrewd man, to the home of my father
Bearing a gold chain strung round with amber beads.   460
The serving maids in the hall and my queenly mother
Felt it with their hands and looked at it with their eyes
And offered his price. He nodded to the woman in silence.
When he had nodded, he went off to the hollow ship.
She took me by the hand and led me from the house outdoors.   465
In the forecourt she found the cups and the tables
Of the men who attended on my father, banqueting.
They were gone to the session and assembly of the district.
At once she concealed three tankards under her bosom
And bore them off. I followed in my thoughtlessness.   470
The sun went down and all the ways were shadowed.
We went swiftly and arrived at the famous harbor
Where there was a swift-sailing ship of the Phoenician men.
They boarded it then and sailed on the watery ways,
When they had boarded us both. And Zeus sent on a breeze.   475
For six days we sailed alike by night and by day.
But when Zeus, the son of Cronos, added the seventh day,
Artemis, who pours forth arrows, struck the woman,
And she crashed as she fell in the hold like a tern of the sea,
And they threw her out to become the prey of seals   480
And fishes. But I was left grieving in my heart.
The wind and the water carried and brought them near Ithaca,
Where Laertes bought me with his resources.
In that way did I see this country with my eyes."
Then Zeus-born Odysseus answered him with a speech: 485
"Eumaeos, you have stirred the heart very much in my
   breast
As you tell the details of the pain you suffered in your heart.
But Zeus has provided good for you along with evil
When, having suffered much, you reached the home of a man
Who was mild, and who furnished you with food and drink   490
Kindly. And you live a good life. But as for me,
I reach here after wandering to many cities of men."
And so they told such stories to one another.
And the two of them did not sleep much time, but a little.
For soon the fair-throned Dawn came on. Telemachos'
   companions
                                                            495
At the mainland, slacked their sails, and took the mast down

Speedily, and pulled the ship to the mooring with the oars.
They threw out the anchor stones and tied the stern cables.
They themselves got out at the surf of the sea,
500 And they prepared a dinner and mixed sparkling wine.
But when they had taken their fill of food and drink,
Sound-minded Telemachos began speaking to them:
"You men, bring the black ship over now toward the town,
And I myself shall hurry to the fields and the herdsmen.
I shall go to the town at evening when I have seen my own
505   lands.
And at dawn I shall provide for you as the journey's pay
A good banquet of meat and of wine sweet to drink."
Then godlike Theoclymenos addressed him:
"But where shall I head, dear child? To what man's house
510 Shall I go, of those who rule over rocky Ithaca,
Or shall I go straight to your mother's house and yours?"
Then sound-minded Telemachos answered him:
"In another case I myself should advise you to go
To our house, for there is no lack of hospitality. Still,
515 It would be worse for you, since I am gone, and my mother
Will not see you. She does not appear often in the house
To the suitors, but apart from them weaves a web in her
    room.
But I shall tell you about another man you may go to:
Eurymachos, noble son of skillful Polybos,
520 Whom the Ithacans look upon as equal to a God.
He is far the most excellent man and is the most eager
To marry my mother and have the honor of Odysseus.
But in that, Olympian Zeus who dwells in the upper air, knows
If he will bring an evil day to pass for them before the marriage."
525 A bird flew to the right of him as he was speaking,
A hawk, swift messenger of Apollo. In his claws
He was plucking a dove he held and strewing its feathers on the
    ground
Between the ship and Telemachos himself.
Theoclymenos called him aside from their companions,
530 Took his hand, and spoke right out directly to him:
"Telemachos, not without a god did that bird fly to the right.
I knew when I saw it head on it was a bird of omen.
There is no other descent more royal than yours
In the land of Ithaca. You are the strongest always."

Then sound-minded Telemachos answered him: 535
"Would that this speech, stranger, might be fulfilled.
And then you would soon know friendship and many gifts
From me, so that someone who met you would call you
    blessed."
And then he shouted to Peiraeos, his trusty companion:
"Peiraeos, son of Klytos, in all else you hearken to me   540
Most of all the companions who followed me to Pylos.
And now bring this guest for me into your house.
Befriend him kindly and honor him until I come."
Then Peiraeos, renowned for his spear, answered him:
"Telemachos, even if you stay here for a long time   545
I will conduct this man, and he shall not lack hospitality."
When he had said this, he went on the ship and called his com-
    panions
To get on board themselves and untie the stern cables.
They got on board at once and took seats at the oars.
Telemachos bound the lovely sandals beneath his feet   550
And took a valiant spear pointed with sharp bronze
From the deck of the ship. They untied the stern cables
And pushed it off and sailed to the city, as Telemachos,
The beloved son of godly Odysseus, had commanded.
His feet bore him forward fast, as he strode, till he reached   555
The farmyard where the numberless swine were, beside which
    slept
The noble swineherd whose mind was mild to his masters.

XVI

Then both Odysseus and the godly swineherd in the hut
Were preparing breakfast at dawn when they had kindled a fire,
And had sent out shepherds along with the droves of swine.
The dogs, prone to bark, fawned around Telemachos
5 And did not bark as he approached. Godly Odysseus noticed
The fawning dogs, and the sound of footsteps carried to him.
Right away to Eumaeos he uttered wingèd words:
"Eumaeos, surely some companion is coming here
Or some other acquaintance, since the dogs do not bark
10 But fawn around him. And I hear the low noise of his feet."
The speech was not yet fully said when his dear son
Was standing in the doorway. The swineherd started,
   dumbstruck.
From his hands the bowls fell that he was tending to
As he mixed the sparkling wine. He went over to his master
15 And kissed him on the head and on both lovely eyes
And both of his hands. A swelling tear fell from him,
As a father receives lovingly the dear son he sees
Coming in the tenth year from a faraway land,
His precious only son, for whom he suffered many pains;
20 So then the godly swineherd embraced and kissed all over
The godlike Telemachos, as if he had escaped from death.
And while he was sobbing he uttered wingèd words:
"Telemachos, you have come as a sweet light. I myself thought
I would never see you again when you went by ship to Pylos.
25 But come in here now, dear child, so that in my heart
I may delight to see you here inside, come afresh from
   elsewhere.
You do not often visit the shepherds and the fields,
But remain in town. Indeed, it has pleased your heart
To look upon the destructive throng of the suitors."
30 Then sound-minded Telemachos answered him:
"So it shall be, father. I have come here on your account,

So that I may see you with my eyes and hear your story
As to whether my mother stays in the halls or already
Some other man has wed her and the bed of Odysseus
Lies with foul spider webs, perhaps, deprived of bedding.   35
Then the swineherd addressed him, the chief of the men:
"Yes, long now indeed does that woman in her enduring spirit
    wait
Within your halls. And the miserable nights
And the days always waste away for her as she sheds tears."
When he had said this, he took the bronze spear from him,   40
Then he himself went in and crossed the stone threshold.
His father Odysseus yielded him a seat as he entered.
But Telemachos, for his part, checked him and spoke out:
"Sit down, stranger. We will find a seat somewhere else
In our hut. Here is a man who will furnish one."   45
So he said. The other went and sat down. Then the swineherd
Spread yellow-green brushwood beneath and fleeces on top.
And there the beloved son of Odysseus took a seat.
The swineherd offered platters of meat slices to them,
Of the roast meat that they had left from eating before.   50
And in baskets he hastily heaped up bread,
And he mixed honey-sweet wine in a bowl of ivy wood.
He himself sat down facing the godly Odysseus.
Then they stretched forth their hands to the food that was laid
    out ready,
But when they had taken their fill of food and drink,   55
Telemachos spoke out to the godly swineherd:
"Father, where did this stranger come from? How did sailors
Bring him to Ithaca? What men did they claim to be?
For I do not think he could have arrived here at all on foot."
Then you addressed him in answer, swineherd Eumaeos: 60
"Well then, my child, I shall tell you all of the truth.
He declares he is of the race of those who live in broad Crete,
And he says he has been to many cities of mortals
In his wandering, for that was the way the god spun his thread.
And now, having escaped from a ship of the Thesprotians,   65
He has come to my hut, and I hand him over to you.
Do as you wish. He declares he is a suppliant to you."
Then the sound-minded Telemachos answered him:
"Eumaeos, this speech you have spoken is distressing.

70 How indeed shall I receive the stranger in my home?
I myself am young and have not yet trusted my hands
To defend me against some man when he outrages me first.
As for my mother, the heart in her breast ponders two ways,
Either that she remain here with me and attend to the house,
75 Respecting the bed of her husband and the talk of the people,
Or that she already go at once with whichever of the Achaians
Is the best man that woos her in the halls and offers the most.
Yet, indeed, since this stranger has come to your house,
I shall clothe him in a mantle and a tunic, lovely garments.
80 I shall give him a two-edged sword and sandals for his feet,
And I shall send him wherever his heart and spirit bid.
But if you wish to, care for him and keep him in your hut.
I shall send the garments here myself and all the food
To eat, so that he will not strain you and your companions.
85 I for my part should not allow him to come there
Among the suitors, for they have too much reckless
     presumption,
Lest they mock him, and that be a dread grief to me.
It is difficult for a single man, even a mighty one,
To succeed at all against many, since they are far stronger."
90 Then godly Odysseus, who had suffered much, answered him:
"My friend, since surely it is proper for me to reply,
My own heart is torn to pieces when I hear
About the reckless deeds you say the suitors contrive
In your halls, against the will of a man as good as yourself.
95 Tell me, are you willingly subjected or do the people
Despise you in the district, yielding to the voice of a god?
Or do you blame your kinsmen, those on whom a man
Should rely for fighting, even if a great quarrel arises?
Would that, with this heart of mine, I were as young as you,
100 Or the child of excellent Odysseus, or that the man himself
Should come roaming; for there is still a share of hope.
And may an alien mortal at once cut off my head
If I did not become a curse to all of those men,
As I come into the hall of Odysseus, son of Laertes.
105 And if they should beat me, a single man, by their numbers,
I would rather be killed in my own halls and die
Than perpetually to look upon these sorry deeds:
Strangers being maltreated, and men disgracefully
Dragging the servant women through the lovely halls,

And wine being drawn off, and men eating bread   110
Rashly this way, and limitlessly, acts without end."
Then sound-minded Telemachos answered him:
"Very well, stranger, I shall speak to you truthfully.
The whole district is not hostile or enraged against me,
Nor do I blame any kinsmen, those on whom a man   115
Should rely for fighting, even if a great quarrel arises;
For thus did the son of Cronos make ours a single line.
Arkesios sired Laertes, a single son,
And his father sired Odysseus alone; Odysseus sired me
Alone, and left me in the halls, and got from me no joy.   120
So now there are countless enemies in the house.
All the noblemen who rule over the islands,
Dulichion and Samê and wooded Zacynthos,
And all those who are masters in craggy Ithaca,
Are paying court to my mother and wearing down my home,   125
She neither refuses the hateful wedding nor can she
Make an end of it. But they are wasting my home away
As they devour it. Soon they will tear me to pieces myself.
Well, all these matters lie in the laps of the gods.
Go quickly, father, to constant Penelope.   130
Tell her I am safe and have arrived from Pylos.
I myself shall remain here, but you come back here
When you have told just her. Let no one else of the Achaians
Find out about it, for many devise evils against me."
And you addressed him in answer, swineherd Eumaeos: 135
"I know, I see; you say this to an understanding man.
But come, tell me this, and speak out truthfully,
Should I go or not by the same path to tell Laertes,
That wretched man, who, while he grieved much for Odysseus,
Used to oversee the fields, and with the servants in his house   140
Ate and drank when the heart in his breast bade him to.
But now from the time you were gone in the ship to Pylos,
They say he no longer eats and drinks the way he did,
Nor looks over the fields, but with groaning and wailing
He sits and laments, and the flesh shrinks round his bones."   145
Then sound-minded Telemachos answered him:
"That is the more painful. Still, let us leave him, though we are
     grieved,
For if all things were somehow free for mortals to choose,
We should first choose the day of my father's return.

150 But you, when you have told the news, come back and do not
     Wander in the fields after that man. But tell my mother
     To send the housekeeper on as soon as possible,
     Secretly. And she may announce it to the old man."
     He spoke, and roused the swineherd. He took sandals in hand,
155 Bound them under his feet, and went to the city; nor did
     The swineherd Eumaeos escape Athene as he went from the
          lodge,
     But she came up close. She likened her body to a woman's,
     Lovely and tall and skilled in excellent tasks.
     She stood and appeared to Odysseus at the hut doorway,
160 Nor did Telemachos see her face to face or perceive her.
     For in no way do the gods appear clearly to all men.
     But Odysseus and the dogs saw her. They did not bark;
     They slunk with a whimpering to the other side of the lodge.
     She signaled with her eyebrows. Godly Odysseus perceived it
165 And went out of the room along the great farmyard wall
     And stood in her presence. Athene addressed him:
     "Zeus-born son of Laertes, Odysseus of many devices,
     Now is the time, say the word to your son, and do not conceal it
     So you may both work death and destruction on the suitors,
170 And come to the renowned city together. Nor shall I
     Myself be long from you, as I desire to fight."
     Athene spoke and touched him with a golden wand.
     At first she placed a cloak and a well-washed tunic
     About his shoulders, increased his body and his youth.
175 His skin became dark again, and his cheeks filled out,
     And the beard around his chin turned into dark blue.
     When she had done this, she went back again, and Odysseus
     Went into the hut. His dear son marveled at him.
     He cast his eyes the other way, alarmed lest it be a god.
180 And he spoke out to him and uttered wingèd words:
     "You appear other to me, stranger, than a moment before.
     You have other garments, and your skin is not as it was.
     You must be some one of the gods who possess broad heaven.
     Well, be gracious, so we may give pleasing sacrifices
185 And well-made golden gifts to you. Be sparing toward us."
     Then godly Odysseus, who had suffered much, answered him:
     "I am not any god. Why liken me to immortals?
     But I am your father for whose sake you are grieving
     And suffer many pains, receiving the assaults of men."

When he had said this, he kissed his son and sent a tear to the
   ground   190
Off his cheeks. Before, he had always held them back without
   blenching.
Telemachos—he did not yet believe him to be his father—
Answered him right away with words and addressed him:
"You surely are not my father Odysseus, but some god
Enchants me, so that I may grieve and lament still more;   195
For in no way would a mortal man in his own mind
Devise these things, unless a god came by in person
Who might easily if he wished make one young or old.
Just recently you were an old man and had on sorry clothes.
And now you resemble the gods who possess broad heaven."   200
Odysseus of many wiles addressed him in answer:
"Telemachos, it is not seemly when your father is within
To wonder exceedingly and to be amazed.
No other Odysseus, indeed, shall ever come to you here.
I am the very man; suffering evils, wandering much,   205
I have come in the twentieth year to my fatherland.
And now this is the work of the forager Athene,
Who has made of me what she wishes, for she can do that,
Sometimes in the semblance of a beggar and sometimes
That of a young man who has lovely clothes on his skin.   210
It is easy for the gods who possess broad heaven
To glorify a mortal man or to disfigure him."
When he had said this he sat down. Telemachos
Embraced his noble father and moaned, shedding tears.
In both of them there arose a longing for lamentation.   215
They wailed piercingly and more incessantly than birds,
Sea eagles or falcons with hooked claws whose children
Farmers have snatched off before they were fully fledged.
So they lamented and shed tears from under their eyelids,
And the light of the sun would have gone down on their
   moaning   220
If Telemachos had not at once spoken out to his father:
"In what kind of a ship, dear father, did sailors
Bring you to Ithaca? Who did they claim to be?
For I do not believe you reached here at all on foot."
Then godly Odysseus, who had suffered much, addressed him: 225
"Well then, my child, to you I shall speak out the truth.
The Phaeacians, famous for ships, brought me, who escort

Other men too, whenever anyone reaches their people.
They brought me sleeping in a swift ship on the ocean,
230 Put me down at Ithaca, and gave me glorious gifts,
Bronze and gold in abundance and woven clothing;
These things now lie in caverns, by the will of the gods.
Now I have come here at Athene's instigations,
So we may plan about slaughter for our enemies.
235 Come now, speak out, and number the suitors for me,
So I may know how many men they are, and what sort.
Then as I deliberate in my own blameless heart
I may consider whether we can oppose them ourselves,
Alone without others, or shall seek for others."
240 Then sound-minded Telemachos spoke to him in answer:
"Father, I have always heard of your great renown
For being a skillful fighter with your hands and prudent in
counsel.
But you speak of something enormous. Awe holds me. It could
not
Be that two men might fight against so many stout men.
245 Truly, there are not ten of the suitors or twenty only,
But far more. You shall soon know their number here:
Out of Dulichion there are fifty-two
Chosen young men, and six servants to follow them.
Out of Samê there are four and twenty mortal men;
250 Out of Zacynthos there are twenty young men of the Achaians;
Out of Ithaca herself, twelve, all of the best;
And Medon is with them as herald, and the godly singer,
And a pair of servants who are skilled at carving the meat.
If we opposed all of those who are within, I fear
255 In bitterness and dread would you avenge their violence
Now that you have come. But if you can, think of some
defender;
Take thought for someone well disposed to defend us."
Then godly Odysseus, who had suffered much, addressed him:
"I shall tell you, then, mark it well and listen to me,
260 And consider whether Athene with Father Zeus
Will protect us, or I shall think up some other defender."
Then sound-minded Telemachos answered him:
"These are excellent defenders of whom you speak,
Both seated high upon the clouds, and the two of them
265 Rule over all others, both men and the immortal gods."

Then godly Odysseus, who had suffered much, addressed him:
"Those two, indeed, shall not be for a long time far
From the mighty combat, when the strength of Ares
Is put to the proof in my halls between us and the suitors.
Well now, you go on home at the appearance of dawn   270
And mingle in with the presumptuous suitors,
And the swineherd will bring me later to the town
In the semblance of a beggar, miserable and old.
And if they dishonor me in the house, let the heart
In your own breast endure it that I suffer evilly.   275
Even if they drag me by the feet through the house out the
    doors
Or throw at me with darts, look on and restrain yourself.
No, just order them to cease their foolishness,
Speaking to them with soothing words. And they will surely
Give no heed at all, because for them the fated day stands at
    hand.   280
I shall tell you another thing, and keep it in mind.
When Athene of many plans puts it in my mind,
I shall nod to you with my head, and then you yourself take
    note
How many weapons of war are lying in the halls;
Pick them up and put them in a nook of the lofty chamber,   285
All of them. And appease the suitors deceptively
With soft speeches when they miss them and ask you questions:
'I have put them out of the smoke, since they no longer look
    like those
That Odysseus once left behind when he went to Troy,
But they are befouled, so much has the smoke of the fire got to
    them.   290
And the son of Cronos, too, has put this greater thought in my
    mind:
That, perhaps, drunk with wine, you may set up a quarrel
Among you, wound one another, and disgrace the banquet
And your wooing. For iron of itself draws a man on.'
And for us alone leave two swords and two spears   295
And a pair of oxhide shields to grasp with our hands
So we may rush upon them and capture them. And then
Pallas Athene will charm them, and the counselor Zeus.
I shall tell you something else, and keep it in mind,
If you are indeed truly my own and of our blood: 300

Let no one at this time hear Odysseus is within;
Let Laertes not know it, and not the swineherd,
No one of the servants, not Penelope herself.
Let you and me alone find out the bent of the women,
305 And we shall further try out certain of the menservants,
To see where one honors us and respects us in his heart,
And who does not heed you and dishonors the man you are."
His illustrious son spoke out to him in answer:
"Father, you shall know my disposition, I think,
310 And soon, for no slackness of mind holds me at all.
But I for my part think this will not be an advantage
To the two of us. I ask you to consider it;
A long time in vain would you go and test each person
By visiting the fields. And they in our halls unharmed
315 Devour goods insolently; there is no restraint.
And I ask you to find out for yourself the women
Who dishonor you, and those who are innocent.
As for the men, I myself would not want us to go
To their lodgings to test them; but attend to these matters
    later
320 If you truly know some portent from aegis-bearing Zeus."
And so such things did they say to one another.
Then the well-made ship was brought up to Ithaca
That had borne Telemachos and all his companions from Pylos.
When they had arrived within the very deep harbor
325 They drew the black ship up upon the land themselves
While proud-spirited servants carried their gear off.
At once they brought beautiful gifts to Klytios' house,
And they sent on a herald to the home of Odysseus
With a message to tell the prudent Penelope
330 That Telemachos was in the fields and had ordered the ship
To sail off to the town, so that the goodly queen
Might not fear in her heart and shed a tender tear.
The herald and the godly swineherd met each other
On account of the very same message they were to tell the
    woman,
335 And when they reached the home of the divine queen
The herald spoke out in the midst of the serving maids:
"Your beloved son, my queen, has already come."
And the swineherd, standing near Penelope,
Told her all her beloved son bade him to say.

And when he had told her all he was to deliver,   340
He went on his way to the swine and left the enclosures and the
    hall.
The suitors were grieving and depressed in their hearts;
They went out of the hall along the great wall of the courtyard
And they sat down there out in front of the portals.
Eurymachos, son of Polybos, began speaking to them: 345
"Friends, a great task is arrogantly achieved
By Telemachos, this voyage. We thought he would not achieve
    it.
Come now, let us drag down a black ship, the one that is best,
And gather seamen as rowers, so they may quickly
Give a message to those men to go swiftly home."   350
He had not said all, when Amphinomos saw the ship,
As he turned in his place, inside the very deep harbor;
And men lowering the sails and holding oars in their hands.
He gave a sweet laugh and said to his companions:
"Never mind sending a message now. Here they are inside;   355
Either some god told them this, or else they themselves
Saw the ship coming in that they were not able to catch it."
So he said, and they stood up and went to the strand of the sea.
They dragged the black ship up at once on the dry land
And proud-spirited servants carried the gear off for them.   360
They themselves went off to the assembly together. Nor did
    they
Allow anyone else to sit with them, of young men or old.
Antinoos spoke to them, son of Eupeithes:
"Well now, the gods have delivered this man from harm!
Lookouts were sitting day by day on the windy heights,   365
In quick succession always, and at the setting sun
We never rested a night on land, but on the ocean,
Sailing in the swift ship we awaited godly dawn,
In ambush for Telemachos that we might capture him
And kill him. And meanwhile some god has brought him home.   370
But let us here think of a woeful destruction
For Telemachos, and let him not escape us. I think
These deeds will not be accomplished while he is alive.
He himself is skilled in deliberation and thought,
But the people no longer wholly bear favor toward us.   375
Well, come now, before he convenes the Achaians
Into assembly—for I think he will not let anything go,

But will be angry. He will stand up among all and tell
How we contrived sheer murder for him and did not catch him.
380 And they will not approve when they hear of the evil deeds.
I fear they will do some evil and drive us out
Of our own land, and we shall reach the country of others.
Let us forestall him and take him in fields far from the city
Or on the path. We should then have his living and property
385 To divide duly among us, and then we might give
The house for his mother and for the one who weds her to
      have.
But if this speech displeases you, and you wish
The man to live and have all his paternal goods,
Let us not then gather here and devour his goods
390 In their pleasing abundance, but let each from his own hall
Woo her and seek her with gifts. And she then may wed
Whoever gives the most and comes as the destined man."
So he said, and they all became hushed in silence.
Amphinomos then spoke out to them and addressed them,
395 The illustrious son of King Nisos, son of Aretias,
Who out of Dulichion, grassy and rich in grain,
Was leader of the suitors and pleased Penelope
The most with his speeches, for he practiced good sense.
With favorable intent he spoke out and addressed them:
400 "My friends, I would not myself at all want to kill
Telemachos. Dreadful it is to kill the race
Of kings. But let us first ask the gods for advice
If the decrees of great Zeus do agree with this,
I shall kill him myself and order all others to do so,
405 But if the gods turn aside, I give the order to cease."
So Amphinomos said, and his speech was pleasing to them.
They got up then at once and went to the home of Odysseus,
And when they got there, they took their seats in polished
      armchairs.
But the prudent Penelope had another thought:
410 To appear to the suitors with their presumptuous pride;
For she had heard death was to be in the halls for her son.
The herald Medon, who found out their plans, had told her.
She went on into the hall along with her serving women.
And when the godly woman arrived before the suitors,
415 She stood beside the pillar of the stoutly fashioned roof;
Holding the glistening headbands before her cheeks

She rebuked Antinoos and spoke right out directly:
"Antinoos, for all your pride and evil devices, they say
You are the best of your peers in the land of Ithaca
For advice and speeches. But you are not really so.   420
You madman, why do you devise murder and death
For Telemachos, and do not heed the suppliants
Who have Zeus for a witness? It is not holy to plot ills for one
 another.
Do you not know that your father came here in flight
And in fear of the people? And they were highly enraged   425
Because he had come along with Taphian pirates
And troubled the Thesprotians, who were our close friends.
They wished to destroy him and to tear out his own heart,
And to devour his great and satisfying livelihood.
But Odysseus held them back and restrained them, though they
 wanted that.   430
Now you devour his home without payment, and woo his wife,
And kill off his son, and you anger me very much.
Well, I tell you to stop and to order the others so.
Eurymachos, son of Polybos, answered her:
"Prudent Penelope, daughter of Icarios,   435
Take heart. Do not give heed to these matters in your mind.
The man does not exist, nor shall, nor come to be,
Who would lay hands on your son Telemachos
While I at least am alive and have sight on the earth.
I declare this to you, and it shall surely come to pass.   440
Right away his black blood shall run on my spear,
Since Odysseus, the sacker of cities, many times
Sat me upon his knees and placed a piece of roast meat
In my hands, and also held the red wine up to me.
And so Telemachos is by far the dearest to me   445
Of all men, and I bid him not to tremble for death,
From the suitors at least. But from the gods it is not to be
 escaped."
So he said, cheering her, and himself wrought destruction for
 him.
But she went on into the shining upper chamber
And wept there for Odysseus, her dear husband, until   450
Bright-eyed Athene cast sweet sleep on her eyelids.
At evening the godly swineherd came to Odysseus
And his son. They were preparing dinner attentively,

Sacrificing a year-old swine. And Athene
455 Stood close beside Odysseus, son of Laertes,
Struck him with a wand, and made him an old man again.
She clothed his skin in wretched garments, lest the swineherd
Look straight at him and know him and go announce it
To constant Penelope, and not keep it back in his mind.
460 Telemachos was the first to address a speech to him:
"You have come, godly Eumaeos. What is the news through the
town?
Are the bold suitors already within and back
From their ambush, or do they still watch for me on my way
home?"
And you addressed him in answer, swineherd Eumaeos:
465 "I did not bother to ask and inquire about these matters
As I went down through the town. My heart bade me at once,
After I had told the message, to come back here again.
The swift messenger from your companions joined me,
A herald, who first gave the word to your mother.
470 I know something else, for I saw it with my eyes.
Just now over the city where the hill of Hermes is,
I was going along when I saw a swift ship coming on
Into our harbor. There were upon her many men.
It was loaded down with shields and with two-edged spears.
475 And I thought it to be those men, but do not at all know them.
So he said, and Telemachos smiled in his sacred strength.
He looked with his eyes at his father and avoided the swineherd.
And when they had ceased from their toil and made dinner,
They dined, nor did their hearts want for a well-shared meal.
480 But when they had taken their fill of food and drink
They remembered rest, and they took the gift of sleep.

XVII

And when the early-born, rosy-fingered dawn appeared,
Telemachos, the dear son of godly Odysseus,
Bound the beautiful sandals underneath his feet,
And he took the stout spear that fitted in his hand,
Heading for the town, and he spoke out to his swineherd: 5
"Uncle, I am going to the city, so that my mother
May see me; I do not believe that she will cease
From hateful wailing and tearful lamentation
Until she sees me in person. I give you this order:
Lead this wretched stranger to the city, so that there 10
He may beg a dinner. Whoever wishes may give him
A loaf and a cup. It is not possible for me to endure
All sorts of men, with the pains in my heart that I have.
And if the stranger gets very angry, it will be the more painful
For himself. Yes, indeed, I like to speak the truth." 15
Odysseus of many wiles addressed him in answer:
"My friend, I do not wish to be held back myself.
It is better for a beggar to beg dinner in the city
Than in the fields. Whoever wishes will give it to me.
I am not yet of an age to remain at the folds, 20
So as to obey in everything a master who gives orders.
But come, this man that you are bidding will lead me
The moment I get warm from the fire and the sun's heat
    comes.
I have miserably poor clothes on, and I fear the frost
Of morning may overcome me. You say the town is far away." 25
So he spoke, and Telemachos went through the lodge
At a brisk pace; he was sowing the seeds of ill for the suitors.
And when he arrived at the well-situated house,
He stood the spear he carried against a tall pillar.
Then he went in himself and crossed the stone threshold. 30
The nurse Eurycleia was by far the first to see him.
She strewed fleeces upon the cleverly wrought armchairs,

And then she broke out in tears and came straight to him.
The other serving women of hardy-minded Odysseus gathered,
35 And they kissed him affectionately on his head and shoulders.
The prudent Penelope went on out of the chamber,
Resembling Artemis or golden Aphrodite.
Weeping, she threw her arms around her beloved son;
She kissed him on the head and on both lovely eyes.
40 And while she was sobbing she uttered wingèd words:
"You have come as a sweet light, Telemachos. I thought
I would see you no more when you went secretly in a ship
Against my will to Pylos for word of your dear father.
But come, tell me in what way you got sight of him."
45 And sound-minded Telemachos answered her:
"Mother, do not raise lamentation in me, nor arouse
The heart in my breast, since I did escape sheer destruction.
But bathe and put pure garments upon your skin
And go on into the upper chamber with the serving women.
50 Vow to all the gods you will sacrifice full hecatombs
If somehow Zeus may bring about deeds of retribution.
And I shall go on to the assembly, so that I may call
On a stranger who accompanied me hence as I came here.
I sent him on myself with my godlike companions,
55 And I ordered Peiraeos to lead him to the house,
To befriend him kindly and respect him till I should come."
So he said, and for her the word was without a wing.
She washed herself and put pure garments upon her skin,
Vowed to all the gods she would sacrifice full hecatombs
60 If somehow Zeus might bring about deeds of retribution.
Telemachos then went on through the hall
Holding a spear, and two swift dogs accompanied him.
Moreover, Athene shed a marvelous grace about him.
All the people wondered about him as he came on.
65 The bold suitors gathered together around him,
Speaking fine words but plotting evils in their minds.
And then he avoided the entire group of them.
But where Mentor sat down, and Antiphos and Halitherses,
Who were his father's companions from the beginning,
70 He went and took a seat. They asked him for the details.
Peiraeos, renowned for the spear, came close to them,
Bringing the stranger through the city to the assembly. Not long

Did Telemachos turn aside from the stranger, but stood beside
   him.
First to him did Peiraeos address his speech:
"Telemachos, go urge the women at once on to my house   75
So that I may send the gifts that Menelaos gave you."
Then sound-minded Telemachos answered him:
"Peiraeos, we do not know how the present acts will come out.
If the bold suitors in the halls secretly
Kill me and divide up all the goods of my father,   80
I would rather you gained them yourself than any of those.
But if I myself breed death and destiny for these men,
Then carry them gladly to the house, and I shall be glad."
When he had said this, he led the long-suffering stranger to the
   house.
And when they reached the well-situated hall,   85
They put their mantles down over the seats and armchairs,
Got into well-polished bathtubs, and washed themselves.
When the serving maids had washed and anointed them with
   olive oil,
And thrown woolen mantles around them, and tunics
They got out of the bathtubs and sat on the seats.   90
A handmaid poured water from a pitcher she was carrying,
A lovely golden one, over into a silver basin,
For washing the hands; she set up a polished table alongside.
A respected housekeeper served bread she was carrying,
Laying out many dishes, gracious with the provisions.   95
His mother sat opposite him by the doorpost of the hall,
Leaning back in her seat, turning the fine threads on the distaff.
They stretched forth their hands to the food that was laid out
   ready,
But when they had taken their fill of food and drink,
The prudent Penelope began speaking to them: 100
"Telemachos, when I have gone up into the upper chamber
I shall lie down in my bed, which is made full of groans for me,
Ever sullied with my tears since the time Odysseus
Went to Troy with the sons of Atreus. Nor did you dare,
Before the bold suitors came into this house   105
To tell clearly of your father's return, if you did hear of it."
And sound-minded Telemachos answered her:
"All right, then, Mother, I shall speak the truth to you.
We went to Pylos and to Nestor, shepherd of the people.

110 The man received me and kindly befriended me
In his lofty home, as a father would his own son
Come afresh after a time from somewhere else. So the man
Kindly entertained me with his glorious sons.
But of hardy-hearted Odysseus, alive or dead,
115 He said he had never heard anything from anyone on earth.
He sent me on with horses and well-jointed chariots
To the son of Atreus, Menelaos, famed for the spear.
There I saw Argive Helen, on whose account
Trojans and Argives suffered much at the will of the gods.
120 Menelaos, good at the war cry, asked me at once
What I had come in search of to godly Lacedemon.
And I declared to him myself the entire truth.
Then he addressed me and answered me with a speech:
'Well now, they who are themselves without courage
125 Have wished to lie down in the bed of a stouthearted man!
As when a deer in the thicket of a mighty lion
Has put her newborn milk-sucking fawns to sleep,
And goes questing over the spurs and the grassy gorges
For grazing, and just then he comes to his own lair
130 And upon the two of them brings a wretched fate;
So upon these men will Odysseus bring a wretched fate.
By Father Zeus, Athene, and Apollo, I wish
He might be as he once was in well-established Lesbos
When he stood up and wrestled in a fight with Philomelides,
135 Threw him down mightily, and all the Achaians rejoiced;
As that sort of man might Odysseus contend with the suitors.
They would all be swift in their doom and bitter in marriage.
As for what you ask and beseech me about, I myself
Will say nothing at all off the point, nor will I deceive.
140 But what the unerring old man of the sea told me,
Not a word of that shall I hide from you or conceal.
He said he saw him on an island, that he had strong pains
In the halls of the nymph Calypso, who by compulsion
Is holding him back. And he cannot reach his fatherland,
145 For he has no ships there with oars, and no companions
Who might convey him over the broad back of the sea.'
So said Atreus' son, Menelaos, famed for the spear.
When I finished this, I went off. The immortals gave me
A breeze, and they brought me swiftly to my dear fatherland."
150 So he said, and he stirred up the heart in her breast.

And the godlike Theoclymenos spoke among them:
"Respected wife of Odysseus, son of Laertes,
Indeed this man has no clear knowledge, but mark my word;
For I shall prophesy to you truthfully and conceal nothing.
May Zeus now be my witness, first of the gods, and this guest
    table,   155
And the hearth of the blameless Odysseus, to which I have
    come,
That Odysseus is already on his fatherland soil.
He is here, sitting still or moving, and is finding out
These evil deeds, and he breeds evil for all the suitors.
Such was the meaning of the bird I observed as I sat   160
On the well-timbered ship, and declared it to Telemachos."
And then the prudent Penelope spoke to him:
"Would that this speech, stranger, might be fulfilled.
Then you would soon know friendship and many gifts
From me, so that one who met you would call you blessed."   165
And so they said such things to one another.
The suitors out in front of the hall of Odysseus
Were amusing themselves by throwing weights and javelins
On the leveled terrace as before, in their insolence.
And when it was time for dinner, and from everywhere   170
In the fields sheep came that the men drove as they did before,
Then Medon spoke to them, who was most pleasing to them
Of all the heralds, and he attended on them for the meal:
"Young men, now that you have all amused your minds with
    contests,
Come into the house so that we may partake of a meal.   175
It is not a bad thing to take dinner at the right time."
So he said. They stood up, went, and obeyed his word.
And when they had arrived at the well-situated house,
They put mantles down on the seats and on the armchairs;
And they sacrificed great sheep and goats rich with fat,   180
They sacrificed sleek hogs and a heifer of the herd,
Preparing the meal. But Odysseus and the godly swineherd
Were hastening on to go from the field to the city.
The swineherd, chief of the men, began speaking to them:
"Stranger, since you do desire to go to the city   185
Today, as my master commanded, I myself would like
To leave you here as a guardian of the folds,
But I hesitate and fear him, lest afterward

He reproach me for it. Harsh are the rebukes of masters.
190 Come now, let us go. The day is mostly past,
And soon it will be colder for you, toward the evening."
Odysseus of many wiles addressed him in answer:
"I know, I see. You say this to an understanding man.
Well, let us go. Lead us all the way on yourself,
195 And give me any staff that may have been cut for you
To support me, since they say the roads are slippery."
He spoke, and put the sorry wallet around his shoulders,
Full of rents. And there was a twisted strap on it;
Eumaeos then gave to him a staff that he liked.
200 The two of them then went on. The dogs and the herdsmen
Who stayed behind guarded the lodge. He led his master
To the city in the likeness of a beggar miserable and old,
Walking with a staff. Sorry clothes were on his skin.
And when, as they went on along the rugged path,
205 They got near the city, they arrived at a spring,
Paved and fair-flowing, whence the townswomen drew water,
Which Ithakos, Neritos, and Polyktor had made.
About it was a grove of poplars nourished by water
In a circle on all sides, and cold water flowed down
210 From the rock above. An altar had been built above
To the nymphs, where all travelers made offerings.
There Melanthios, son of Dolios, came upon them
While he was leading goats that were best among all the herds,
As dinner for the suitors. And two herdsmen followed along.
215 When he saw them he upbraided them and spoke directly,
A striking, disgraceful speech. He stirred Odysseus' heart.
"Now a man wholly foul leads a man who is foul;
So the god always brings a like to his own like.
Miserable swineherd, where are you leading this wild pig,
220 This tiresome beggar, desecrator of feasts,
Who stands by many door posts and rubs his shoulders on them,
Begging for morsels, but not for basins or swords?
If you give him to me to become a guard of the folds,
To be a stall sweeper and carry greens for the kids,
225 Then he could drink whey and put on a great thigh.
But since he has learned foul deeds, he will not wish
To approach work, but wants to beg through the district
And to ask food for his insatiable belly.
I tell you this straight out and it will be fulfilled:

If he ever comes to the home of godly Odysseus,   230
Many stools about his head thrown from the hands of men
Will his ribs wear out as he is tossed through the hall."
So he said, and in his foolishness rushed with a kick
On his flank. But he did not drive the man off the path;
Odysseus stood steadfast. And he deliberated   235
Whether to rush on the other with the staff and take his life
Or to lift him by the middle and dash his head to earth.
But he braced himself and checked his mind. The swineherd
Looked at the other and scolded him; he raised his hands and
    prayed aloud;
"Nymphs of the springs, Zeus's daughters, if ever Odysseus   240
Burned thighs to you, enclosing them in rich fat,
Of lambs or of kids, bring this wish of mine to pass:
May the man himself come, and may some god bring him.
Then he would scatter all these vainglories far and wide
That you bring now in your insolence, forever straying   245
To the town. And evil herdsmen are destroying the flock."
Then Melanthios, herdsman of the goats, spoke to him:
"Well now, what has this dog of pernicious mind said!
Someday I shall take him on a black, well-timbered ship
Far from Ithaca, where he might get me a large fortune.   250
Would that silver-bowed Apollo might shoot Telemachos
Today in the halls, or he be overcome by the suitors,
As Odysseus' day of return has been lost afar."
When he had said this, he left them there as they walked quietly
    on.
Then he went on and swiftly reached the master's house.   255
He went in at once and sat down among the suitors
Opposite Eurymachos, for the man liked him very much.
Those who were serving offered him a portion of the meat
And a respected housekeeper offered bread she was carrying,
To eat. Both Odysseus and the godly swineherd   260
Stood still as they got near. About them came the sound
Of the hollow lyre. For Phemios struck up a song among them.
The other took the swineherd by the hand and addressed him:
"Eumaeos, this is surely the lovely home of Odysseus,
Easy to recognize when seen, even among many.   265
One part is right next to another, and its court is finished off
With wall and copingstones. And there are doors well fenced
In a double gate. No man could look down upon them.

I know that many men are holding banquets
270 In the place, since meat smoke rises from it, and the lyre
Sounds there, which the gods make the companion of a
        banquet."
And you addressed him in answer, swineherd Eumaeos:
"You know it clearly, as you are not otherwise without sense.
So come now, and let us discuss how these acts shall be.
275 Either you first enter the well-situated house
And go among the suitors, and I shall be left behind here,
Or, if you wish, stay back, and I shall go forward myself.
Do not linger, lest someone perceive you outside
And hit you or drive you; I bid you to consider this."
280 Then godly Odysseus, who had suffered much, answered him:
"I know, I see. You say this to an understanding man.
Go forward now, and I shall remain here behind,
For I am not unacquainted with tosses or with blows.
My heart is enduring, since I have suffered many ills
285 On the waves and in war. Let this one be added to them.
There is no way of concealing an eager stomach,
The accursèd thing that gives many evils to men,
On whose account also well-rigged ships set out
Over the barren ocean, carrying evils for enemies."
290 And so such things did they say to one another,
And the dog held his head and his ears up where he lay,
Argos, stout-hearted Odysseus', that he himself
Had once reared and did not enjoy, but he went off beforehand
To holy Ilion. Some time back, young men used to take him out
295 After the wild goats and the rabbits and the deer.
But now he was lying unwanted while his master was gone,
In much dung from mules and oxen, which was heaped
In abundance before the gates, till Odysseus' servants
Should bring it when they had a great plot to fertilize.
300 There the dog Argos lay, full of the vermin of dogs;
And then, when he perceived that Odysseus was nearby,
He fawned over him with his tail and dropped both his ears.
But then he was no longer able to go closer
To his master. The man looked away and wiped off a tear.
305 He hid easily from Eumaeos, and he at once asked a question:
"Great wonder is it, Eumaeos, that this dog lies here in the
        dung;
He is handsome in body, but I do not clearly know

Whether along with this look he used also to be swift to run
Or was simply the sort of table dog that belongs to men
And that masters take care of on account of their graceful look." 310
And you addressed him in answer, swineherd Eumaeos:
"Ah yes, this is the dog of a man who died far away,
And if he were the same in body and in his actions
As when Odysseus left him behind on his way off to Troy,
You would wonder at once when you saw his speed and his
    force.   315
No wild beast that he chased could escape him at all
In the recesses of the deep woods. And tracks he knew well.
Now he is caught in misery, and his master is dead somewhere
Far from his fatherland. The careless women do not tend him.
And the servants, since the masters are holding sway no more, 320
Hence are no longer willing to perform proper tasks.
And broad-seeing Zeus takes away half the excellence
Of a man, from the time the day of slavery comes upon him."
When he had said this he entered the well-situated halls,
And he went straight through the hall to the noble suitors. 325
But the fortune of black death took Argos away
Once he had seen Odysseus in the twentieth year.
God-like Telemachos was by far the first to see
The swineherd coming to the house; and then he quickly
Nodded and called him. The man looked around and took a
    stool   330
That was lying where a server usually sat and carved
Many pieces of meat for the suitors as they dined in the hall.
He brought it to Telemachos' table on the other side,
Put it down, and sat on it himself. And a herald
Brought him a share, set it down, and lifted bread out of a
    basket.   335
Odysseus entered the halls close behind him
In the semblance of a beggar, miserable and old,
Walking with a staff. Sorry garments clothed his skin.
He sat at the ashwood threshold inside of the portals
Leaning on a cypress post that a workman once   340
Had skillfully planed and drawn straight to the line.
Telemachos called the swineherd to him and addressed him;
He took an entire loaf from the beautiful basket
And as much meat as his hands held around it could contain:
"Bring this and give it to the stranger and tell him   345

To go around to all the suitors and beg in turn,
For shame is not a good thing for a needy man."
So he spoke, and the swineherd went when he had heard what
    he said.
He stood close to the man, and uttered wingèd words:
350 "Telemachos gives this to you, stranger, and tells you
To go around to all the suitors and beg in turn,
Since shame, he says, is not good for a needy man."
Odysseus of many wiles addressed him in answer:
"Lord Zeus, grant me that Telemachos be blessed among men,
355 And all that he wants in his mind come about for him."
So he said, and received it with both hands, and set it down
In front of his feet there, upon the disgraceful wallet.
And he ate while the singer was singing in the halls.
When he had had dinner and the godly singer had ceased,
360 The suitors made a din through the halls. And Athene
Stood close beside Odysseus, son of Laertes,
And urged him on to gather loaves from the suitors,
So he might know who were righteous and who lawless;
And yet she did not intend any to escape from misfortune.
365 He went along begging of each man, from left to right,
Stretching his hand every way as though he had long been a
    beggar.
They pitied and they gave, and they marveled at him
And asked one another who he was and whence he came.
And then Melanthios, the goatherd, spoke out among them:
370 "Suitors of the famous queen, listen to what I say
About this stranger here. For I have seen him before.
And surely the swineherd guided him to this place.
But I do not know him clearly, or whence he declares his birth
    to be."
So he said, and Antinoos upbraided the swineherd with a
    speech:
375 "Notorious swineherd, why did you lead this man
To the city? Are there not enough vagrants for us,
Insatiable beggars, defilers of the banquet?
Do you treat it lightly that those who are gathered here
Devour your master's living, that you called this man here too?"
380 And you addressed him in answer, swineherd Eumaeos:
"Antinoos, though you are noble, you have said what is not
    good.

For who invites some other stranger when he comes himself
From elsewhere, unless he is one of the district craftsmen,
A prophet or a healer of ills or a worker of wood
Or a wonderful singer who gives delight as he sings?   385
These are invited among mortals throughout the boundless
    earth.
No one would invite a beggar to eat his substance away!
But always you are harsh beyond the other suitors
To the servants of Odysseus, and especially to me.
I do not care, though, while constant Penelope   390
And god-like Telemachos are alive for me in the halls."
Then sound-minded Telemachos answered him:
"Silence, and please do not answer this man so much with
    words.
Antinoos has the habit of always giving evil provocation
With harsh speeches, and he urges others also to do it."   395
So he said, and he uttered wingèd words to Antinoos:
"Antinoos, you care for me nicely as a father for his son
When you order me to drive the stranger from the halls
With a word of constraint. Let a god not bring this to pass.
Take and give to him; I begrudge it not. In fact, I command it.   400
And do not stand in awe of my mother, or of anyone else
Among the servants who are in the halls of godly Odysseus.
And yet you have no such intention in your breast.
You would rather eat yourself than give to another."
In answer to him, Antinoos addressed him: 405
"High-talking Telemachos, unchecked in your anger, what have
    you said?
If all the suitors should offer him as much as this,
The house would keep him at a distance for three months."
So he said, and out from under the table he brought a footstool
That lay there, on which he held his glossy feet while feasting.   410
All the others gave and filled his wallet with bread and meat.
And soon Odysseus was again ready to go back again
To the threshold and get a taste from the Achaians free.
He stood by Antinoos and addressed a word to him:
"Give, my friend; you do not seem to me to be the worst   415
Of the Achaians, but the best, since you look like a king.
And so you ought to give bread more liberally
Than the others. I shall speak your fame through the boundless
    earth.

For I myself was once blessed, and I inhabited
420 A rich house among men, and gave to a tramp like this
Many times, no matter who came, whatever he needed.
I had numberless servants and many other things
Men have who live well and are called prosperous.
But Zeus, son of Cronos, destroyed me, as he somehow wished;
425 He sent me along with pirates who wandered much,
To go to Egypt, a long journey, so I might die.
I beached my bobbing ships by the Egyptian river,
And then I called upon my trusty companions
To remain there beside the ships and to guard the ships.
430 And I ordered spies to go up on places of lookout,
But they gave in to excess, and, relying on their own strength,
They sacked the beautiful fields of the Egyptians
At once and carried their women and infant children off.
They killed the men. And soon the noise reached the city.
435 They perceived the shouting, and at the appearance of dawn
Came on. The whole plain was filled with foot soldiers and
     horses,
And the flash of bronze. Zeus who hurls the thunderbolt
Threw evil panic among my companions, nor could any
Bear to stay face to face. Ills surrounded us on all sides.
440 Then they slaughtered many of us with the sharp bronze
And led some off alive to work for them under constraint.
But they gave me to a stranger they met bound for Cyprus,
Dmetor, son of Iasos, who ruled over Cyprus by force.
From there have I now come here this way, suffering troubles."
445 Then Antinoos answered him and addressed him:
"What god has brought this trouble, this annoyance at the
     banquet?
Stand as you are in the middle, apart from my table,
Lest you soon arrive at a bitter Egypt and Cyprus,
Because you are some bold and shameless beggar.
450 You stand beside all in turn. And they give to you
Wantonly, since they have no restraint or remorse
At giving of others' goods freely, since each has much."
Odysseus of many wiles withdrew and addressed him:
"Well now, your mind is not a match for your appearance.
455 You would not give salt from your house to your own suppliant,
You who now sit among others' things and cannot bear
To take off a little bread and give it to me; yet much is there."

So he said, and Antinoos was very angry in his heart,
And glaring at him, he uttered wingèd words:
"I think you will no longer withdraw through the hall;   460
In peace, since you are even uttering reproaches."
So he said, and took the footstool and hit his right shoulder
At the very base of his back. He stood there just like a rock,
Steadfast. Nor did the throw of Antinoos make him fall,
But he moved his head in silence, plotting evils deep inside.   465
He went back to the threshold and sat down, and he put
His full wallet beside him and spoke to the suitors:
"Listen to me, suitors of the illustrious queen,
So that I may say what the heart in my breast bids me to.
There is no pain in a man's mind or any grief   470
When he battles over possessions of his own
And is wounded for the sake of his oxen or shining sheep.
But Antinoos hit me on account of my woeful belly,
A cursed thing that gives many evils to men.
But if perchance gods and Furies exist for beggars,   475
May the end of death find Antinoos sooner then marriage."
Then Antinoos, son of Eupeithes, addressed him:
"Sit and eat in peace, stranger, or go somewhere else,
Lest the young men drag you through the halls for what you say,
By the foot or by the hand, and tear you all to pieces."   480
So he said, and they all grew presumptuously angry.
And this is what one of those overbearing young men would
    say:
"Antinoos, you did not do well to hit a hapless wanderer.
You are cursed, if perchance he is some heavenly god.
Yes, the gods in the semblance of alien strangers   485
Do appear in all forms and go about among cities
Looking upon the excess and the good order of men."
So said the suitors, and he did not attend to their speech.
Telemachos was nursing a great grief in his heart
For the struck man, but he cast no tear on the ground from his
    eyelids;   490
But in silence moved his head, plotting evils deep inside.
When the prudent Penelope heard that the man
Was struck in the hall, she spoke out to her servants:
"Would that bow-famed Apollo might so strike the other
    himself."
Then Eurynome, the housekeeper, addressed her in a speech: 495

"Would that there might come a fulfillment for our prayers!
None of these men would get as far as the fair-throned Dawn."
Then the prudent Penelope spoke to her:
"Good mother, they are all foes, since they devise evils.
500 Antinoos most of all is like a black fate.
Some hapless stranger wanders into the house
Begging from the men. Lack of means calls him on.
Then all the others filled him up and gave to him there,
And this one hit him with a footstool at the base of the right
    shoulder."
505 And so did she speak among her serving women,
Seated in her chamber. And godly Odysseus was eating dinner.
She called out to the godly swineherd and addressed him:
"Come, godly Eumaeos, go order the stranger
To come, so that I may embrace him in some way and ask of
    him
510 If he has perchance heard news of stouthearted Odysseus,
Or seen him with his eyes. He looks like a man who has much
    roamed."
And you addressed her in answer, swineherd Eumaeos:
"Well then, my queen, let the Achaians be silent.
The man tells such tales as would enchant your own heart.
515 Three nights I had him, and I held him for three days
In my hut. He first came to me running away from a ship.
Nor did he ever make an end of telling his misfortune.
As when a man looks upon a singer who sings
The words pleasing to mortals that he has learned from the gods,
520 And they endlessly long to hear him whenever he sings:
So that man enchanted me as he sat in the halls.
He says he is a paternal guest-friend of Odysseus
And he dwells in Crete, where the race of Minos is.
And now he has come here this way, suffering pains,
525 Rolling on and on. He claims to have heard news of Odysseus
Near us, in the fertile land of the Thesprotians;
That he is alive and is bringing many treasures to his home."
Then the prudent Penelope spoke to him:
"Come, call him here, so he may speak himself, face to face.
530 And let these men sit sporting either at the doors
Or here through the halls, since their hearts are merry.
Their own possessions lie undisturbed at home,

Bread and sweet wine. These are what their house servants eat,
But they themselves cluster to our house day after day
Slaughtering oxen and sheep and fat goats.   535
They carry on their revel and drink the sparkling wine
Wantonly. Many things are wasted. And there is no man
Of the kind Odysseus was, to ward off harm from the house.
But if Odysseus were to come and reach his fatherland,
With his son he would at once avenge the men's violence."   540
So she said, and Telemachos sneezed loud. About the house
It resounded terribly. And Penelope laughed.
At once to Eumaeos she uttered wingèd words:
"Come to me, and summon the stranger so, face to face.
Did you not see that my son sneezed at all the words?   545
So death will come not unfulfilled for the suitors,
All of them, nor will any ward off death and destiny.
I shall tell you something else; keep it well in mind.
If I acknowledge that he says everything truthfully,
I shall clothe him in a mantle and a tunic, lovely clothes."   550
So she said; the swineherd went when he heard the speech,
Stood close beside him, and uttered wingèd words:
"Father stranger, the prudent Penelope calls to you,
The mother of Telemachos. Her heart bids her to ask
Something about her husband, though she has suffered cares.   555
If she acknowledges that you say everything truthfully,
She will clothe you in a mantle and a tunic, the things that you
    need
The most. And then, begging bread through the district,
You will feed your belly; whoever wishes will give to you."
Then godly Odysseus, who had suffered much, spoke to him: 560
"Eumaeos, straight off I would tell all truthfully
To the prudent Penelope, daughter of Icarios.
For I know well about that man; we have got the same woe.
But I fear the throng of the difficult suitors
Whose insolence and force reach iron heaven.   565
Why, just now, when this man, as I was going to the house
Doing no evil, struck me and presented me with pains,
Telemachos could not at all prevent it, or anyone else.
So now go bid Penelope to remain in the halls,
Though she is eager, till the setting of the sun.   570
Then let her ask me about the day of her husband's return,

Seating me closer to the fire. For the clothes I have
Are woeful. You yourself know it too, since I besought you
     first."
So he said. And the swineherd went when he heard the speech.
575 Penelope spoke to him as he went over the threshold:
"Do you not bring him, Eumaeos? What does the wanderer
     mean by this?
Does he fear someone excessively, perhaps, or otherwise
Feel ashamed in the house? A tramp who feels shame is a bad
     one."
Then you addressed her in answer, swineherd Eumaeos:
580 "He speaks in measure, as anyone else would think
Who would avoid the insolence of presumptuous men.
But he bids you to wait until the setting of the sun;
And this way, queen, it will be far better for yourself
To speak alone to the stranger and to hear his speech."
585 Then the prudent Penelope addressed him:
"The stranger is not senseless; he thinks the way it may be.
For never, in this way, surely, did any among mortal men
So devise reckless deeds in their insolence."
So the woman spoke, and the godly swineherd went off
590 To the conclave of suitors, when he had told her everything.
And at once he uttered wingèd words to Telemachos,
Holding his head close, so the others could not hear:
"My friend, I am going off to guard the swine and the other
     things there,
Your living and mine. Let everything here be your affair;
595 Protect yourself first and give heed in your heart
Lest you suffer something. Many Achaians plot evils.
May Zeus destroy them before trouble comes upon us."
And then sound-minded Telemachos answered him:
"So it will be, father. Go when you have had supper.
600 Come at dawn and bring fine victims for sacrifice.
But all these things will be my affair, and the immortals'."
So he said, and the man at once sat on the polished stool,
When he had filled his heart with eating and with drinking.
He went after the swine, and left the enclosures and the hall
605 Full of banqueters. They were enjoying themselves with dancing
And with song, for the evening of the day was already coming.

XVIII

Then up came the beggar of the whole district, who begged
Through the town of Ithaca; he was outstanding for his greedy
   belly,
For incessantly eating and drinking. Nor did he have
Strength or force, but his form was very large to behold.
Arnaios was his name. His queenly mother gave it   5
At the time of his birth. But all the young men called him Iros,[1]
Because he went with a message when anyone asked him.
He came up and tried to drive Odysseus from his own home,
And, upbraiding him, he uttered wingèd words:
"Leave the doorway, old man, lest you soon be dragged off by
   the foot.
Don't you understand that they are all winking at me   10
And call on me to drag you? Still, I am ashamed to.
But get up, lest our quarrel soon come even to fists."
Odysseus of many wiles glowered at him and addressed him:
"My fine friend, I do not do or speak any wrong to you.   15
Nor do I begrudge anyone's giving, even if much is taken.
This threshold can contain us both. There is no need
To begrudge what others have. You seem to me to be
A tramp, like me; and the gods are supposed to bestow wealth.
But do not challenge with your fists too much, lest you anger
   me;   20
Lest, old man though I am, I stain your chest and your lips
With blood. And then there would be still greater peace for me
Tomorrow. And indeed I think you will not return at all
A second time to the house of Odysseus, son of Laertes."
Getting angry at him, the tramp Iros spoke to him: 25
"Well now, how fluently does the wild pig talk,
Like an oven woman; I should devise evils for him,
And beat him with both hands, and knock all his teeth
Out of his jaw to the ground like a crop-devouring sow's.
1. The messenger of the gods.

30 Gird yourself now so all these men may look upon us
As we fight. How would you contend with a younger man?"
And so outside in front of the lofty portals,
On the polished threshold, they grew fierce in full wrath.
Antinoos noticed them in his sacred might,
35 Laughed out sweetly, and spoke before the suitors:
"My friends, nothing like this has ever happened before.
Such a delight has the god brought to this house!
The stranger and Iros are quarreling with one another
To battle with their fists. Let us quickly set them together."
40 So he said, and all of them sprang up in laughter
And clustered about the beggars in their foul clothes.
Antinoos, son of Eupeithes, spoke out to them:
"Listen to me, bold suitors, so I may say something.
These stomachs of goats are lying in the fire that we
45 Have stuffed with fat for dinner and filled up with blood.
Whoever wins and turns out to be the better man,
Let him stand up and take whichever one of them he wishes.
And he may always dine with us, nor shall we allow
Any other beggar inside to mingle and make requests."
50 So Antinoos spoke, and his speech was pleasing to them.
Odysseus of many wiles spoke to them with a plan in his mind:
"My friends, there is no way for an old man worn out with grief
To fight against a younger. Still, my criminal belly
Urges me on, that I be overcome with blows.
55 But come, all of you, and swear a mighty oath,
That no one favoring Iros will recklessly
Strike me with heavy hand and overpower me for him."
So he said, and all of them swore as he had asked.
But when they had sworn and had completed the oath,
60 Telemachos again addressed them in his sacred might:
"Stranger, if your heart and bold spirit urge you on
To ward this man off, do not fear any of the other
Achaians, since he who smites you shall fight with many.
I am myself the host, and the two kings agree,
65 Antinoos and Eurymachos, both sound-minded men."
So he said, and they all assented. Then Odysseus
Girded his rags round his private parts and displayed his thighs,
Handsome and large; and his broad shoulders appeared,
And his chest and his powerful arms. Then Athene

Stood near and filled out the limbs of the shepherd of the
    people,   70
And all the suitors were exceedingly amazed.
So one of them would look at his neighbor and say:
"Soon Iros, un-Irosed, shall have an ill he brought on himself,
So great a thigh muscle does the old man show from his rags."
So they said, and the heart in Iros was sorely stirred.   75
And so the servants, when they had girded him, led him by
    force
In his fright. And the flesh trembled all over his limbs.
Antinoos rebuked him and spoke out to him directly:
"You ought not to exist now, ox-braggart, or have been born,
If you tremble before this man and dreadfully fear him,   80
An old man overwhelmed with the grief that has come upon
    him.
But I shall tell you this, and it shall be brought to pass;
If this man overcomes you and turns out the better man,
I shall throw you on a black ship and send you to the mainland,
To King Echetos, destroyer of all mortal men,   85
Who will cut off your nostrils and ears with a sharp bronze
    sword;
He will tear off your private parts and give them to dogs to eat
    raw."
So he said, and still greater trembling seized the other's limbs.
They led him out to the middle; both men held out their hands.
And then godly Odysseus, who had endured much, considered   90
Whether to strike him so his soul would leave him as he fell
Or to strike him softly and stretch him out on the ground;
And as he thought, it seemed to him to be better this way:
To strike softly so the Achaians would not take note of him.
Then they both drew themselves up. On the right shoulder   95
Iros hit him. But the other struck his neck under the ear and
    crushed
The bone inside. At once gory blood came out of his mouth.
He fell bellowing in the dust. He knocked his teeth together,
As he kicked the ground with his feet. Then the noble suitors
Held their hands up and died with laughter. And Odysseus   100
Took him by the foot and dragged him through the door till he
    reached
The courtyard and the doors of the porch. He leaned him up

Against the fence of the courtyard, put his staff in his hands,
And speaking to him, he uttered wingèd words:
105 "Sit there from now on and keep off the swine and the dogs,
And do not be a lord over strangers and beggars,
Woeful as you are, lest you incur a greater evil."
He spoke, and put his sorry wallet around his shoulders,
Full of rents. And there was a twisted strap on it.
Then he went back to the threshold and sat down. But they
110 went inside,
Sweetly laughing, and they welcomed him with speeches.
And this is what one of the overbearing young men would say:
"Stranger, may Zeus and the other immortal gods
Grant you what you wish and is most dear to your heart,
115 Since you have stopped this insatiable man from wandering
In the district. And soon we will bring him to the mainland,
To King Echetos, destroyer of all mortal men."
So he said, and godly Odysseus rejoiced at the omen he heard.
Antinoos put a large stomach before him
120 Full of fat and blood. And Amphinomos
Lifted two loaves out of the basket and gave them to him.
He toasted him with a golden cup and spoke forth:
"Hail, father stranger, henceforth may prosperity
Be yours in the future. But you are held now in many ills."
125 Odysseus of many wiles addressed him in answer:
"Amphinomos, you seem to me to be quite sound minded,
For such was your father, because I heard of his noble renown,
That Nisos of Dulichion was prosperous and good.
They say you are his son; you seem like a discreet man.
130 So I shall speak to you; pay attention and listen to me.
Earth nourishes nothing of slighter account then man
Of all the things that breathe and move on the earth.
For he thinks he will not suffer any evil in the future
As long as the gods provide excellence and his limbs stir.
135 But whenever the blessed gods bring woeful things to pass,
He bears them, too, against his will, in his enduring heart.
The disposition of men who dwell on earth is the same
As the kind of day the father of men and gods may bring.
And I myself was accustomed to be happy among men;
140 But I did much recklessly, yielding to my strength and might,
Relying on my father and on my relatives.
And so let no man ever be lawless by any means.

He should keep the gods' gifts in silence, whatever they give.
So I see the suitors devising such reckless deeds,
Consuming the property and dishonoring the wife   145
Of a man who I think will not be away much longer
From his dear ones and his fatherland. He is very near. May
    some god
Lead you back safely, and may you not encounter that man
At the time he returns to his dear fatherland.
I think when that man enters his hall, the suitors   150
And he shall not be pulled apart without bloodshed."
So he said; he poured libation, and drank honey-sweet wine.
Then he put the cup back in the hands of the chief of the
    people.
The other went through the house, grieving in his own heart,
Nodding his head. For indeed in his spirit he apprehended evil. 155
Yet not even so did he flee fate. Him too had Athene bound
To be overcome in power by the hands and spear of
    Telemachos.
Then he sat down again in the chair from which he had stood
    up.
The bright-eyed goddess Athene put it in the mind
Of Icarios' daughter, the prudent Penelope,   160
To appear to the suitors so she might the most expand
The hearts of the suitors, and might get more honor
From her husband and her son than she had before.
She laughed inanely and spoke quite directly out:
"Eurynome, my spirit longs, as it did not before,   165
To appear to the suitors, though they are detestable;
And I shall say something to my son, that it would be better
Not always to associate with the presumptuous suitors,
Who speak nicely but are thinking of evil for the future."
Then the housekeeper Eurynome addressed a speech to her: 170
"Yes, indeed, child, you have spoken all this properly;
But go, say the word to your son and do not conceal it,
When you have wiped off your skin and anointed your cheeks.
Do not go with your countenance befouled this way
By tears, since it is very wrong to mourn endlessly.   175
Already your son is of the age that you have most
Prayed to the gods to see him at, growing a beard."
And then the prudent Penelope addressed her:
"Eurynome, do not say this, though you care for me,

180 That I should wipe off my skin, and anoint me with oil.
The gods who possess Olympos have destroyed in me
My charm, from the time he went off in the hollow ships.
But give the order for Autonoe and Hippodameia
To come to me, so they may stand by me in the halls.
185 I shall not go alone among the men. I am ashamed."
So she said, and the old woman went out through the hall
To give the word to the women and urge them to come.
But the bright-eyed goddess Athene had another thought.
She shed sweet sleep over the daughter of Icarios.
190 And she sank back in sleep, and all her joints relaxed
There in her armchair, while the divine goddess gave her
Ambrosial gifts, so the Achaians might wonder at her.
First she purified her lovely face with ambrosial beauty
Like that with which the well-crowned Cytherea anoints herself
195 When she goes to the delightful dancing of the Graces;
And then she made her taller and fuller to look upon
And made her to be whiter than sawn ivory.
When she had done that, the divine goddess went off,
And the white-armed servants came out of the hall,
200 Coming up with their voices. Sweet sleep let go of her.
And she wiped her cheeks off with her hands and spoke out:
"In my dread suffering a soft slumber covered me round.
Would that chaste Artemis might bring soft death upon me
At once now, so that I should no longer waste my life away
205 Mourning in my heart and longing for my dear husband,
Who had excellence of all kinds, since he was foremost of the
Achaians!"
When she had said this, she went down from the glistening
upper chambers,
Not alone, but two servants followed along with her.
And when the godly woman had come to the suitors,
210 She stood by the pillar of the stoutly fashioned roof,
Holding the glistening headbands before her cheeks.
A devoted servant maid stood near her on either side.
The men's knees were loosened on the spot and their hearts
were charmed with desire,
And they all voiced the prayer of lying beside her in bed.
215 Then she addressed Telemachos, her beloved son:
"Telemachos, your mind and intent are steadfast no longer.

While you were still a child you managed plans in your mind
    better.
But now that you are big and have reached the measure of
    youth,
And one would say you were the offspring of a prosperous man:
For so an alien mortal would say who saw your beauty and
    stature,   220
Yet your mind and intent are no longer correct,
Since a deed of this sort has been performed in the halls,
In that you have allowed the stranger to be outraged this way.
What now, if the stranger seated in our halls as he is
Should suffer some harm from the miserable maltreatment?   225
Shame and disgrace would come about for you among men."
Then sound-minded Telemachos answered her:
"Mother, I do not hold it against you for being angry.
But I perceive in my heart and know about every matter,
The good and the worse. Until now I was a child.   230
Still, I cannot always have ideas that are sound,
For they dismay me, seated on one side and the other,
Those men who plot evils. And there is no one to help me.
The struggle between the stranger and Iros did not come out
To the suitors' liking—but he was the stronger in might.   235
By Father Zeus, Athene, and Apollo, I wish
The suitors that are now in our house in the same way
Might nod their heads, overcome: both those in the courtyard
And those within the house, and the limbs of each might be
    loosed,
The way that man Iros at the door of the courtyard now   240
Sits nodding with his head like a drunken man,
And cannot stand up straight on his feet or return home,
Wherever that may be, since his precious limbs are loosed."
And so such things did they say to one another.
But Eurymachos addressed a speech to Penelope: 245
"Daughter of Icarios, prudent Penelope,
If all the Achaians through Iasian Argos should see you,
More suitors still would be dining in your halls
From the morning on, since you excel among women
For form and stature, and for a mind well balanced within."   250
Then the prudent Penelope addressed him in answer:
"Eurymachos, the immortals destroyed my excellence

Of form and body at the time the Argives went aboard ship
Toward Ilion, and with them went my husband Odysseus.
255 If that man should come and minister to my life,
My renown would be greater that way, and lovelier,
But now I am grieved. So many ills some god has sent me!
Yes indeed, at the time when he went to leave his fatherland
He took me by the right hand at the wrist and said to me:
260 'My wife, I do not believe the well-greaved Achaians
Will all get back safely uninjured out of Troy,
For they say that the Trojans are men who are fighters,
Both as throwers of javelins and as drawers of arrows,
And mounters of swift horse chariots, such as most quickly
265 Decide the great contention of impartial war.
So I know not if the god will restore me, or I shall be taken
There in Troy. But do look after everything here.
Remember my father and my mother in the halls
As you do now, or even more, when I am gone away.
270 And when you see that my son is growing a beard,
Marry whom you may wish to and leave your own home.'
So the man said. Now all these things are brought to pass.
And there will be a night when hateful marriage shall come
Upon my cursèd self, whose bliss Zeus has taken away.
275 And the dreadful grief reaches my heart and spirit.
This is not the just way established in the past for suitors
Who wish to rival one another and pay court
To a good woman and the daughter of prosperous man.
Such men as those are bring oxen and goodly sheep,
280 A banquet for the lady's friends, and give glorious gifts,
But they do not consume another's livelihood scot free."
So she said; godly Odysseus, who had endured much, rejoiced
That she extracted their gifts from them and charmed their
    hearts
With soothing speeches, but her mind devised other things.
285 Then Antinoos, the son of Eupeithes, addressed her:
"Daughter of Icarios, prudent Penelope,
Let whoever of the Achaians wishes bring gifts here,
And you receive them. For it is not good to refuse a gift.
And we shall not go to our fields or anywhere else
290 Until you have married the noblest of the Achaians."
So Antinoos said, and his speech was pleasing to them.
Each one sent for a herald to bring his gifts.

For Antinoos one brought a great, beautiful tunic,
Embroidered. And twelve brooches were on it in all,
Made of gold, fitted with well-fastening clasps.   295
One brought for Eurymachos a necklace cunningly wrought
Of gold, strung with amber beads, and it was like the sun.
For Eurydamos two servants brought in earrings
With three droplets, clustering. Much grace shone from them.
And from the lord Peisander, son of Polyktor,   300
A servant brought a necklace, a beautiful ornament.
Each of the Achaians brought some other lovely gift.
Then the godly woman went up to the upper chambers,
Where servants followed her bearing the beautiful gifts.
The men turned then to dancing and delightful song   305
And took their pleasure, and waited for evening to come.
As they took their pleasure black evening came upon them.
Right away they stood three braziers up in the halls
To give light: they put seasoned pieces of wood around,
Dried a long time, very parched, newly split with the ax.   310
And they mixed torches between. The maids of stouthearted
    Odysseus
Kept their light up high, taking turns. But he himself,
Zeus-born Odysseus of many wiles, spoke out to them:
"You maids of Odysseus, the master who is gone so long,
Do come to the halls where the respected queen is;   315
Twist up her distaff wool for her and do her pleasure,
Seated in the hall, or else card the wool with your hands,
And I myself shall furnish light to all these people.
Even if they wish to await the fair-throned dawn,
They will not overcome me; I can hold out very well."   320
So he said, and they laughed and looked at one another.
But fair-cheeked Melantho upbraided him shamefully;
Dolios fathered her, and Penelope cared for her,
And reared her as her own child, and gave her toys to her liking;
Yet even with that, she did not keep Penelope's grief in mind;   325
But she had lain with Eurymachos, and loved him.
And with reproachful speeches she rebuked Odysseus:
"Wretched stranger, you are a man knocked out of his mind,
As you do not wish to go and sleep in the bronzesmith's house,
Or, say in the public court; but you speak very much here   330
Boldly among many men, nor are you at all frightened
In your heart. Wine possesses your mind, or your mind is always

The way it is now, so that you utter vanity.
Are you beside yourself for beating the tramp Iros?
Take heed lest a better man than Iros soon stand up against
335   you
Who would beat you around the head with his stout hands
And send you from the house, defiling you with much blood.'
Odysseus of many wiles glowered at her and spoke:
"Soon I shall tell Telemachos what you say, bitch,
340 When he comes here, so he may cut you up limb from limb."
When he had said this he terrified the women with his words.
They went through the hall, and the limbs of each one went
      slack
In alarm. For they thought that he had spoken the truth.
And he himself stood by the flaming braziers keeping the light
      up
345 And looked at all the men. The heart in his breast planned
Other matters, and those were not to be unachieved.
Athene by no means allowed the bold suitors
To keep from grievous outrage, so that still more pain
Might enter the heart of Odysseus, son of Laertes.
350 Eurymachos, son of Polybos, began speaking to them,
Abusing Odysseus, and he caused laughter in his companions.
"Listen to me, suitors of the illustrious queen,
So I may tell you what the heart in my breast bids me to.
Not without the gods has this man reached the house of
      Odysseus;
355 Indeed, the light of the torches seems to me to be his own,
From his head, since there are no hairs on it in the least."
He spoke, and addressed Odysseus, sacker of cities:
"Stranger, would you like to labor, if I should take you on,
At the field's very verge—the pay will be enough for you—
360 Gathering stones for the walls and planting tall trees?
There I myself shall furnish unfailing bread,
Clothe you in garments, and give you sandals for your feet.
But since you have learned foul deeds, you do not wish
To approach work, but want to beg through the district
365 So that you may have food for your insatiable belly."
Then Odysseus of many wiles addressed him in answer:
"Eurymachos, I wish a contest of work might come between us
In the spring season, when the long days come around,
In the grass, and I held a well-bent sickle myself

And you held the same kind, so we might test us at the work, 370
Fasting right up until dusk, and the grass should still be there;
And if there were oxen to drive, the best there are,
Great tawny ones, the pair of them filled up on grass,
The same age, equal at plowing, their strength not slight,
And the field were four lengths and the clod should yield to the
    plow;   375
Then you should see if I cut ahead an unbroken furrow.
And if the son of Cronos should raise up a battle somewhere
On this day, and I should have a shield and two spears
And a helmet all of bronze and fitted to the temple;
Then you should see me mingling in the forefront of combat,   380
Nor would you address me in reproach of my belly.
But you are quite insolent and your mind is unbending.
Perhaps you think yourself a great and mighty man
Because you associate with small men of no worth.
But if Odysseus should come and reach his fatherland,   385
Right away the portals, although they are very broad,
Would be narrow for you as you fled through the entrance
    outdoors."
So he said, and Eurymachos got still angrier in his heart.
Glowering at him, he uttered wingèd words:
"Wretch, I soon shall bring evil to pass for you, since you   390
Speak boldly among many men. Nor are you at all frightened
In your heart. Wine posesses your mind, or your mind is always
The way it is now, so that you utter vanity.
Are you beside yourself for beating the tramp Iros?"
So he said, and he took hold of a footstool. Odysseus   395
Sat down at the knees of Dulichian Amphinomos
In fear of Eurymachos. But that one struck the wine server
On his right hand; the pitcher clattered as it fell on the ground.
The man himself groaned and fell on his back in the dust.
The suitors made a din through the shadowy halls.   400
And this is what one of them, looking at his neighbor, would
    say:
"I wish that the stranger had strayed elsewhere and perished
Before coming. So he would not have set such a noise among us.
And now we are contending over beggars, and no delight
Shall be in the noble banquet, but worse matters win out."   405
And Telemachos spoke to them in his sacred might:
"You fools, you are enraged and no longer hide in your hearts

Your eating and drinking. One of the gods stirs you up.
But since you have dined well, go on home and lie down,
410 Whenever the spirit bids. I shall not pursue anyone."
So he said, and they all bit their lips with their teeth
And wondered at Telemachos, that he spoke boldly.
Then Amphinomos spoke to them and addressed them,
The illustrious son of lord Nisos, the son of Aretias:
415 "My friends, surely no one should become enraged
At a just saying, and rebuke someone with hostile words.
Do not maltreat the stranger at all, or any one
Of the servants who are in the halls of godly Odysseus.
Come now, let a wine server pour the first drops in the cups,
420 So we may pour libation and go on home to sleep.
And let the stranger go into the halls of Odysseus,
In the care of Telemachos; for he has reached his dear home."
So he said, and spoke a speech pleasing to all of them.
The hero Moulios, the herald from Dulichion, mixed
425 A bowl up for them. He was a servant of Amphinomos.
He gave it in order to all. They poured libation
To the blessed gods and drank the honey-sweet wine;
But when they had poured libation and drunk all they wished
They went off, each one to his own home to sleep.

XIX

So godly Odysseus was left behind in the hall
Devising slaughter for the suitors, with Athene's aid.
At once he uttered wingèd words to Telemachos:
"Telemachos, we must put the weapons of war inside,
All of them, and beguile the suitors deceptively   5
With soft speeches, when they miss them and ask you questions:
'I put them out of the smoke since they no longer look like those
That Odysseus once left behind when he went to Troy.
But they are befouled, so much has the smoke of the fire got
     to them.
And some god has put this other, greater thought in my mind: 10
That besides, drunk with wine, you might set up a quarrel
Among you, wound one another, and disgrace the banquet,
And your wooing too. For iron of itself draws a man on.' "
So he said. And Telemachos obeyed his dear father.
He called the nurse Eurycleia and spoke to her: 15
"Good mother, come hold the women back in the halls,
So that we may put away the weapons of my father up into the
     chamber,
The fine ones that smoke tarnishes uncared for in the house
Since my father went off, and I was still a foolish child.
Now I wish to put them away where the fire's smoke will not get
     to them."   20
Then his dear nurse Eurycleia spoke to him:
"My child, would that some time you might get hold of
     prudence
To take care of your house and watch over all your goods.
But come, who will go get a light and carry it for you?
You do not let the maids, who might have given light, go
     ahead."   25
Then sound-minded Telemachos answered her:
"This stranger. I shall not let any man go idle

Who has touched my rations, though he has come from far
    away."
So he said, and for her the word was without a wing.
30 She shut the doors of the well-situated halls.
Odysseus and his illustrious son both leaped up
And carried the helmet plumes and the bossed shields in,
And the pointed spears. Pallas Athene in front of them
Held a golden lantern and made a beautiful light.
35 Then Telemachos at once spoke to his father:
"Father, this is a great wonder I see before my eyes.
Indeed, the walls of the halls and the lovely pedestals,
The fir-wood beams and the pillars holding them high,
Appear bright to my eyes as if from a glittering fire.
Some god must be inside, one of those who possess broad
40   heaven."
Then Odysseus of many wiles addressed him in answer:
"Silence. Keep this in your mind and ask no question.
This is the rule of the gods who possess Olympos.
You go lie down, and I shall stay behind here,
45 So I may stir up still more your mother and the serving maids.
And she, as she laments, will ask me for details."
So he said, and Telemachos went out through the hall
Under the shining torches to lie down, to the chamber
Where he went to bed before whenever sweet sleep came upon
    him.
50 He lay down there then also and awaited the godly dawn.
But godly Odysseus was left behind in the hall
Devising slaughter for the suitors with Athene's aid.
And the prudent Penelope went out of her chamber
In the semblance of Artemis or golden Aphrodite.
55 They put a chair by the fire for her where she used to sit,
A chair whorled with ivory and silver that Ikmalios
The craftsman had once fashioned; to it he had attached
A footstool under the feet; and over it a large fleece was
    thrown.
Then the prudent Penelope sat down on it.
60 White-armed serving women came out of the hall
And were taking away a great amount of bread, and the tables,
And the cups from which the insolent men had drunk.
They threw the fire from the braziers to the ground and heaped
Much fresh wood upon them for light and for warming.

Melantho upbraided Odysseus again a second time;   65
"Stranger, will you still bother us here even now through the
      night,
Prowling through the house; and will you be ogling the women?
Well, go on outdoors, you wretch, and enjoy your meal,
Or soon you will be struck with a firebrand and go outdoors."
Odysseus of many wiles glowered at her and spoke: 70
"You terror, why do you hold at me so in rancorous spirit?
Is it because I am dirty and wear foul garments on my skin
And beg through the district? Necessity drives me on.
This is the way that beggars and wandering men are.
I myself was once blessed, and I inhabited   75
A rich house among men, and gave to such a wanderer
Many times, no matter who came, whatever he needed.
I had numberless servants and many other things
Men have who live well and are called prosperous,
But Zeus, son of Cronos, destroyed me, as he somehow wished. 80
So take heed, woman, lest soon you, too, lose all the grace
In which for the present you excel among the serving maids,
Lest perhaps your mistress get angry and bear hard on you,
Or lest Odysseus come. For there is still a share of hope.
And if he has died, as you think, and is no more to return,   85
Yet already, thanks to Apollo, he has a son like himself,
Telemachos. And no women in the halls who acts recklessly
Escapes his notice, because he is no longer so young."
So he said, and the prudent Penelope heard him.
She rebuked her servant and spoke out to her directly: 90
"Bold woman, fearless bitch, you indeed do not escape my
      notice
When you do this enormous deed, that you shall wipe off on
      your head.
And you know this full well, as you heard me say it myself,
That I intended to ask the stranger in my halls
About my husband, since my griefs come thick and fast."   95
She spoke, and said a speech to the housekeeper Eurynome:
"Eurynome, bring a chair and a fleece upon it here
So that the stranger may sit down and speak with me,
And listen; I should like to ply him with questions."
So she said, and the woman very quickly brought a well-planed
      chair   100
And set it up, and upon it she threw a fleece.

Then godly Odysseus, who had endured much, sat down there.
And the prudent Penelope began speaking between them:
"Stranger, I myself shall ask you this question first:
105 What men are you from? Where are your city and parents?"
Odysseus of many wiles addressed her in answer:
"My good woman, no one among mortals on the boundless
    earth
Would find fault with you. Your renown reaches broad heaven,
As though of some blameless king who in a god-fearing way
110 Holds sway over numerous and valiant men,
Who upholds good laws, and his black earth produces
Wheat and barley, and his trees are laden with fruit.
His sheep bear young without fail, and the sea provides fish
From his good leadership, and the people excel under him.
115 And so ask me anything else now in your house,
But do not inquire of my race and my fatherland,
So that you may not fill my heart up further with pains
While I remember. I am a man of much grief. There is no need
For me to sit wailing and moaning in another's home,
120 Since it is always worse to grieve endlessly,
Lest one of the maids resent it, or you yourself,
And say my tears flow because my mind is heavy with wine."
And then the prudent Penelope answered him:
"Stranger, truly the immortals destroyed my excellence
125 Of form and body at the time the Argives went aboard ship
Toward Ilion, and with them went my husband Odysseus.
If that man should come and minister to my life,
My renown would be greater that way, and lovelier.
But now I am grieved, so many ills has some god sent me!
130 All the noblemen who rule over the islands
Of Dulichion and Samê and wooded Zacynthos,
And who dwell round about sunny Ithaca itself,
Woo me against my will and are consuming my house.
And so I have no regard for strangers or suppliants,
135 Nor for heralds at all, who are craftsmen of the district;
But, longing for Odysseus, I pine away in my heart.
They are eager for marriage, and I weave deceits.
First some god inspired my mind with the thought of a robe;
I should set up a great loom in the halls and weave on it
140 A large and delicate fabric. I told them at once:
'Young men, my suitors, since godly Odysseus is dead,

Wait, though you are eager for this marriage of mine, till I finish
This robe, so that the yarn may not waste in vain,
This burial sheet of hero Laertes for the time
When the ruinous fate of long-sorrowful death seizes him,   145
Lest one of the Achaian women in the district blame me
If he who had won so much lie without covering.'
So I said, and the bold spirit was persuaded in them.
Every day I kept weaving there on the great loom,
And the nights I undid it when I had the torches set up.   150
So for three years I fooled the Achaians and persuaded them.
But when the fourth year came and the seasons came on
As the months waned, and many days came to an end,
Then indeed through my maid servants, uncaring bitches,
They came and caught me, and all shouted at me together.   155
And so I finished it, though unwilling and under duress.
And now I can neither escape marriage nor find
Any further plan. My parents urge me on very much
To marry, and my son chafes at those who devour his living,
And he notices it; for he is already a man quite able   160
To care for the sort of house to which Zeus gives renown.
But tell me of your descent, wherever you are from,
For you are not from the oak of ancient tale or from rock."
Odysseus of many wiles addressed her in answer:
"Respected wife of Odysseus, son of Laertes,   165
Will you never leave off inquiring of my descent?
Well, I shall speak out to you, and you will give me to more
     woes
Than those I am held in. For this is the rule, when a man
Has been away from his fatherland as long as I now have,
Wandering to many cities of mortals, suffering pains.   170
Yet even so I shall tell you what you ask and inquire about:
There is a certain land, Crete, in the midst of the wine-faced
     ocean,
Lovely and fertile, circled by the sea. Many men
Are in it, innumerable, and ninety cities are there;
One tongue is mingled with others. There are Achaians,   175
Great-hearted true Cretans and Cydonians,
Dorians, of three settlements, and godly Pelasgians.
And among those is Cnossos, a great city, where Minos,
The intimate of great Zeus, ruled nine years as king.
The father of my father, great-hearted Deucalion.   180

Deucalion begat me and the lord Idomeneus.
And that man went off up to Ilion in the curved ships
With the sons of Atreus. Aithon is my well-known name.
I was the younger by birth; he was older and more valiant.
185 And there I myself saw Odysseus and gave him guest gifts.
For in fact, the force of the wind had brought him over toward
      Crete
When he was eager for Troy, driving him off course past Malea.
He anchored at Amnisos, where the cave of Eileithyia is,
A difficult harbor, and he barely escaped the storms.
190 He went up to the city at once and asked for Idomeneus
And said he was his guest friend, a dear and respected one.
But the tenth or eleventh dawn had already come for the man
Since he had been gone in the curved ships to Ilion.
I led him to my house and entertained him well,
195 Befriending him kindly, as there was much in my home.
To him and to the others, his companions who followed him
I gave barley gathered from the region and sparkling wine
And oxen for sacrifice so their hearts might be satisfied.
There the godly Achaians remained for twelve days.
200 A great North Wind held them back, and did not allow them
To ride at anchor near land; some harsh god raised it up.
The thirteenth day the wind fell, and they put to sea."
He spoke many falsehoods and made them seem like the truth.
Tears flowed from her as she listened and her flesh melted.
205 Just as snow melts down upon the peaks of the mountains
Which the East Wind melts when the West Wind pours it
      down,
And when the snow melts the flowing rivers are full;
So her lovely cheeks melted as she poured down her tears,
Weeping for her husband who was sitting by. Odysseus
210 Felt pity in his heart for his wife as she lamented,
But his eyes stood fast, as though they were horn or iron
Untrembling in his eyelids. And by guile he hid his tears.
But when she had her fill of tearful lamentation,
She once more answered him and addressed him, saying:
215 "And now, stranger, I think I shall test you out,
If truly in that place with his godlike companions
You entertained my husband in your halls, as you say.
Tell me what sort of clothes he had on over his skin,

What sort of man he was, and what companions went with
    him."
Odysseus of many wiles addressed her in answer: 220
"My good woman, it is hard to say, for a man who has been so
    long
Parted, since already it is the twentieth year
From the time he went thence and left my fatherland.
But I shall tell you the way my heart pictures it for me:
Godly Odysseus had on a purple mantle of wool,   225
A double one. And the brooch upon it was made of gold,
With twin sockets. And on its face it was skillfully wrought:
In his front paws a dog was holding a dappled fawn
And gazed at it while it writhed. All men marveled to see
How the one, being of gold, gazed at the fawn he throttled,   230
And the other strove to get away as he writhed with his feet.
I noticed the tunic over his flesh glistening
The way the husk does on an onion that is dried,
So soft it was, and it was shining like the sun.
Many women indeed looked with wonder upon him.   235
I shall tell you something else, and keep it well in mind:
I do not know if Odysseus had these clothes on his skin from
    home,
Or if some companion gave them as he went on the swift ship,
Or perhaps some guest friend, since Odysseus was dear
To many men. For few of the Achaians were equal to him.   240
And I myself gave him a bronze sword and a lovely double-
    folded
Cloak of purple and a tunic with a fringe on it,
And I sent him off with honor on his well-timbered ship,
And a herald a little older than he was himself
Followed him. I will tell you the sort of man he was, too: 245
He was bent in the shoulders, black-skinned, with a wooly crown;
Eurybates was his name. Odysseus honored him foremost
Among his companions, because he had a mind that matched
    his own."
So he said, and roused in her still more desire for weeping
When she recognized as sure ones the signs Odysseus gave her.   250
And when she had her fill of tearful lamentation,
She replied to him with a speech and addressed him:
"And now, stranger, though you were pitied by me before,

You shall now be beloved and respected in my halls.
255 I myself gave him those garments that you speak about
From my chamber, after folding them; and I put on the shining
  brooch
To be an ornament for him. But I shall not welcome him again
On his return home to his dear fatherland.
So did Odysseus go off by an evil fate on a hollow ship
260 On his way to see evil Ilion, the unspeakable."
Odysseus of many wiles addressed her in answer:
"Respected wife of Odysseus, son of Laertes,
No longer mar your lovely skin, nor waste your heart
Lamenting for your husband. I do not blame you at all.
265 For indeed one would mourn a wedded husband she had lost,
To whom she had coupled in love and borne children, even
Another sort than Odysseus, who they say is like the gods.
But cease from lamentation and hearken to my speech.
I shall tell you unerringly and shall not conceal
270 That I have already heard about the return of Odysseus;
He is nearby in the rich land of the Thesprotians,
Alive. And he is bringing many excellent treasures,
Begging them through the land. But his trusty companions
And his hollow ship he lost on the wine-faced ocean.
275 Going from the island Thrinacria. At him did Zeus
And the Sun get angry, for the companions killed his cattle.
All of them perished in the much-surging sea.
But a wave threw him on the ship's keel upon the mainland,
The country of the Phaeacians, who are close kin to the gods.
280 They honored him heartily as they would a god,
And gave him many things, and wished themselves to send him
Homeward unharmed. And long ago would Odysseus have
  been here,
But this course seemed to him in his heart to be better:
To get together goods while going to many lands,
285 Because Odysseus knows beyond all mortal men
About great gains, and no other person might contend with
  him.
So Pheidon the king of the Thesprotians told me.
He swore to me personally, pouring a libation in his house,
That a ship had been drawn down and companions were ready
290 Who would conduct him to his beloved fatherland.
But he sent me off first. For a ship happened to come

Of Thesprotians headed for Dulichion, rich in wheat,
And he showed me all the possessions Odysseus had gathered.
They would support each man in turn to the tenth generation,
So many were the treasures that lay in the lord's halls.   295
He said that man had gone to Dodona in order to hear
The plan of Zeus from the lofty-leaved oak of the god
As to how he might return to his beloved fatherland,
Openly or in secret, as already he had been long away.
And so he is safe and very near, and he will come   300
Soon, nor will he be absent much longer, far
From his friends and fatherland. Indeed, I shall give you an oath:
Zeus now be my first witness, the highest and best of the gods,
And the hearth of blameless Odysseus to which I have come:
That all these things shall come to pass as I say.   305
Within the light of this very month will Odysseus be coming
    here
While one moon is waning and another is on the rise."
Then the prudent Penelope answered him:
"Would that this saying, stranger, might be brought to pass,
And then you would soon know friendship and many gifts   310
From me, so that a man who met you might call you blessed.
And yet it seems to me in my heart it will be this way:
Odysseus will not come home again, nor shall you be granted
An escort, since there are no masters in the house of the sort
That Odysseus was among men, if he ever existed,   315
To send respectable strangers off and receive them.
Well now, servants, wash him off and lay him down a bed
Of bedclothes and of mantles and of glistening blankets
So that he may reach, well-warmed, Dawn of the golden throne.
And very early in the dawn wash him and anoint him,   320
So he may think of a meal seated in the hall within
Beside Telemachos. And it will be very painful
For whoever of these grievous men annoys him. He shall not
Gain anything here any more, though he be dreadfully angry.
How shall you learn about me, stranger, that I at all excel   325
Among other women for purpose and a thoughtful plan,
If, squalid and clothed in evil garments, you dine
In the halls? Men come to their growth just a tiny while.
On whoever is himself harsh and versed in what is harsh
Do all mortal men invoke the curse of future pains   330
While he is alive, and all jeer at him when he dies.

Whoever is himself blameless and versed in what is blameless,
For him do strangers carry renown far and wide
Among all men, and many speak of him as noble."
335 Then Odysseus of many wiles addressed her in answer:
"Respected wife of Odysseus, son of Laertes,
Mantles and glistening blankets have in fact been hateful to
    me
From the time when I first left behind the snowy mountains
Of Crete, going upon the ship with its long oars.
340 I shall lie down, as indeed I spent slumberless nights before.
Yes, for many nights in an ill-favored bed
I have rested and waited for the fair-throned Dawn.
No water for washing my feet is at all pleasing
To my heart. Nor shall any woman touch our feet
345 Among those who are active for you in your house,
Unless there is some agèd woman with a sense of devotion,
Someone who has suffered in mind as much as I have myself:
I shall not hold it against her if she touches my feet."
And then the prudent Penelope spoke to him:
350 "Dear stranger, never yet has a man so sound in mind
Of strangers from far away come more welcome to my house,
Because you so thoughtfully speak of all that is sound.
I have an old woman whose mind is packed with thoughts,
Who nourished that hapless man well and brought him up,
355 Taking him in her own hands when his mother first bore him.
She shall wash your feet, though indeed her strength is slight.
Come and stand up now, prudent Eurycleia;
Wash a man the same age as your master. Perhaps Odysseus
By this time is just like him in his hands and feet,
360 For quickly in misfortune do mortals become old."
So she said, and the old woman covered her face with her hands,
Shed hot tears, and uttered a speech of lamentation:
"Alas, for you, my child, I am helpless. Zeus hates you
Beyond other men, though you have a god-fearing heart.
365 No mortal ever yet burned so many fat thighs or sacrificed
Such choice hecatombs to Zeus, who hurls the thunderbolt,
As you bestowed on him, praying that you might come
To a sleek old age and rear your illustrious son.
For you alone is the day of return now all taken away.
370 And so perhaps the women jeered at him also
Among far-off strangers when he reached someone's home,

As these bitches, all of them here, are jeering at you.
And now, to avoid their reproach and their many insults,
You do not allow them to wash you. But me did Icarios'
    daughter,
The prudent Penelope, ask, and not against my will.   375
So I will wash your feet on Penelope's own account,
And on your own, since the heart is aroused within me
By sorrow. And now understand the speech that I speak:
Many long-suffering strangers have reached this place:
I think I have never yet seen one who resembles him   380
As you resemble Odysseus, in voice, body, and feet."
Odysseus of many wiles addressed her in answer:
"Old woman, that is what all men say who have seen us both
With their eyes, that we are very similar to one another,
As, indeed, you yourself have discerned and said."   385
So he spoke, and the old woman took a glittering basin
That she used for washing feet; she poured in much water,
The cold; then she transferred in the hot. Odysseus
Was sitting by the hearth, and suddenly turned toward the
    darkness.
For at once he was apprehensive in heart lest when she touched
    him   390
She notice his scar and the facts become apparent.
She went near and was washing her master, and right away knew
The scar which once a boar dealt him with its shining tusk
When he had come to Parnassos to see Autolycos and his sons,
His mother's noble father who excelled among men   395
In trickery and oath making. The god Hermes himself
Endowed him, for he burned the thighs of lambs and kids
Pleasing to the god, who zealously attended the man.
Autolycos had gone to the rich land of Ithaca
And found a son newly born to his own daughter.   400
Eurycleia placed him upon the man's own knees
As he finished dinner, and spoke out to him directly:
"Autolycos, now find yourself a name you may give
To the dear son of your child; he has been much prayed for."
Then Autolycos answered her and addressed her: 405
"My son-in-law and daughter, give him the name I say.
I myself come here as one who has been enraged at many,
At men and at women, throughout the much-nourishing earth,
And let him be named Man of Wrath: Odysseus. For my part,

410 When he reaches his prime, and comes to the great house
Of his mother, to Parnassos where I have my possessions,
I shall give him some from them and send him back in joy."
Odysseus went for them, so the man might give him glorious
          gifts.
Autolycos and the sons of Autolycos greeted him
415 With handclasps and welcomed him with soothing speeches.
The mother of his mother, Amphithea, embraced Odysseus
And kissed him on the head and on both lovely eyes.
Autolycos called to his illustrious sons
To get dinner ready. They heeded as he urged them on.
420 And at once they drove in a male ox five years old.
They flayed it and worked round it and dismembered it all
And cut it up skillfully and pierced it on spits,
Roasted it carefully, and distributed the portions.
So then for the whole day till the setting of the sun
425 They dined, nor did their hearts want for a well-shared meal.
And when the sun went down and the darkness came on,
They lay down to sleep and took the gift of slumber.
And when the early-born, rosy-fingered dawn appeared,
They went on the hunt, both the dogs and themselves,
430 The sons of Autolycos. With them godly Odysseus
Went along. They approached the sheer mountain covered with
          woods
Of Parnassos, and soon they reached the windy ravines.
At that moment the Sun was freshly striking the fields
Up from the deep stream of gently flowing Oceanos,
435 And the beaters reached the glen. In front of them
Dogs moved on, tracking the footprints, and behind them
Came the sons of Autolycos. With them godly Odysseus
Moved close to the dogs, brandishing a long-shadowed spear.
And there in a thick-copse was lying a great boar.
440 The blowing winds' watery force did not blow through to it,
Nor did the Sun strike it with the beams of his rays,
Nor did the rain get all the way through, so thick
It was, and a plentiful deposit of leaves was there.
The beating of the feet of men and dogs came round to him
445 As they came rushing on. Facing them out of the thicket
He bristled his back well, glanced fire with his eyes,
And stood very close to them. Odysseus first of all
Rushed on, holding the long spear up in his stout hand,

Eager to hit him. The boar got the start and struck him
Above the knee, and gashed his flesh deep with a tusk,   450
Charging at him slantwise, but did not get to the man's bone.
Odysseus wounded him, hitting him on the right shoulder.
And the point of his shining spear went straight on through
　　him.
He fell in the dust, squealing, and his spirit flew off.
The beloved sons of Autolycos attended to the boar   455
And bound up the wound of excellent, godlike Odysseus
Skillfully. And with an incantation they held back
The black blood. At once they reached their dear father's home.
Autolycos and the sons of Autolycos healed him
Well, and they provided him with glorious gifts,   460
And sent him in joy speedily to his dear fatherland,
To Ithaca. His father and queenly mother welcomed him
On his return, and they inquired about the details
Of how he had suffered the scar. He told them about it fully.
How the boar had struck him with his shining tusk while he was
　　hunting   465
When he had gone to Parnassos with the sons of Autolycos.
The old woman took the scar in the palms of her hands and
　　knew it
As she touched it; she let the foot drop that she held,
And his shin fell into the basin and the bronze clattered.
It tipped back to one side and the water spilled out onto the
　　ground.   470
Both delight and pain gripped her mind, and her two eyes
Filled with tears, and her resonant voice was held back.
She touched Odysseus' chin and spoke to him:
"Indeed you are Odysseus, dear child; not even I
Knew you at first, till I had touched my master all over."   475
She spoke, and then glanced at Penelope with her eyes,
Wishing to tell her that her dear husband was within.
But the other could not sight her face to face or perceive her,
For Athene had turned her mind. Odysseus groped for her
With his hands and took her by the throat with his right hand,   480
And with the other he drew her closer to himself and spoke:
"Good mother, why do you wish to destroy me? You brought
　　me up
At your breast yourself. Now, having suffered many pains,
I have come in the twentieth year to my fatherland.

485 Since you have recognized me, and a god put it in your heart,
Be quiet, lest someone else in the halls find out.
For I shall speak out as follows, and it shall be fulfilled;
If a god does subdue the noble suitors underneath me,
I shall not hold off from you for being my nurse
490 When I kill the other serving women in the halls."
And then the prudent Eurycleia addressed him:
"My child, what sort of a speech has got past the bar of your
teeth?
You know how much my strength is steadfast and unyielding.
I shall hold out like iron or some rigid stone.
495 I shall tell you another thing, and keep it well in mind.
If a god does subdue the noble suitors underneath you,
Then I shall tell you about the women in the halls,
Those that dishonor you and those that are innocent."
Odysseus of many wiles addressed her in answer:
500 "Good mother, why tell me of them? There is no need.
I myself shall observe and know each one quite well.
But keep your story in silence and turn it over to the gods."
So he said, and the old woman went on through the halls
To bring water for the feet, since the first had all been spilled.
505 And when she had washed him and anointed him richly with oil,
Then Odysseus drew the chair up closer to the fire
To warm himself. And he hid the scar in his rags.
Then the prudent Penelope began speaking between them:
"Stranger, I myself shall ask just this little thing;
510 For indeed it shall soon be the hour for pleasant slumber.
Sleep is sweet, whomever it seizes, though he has cares.
However, to me some god has given unmeasured grief.
For I enjoy my days in lamentation, mourning
And looking after my tasks and those of the servants in the
house.
515 But whenever night comes and slumber seizes them all
I lie in my bed, and thronging about my throbbing heart,
The sharp anxieties plague me as I lament.
As when the daughter of Pandareus, the nightingale of the
green,[1]
Sings beautifully when spring has freshly risen,
520 Seated amid the thick foliage of the trees,

1. Aedon ("nightingale, singer") killed her son Itylos by mistake and was
turned into a bird.

And, often modulating, pours out her loud-sounding song,
Lamenting her dear son Itylos, child of lord Zethos,
Whom one day she killed with a sword unwittingly;
So my heart is aroused, divided this way and that,
Whether I should wait with my son and steadfastly guard   525
All my property, the maids and the high-roofed house,
Respecting the bed of my husband and the talk of the people,
Or by this time should follow the best of the Achaians
Who woos me in the halls and offers endless bridal gifts.
My son while he was yet childish and weak of mind   530
Would not let me marry and leave my husband's home;
But now that he is big and has reached the measure of youth,
He implores me to go home again out of the hall,
Chafing at the property that the Achaians consume.
But come, listen to this dream and interpret it for me: 535
Twenty geese are eating the wheat in my house,
Out of the water, and I am warmed to look on them.
Then a great crooked-beaked eagle came off a mountain,
Broke all their necks and killed them. They were heaped
Together through the halls, and soared to the divine air.   540
But I wept and lamented in the very dream,
And the fair-haired Achaian women gathered about me,
As I piteously grieved that the eagle killed my geese;
But he came back and perched on a projecting rafter,
And he checked me and spoke out with a mortal voice: 545
'Take courage, daughter of widely renowned Icarios,
Not a dream it is, but a good vision, that will come to pass:
The geese are the suitors, and I who previously
Was the eagle have come back now as your own husband,
Who shall inflict on all the suitors a sorry destiny.'   550
So he said, and then honey-sweet sleep let me go.
And looking over the geese in the halls, I perceived
That they were pecking up wheat at the trough where they
   did before."
Then Odysseus of many wiles addressed her in answer:
"My good woman, there is no way to interpret this dream   555
By twisting it off another way, since Odysseus himself
Has shown how he will achieve it. Destruction is plain for the
   suitors,
All of them; and not one shall ward off destiny and death."
And then the prudent Penelope spoke to him:

"Stranger, hard to handle and confused in their stories do
560   dreams
Come, and not all in them is brought to pass for men.
For double are the portals of flickering dreams.
One set is made of horn, the other of ivory.
And as for those that come through the sawn ivory,
565 They deceive, carrying words that will not be fulfilled;
But those that pass on outside through the polished horn
Do fulfill the truth whenever any mortal sees them.
But I do not think my awesome dream has come
From these gates. That would truly be welcome to me and to
    my son.
570 I shall tell you something else, and keep it well in mind:
This dawn of evil name shall come that will make me leave
The home of Odysseus, for now I will set up a contest
Of axes, which the man used to stand up in a row
In his halls, as trestles, all twelve of them.
575 He would stand at a great distance and shoot an arrow through.
And now I will set up this contest for the suitors:
The one who most nimbly strings the bow in his hands
And shoots an arrow through all twelve of the axes,
Him will I follow, leaving this very lovely
580 Home of my marriage, full of the goods of life,
Which I think I shall ever remember even in dreams."
Odysseus of many wiles addressed her in answer:
"Respected wife of Odysseus, son of Laertes,
Do not delay this contest any longer in the house.
585 Odysseus of many wiles shall come to you in this place
Long before these men who handle this well-made bow
Have stretched the bowstring and shot an arrow through the
    iron."
And then the prudent Penelope spoke out to him:
"Stranger, if you should like to sit by me in the halls
590 And delight me, sleep would never be shed on my eyelids.
But it is not possible for men to be without sleep
Forever. The immortals have set down a limit
For everything among mortals on the grain-giving earth.
Well, I shall go up myself into the upper chamber
595 And lie down in my bed, which is made full of groans for me,
Ever sullied with my tears since the time Odysseus
Went off to see evil Ilion, the unspeakable.

There I shall lie down. You lie down in this house,
Spreading a bed on the ground; or let them put bedding down
    for you."
When she had said this, she went up to the glistening upper
    chambers,   600
Not alone, but with her went the others, her serving women.
She entered the upper chamber with her serving women
And then wept for Odysseus, her dear husband, until
Bright-eyed Athene cast sweet sleep upon her eyelids.

XX

But godly Odysseus went to bed in the portico.
Under him he spread an undressed hide, and above
Many fleeces of the sheep the Achaians had been sacrificing.
Eurynome threw a mantle on him when he lay down.
5 Then Odysseus lay awake devising evils in his heart
For the suitors. And the women who up to then
Used to lie with the suitors went out of the hall,
Entertaining one another with laughter and with mirth.
As for him, the heart was aroused in his own breast.
10 He deliberated much in his mind and in his heart,
Whether to rush among them and bring death on each one
Or else allow them to lie with the bold suitors
A last and final time. The heart within him growled;
As when a bitch standing over her feeble puppies,
15 Not recognizing a man, growls and is eager to fight,
So his heart growled within him, indignant at their evil deeds.
But he struck his breast and rebuked his heart in a speech:
"Stand it, my heart. You stood something still more shameful
On the day the Cyclops with irresistible force devoured
20 My mighty companions. And you endured, until a plan
Led you out of the cave when you thought you were to die."
So he said, and upbraided the heart in his own breast,
And so his heart kept enduring steadfastly
In submission. But he himself turned this way and that,
25 As when a man shifts an intestine full of fat and blood
On a great blazing fire quickly this way and that
And longs for it to be roasted very rapidly;
So this way and that did he toss about, pondering
How he might lay his hands upon the shameless suitors,
30 Being one man against many. Athene came close to him,
Descending from the sky; she likened her body to a
    woman's.
She stood above his head and addressed a speech to him:

"Why are you awake, ill-fated beyond all mortal men?
This is your house, and this is your wife in the house,
And your child, the kind anyone would long to have for a son."   35
Odysseus of many wiles addressed her in answer:
"Yes, in all this, goddess, you have spoken properly.
But this is what the heart in my breast worries somewhat about:
How I might lay my hands upon the shameless suitors,
Being a single man, but they are always within, in a body,   40
And I also think over this greater point in my mind:
If I were to slay them with your help and that of Zeus,
Where would I get away? I ask you to think of that."
Then the bright-eyed goddess Athene addressed him:
"Stubborn man, some will trust an inferior companion   45
Who is a mortal and does not know such wisdom as mine.
But I myself am a god, who constantly protects you
In all your trials. I shall speak to you openly.
If fifty troops of articulate men in ambush
Were to stand around us, striving to kill us in war,   50
Yet should you drive off their cattle and goodly sheep.
But let sleep take you. It is also a trouble to keep watch
And lie awake all night. You shall soon rise up from your ills."
So she said. And she shed sleep over his eyelids;
Then the divine goddess herself went back to Olympos.   55
While sleep, the looser of the limbs, seized him, loosing
The troubles of his heart, his wife, who had a sense of
    devotion,
Woke up and wept while sitting up in her soft bed.
And when she was sated in her own heart with weeping,
The divine woman prayed to Artemis first of all: 60
"Artemis, queenly goddess, daughter of Zeus, would that now
You might strike my chest with an arrow and take my life away
At this very time, or that a storm would now snatch me up
And depart carrying me forth upon the murky ways,
And throw me in the streams of backward-flowing Oceanos;   65
As when storms snatched up the daughters of Pandareus,
Whose parents the gods destroyed, and they were left
    themselves
Orphaned in the halls. Divine Aphrodite tended them
With cheese and with sweet honey and with pleasant wine.
Hera endowed them beyond all other women   70
With form and wisdom. Chaste Artemis gave them stature,

And Athene taught them how to do illustrious tasks.
When divine Aphrodite proceeded to tall Olympos,
To Zeus who hurls the thunderbolt, to ask for an outcome
75 Of lusty marriage for the maidens, as he knows all things well—
What is fated and what not fated for mortal men—
At that time did whirlwinds snatch the maidens away
And give them to the hateful Erinyes to take care of.
So may those who hold Olympos's hall annihilate me,
80 Or may fair-braided Artemis strike me, so that
With Odysseus in my mind's eye, I may go beneath the hateful
    earth,
Lest perchance I gladden the thought of a lesser man.
But it is an unendurable evil when anyone
Weeps by day, when his heart is abundantly grieved,
85 And sleep holds his nights: it brings forgetting of all
Things good and evil when it closes about his eyelids,
But even the dreams that some god sent me were evil.
For this night again there slept beside me one like the man
    himself,
As he was when he went off with the host. And my heart
90 Rejoiced, since I thought it not a dream, but a waking fact."
So she said. And at once the golden-throned Dawn came.
Godly Odysseus heard her voice as she was weeping,
And then he thought it over; she seemed to him in his heart
Already to know him and be standing at his head.
95 He gathered up the mantle and the fleeces in which he slept
And put them on a chair in the hall; he carried the hide out,
Set it outside, and raised his hands in prayer to Zeus:
"Father Zeus, if you gods have brought me willingly,
Over dry ground and wet sea, to my land, when you had hurt
    me much;
100 Let someone inside wake up and tell me an omen,
And outside let another portent appear from Zeus."
So he said in his prayer, and the counselor Zeus heard him,
And he thundered at once from glittering Olympos
High up out of the clouds. Godly Odysseus rejoiced,
105 And a woman grinding sent an omen out of the house nearby
Where the mills were set for the shepherd of the people,
And at them twelve women in all usually plied the work,
Producing barley grain and wheat flour, marrow of men.

The others were sleeping, since they had ground up the
  wheat.
But one had not yet ceased, the weakest; she was still working. 110
She stopped the mill and said a word, a sign to her master:
"Father Zeus, you who rule over the gods and men,
Greatly have you thundered out of the starry heaven,
Nor is there a cloud anywhere. You show this as a portent to
  someone.
Fulfill now, even for my poor self, what I say: 115
May the suitors this day for the last and final time
Partake of a delightful banquet in the halls of Odysseus,
Those who have undone my knees in heart-hurting toil
To make barley flour. May they dine now for the last time."
So she said, and godly Odysseus rejoiced at the omen and
  thunder   120
Of Zeus. For he expected him to take vengeance on the guilty.
The other serving women in the lovely house of Odysseus
Woke up and kindled an unwearying fire on the hearth.
Telemachos, a man like a god, rose up from his bed
And put on his clothes. He put his sharp sword round his
  shoulder   125
And bound the lovely sandals beneath his shining feet.
Then he took his stout spear pointed with sharp bronze,
Went to stand on the threshold, and spoke to Eurycleia:
"Good mother dear, how have you honored the stranger in the
  house?
With bed and food? Or does he lie uncared for entirely?   130
For that is the way my mother is, though she be discreet;
Indeed, among articulate men she honors the worse one
Impulsively, and the better man she sends off with no honor."
And then the prudent Eurycleia addressed him:
"Child, please do not now blame one who should not be
  blamed.   135
He sat and drank wine, in fact, as long as he wished to.
He said he was not hungry for food, for she asked him.
But when he would think about going to bed and sleep,
She ordered the servants to spread the bedding down.
Then, like a man wholly woeful and lacking his fate,   140
He did not wish to lie down to sleep on a bed and in blankets,
But on an undressed oxhide and the fleeces of sheep

He lay down in the portico. We put a mantle on him ourselves."
So she said, and Telemachos went out through the hall
145 Holding his spear. And two swift dogs followed with him.
He went on to the assembly to join the well-greaved Achaians.
Then to the serving maids the godly woman called,
Eurycleia, daughter of Ops, the son of Peisenor:
"Come here. Some of you get busy and sweep the house,
150 Sprinkle it, and throw down purple coverlets
On the well-fashioned chairs; others wipe off with sponges
All of the tables, and clean the mixing bowls out,
And the well-wrought two-handled cups. Others of you go
To the spring for water, and come bringing it quickly.
155 For the suitors will not be long absent from the hall:
They will come very early, since it is a feast day for one and all.
So she said. They listened closely to her and obeyed her.
Twenty of them went on to the dark-watered spring,
And the rest busied themselves skillfully through the house.
160 Then the lordly menservants came in. And these
Split pieces of wood up skillfully and well. The women
Came back from the spring. The swineherd came after them,
Leading on three porkers who were the best of all.
And he let them out to feed in the lovely enclosures.
165 Then he himself spoke to Odysseus with soothing words:
"Stranger, do the Achaians look on you in any way better?
Or do they dishonor you in the halls as they did before?"
Odysseus of many wiles addressed him in answer:
"Eumaeos, may the gods avenge the injury
170 That those insolent men have recklessly devised
In another's home, and they have no share of shame."
And so they said such things to one another;
But Melanthios the goatherd came up close to them,
Leading goats that were outstanding in all the flocks
175 As a meal for the suitors. Two herdsmen followed with him,
And they tied the goats up inside the resounding portico;
And then he himself spoke out to Odysseus with taunts:
"Stranger, will you now still give trouble in the house,
Begging of the men, and you will not go on outdoors?
180 I think the two of us will not be separated wholly
Till we have tasted fists, since indeed you do not beg
Decently. And there are other banquets of the Achaians, too."
So he said, and Odysseus of many wiles said nothing,

But moved his head in silence, deliberating evils.
Philoitios, a chief of men, came up as a third among them,   185
Driving a sterile heifer for the suitors, and fat goats.
Ferrymen had brought them over, who also conduct
Other men, whoever may come up to them.
And he tied the beasts up well under the resounding portico.
He himself stood close by and questioned the swineherd: 190
"Who is this stranger, swineherd, who is newly arrived
At our house? Out of what men does he declare he is?
Where indeed are his race and his fatherland soil?
He is ill-fated, yet he looks in form like a lordly king.
But the gods do afflict much-wandering men   195
Whenever they weave a fate of sorrow, even for kings."
So he said, stood close, and pledged him with his right hand,
And speaking out to him he uttered wingèd words:
"Hail, father stranger; may bliss come to pass for you
Hereafter. But, now at least, you are held in many ills.   200
Father Zeus, none of the gods is more destructive than you.
You do not pity men when once you yourself give them birth,
Getting them involved in misfortune and wretched woes.
I sweated when I thought, and my eyes were filled with tears
To remember Odysseus, since I believe he too   205
Wanders among men wearing such tatters as these,
If he is yet alive and sees the light of the sun.
But if he is already dead and in the halls of Hades,
Alas then for blameless Odysseus who put me as a small boy
In charge of oxen in the land of the Cephallenians.   210
Now they have grown numberless, nor did any race
Of broad-browed cattle give better increase for any man.
Others order me to drive them in for themselves to eat,
Nor do they care in any way for the son in the halls,
Or tremble at the surveillance of the gods. They strive even now 215
To divide the goods of the master who is gone so long.
But this thing the heart inside my own breast turns over
Many times: it is very bad while the son is alive
To go off to the land of others with the oxen and all
Among alien men. But it is more dreadful to remain here   220
And undergo pains while abiding by the oxen of others.
Indeed, I would have fled long ago and come to another
Proud king, since matters are no longer to be borne.
But still I think of that hapless man, if from somewhere

225 He may come and make the suitors scatter through the halls."
Then Odysseus of many wiles addressed him in answer:
"Herdsman, you do not seem like a bad or senseless man,
And I know for myself that prudence attains your mind.
So I shall speak out to you and swear a great oath on it:
May Zeus now be my witness first of the gods, and this guest
230   table,
And the hearth of blameless Odysseus, to which I have come;
While you are in this place Odysseus shall come home
And you shall see with your own eyes, if you desire,
The suitors being slaughtered who are lording it here."
235 Then the man who was a herdsman of the oxen spoke to him:
"Stranger, would that the son of Cronos might bring this to pass!
You should learn what my strength is and how my hands go
    with it."
And so Eumaeos prayed the same way to all the gods
That many-minded Odysseus should return to his own home.
240 Such matters did they speak of to one another.
Meanwhile the suitors were contriving death and destiny
For Telemachos; still a bird came to him on the left,
A lofty-flying eagle and he held a trembling dove.
Amphinomos spoke out to them and addressed them:
245 "My friends, this plan shall not concur with our wish,
The murder of Telemachos. Let us take thought for a banquet."
So Amphinomos said, and his speech was pleasing to them.
They went into the house of godlike Odysseus,
And they put mantles down on the seats and on the armchairs.
250 Then they sacrificed great sheep and goats rich with fat,
They sacrificed sleek hogs and a heifer of the herd.
Then they roasted the entrails and distributed them
And mixed wine up in bowls. And the swineherd passed the
    cups.
Philoitios, a chief of men, passed out bread to them
255 In lovely baskets, and Melanthios poured the wine.
Then they stretched forth their hands to the food that was
    laid out ready.
Telemachos, managing for advantage, sat Odysseus down
Inside the well-built hall next to the stone threshold,
Setting down an insignificant stool and small table.
260 Beside him he put portions of entrails and poured wine
In a golden cup, and addressed a speech to him:

"Sit in this place now and drink your wine among the men.
I myself shall personally hold off the jibes and the fists
Of all the suitors, since this house is not public
But belongs to Odysseus, and he gained it for me.   265
As for you, suitors, keep your hearts in check from taunting
And from using your fists, so no strife or quarrel may arise."
So he said, and they all bit their lips with their teeth
And wondered at Telemachos that he spoke boldly.
Then Antinoos, the son of Eupeithes, addressed them: 270
"Achaians, let us accept the speech of Telemachos,
Though it is a harsh one. He speaks with great threat to us.
For Zeus, son of Cronos, did not allow it, or by now
We would have stopped him in the halls, clear speaker though
       he be."
So Antinoos said. But the man gave no heed to his speech.   275
Meanwhile, heralds were leading a sacred hecatomb to the gods
Through the town. And the long-haired Achaians gathered
Under the shadowy grove of far-darting Apollo.
When they had roasted the top parts of meat and drawn it off,
They divided up the portions and shared in the glorious feast.   280
Those who were serving placed beside Odysseus a portion
Equal to what they got themselves, as Telemachos,
The beloved son of godly Odysseus, had ordered.
And Athene by no means allowed the bold suitors
To refrain from grievous outrage, so that still more pain   285
Might enter the heart of Odysseus, son of Laertes.
There was a man among the suitors who had a lawless mind.
Ktesippos was his name, and in Samê he made his home.
Relying on his own prodigious property,
He wooed the wife of Odysseus who was gone so long.   290
He then spoke out before the insolent suitors:
"Listen to me, bold suitors, so I may say something.
This stranger has long had, as is seemly, a share
Which is equal. It is not good or just to slight
The guests of Telemachos, whoever comes to this house.   295
Come then, I too shall give him a gift, so that he also
May give a prize to the water pourer or someone else
Of the servants who are in the home of godly Odysseus."
When he said this he threw an ox's foot from his stout hand,
Picking it up from the basket where it lay. And Odysseus   300
Dodged it by quickly ducking his head, and smiled in his heart

A very scornful smile. It struck the well-built wall.
Telemachos rebuked Ktesippos in a speech:
"Ktesippos, this was much better for you in your heart
That you did not hit the stranger. He dodged the missile
305   himself.
For I would have struck you through the middle with my sharp
    spear,
And your father would be arranging a tomb for you, not a
    wedding,
Right here. So let no one show any unseemly deeds
In my house. For I am now aware and know the facts,
310 The good ones, and the worse. I was a foolish child before,
And still we endure these things as we look on them,
While sheep are being slaughtered, wine is being drunk, and
    bread
Being eaten. It is hard for one man to check many men.
Come then, do me no more evil in your hostility.
315 If you are already eager to kill me with the bronze,
I should prefer that; it would be better by far to die
Than perpetually to look upon these sorry deeds,
Strangers being maltreated and men disgracefully
Dragging the servant women through the lovely halls."
320 So he said, and all of them grew hushed in silence.
Finally Agelaos, son of Damastor, spoke out:
"My friends, surely no one should become enraged
At a just saying and rebuke someone with hostile words.
Do not maltreat the stranger at all, or any one
325 Of the servants who are in the halls of godly Odysseus.
I myself would say to Telemachos and his mother
A mild speech that should please the hearts of both of them.
So long as the spirits in your breasts were expecting
That many-minded Odysseus would return to his own home,
330 There was no resentment that you waited and kept the suitors
In check within the house, since that was preferable
If Odysseus had returned and did get back to his house.
But now it is clear already he is to return no more.
Come then, sit beside your mother and tell her this:
335 To marry him who is the best man and provides the most,
So you may possess all your paternal goods in joy,
Eating and drinking, and she may tend to the house of another."
Then sound-minded Telemachos answered him:

"Agelaos, by Zeus and the pains of my father, who may
Have perished or have wandered far from Ithaca,   340
I shall not delay my mother's wedding at all. I bid her
To marry whom she wishes, and I shall add on endless gifts.
But I am ashamed to drive her out of the hall against her will
By a word of constraint. May a god not bring this to pass."
So Telemachos said. But Pallas Athene aroused   345
Quenchless laughter in the suitors and set their wits astray.
They were already laughing with the jaws of other men,
And they were eating meat spattered with blood. Their eyes
Filled up with tears and their hearts sensed an anguish coming.
Godlike Theoclymenos also spoke out among them: 350
"Wretched men! What evil is this you suffer? Your heads
And faces are shrouded in night, and your knees beneath;
Wailing blazes up, and your cheeks are covered with tears,
The walls and the lovely pedestals are sprinkled with blood.
The porch is full of phantoms; the courtyard is also full   355
Of those eager for Erebos under the dusk. The sun
Has perished out of heaven, and an evil mist has rushed in."
So he said, and all of them laughed sweetly at him.
Eurymachos, son of Polybos, began speaking to them:
"This stranger newly come from elsewhere is out of his mind.   360
So send him at once, young men, out of the house outdoors
To go to the place of assembly, since it seems like night to him
   here."
Then godlike Theoclymenos addressed him:
"Eurymachos, I do not ask you to furnish guides for me.
I have my eyes and my ears and both of my feet,   365
And the thought in my breast is not at all shabbily formed.
With their help I shall go on outdoors, since I perceive
An evil coming on you, that no one of you suitors
Who outrage men in the home of godlike Odysseus
And devise reckless deeds shall escape from or avoid."   370
When he said this he went out of the well-situated house
And came to Peiraeos, who kindly welcomed him.
Then all the suitors, looking at one another,
Provoked Telemachos, laughing about his guests.
And this is what one of those overbearing young men would say: 375
"Telemachos, no one is worse off with guests than you;
Insofar as you have for one of them this filthy tramp
Who requires bread and wine and is not at all skilled

At tasks or in strength, but is just a burden on the land.
380 Moreover, this other man has stood up to prophesy.
But if you listen a little to me it would be far better.
Let us throw the guests into a ship with many oarlocks
And send them to Sicily, where you would get a worthwhile
    price."
So the suitors said. But he did not heed their speeches.
385 No, he glanced at his father in silence, ever on watch
For the time when he might lay hands on the shameless
    suitors.
The daughter of Icarios, prudent Penelope,
Put down a beautiful stool opposite
In the halls where the men were and listened to the words of
    each.
For the men themselves while they laughed and prepared a
390   dinner,
Sweet and satisfying since they had sacrificed many animals.
No other more joyless supper might ever come to be
Than the one the goddess and the mighty man were soon
To set out. For the others were first to contrive sorry deeds.

XXI

Now the bright-eyed goddess Athene put it into the mind
Of Icarios' daughter, the prudent Penelope,
To set the bow before the suitors and the gray iron
In Odysseus' halls as a contest and a start for slaughter.
She stepped up on the high stairway of her quarters   5
And in her stout hand took hold of the well-curved key,
A lovely one of bronze. And an ivory handle was on it.
And she went on with her serving women into a chamber,
The last room, where the treasures of her lord were lying,
Bronze and gold and iron that was highly wrought.   10
There a springy bow was lying, and also a quiver
For arrows, and in it were many arrows that bring grief;
These gifts a friend had given him who met him in Lacedemon,
Iphitos, son of Eurytos, who was like the immortals.
The two of them came upon each other in Messene,   15
In the house of skillful Ortilochos. Odysseus
Had gone there after a debt that the whole people owed him.
Messenian men had taken up three hundred sheep
And their shepherds out of Ithaca in many-oared ships.
For their sake Odysseus had gone a long way on his errand   20
While a boy. His father and the other elders had sent him forth.
And Iphitos came after horses, twelve females of his
That he had lost, along with unweaned, work-enduring mules.
Then these, indeed, brought upon him murder and destiny
When he went in the presence of the stout-hearted son of Zeus, 25
The mortal Heracles, who was experienced in huge deeds
And slaughtered the man as a guest in his own house,
A cruel wretch, as he did not respect the gods' wrath or the
    table
That he had set before him. And then he killed the man himself.
He himself kept the mares with the powerful hooves in his halls. 30
Seeking these, the man met Odysseus and gave him the bow,

Which great Eurytos had carried before, and then
Had left when he died to his son in the lofty house.
Odysseus gave him a sharp sword and a mighty spear,
35 The start of a close-binding friendship; but they did not know
One another at the table, since before that Zeus's son slew
Iphitos, son of Eurytos, a man like the immortals,
Who gave him the bow. And never would godly Odysseus
Take it when he went off on the black ships to war.
40 But he left it lying there in the halls as a reminder
Of his dear friend. And he did carry it in his own land.
And when the divine woman had arrived at her chamber
And had gone over the oak threshold that a craftsman once
Skillfully planed for her and straightened with a line—
45 He fitted doorposts up and set shining doors on them—
Right away she quickly took the thong from the hook,
Inserted the key, and shot back the bolts of the door,
Aiming them straight; and they groaned like a bull
Feeding in a meadow, so loud did the lovely door sound
50 As it was struck by the key and was quickly opened wide.
She stepped up on the lofty planking. And there chests
Were standing, inside of which fragrant clothing was stored.
From there she stretched herself up and reached the bow
    from its peg,
Along with the bow case that surrounded it handsomely.
55 She sat down right there, putting it on her own knees,
And wept aloud as she took down her husband's bow.
And when she had her fill of tearful lamentation,
She went on into the hall among the noble suitors,
Holding in her hand the springy bow and the quiver
60 For arrows. In it were many arrows that bring grief.
Her servants brought her a case in which iron lay
In plenty, and so did bronze, the prizes of her lord.
And when the godly woman had come to the suitors,
She stood beside the pillar of the stoutly fashioned roof,
65 Holding the glistening headbands before her cheeks.
A devoted servant maid stood near her on either side.
At once she spoke out to the suitors and addressed a speech to
    them:
"Listen to me now, bold suitors, you who have always
Beset this house, perpetually eating and drinking
70 While my husband has been gone away for a long time.

You could make up no other story as an excuse
Than that you wanted to marry me and make me your wife.
Well, come now, suitors, since this appears as your prize.
I will set up the great bow of godly Odysseus.
The one who most nimbly strings the bow in his hands   75
And shoots an arrow through all twelve of the axes,
Him will I follow, departing from this very lovely
Home of my marriage that is full of the goods of life,
Which I think I shall ever remember, even in dreams."
So she said, and she called to Eumaeos, the godly swineherd,   80
To set up for the suitors the bow and the gray iron.
Eumaeos took them, weeping, and he set them out.
The herdsman for his part wailed when he saw his master's bow.
Then Antinoos rebuked them and spoke out to them directly:
"Foolish yokels, who consider only the things of the day.   85
You wretches, why are you dripping tears? Why arouse
The heart in the breast of a woman whose heart lies in pain
In any case, since she has lost her dear husband?
But sit down and eat in silence, or else go on
And wail outdoors, leaving the bow behind right here,   90
An inviolable contest for the suitors. So I think
This polished bow is not to be strung easily,
And there is no man present among all of you
Of the kind Odysseus was. I saw him my own self,
And I do remember him though I was still a foolish child."   95
So he said, but even so the heart in his breast hoped
To string the bowstring and shoot an arrow through the iron.
Yet he was destined to be the first to taste an arrow
From the hands of blameless Odysseus, whom he was flouting
     just then
As he sat in the halls, and he was rousing all his companions. 100
Telemachos spoke out to them in his sacred might:
"Well, Zeus, son of Cronos, has made me lacking in sense.
My dear mother says, even though she is prudent,
That she will follow another and leave this house behind.
Yet I am laughing and am pleased in my senseless heart.   105
Come now, you suitors, since this appears as the prize,
A woman whose like now exists not in the Achaian land,
Not in sacred Pylos or in Argos or Mycenae,
Or in Ithaca herself, or upon the black mainland.
You know it yourselves. Why need I praise my mother?   110

Come, do not put it off with excuses or turn away
From stringing the bow any more, so we may see.
And I my very own self might make a try at the bow.
If I were to string it and shoot an arrow through the iron,
115 My queenly mother would not leave me in any grief
If she went off with another, since I should be left behind
As already one able to take up my father's fine weapons."
He spoke, and put the purple tunic off his shoulders,
Sprang upright, and off his shoulders took the sharp sword.
120 First he stood up the axes, digging one long trench through
For all of them, and he straightened it with a line,
And stamped earth down about them. Wonder seized all who
     saw
How neatly he stood them, but he had never viewed them
     before.
He went and stood on the threshold and tested the bow.
125 Three times he made it quiver, striving to draw it,
And three times he slackened his strength, hoping in his heart
To string the bowstring and shoot an arrow through the iron.
And he would have drawn it the fourth time, bending it with
     his strength.
But Odysseus nodded and checked him, impelled as he was.
130 Then Telemachos spoke out to them in his sacred might:
"Well, how weak and cowardly I shall be even in the future,
Or else I am too young and cannot yet rely on my hands
For warding some man off if he gets angry first.
Come now, you who are superior to me in strength,
135 Try the bow out and let us conclude the contest."
So he said, and put the bow away from him on the ground,
Leaning it against the tight-fitted, well-made doors.
And then he leaned a swift dart against its fine tip.
Then he sat back down on the chair from which he had stood.
140 Antinoos, the son of Eupeithes, spoke out to them:
"Rise, all my companions, in order, from left to right,
Beginning at the place from which the wine is poured."
So Antinoos said, and his speech was pleasing to them.
Leodes, son of Oinops, was the first to stand up.
145 He was their soothsayer, and he always sat
Furthest in by the lovely mixing bowl. To him alone
Was recklessness hateful; he resented all the suitors.
He was the first then to take the bow and the swift dart.

He went and stood on the threshold and tried out the bow.
He did not string it. Before that, drawing it up,   150
He tired his soft, unworn hands. And he spoke to the suitors:
"My friends, I cannot string it. Let another take it.
Many excellent men shall this bow have bereaved
Of life and spirit, since it is better by far
To die than to live and miss what perpetually   155
We are gathered for here, expectant day after day,
And even now someone hopes in his mind and desires
To marry Penelope, the wife of Odysseus.
But when he has seen the bow and tested it out,
Let him then woo some other of the well-gowned Achaian
     women   160
And seek her in marriage with gifts. She then may wed
Whoever gives the most and comes as the destined man."
When he had said this he put the bow away from him,
Leaning it against the tight-fitted, well-made doors.
And then he leaned the swift dart against its fine tip.   165
Then he sat back down on the chair from which he had stood.
But Antinoos rebuked him and spoke out to him directly:
"Leodes, what sort of speech has got past the bar of your teeth?
A wretched and grievous one. I am angered as I hear it,
If this bow indeed shall deprive excellent men   170
Of spirit and life, when you cannot string it yourself.
Your queenly mother did not bear you as the sort of man
Who would be capable of drawing a bow and arrows;
But other noble suitors shall quickly string it."
So he said, and he called to Melanthios, the goatherd.   175
"Come, Melanthios, and kindle a fire in the halls.
Put a large stool down alongside and a fleece upon it,
And bring in a great round piece of the fat from inside,
So we young men, when we have warmed it and rubbed it with
     grease,
May try the bow out and may conclude the contest."   180
So he said. Melanthios at once kindled a quenchless fire,
Brought in a stool, put it down, and set a fleece upon it.
Then he carried in a great round piece of the fat from inside.
This the young men tried, when they had warmed it. But they
     were not
Able to string it: they were far too lacking in strength.   185
Antinoos and godlike Eurymachos, chief of the suitors,

Still held back. They were by far the best in excellence.
Accompanying each other, the oxherd and the swineherd
Of godly Odysseus had both gone out of the house.
190 Divine Odysseus came after them from the house himself.
And when they were outside of the doors and the courtyard
He raised his voice and addressed them with soothing speeches:
"Oxherd, and you, swineherd, shall I tell you something
Or keep it to myself? My heart bids me to speak.
195 How would you fend for Odysseus if he came from somewhere
Very suddenly this way and some god had brought him in?
Would you fend for the suitors or fend for Odysseus?
Speak the way your heart and your spirit command you to."
Then the man who was in charge of the oxen addressed him:
200 "Father Zeus, would that you might fulfill this wish,
That the man himself might come, and some god might bring
him.
You would learn what my strength is and how my hands go with
it."
And so Eumaeos prayed the same way to all the gods
For many-minded Odysseus to return to his own home.
205 And when he had recognized their unerring intent,
He answered them right away and addressed them with a
speech:
"Here I am, home, myself, having suffered many pains;
I have come in the twentieth year to my fatherland.
I realize that you alone of the servants I come to
210 Are longing for me. I have heard none of the others
Praying for me to reach home again on my return,
And I shall speak the truth to you both as it shall be.
If a god indeed subdues the noble suitors beneath me,
I shall give you both wives and provide you with property
215 And houses built close to my own. Then you shall be
Companions and kinsmen of Telemachos and myself.
Come now, I shall show you another manifest sign
So you may know me well and trust me in your hearts:
A scar a boar once inflicted on me with his shining tusk
220 When I went to Parnassos with the sons of Autolycos."
When he had said this he drew his rags away from the great scar.
Both of them, when they had seen and well noted the details,
Wept and threw their arms around the skillful Odysseus,
And they kept kissing him, embracing his head and shoulders.

Odysseus kept kissing their heads and hands the same way.   225
The light of the sun would have gone down on them as they
     moaned
If Odysseus himself had not checked them and spoken out:
"Stop wailing and lamenting, lest someone come out
Of the hall, see us, and then tell it within too;
But go inside, each in turn and not all together,   230
I first, and you afterward. And let this be made the sign.
When all the others, the whole number of noble suitors,
Will not allow the bow and quiver to be given to me,
Then you, godly Eumaeos, carry the bow through the house,
Place it in my hands, and then tell the women   235
To lock up the closely fitted portals of the hall,
And if anyone inside hears in our enclosures
A groaning and beating of men, let her not go forth
Out the door at all, but be there in silence at the task.
And you, godly Philoitios, I order to bolt the gates   240
Of the courtyard with a bolt, and quickly lash on the cord."
When he had said this he entered the well-situated halls.
Then he went and sat down on the stool from which he had
     stood,
And the two servants of godly Odysseus also went in.
Eurymachos was already turning the bow in his hands,   245
Warming it here and there in the fire's flame. But he could not
String it that way; his mighty heart swelled heavily.
Angered, he uttered a speech and spoke out directly:
"Well now, there is grief in me for myself and for all.
Not for the marriage, though distressed, do I moan so greatly.   250
There are many other Achaian women, some in this very
Sea-circled Ithaca; and some in other cities.
But if we are to such a degree lacking in the force
Of godlike Odysseus that we cannot string his bow,
It is a disgrace even for men in the future to hear of."   255
Then Antinoos, son of Eupeithes, spoke to him:
"Eurymachos, it will not be so. And you know it yourself.
For now through the district is a feast day of that god,
A holy one. And who would bend the bows? Put them down
Quietly. But as for the axes, suppose we let them   260
All stand. For I think no one will come into the hall
Of Odysseus, son of Laertes, and carry them off.
Come now, let the wine-pourer begin the rite with the cups,

So we may pour libation and lay down the curved bows.
265 And at dawn summon Melanthios, the goatherd,
To bring the goats that are far outstanding in all the herds,
So that, setting out thighs to Apollo, famed for the bow,
We may try the bow out and conclude the contest."
So Antinoos said, and his speech was pleasing to them.
270 Heralds poured out water for them over their hands.
Young men were filling bowls up to the brim with drink.
And served round to all, putting the first drops in the cups.
When they had poured libation and drunk what their hearts
    wished,
Odysseus of many wiles spoke to them with a trick in mind:
275 "Listen to me, suitors of the illustrious queen,
So I may tell you what the heart in my breast bids me to.
Eurymachos especially and godly Antinoos
Do I beseech, since he spoke properly when he said:
We should let the bow go now, and leave the matter to the gods,
280 And at dawn the god will give the strength to the one he wishes.
Come then, give me the polished bow, so that among you
I may test out my strength and hands, whether the force
Is in me still that once was in my supple limbs,
Or whether wandering and lack of care have ruined me already."
285 So he said, and they all grew insolently angry,
Fearing that he might put the string on the polished bow.
Antinoos rebuked him and spoke out to him directly:
"Wretched stranger, you have no sense, none in the least.
Are you not content to dine among us exalted men,
290 Secure, not to be deprived of food at all, and to hear
Our speeches and our discourse? Nor does anyone else,
Whether stranger or beggar listen to our speeches.
Honey-sweet wine besets you, that harms other men, too,
Whoever takes it down in gulps and drinks to excess.
295 Wine blinded the Centaur too, illustrious Eurytion,
In the hall of great-spirited Perithöus,
When he came to the Lapiths. After his mind was blinded with
    wine
He went mad and did evils in the house of Perithöus.
Distress seized the heroes. They leaped and dragged him
    outdoors
300 Through the forecourt and sheared his ears and nostrils off
With the pitiless bronze. Then he grew reckless in his mind

And went on, bearing madness in his impetuous heart.
From that came the quarrel between Centaurs and men.
But first for himself he found evil, being heavy with wine,
And so I declare great trouble for you if you should string   305
This bow. You would not encounter any gentle use
In our district. We should send you speedily
To King Echetos, the destroyer of all mortal men,
In a black ship. And you would not be saved there. But drink
Quietly, and do not wrangle with men younger than you."   310
And then the prudent Penelope answered him:
"Antinoos, it is not good or just to slight
The guests of Telemachos, whoever comes to this house.
Do you think, if this stranger does string the great bow
Of Odysseus, relying on his hands and his mighty force,   315
That he will lead me to his home and make me his wife?
He himself has never yet thought this in his breast.
Let no one of you dine here grieving in his heart
On that account, since it is not seemly at all."
Eurymachos, son of Polybos, answered her: 320
"Daughter of Icarios, prudent Penelope,
We do not think this man will lead you home. It is not seemly,
But we are ashamed at the rumor among men and women,
Lest sometime some other foul person of the Achaeans may say:
'Yes, far inferior men are wooing the wife   325
Of an excellent man and cannot string his polished bow.
But someone else, a beggar, who came on his wanderings,
Easily strung the bow and shot through the iron.'
So they would say, and this would be a reproach to us."
Then the prudent Penelope spoke to him: 330
"Eurymachos, there is no way that good reports may exist
In the district for those who dishonor and devour
A noble man's home. And why make a reproach of this?
The stranger here is very large and of a well-knit frame.
He declares he is by descent a good father's son.   335
Come now, give him the polished bow, so we may see.
For this do I proclaim, and it shall be brought to pass.
If he does string it and Apollo gives him the praise,
I shall clothe him in a mantle and a tunic, lovely clothes.
I shall give him a sharp javelin, a defense against dogs and men, 340
And a two-edged sword. I shall give him sandals for his feet
And send him wherever his heart and spirit bid."

Then sound-minded Telemachos addressed her in answer:
"My mother, as for the bow, none of the Achaians has more
    power
345 Then I have to give or refuse it to whomever I wish.
Not any of those who rule in craggy Ithaca
Or who rule over the islands towards horse-pasturing Elis.
None of them will compel me against my will even from giving
This bow once for all to the stranger to take off, if I wish.
350 But go into the house and attend to your own tasks,
The loom and the distaff, and give orders to your servants
To set at the work. The bow shall concern all the men
But me especially. For the power in the house is mine."
She was amazed at him, and back into the house she went.
355 The sound-minded speech of her son she took to heart.
She went into the upper chamber with her serving women,
And then wept for Odysseus, her dear husband, until
Bright-eyed Athene cast sweet sleep upon her eyelids.
Then the divine swineherd took the curved bow, and was
    carrying it,
360 And all the suitors made an outcry in the halls.
This is what one of those overbearing young men would say:
"Where are you carrying the curved bow, miserable swineherd,
You vagabond? Soon the swift dogs you reared yourself,
Shall eat you amid the swine, apart from men, alone,
365 If Apollo is gracious to us, and the other immortal gods."
So they said; but he carried it and put it right where he was,
Afraid because many made an outcry in the halls.
But Telemachos from the other side shouted a threat:
"Uncle, bring the bow out. You will soon not do well to heed
    all,
370 Lest, though younger than you, I drive you to the fields
And throw stones at you. I am mightier than you in strength.
Would I were that much mightier in strength and with my hands
Than all of the suitors who are inside the halls.
Then I should soon send one of them grimly on his way
375 Out of our house, since they are devising evils."
So he said, and all of the suitors sweetly laughed
At him, and they relaxed their oppressive anger
Toward Telemachos. The swineherd carried the bow through
    the house,
Stood beside skillful Odysseus, and put it in his hands.

Then he called forth the nurse Eurycleia and addressed her: 380
"Prudent Eurycleia, Telemachos orders you
To lock up the closely fitted portals of the hall.
And if anyone inside hears in our enclosures
A groaning and a beating of men, let her not go forth
Out the door at all, but be there in silence at the task."   385
So he said, and for her the word was without a wing.
She locked up the doors of the well-situated halls.
Philoitios hastened in silence out of the house,
Outdoors, and locked up the gates of the well-fenced court.
Under the portico lay the papyrus-fiber cable   390
Of a bobbing ship. With it he tied the gates, entered,
And then went and sat down on the stool from which he had
     stood
And looked at Odysseus. He was already handling the bow,
Turning it in all directions, testing it this way and that,
For fear worms had eaten the horns while the master was away.   395
And this is what one of them, looking at his neighbor would
     say:
"This is some fancier and an expert with bows,
And perhaps such as these are lying in his home too,
Or else he wants to make one, he handles it so
This way and that in his hands, the beggar skilled in evils."   400
And another of the overbearing young men would say:
"Would that he might encounter profit only to the degree
That he shall ever be able to string this bow himself."
So the suitors said. But Odysseus of many wiles,
At once when he raised the great bow and viewed it on all
     sides—   405
As when a man skilled at the lyre and at singing
Easily stretches a string over a new peg,
Tying at both ends the flexible gut of the sheep—
So without effort did Odysseus string the great bow.
He took it in his right hand and tested the cord.   410
It sang sweetly beneath like a swallow in its sound.
Great distress came upon the suitors, and the skin of all
Turned color. Zeus thundered greatly, showing signs.
Then godly Odysseus, who had endured much, rejoiced
That the son of crooked-counseling Cronos sent him a portent.   415
He took a swift arrow that lay by him on the table,
Bare. The others were lying within the hollow quiver,

The ones the Achaians were soon to experience.
He put it to the bridge, drew the string and the notches,
420 And shot the arrow right from there, sitting on the stool,
Aiming it straight, and he did not miss one handle tip
Of all of the axes. The arrow heavy with bronze
Went straight on out the end. He spoke to Telemachos:
"Telemachos, the stranger seated in the halls
425 Does not discredit you. I did not miss my aim,
Nor did I toil long to string the bow. My strength is steadfast
　　still
And is not such as the suitors scorn, despising me.
And now it is time for the Achaians to have a meal prepared
In the light, and then to make sport in other ways
430 With singing and the lyre; they are the ornaments of a feast."
So he said, and signaled with his eyebrows. Telemachos,
The dear son of godlike Odysseus, girded on his sharp sword,
Put his own hand round his spear, and stood close to him
Beside his armchair, equipped with the glittering bronze.

XXII

Then Odysseus of many wiles bared himself from his rags
And sprang upon the great threshold, holding the bow
And the quiver full of arrows. He poured the swift shafts out
There before his feet. And he spoke out among the suitors:
"This inviolable contest has been brought to an end.   5
And now I shall know another mark that no man has ever hit,
If I happen to hit it, and Apollo grant me glory."
So he said, and aimed a bitter arrow at Antinoos.
The man was about to lift up the lovely libation cup,
A gold double-eared one, and he held it up in his hands   10
So that he might drink wine. There was no thought of slaughter
In his heart. Who would think a single man among so many
As the banqueters were, though he was very powerful,
Would bring upon him an evil death and black fate?
Odysseus took aim and shot him with an arrow in the throat;   15
The point of it went straight on through his tender neck.
He leaned to one side and the cup fell from his hand
As he was hit; at once a thick spurt of human blood
Came through his nostrils. He quickly pushed the table from
    him,
Striking it with his foot. He spilled the food on the ground,   20
And the bread and roast meat were defiled. The suitors made
A din through the halls when they saw the man fall.
They rose up from their chairs, panicking through the house,
Peering on all sides along the well-constructed walls.
And nowhere was there a shield or stout spear to be grasped.   25
They upbraided Odysseus with words full of rage:
"Stranger, to your ill do you shoot at men. You shall no longer
Enter other contests; now your sheer destruction is certain.
Now you have slain the mortal who was the greatest by far
Of the young men in Ithaca. So vultures shall eat you here."   30
Each man guessed so, since they thought he had killed the man
Without wanting to. And the fools did not perceive

That already the bonds of destruction were fastened on them all.
Odysseus of many wiles glared at them and spoke:

35 "Dogs, you thought I would no longer come home in return
From the land of the Trojans, in that you wore my house away
And slept alongside my serving women by force
And underhandedly courted my wife while I was myself alive,
And you did not fear the gods who possess broad heaven,

40 Or that there would be any vengeance of men in time to come.
Now the bonds of destruction are fastened on you all."
So he said, and sallow fear got a grip on all of them.
Each one peered for where he might flee sheer destruction.
Eurymachos alone spoke to him in answer:

45 "If indeed you are Ithacan Odysseus, who have come,
You have rightfully told all this that the Achaians have done:
Many wicked things in the halls, and many in the fields.
And here he lies already who was guilty of them all,
Antinoos. He it was who instigated these deeds,

50 Not so much wanting or desiring the wedding at all,
But plotting other acts which the son of Cronos did not bring
    about
For him: that over the well-tilled land of Ithaca
He might himself be king, and might kill your son in ambush.
Now he is slain, as was his due. Spare your people

55 And we shall give satisfaction in the land hereafter
For all that has been drunk up and eaten in the halls,
Each one bringing separately a recompense worth twenty oxen,
And we shall give bronze and gold in return till your own heart
Is softened. Till then no one would blame you for getting
    angry."

60 Odysseus of many wiles glared at him and spoke:
"Eurymachos, not if you gave me all the paternal goods
That you possess, and any others you added from somewhere,
Not even then should I yet stay my hands from slaughter
Until the suitors had paid for all their insolence.

65 And now it lies with you either to fight face to face
Or to flee, whoever would avoid death and destiny.
But I think that no one shall escape sheer destruction."
So he said; and their knees and their own hearts went slack
On the spot. And Eurymachos addressed them yet again:

70 "My friends, this man will not check his invincible hands,
But once he has taken the polished bow and quiver

He will shoot from the smooth threshold until he has killed
All of us. But let us remember the ardor of battle;
Draw your swords out and hold the tables up in the way
Of the swift-fated arrows. And let us all go at him   75
In a body, hoping we may force him from the threshold and the
    doorway.
And may come to the town, and an alarm quickly be raised.
And soon then this man would have shot for the last time."
When he had spoken so, he drew out his keen sword
Of bronze, sharpened on both sides; and sprang on the man   80
With a terrible cry. At the same time godly Odysseus
Shot off an arrow, and he hit his chest by the nipple;
He drove the swift shaft into his liver. And from his hand
He let the sword drop to the ground. He fell down sprawling
Doubled up on the table. He spilled the food on the ground,   85
And the two-handled cups. He beat the earth with his forehead,
Agonized in his heart. He kicked the armchair with both feet.
And made it shake. A mist was shed over his eyes.
Amphinomos charged upon the mighty Odysseus
Rushing up against him, and he drew his sharp sword   90
That the man might somehow yield the door to him.
    Telemachos
Was too fast for him, and hit him from behind with a bronze
    spear
In the middle of the shoulders, and drove it through his chest.
He made a noise falling and struck the ground flat with his
    forehead.
Telemachos sprang away, leaving his long-shadowy spear   95
There in Amphinomos. For he greatly feared that, as he drew
    out
The long-shadowy spear, some Achaian might thrust him
    through
By rushing on with a sword, or hit him as he stooped forward.
He ran on and very quickly reached his dear father.
He stood close beside him and uttered wingèd words: 100
"Father, I shall now bring you a shield and two spears,
And a helmet all of bronze, fitted to the temples.
I shall put it on me when I come, and I shall give other
    arms
To the swineherd and the oxherd. It is better to be armed."
Odysseus of many wiles addressed him in answer: 105

"Bring them on the run, while the arrows may defend me,
Lest they force me out the doors, single man that I am."
So he said, and Telemachos obeyed his dear father.
He went on into the chamber where lay the glorious arms.
110 And from that place he took away four shields, eight spears,
And four bronze-fitted helmets with shaggy horsehair plumes;
He came carrying them and very soon reached his dear father.
He himself put the bronze on over his flesh first of all.
The two servants put their fine armor on the same way.
115 They flanked the skillful and subtle-minded Odysseus.
He himself, so long as there were arrows to defend him,
Kept aiming at the suitors in his house one by one
And always hit his mark. They fell one after another.
But when the arrows had all left the master as he shot,
120 He leaned the bow to stand it up against the doorpost
Of the well-built hall, against the resplendent walls.
He himself put the four-layered shield round his shoulders
And placed on his mighty head the well-fashioned helmet
With a horsehair crest; terribly the plume nodded on top of it.
125 And he took two valiant spears fitted out with bronze.
There was a certain side door in the well-built wall
Along the highest point of the well-based hall's threshold.
It was a way to the passage, and well-fitted doors held it.
Odysseus ordered the godly swineherd to stand close to it
130 And watch over it. It was the one single way of approach.
Then Agelaos spoke to them, declaring his speech to all:
"My friends, will not someone go up through the side door
And tell the people, so an alarm may quickly be raised,
And then this man would soon have shot now for the last time."
135 Then Melanthios, herdsman of the goats, spoke to him:
"There is no way, Zeus-bred Agelaos. The court's fine doors
Are dreadfully close, and the mouth of the passage is hard,
And a single man who was valiant could hold back all.
But come, I shall bring you arms to gird yourselves with
140 From the chamber. Within, I think, and nowhere else
Have Odysseus and his glorious son put their armor up."
When he had said this, Melanthios, the goatherd, went up
To Odysseus' chambers through the slits of the hall.
There he took out twelve shields and as many spears
And as many bronze-fitted helmets with shaggy horsehair
145 　　plumes.

He came out and brought them quickly and gave them to the
    suitors
Then Odysseus' knees and his heart went slack
When he saw them putting on the armor and brandishing
The long spears in their hands. It seemed to him a great task.
Right away he uttered wingèd words to Telemachos: 150
"Telemachos, some one of the women in the halls
Stirs up an evil battle against us, or Melanthios does."
Sound-minded Telemachos addressed him in answer:
"Father, I myself made this mistake, and no one else
Is guilty. I left the closely fitted door of the chamber   155
Hanging open. One of them spied it better than I.
But go, godly Eumaeos, and close the door
And observe whether one of the women is doing this,
Or Melanthios, son of Dolios, the one I think."
And so they said such things to one another.   160
Then Melanthios, the goatherd, went again to the chamber
To bring the fine armor. The godly swineherd perceived him
And at once he addressed Odysseus, who was near:
"Zeus-born son of Laertes, Odysseus of many devices,
That destructive man who we ourselves think is the one   165
Is going to the chamber. And tell me unerringly
Whether I should kill him if I am more powerful,
Or bring him here to you to pay for the many
Insolences this man has plotted in your house."
Odysseus of many wiles addressed him in answer: 170
"Indeed, Telemachos and I shall hold the noble suitors
Inside of the halls, though they may struggle very much.
But both of you twist his feet behind him and his hands
    above,
Throw him into the chamber, and bind planks behind him,
And then fasten a plaited rope to the man himself.   175
Drag him up the lofty pillar and bring him near the beams
So he may long be alive and suffer oppressive pains."
So he said. They hearkened closely to him and obeyed him.
They went on into the chamber unseen by the man inside;
He in fact was searching a corner of the chamber for the arms.   180
The two remained standing on either side of the posts.
When Melanthios, the goatherd, was going over the threshold
Carrying a fine-horned helmet in one of his hands
And in the other a broad, old shield spattered with mold

185 Of the hero Laertes, which he used to bear as a young man—
But at this time it was laid by, and the seams of its thongs were
  loose—
The two rushed upon him, seized him, and dragged him inside
By the hair; they threw him, grieved at heart, on the ground.
They bound his hands and his feet with a spirit-hurting bond,
190 Turning it around very thoroughly and well, as the son
Of Laertes had ordered, godly Odysseus, who had endured
  much.
They fastened a plaited rope to the man himself,
Dragged him up the lofty pillar, and brought him near the
  beams.
Then you spoke and taunted him, swineherd Eumaeos:
195 "Now, indeed, Melanthios, you will keep watch the whole night,
Lying down in a gentle bed, as is fitting for you.
Nor shall the early-born, golden-throned one as she comes
From the streams of Oceanos escape your view at the time
You drive goats for the suitors to prepare a feast in the house."
200 And so he was left there, stretched in the ruinous bond.
The two put on armor, closed the shining door,
And went to the skillful crafty-minded Odysseus.
There did they stand, breathing force, the four of them
On the threshold, but there were many noblemen within the
  house.
205 Athene, daughter of Zeus, came to close quarters with them,
Likening herself to Mentor in form and in voice.
Odysseus rejoiced to see her, and spoke to her:
"Mentor, fend off harm; remember the dear companion
Who used to do you good. You are the same age as I."
210 So he said, thinking it was Athene, rouser of the people.
The suitors on the other side made a din in the halls.
Agelaos, son of Damastor, reproached her first:
"Mentor, let Odysseus not win you over with speeches
To fight against the suitors and to defend himself,
215 For I think our own purpose shall be carried out this way;
When we have killed these men, the father and the son,
Then you yourself shall be slain with them for what you plan
To do in the halls. You will pay it here with your own head,
And when we have deprived you of your power with the sword,
220 All the possessions you have, both indoors and out
We shall mix with those of Odysseus, and we shall not

Allow your sons to live in the halls or your daughters
Or your devoted wife to move round in the city of Ithaca."
So he said, and Athene grew very angry in her heart,
And she upbraided Odysseus with angry words: 225
"No longer, Odysseus, have you a steadfast mind or strength
As when, over white-armed Helen, who had a noble father,
You fought the Trojans, always relentlessly, for nine years
And in the dreadful combat slaughtered many men,
And Priam's broad-streeted city was taken by your plan.   230
How is it that now, when you have reached your home and
    possessions,
You wail about being valiant against the suitors?
Come now, old friend, stand by me and see the deed,
So you may see what sort Mentor, son of Alkimos, is
To repay well-doing in the midst of hostile men."   235
So she said, and did not yet wholly give him victory
With decisive strength, but still tested the power and strength
Both of Odysseus and of his glorious son.
Then she herself rushed up and sat upon the roof
Of the smoky hall facing them, in the form of a swallow.   240
Agelaos, the son of Damastor, urged on the suitors,
And so did Eurynomos, Amphimedon, Demoptolemos,
Peisander, the son of Polyktor, and skillful Polybos,
Who were by far the best of the suitors for excellence
Of those who were still living and fighting for their lives.   245
The bow and frequent arrows had already overcome the others.
Agelaos spoke to them, declaring his speech to all:
"My friends, this man shall soon hold back his invincible
    hands.
Mentor has gone from him, uttering empty boasts,
And they are left alone out in front of the gates.   250
Do not all of you let your long spears fly together.
Come now, you six hurl your javelins first, so that Zeus
May perchance grant that Odysseus be hit and we gain glory.
For the rest there will be no trouble when this man has
    fallen."
So he said, and they all threw their javelins as he bade,   255
Eagerly. But Athene made them all of no effect.
One of them hit against the pillar of the well-based hall,
Another one hit against the closely fitted door
And another's bronze-heavy ash spear fell on the wall.

260 And then, when they had avoided the spears of the suitors,
Godly Odysseus, who had endured much, began speaking to
them:
"My friends, let me say myself that we, too, right now
Should shoot into the throng of suitors who are striving to kill
us
And strip our armor, adding this to their former evils."
265 So he said, and all of them hurled their sharp spears,
Aiming them straight. Odysseus slew Demoptolemos;
Telemachos, Eurypades; and the swineherd, Elatos;
The man who was in charge of the oxen slew Peisander.
All these together bit the broad floor with their teeth,
270 And the suitors drew away into the corner of the hall.
But the others rushed on them and drew spears out of the dead.
Then the suitors hurled their sharp spears right away,
Eagerly. But Athene made their number of no effect.
One of them hit against a pillar of the well-based hall,
275 Another one hit against the closely fitted door,
And another's bronze-heavy ash spear fell on the wall.
Yet Amphimedon hit Telemachos' hand at the wrist
With a glancing blow, and the bronze wounded his outer skin.
Ktesippos grazed Eumaeos with a long spear on the shoulder
280 Above his shield. It leaped off and fell to the ground.
Then those round the skillful and subtle-minded Odysseus
Hurled their sharp spears into the throng of the suitors.
Then Odysseus, sacker of cities, hit Eurydamas.
Telemachos hit Amphimedon, and the swineherd hit
Polybos;
285 And then the man in charge of the oxen hit Ktesippos
Upon the chest, and he spoke right out with a boast:
"Son of Polytherses, you lover of jeers, never again
Yield wholly to folly and talk big; but turn the tale over
To the gods, since they are more powerful by far.
290 This is a guest gift in return for the foot you once gave
To godlike Odysseus as he went begging in the house."
So said the driver of the crumple-horned cattle. Odysseus
Wounded the son of Damastor at close hand with a long spear.
Telemachos wounded Leocritos, son of Euenor,
In the middle of the flank with a spear; he drove the bronze
295   through him.

The man fell on his face and struck the ground flat with his
    forehead.
Then Athene held up the aegis deadly to mortals,
On high from the roof. The minds of the men were dismayed.
They fled through the hall like cattle in a drove
That a darting gadfly, when it is stirred up, stampedes   300
In the season of spring, when the days are getting long.
And then, as falcons with bent claws and hooked beaks
Come down from the mountains and dash upon the birds—
These are driven over the plain cowering from the clouds,
But the others pounce on them and kill them; and no help   305
Comes, and no escape, and men rejoice at the chase—
So they rushed on through the house upon the suitors
And struck them one after another. Their wretched groaning
Rose as their heads were struck. The whole ground ran with
    blood.
Leiodes rushed on and seized Odysseus by the knees,   310
And imploring him, he uttered wingèd words:
"I pray to you, Odysseus, respect me and pity me.
Never yet, I say, have I spoken or done anything reckless
To any woman in the halls. But I kept stopping
The other suitors when anyone did such things.   315
But they did not heed me and keep their hands from evil,
And so in their recklessness they have come to a wretched fate.
Yet I who as a soothsayer among them did nothing evil
Shall be laid low, since there is no future grace for good deeds."
Odysseus of many wiles glared at him and spoke: 320
"If you indeed declare you are a soothsayer among them,
You are likely to have prayed many times in the halls
That the end of a sweet return be kept far from me;
That my beloved wife follow you and bear you children.
And so you may not escape death that brings bitter pain."   325
When he had said this, he seized in his stout hand a sword lying
    there
That Agelaos had let fall to the ground when he was killed.
With it he drove through the middle of the man's neck.
His head as he spoke was mingled with the dust.
And the son of Terpes, the singer, still tried to avoid black
    death,   330
Phemios, who sang for the suitors under constraint.

He stood holding the clear-toned lyre in his hands
Close to the side door, and he was thinking two ways in his
    mind,
Whether to abandon the hall and take a seat
335 At the well-made altar of the great Zeus of the Court,
Where Laertes and Odysseus had burned many thighs of oxen,
Or to rush up and implore Odysseus at his knees.
And so, as he thought, it seemed to him to be better
To take hold of the knees of Odysseus, son of Laertes.
340 He put his hollow lyre down upon the ground
Between the mixing bowl and the silver-studded chair
And rushed up himself and took Odysseus by the knees,
And imploring him, he uttered wingèd words:
"I pray to you, Odysseus; respect me and pity me.
345 There will be grief for yourself hereafter if you slay
A singer like me who sings for gods and for men.
I am self-taught, and a god has planted all kinds
Of lays in my mind. I am fit to sing before you
As before a god. And so do not be eager to cut my throat.
350 And Telemachos, your beloved son, may tell you this:
That not at all by my wish or need did I frequent
The suitors in your house to sing for them at their feasts.
But, being far more, and stronger, they brought me by
    constraint."
So he said, and Telemachos in his sacred might heard him.
355 At once he addressed his father, who was close beside him:
"Hold off, do not wound this guiltless man with the sword.
Let us also spare the herald Medon, who always
Looked after me in our house when I was a child,
Unless indeed Philoitios or the swineherd has slain him
360 Or he came on you as you were stirred up in the house."
So he said, and Medon, who was sound of mind, heard him.
He lay crouching underneath an armchair and had covered
    himself
With the new-flayed skin of an ox, to avoid black fate.
He rose at once from beneath the chair, took the oxhide off,
365 Then rushed up and grasped Telemachos by the knees,
And imploring him, he uttered wingèd words:
"My friend, here I am, myself. Hold! Tell your father;
Lest in his greater strength he kill me with the sharp sword,
From his anger at the suitors who have devoured his goods

In the halls, and the fools did not honor you at all."   370
Odysseus of many wiles smiled at him and spoke:
"Take courage, as indeed this man has rescued you and saved
    you,
So that you may know in your heart and even tell someone else
How doing good deeds is much better than doing bad.
But come out of the hall and sit down outdoors in the court   375
Away from slaughter, you and the singer full of stories,
Till in the house I have myself taken care of what I must."
So he said, and the two of them went out of the hall.
They both sat down before the altar of great Zeus
And peered round on all sides, ever expecting slaughter.   380
Odysseus peered round his house lest some one of the men
Might still be concealed alive, avoiding black fate.
But he saw they had all fallen, in great numbers,
In blood and dust, like fish that the fishermen
Have drawn up on the curved beach out of the hoary sea   385
In a net that has many meshes; and all of them
Are heaped up on the sands longing for the waves of the sea;
But the sun in his shining is taking away their life;
So then the suitors were heaped up on one another.
Then Odysseus of many wiles addressed Telemachos: 390
"Telemachos, go and call the nurse Eurycleia for me,
So that I may tell her what it is my desire to tell."
So he said, and Telemachos obeyed his beloved father.
He shook the door and spoke to the nurse Eurycleia:
"Rise and come here, old woman, you who were born long ago, 395
And who watch over our serving women in the house.
Come, my father calls you, so he may tell you something."
So he said, and for her the word was without a wing.
But she opened up the doors of the well-situated halls
And came on out. Telemachos went on ahead to lead.   400
Then she found Odysseus among the bodies of the slain,
Bespattered over with blood and with gore like a lion
Who goes along when he has eaten from an ox of the field,
And all his breast and also his cheeks on either side
Are bloody, and his face is terrible to look upon;   405
So was Odysseus bespattered, on his feet and his hands above.
Now when she saw the corpses and the unspeakable blood,
She made ready to exult, since she beheld a huge deed.
But Odysseus checked her and held her, eager as she was,

410 And speaking out to her, he uttered wingèd words:
"Old woman, rejoice in your heart; hold back and do not exult.
It is not holy to boast over men who have been slain.
The gods' fate has worsted these men, and their cruel deeds,
For they honored no one of the men upon the earth,
415 Either evil or noble, whoever encountered them.
And so in their recklessness they met a sorry fate.
Come now, and tell me about the women in the house,
Which ones dishonor me and which ones are innocent."
Then his beloved nurse Eurycleia spoke to him:
420 "All right, then, my child, I shall tell you the whole truth:
There are fifty women of yours inside the halls,
Serving women whom we have taught how to do their tasks,
How to card wool and how to endure servitude;
Of these, twelve in all have gone the way of shamelessness
425 And do not honor me or Penelope herself.
Telemachos grew up recently, and his mother has not
Allowed him to give orders to the serving women.
Well, now, let me go up to the glistening upper chamber
And tell your wife, in whom some god has induced sleep."
430 Odysseus of many wiles addressed her in answer:
"Do not wake her up yet. Go in and tell the women
To come, the ones who devised sorry deeds in the past."
So he said, and the old woman went on through the hall
To announce this to the women and to hasten their coming.
435 But he himself called Telemachos and the oxherd
And the swineherd to him and uttered wingèd words:
"Begin now to carry the corpses, and command the women;
And then have the tables and the beautiful armchairs
Cleaned off with water and with the porous sponges.
440 And when you have set in order the entire house,
Bring the serving women on out of the well-based hall
Between the round-room and the excellent fence of the
        courtyard,
And strike them with the long-edged swords until you have
        taken
The lives of all away, and they have forgotten the love
They had under the suitors, when they lay with them
445   secretly."
So he said, and the women all came in a body together,
Lamenting dreadfully and shedding a swelling tear.

Then they first carried away the bodies of those who were dead
And they set them down under the portico of the well-fenced
  court,
Propping them on one another. Odysseus gave the orders,   450
Urging them on himself. They bore them out by constraint.
And then the tables and the beautiful armchairs
They cleaned off, with water and the porous sponges.
Then Telemachos, the oxherd, and the swineherd
Scraped down the floor of the stoutly built house with shovels. 455
Those servants kept carrying the scrapings and put them
  outdoors.
And when they had set in order the entire hall
They led the serving women out of the well-based hall
Between the round-room and the excellent fence of the court.
They cooped them in a narrow place, from which was no way to
  escape.   460
And sound-minded Telemachos began speaking to them:
"I would not take away with a clean death the lives
Of these women who have heaped reproaches on my head
And upon my mother, and have slept with the suitors."
So he said, and a cable from a dark blue-prowed ship   465
He threw round a pillar of the great round-room and tied
  it on,
Tightening it high up, so none could reach the ground with her
  feet.
As when either thrushes with their long wings or doves
Rush into a net that has been set in a thicket,
As they come in to roost, and a dreadful bed takes them in;   470
So they held their heads in a row, and about the necks
Of all there were nooses, that they might die most piteously.
They struggled a little with their feet, but not very long.
They brought Melanthios through the forecourt and the yard,
Cut off his nose and ears with the pitiless bronze,   475
And tore off his private parts for the dogs to eat raw,
And chopped off his hands and feet in their furious spirit.
Then, when they had washed off their hands and their feet,
They went into the house of Odysseus, and the work was done.
And he addressed Eurycleia, his beloved nurse: 480
"Bring brimstone, old woman, the cure of ills; bring me fire
So that I may purge the hall. You yourself go tell
Penelope to come here with her attendant women

And urge all the serving women in the house to come."
485 Then the dear nurse Eurycleia spoke to him:
"Yes, my child, you have said these things properly.
Come now, I shall bring you a tunic, a mantle and clothes
So your broad shoulders may not be covered with rags this way
As you stand in the halls. It would be a cause of blame."
490 Odysseus of many wiles addressed her in answer:
"First of all now let a fire be made for me in the halls."
So he said, and his dear nurse Eurycleia did not disobey.
Then she brought in fire and brimstone, and Odysseus
Thoroughly purged house and courtyard and hall.
495 The old woman went off through the fine halls of Odysseus
To announce this to the women and hasten their coming.
They came out of the hall bearing torches in their hands.
They gathered round Odysseus and greeted him in welcome;
They kissed him and embraced his shoulders and his head
500 And his hands. And a sweet longing took hold of him
For moaning and wailing; in his mind he recognized them all.

XXIII

The old woman went chuckling on into the upper chamber
To tell her dear mistress that her husband was inside.
Her knees moved quickly and her feet stumbled along.
She stood above her head and addressed a speech to her:
"Wake up, Penelope, dear child, so you may see   5
With your own eyes what you desire all your days.
Odysseus has come and reached home, though arriving late.
He has killed the bold suitors who disturbed his house
And devoured his property and oppressed his son."
And the prudent Penelope spoke to her: 10
"Dear mother, the gods have made you mad, who have the
    power
To make a man senseless, even one who is quite sensible;
And also they put the slack-minded on the way of prudence.
They have injured you, you were balanced in mind before.
Why do you mock me who have a heart full of grief,   15
To tell me these wild things and wake me out of the sweet
Sleep, which has bound me and shrouded my own eyelids?
Never have I had such a sleep from the time Odysseus
Went off to see evil Ilion, the unspeakable.
But come now, depart and go back into the hall.   20
For if anyone else of the women who belong to me
Had come to tell me this and waked me from sleep,
I myself should soon have sent her off hatefully
To go back again to the hall. In this, old age shall help you."
The beloved nurse Eurycleia then spoke to her: 25
"I am not mocking you, dear child, but it is true;
Odysseus has come and reached his home, as I say;
He is that stranger whom they all dishonored in the halls.
Telemachos has known for a long time he was within
But concealed out of prudence the purpose of his father   30
Till he might take revenge on the insolent men for their
    presumption."

So she said. The woman rejoiced, leaped out of her bed,
Embraced the old woman, and shed a tear from her eyelids.
Speaking out to her, she uttered wingèd words:
35 "Come now, dear mother, and tell me unerringly,
If he has truly arrived at his home, as you say,
How did he set his hands upon the shameless suitors,
A lone man, when they always stayed in a body inside?"
Then the beloved nurse Eurycleia spoke to her:
40 "I did not see or learn it, but I heard only the noise
Of men being killed. In a corner of the well-built chambers
We sat terrified, and the well-fitted doors held us
Until the time when your son Telemachos called me
From the hall. His father sent him out to call me.
45 Then I found Odysseus standing among the bodies
Of the slain. They surrounded him on the hard-stamped ground
Lying one upon the other. Your heart would have warmed to see
   him
Bespattered over with blood and with gore like a lion.
And now all of them are at the gates of the courtyard
50 In a heap, and he is purging the beautiful house,
Having kindled a great fire. He sent me to call you.
But come with me so you may both enter into gladness
In your own hearts, since you have suffered many ills.
And now this long desire is already fulfilled;
55 He has himself come alive to his hearth and found in the halls
Both you and his son. Though the suitors acted to him
Evilly, he has punished them all in his own house."
And then the prudent Penelope spoke to her:
"Dear mother, do not chuckle yet and make a great boast,
60 For you know how welcome in the halls he would appear to all,
And especially to me and the son that we both had.
But this story is not really so, the way that you tell it.
Some one of the immortals has killed the bold suitors,
Offended at their heart-hurting insolence and evil deeds,
65 For they honored no one of the men upon the earth,
Either evil or noble, whoever encountered them.
So they suffered evil through their recklessness. And Odysseus,
Far from Achaia lost his return, and is lost himself."
Then the beloved nurse Eurycleia answered her:
70 "My child, what sort of word has got past the bar of your teeth,
To say that your husband who is within at the hearth

Would never come home? Your heart is ever untrusting.
Well, then, I shall tell you another manifest token:
The scar a boar once dealt on him with a shining tusk
I noticed as I washed it. And I wanted to tell it   75
To you yourself. But he seized my mouth with his hands
And did not let me speak, in his resourcefulness of mind.
Come along, then, and I shall myself stake my own person.
If I deceive you, kill me with a most piteous death."
And then the prudent Penelope answered her: 80
"Dear mother, the counsels of the ever-living gods
Are hard for you to comprehend, though you are very shrewd.
In any case let us go to my son, so I may see
The suitors dead and also the man who has killed them."
When she had said this she went down from the upper chamber.
Her heart   85
Pondered much whether to question her dear husband at a
    distance
Or to stand beside him and clasp and kiss his hands and head.
When she had gone on in and crossed the threshold of stone,
She sat across from Odysseus, in the gleam of the fire
By the other wall. And he sat against a tall pillar   90
Looking down, waiting to see if his goodly wife
Would say something to him when she saw him with her eyes.
But she sat a long time in silence, and stupor came over her
    heart.
With her gaze sometimes she looked him full in the face,
And sometimes did not know him for the vile clothes he had on
    his skin.   95
Telemachos rebuked her and spoke out to her directly:
"My mother, cruel mother, you have a heart that is harsh!
Why do you turn from my father so and do not sit
Beside him and ply him with speeches and question him?
No other woman, indeed, with a resisting heart   100
Would so stand off from the husband who had suffered many
    ills
And come back for her in the twentieth year to his fatherland.
Always the heart in you is harder than a stone."
And then the prudent Penelope spoke to him:
"My child, the heart within my breast is amazed,   105
And I am not at all able to speak a word or to ask
Or to look him in the face directly. If really

He is Odysseus and he has arrived home, we two
Shall know one another, and more fully. There are signs
110 For us that the two of us know, hidden from others."
So she said, and godly Odysseus, who had endured much, smiled.
At once he uttered wingèd words to Telemachos:
"Telemachos, permit your mother to test me out
Within the halls. She shall quickly discern even better.
115 Now, because I am dirty and have bad clothes on my skin,
She does not respect me and does not yet say I am he.
But let us consider how it shall come out for the best.
For whosoever kills a single man in the district,
Though there be not many advocates for man thereafter,
120 He flees, abandoning his kinsmen and fatherland.
And we have killed the mainstay of the city, the very best
Of the youth in Ithaca. I bid you to consider this."
Then sound-minded Telemachos answered him:
"Look to these matters yourself, dear father. They say
125 Your counsel is the best among men, nor could any
Other man among mortal men contend with you.
We shall follow along with you eagerly; I do not think
We should lack any courage so far as we do have power."
Odysseus of many wiles addressed him in answer:
130 "Well then, I shall tell you what seems to me to be best,
First of all wash yourselves and put tunics on,
And order the serving women in the halls to take their clothes.
Then let the godly singer, holding his clear-toned lyre,
Be the leader for us in a reveling dance,
135 So a listener outside would think this was a wedding,
One who walked on the road, or one of those who dwell
        round about;
So that a wide report about the slaughter of the suitors
Shall not first get through the town, before we have gone outside
To our own well-wooded land. And then afterward
140 We may think of any advantage the Olympian may bestow."
So he said, and they listened closely and did not disobey.
And first they washed themselves off and put on tunics,
And the women adorned themselves, and the godly singer took
The hollow lyre and aroused the desire among them
145 For sweet melody and also for excellent dancing.
The great house about them resounded at the feet
Of men frolicking and of women with lovely gowns.

And this is what a man who heard them outside the house
    would say:
"Someone indeed must have married the much-wooed queen.
The cruel woman, she did not hold out for her wedded husband 150
And tend the great house steadfastly till he arrived."
So a man would say: they did not know what had been done.
But the housekeeper Eurynome washed great-hearted Odysseus
Inside his own house and anointed him with olive oil.
She put a lovely mantle and a tunic over him.   155
Then Athene poured much beauty upon his head,
Made him bigger to look at and stouter, and made his hair
Flow in curls upon his head like the hyacinth flower.
As when some man overlays gold upon silver,
A skilled man whom Hephaistos and Pallas Athene have taught 160
Art of all kinds, and he turns out graceful handiwork;
So she poured grace upon his head and his shoulders.
He stepped from the bathtub in form like the immortal gods,
And he sat back down on the chair from which he had risen,
Across from his wife, and he addressed a speech to her: 165
"Strange woman, those who have their home on Olympos put in
    you
A heart implacable beyond that of womankind.
No other woman, indeed, with a resisting heart
Would so stand off from the husband who had suffered
    many ills
And come back for her in the twentieth year to his fatherland. 170
Come now, old mother, spread me a bed, so that I
May lie down alone, for the heart in this woman's breast is iron."
And then the prudent Penelope answered him:
"Strange man, I do not at all exalt myself or slight you,
Nor am I too much amazed. I know well the sort of man you
    were   175
When you went off from Ithaca on the long-oared ship.
Come now, Eurycleia, spread for him the thick bed
Outside the well-based bedroom which the man made himself.
Put the thick bed out for him there and throw bedding on,
Blankets and mantles and the glistening coverlets."   180
So she said, testing her husband. But Odysseus
Grew angry and spoke to his wife, who had a sense of devotion:
"My wife, this is a heart-hurting speech you have made.
Who has put my bed elsewhere? That would be hard

185 Even for one very skilled, unless a god came in person,
And easily, if he wished, might put it in another place.
No mortal man alive, not even one in his vigor,
Could dislodge it easily, since a great token was made
In the well-wrought bed. I worked on it, and nobody else.
190 The long-leaved bush of a wild olive grew inside the yard
Flourishing in bloom. It was thick as a pillar is.
So I built the bedroom round it till I finished it
With close-fitted stones and roofed it well up above.
And I put portals on it, jointed and closely fitted.
195 Then I cut off the crown of the long-leaved wild olive;
Chopping the stump from the root up, I hewed it with the
bronze ax
Well and skillfully, and straightened it with a line.
When I had fashioned the bedpost, I bored it all with an auger.
Starting with that, I hewed out a bed till I finished it,
200 Adorning it with gold and silver and ivory.
And I stretched over it an oxhide thong shining with purple.
So I declare this token to you. I do not know at all
Whether the bed is still steadfast, wife, or already
Some man has put it elsewhere, cutting the olive base beneath."
205 So he said, and her knees and her own heart went slack
As she recognized the steadfast tokens Odysseus had shown to
her.
Then she wept, ran straight over, and threw her arms
About the neck of Odysseus, kissed his head and spoke:
"Do not scowl at me, Odysseus, since in everything else
210 You have been the wisest of men. The gods have given us woe
Who begrudged it to us that, staying with one another,
We should enjoy our vigor and reach the threshold of age.
But be not angry at me now for this, and do not resent
That I did not embrace you this way when I saw you first,
215 For always the spirit in my precious heart went cold
Lest someone among mortals come and deceive me
With speeches. Many men think up evil devices.
Nor would Argive Helen, who was a child of Zeus,
Have lain in love and in bed with an alien man
220 If she had known that the warlike sons of the Achaians
Were to bring her back home to her dear fatherland.
Yes, a god stirred her up to do a sorry deed.

She did not lay up in her heart beforehand that woeful
Madness, out of which, from the first, sorrow reached us too.
But now, since already you have declared very plain tokens   225
About our bed, which no other mortal has seen,
But you and I alone, and one single handmaiden,
Aktoris, whom my father gave me when I came here,
She who tended for us the doors of the stout bedchamber;
Now you have convinced my heart, harsh indeed though it be." 230
So she said. In him rose a still greater desire for wailing.
He wept, holding his pleasing wife, who had a sense of devotion.
As when land appears welcome to men who are swimming,
Whose well-made ship Poseidon has dashed in the ocean
As it was driven on by wind and a solid wave,   235
And few have escaped from the hoary sea onto the mainland
By swimming, and much brine has caked upon their skin,
And they walk up on land glad, having fled misfortune,
So welcome was her husband to her as she looked upon him.
In no way could she quite let her white arms go from his neck, 240
And rosy-fingered Dawn would have appeared while they
      wept
If the bright-eyed goddess Athene had not had another thought.
She held the night long on its course, and then kept
The golden-throned Dawn upon Oceanos, and did not allow her
To yoke her swift-footed horses that bear light to men,   245
Lampos and Phaethon, who are the colts that bring the dawn.
Then Odysseus of many wiles spoke to his wife:
"My wife, we have not yet come to the end of all
Our trials, but a measureless labor yet remains,
A long and a hard one that I must wholly carry out.   250
So did the soul of Tiresias prophesy to me
On the day when I went down into the house of Hades
Seeking a return for my companions and myself.
But come, let us go to bed, my wife, so that now
We may lie down and take pleasure beneath sweet sleep."   255
And then the prudent Penelope addressed him:
"The bed shall be for you indeed whenever you wish
In your heart, since the gods have made you to arrive
At your well-established home and your fatherland.
But since you have thought of it and a god has put it in your
      heart,   260

Come tell me of the trial, since hereafter I think,
I too shall hear of it; and it is no worse for me to learn of it at
     once."
Then Odysseus of many wiles addressed her in answer:
"Strange woman, why do you strongly urge me and bid me to
     speak?
265 Well, I will tell it myself and shall not conceal it.
But your heart shall not rejoice, nor do I myself
Rejoice, since he ordered me to visit many towns
Of mortals, holding in my hands a well-fitted oar,
Till the time I come unto those who do not know
270 The sea and do not eat a food that has been mixed with salt,
And where they do not know about ships with purple cheeks
Or about well-fitted oars that are the wings for ships.
He told me a very clear token; I shall not conceal it:
When another wayfarer has confronted me
275 And said I had a winnowing fan on my gleaming shoulder,
He bade me to fix my oar then into the earth
And offer fine sacrifices to lord Poseidon,
A ram, a bull, and a boar, the mounter of sows,
Then to go back home and sacrifice sacred hecatombs
280 To the immortal gods who possess broad heaven,
To all of them in order. Far from the sea will death come
Ever so gently, to my person, and slay me
Worn out with sleek old age. And the people about me
Will be happy. He told me all this would come to pass."
285 And then the prudent Penelope spoke to him:
"If the gods do bring a better old age to pass,
Then there is hope for you there will be an escape from evils."
And so they said such things to one another.
Meanwhile Eurynome and the nurse prepared the bed
290 With soft bedclothing, underneath shining torches.
And when they had made haste and strewn the thick bed,
The old woman went back into the house to lie down
And Eurynome, servant of the chamber, conducted them
With a torch in her hand as they went on to bed.
295 She led to the bedroom and went away again. They then
Arrived happily at the site of their old bed.
But Telemachos, the oxherd, and the swineherd
Stopped the men's feet from dancing and stopped the women
     too,

And went to bed themselves through the shadowy halls.
The two, when they had taken their pleasure of delightful love, 300
Enjoyed themselves with stories, talking to one another:
She, the godly woman, told how much she endured in the
  halls
To look upon the destructive throng of the suitors
Who on her account had slaughtered oxen and goodly sheep
In numbers, and much wine had been drawn off from the jars.   305
And Zeus-born Odysseus told of the many cares he had brought
Upon men, and the many he had suffered himself in his woe.
He told them all, and she enjoyed hearing, nor did sleep
Fall upon her eyelids before he had told it all.
He began how first he had conquered the Cicones and then   310
Had gone to the fertile land of the Lotus-eating men,
And all the Cyclops did, and how he made him pay the
  penalty
For the valiant companions he ate and did not pity.
And how he got to Aeolos who at first kindly received him
And sent him on. But it was not yet his lot to reach   315
His dear fatherland; but a storm snatched him up again
And bore him heavily groaning on the fish-laden ocean.
And he told how he reached Lestrygonian Telepylos,
Whose men destroyed his ships and all his well-greaved
  companions.
Odysseus alone got away from them with his black ship.   320
And he told about Circe's wiles and resourcefulness,
And how he went down to the dank dwelling of Hades
So he might consult the soul of Theban Tiresias
In a ship with many oarlocks and saw all his companions
And the mother who bore him and reared him when he was
  small,   325
And how he listened to the voice of the chanting Sirens,
And how he reached the Wandering Rocks and dread Charybdis
And Scylla, which men have never yet escaped unharmed.
And how his companions slew the oxen of the Sun,
And how high-thundering Zeus struck the swift ship   330
With a smoldering thunderbolt, and his noble companions died
All together, but he himself escaped the evil fates.
And how he reached the island Ogygia and the nymph Calypso.
She held him back, longing for him to be her husband
In the hollow caves, and she nourished him and said   335

She would make him immortal and ageless all his days,
But she never persuaded the heart within his breast.
And he told how, having suffered much, he came to the
    Phaeacians
Who honored him heartily the way they would a god
340 And conducted him in a ship to his dear fatherland,
Giving him bronze and gold and clothing in abundance.
This was the last tale he told, when sweet, limb-loosing sleep
Came upon him, releasing the cares of his heart.
Then the bright-eyed goddess Athene had another thought.
345 When she had supposed in her heart that Odysseus
Had taken pleasure with his wife of the bed and of sleep,
At once from Oceanos she roused the early born one
Of the golden throne to bring light to men. Odysseus
Rose from his soft bed and laid a charge on his wife:
350 "My wife, we are already glutted, the two of us,
With many trials. Here you wept for my troublesome return,
But, while I was wanting to go, Zeus and the other gods
Held me back in pains from my own fatherland.
Now since we have arrived at the bed of much desire,
355 Give heed to the goods which are mine in the halls.
As for the sheep of mine the presumptuous suitors pillaged,
Many others I shall myself plunder back; still others the
    Achaians
Shall give me until they have filled up all the folds.
And then I shall go on myself to the well-wooded land
360 To see my noble father, who is heavily grieved for me.
And, my wife, I charge you this, prudent as you are:
At once at the rising of the sun the report will travel
About the suitors whom I slaughtered in the halls.
Go into the upper chamber with your serving women
365 And sit, and do not look at anyone or ask any question."
He spoke, and put the lovely armor about his shoulders.
He roused Telemachos, the oxherd, and the swineherd
And ordered them all to take the war gear in their hands.
They did not disobey, but armed themselves in bronze.
370 They opened the doors and went out. Odysseus led.
Light was on the earth already, and Athene hid them
In night and led them rapidly out of the city.

XXIV

And Hermes of Cyllene summoned forth the souls
Of the suitors, and he held in his hand the lovely gold wand
With which he enchants the eyes of those men he wishes,
And others he wakens even when they are asleep.
He stirred them with it and drove them. They followed
    squeaking,   5
As when bats in the corner of a prodigious cave
Squeak as they fly when one of them falls away
From the cluster on the rock where they cling to one another;
So they squeaked as they went together. And Hermes,
The deliverer, led them on along the dank ways.   10
They went past the streams of Oceanos, past the White Rock;
Past the gates of the Sun also, and the district of dreams
Did they go. And at once they reached the asphodel meadow
Where the souls dwell, phantoms of those who are worn out.
They came upon the soul of Achilles, son of Peleus,   15
The soul of Patroclos and of excellent Antilochos,
And of Ajax, who was the finest in body and form
Of all the Danaans, after the excellent son of Peleus.
So they thronged around that man, and right close to them
The soul of Agamemnon came on, the son of Atreus,   20
Grieving. And the others drew in together, all those
Who had died with him and met their fate in Agisthos' house.
The soul of the son of Peleus spoke out to him first:
"Son of Atreus, we thought you were dear beyond other heroes
To Zeus who hurls the thunderbolt, for all your days,   25
Because you were lord over many valiant men
In the land of the Trojans where we Achaians suffered pains.
And yet the destructive fate that no one who is born
Can avoid was destined to come early upon you as well.
Would that when you were enjoying the honor of which you
    were master   30
In the land of the Trojans, you had met death and destiny!

Then all the Achaians would have made you a funeral mound
And you would have won great glory for your son hereafter.
As it is, you were fated to be caught in a grievous death."
35 Then the soul of the son of Atreus spoke to him:
"Blessed are you, son of Peleus, godlike Achilles,
You who died in Troy far from Argos. Around you, others,
The best sons of the Achaians and of the Trojans were killed
Contending over you. You in a whirling cloud of dust
40 Lay great and greatly fallen, having forgotten horsemanship.
And we contended the whole day. Nor would we at all
Have stopped the battle if Zeus had not stopped it with a storm.
But when we had brought you up on the ships out of battle,
We set you down upon a bier and cleaned off your lovely
skin
45 With warm water and oil, and the Danaans shed
Many hot tears over you and sheared off their hair.
Your mother came from the sea with the deathless girls of the
sea
When she heard the report. A prodigious cry arose
Over the ocean, and a trembling seized all the Achaians,
And they would have sprung up and gone to the hollow
50 ships
If a man had not restrained them who knew many ancient
matters,
Nestor, whose advice had also before seemed best.
With good intent he spoke out to them and addressed them:
"Hold back, Argives; do not flee, young Achaians. His mother
55 This is, here from the sea with the deathless girls of the sea;
She has come to be beside her son who has died."
So he said, and the great-hearted Achaians were held back
from flight.
About you stood the daughters of the old man of the sea,
Wailing piteously; they clothed you in ambrosial garments.
60 All the nine Muses, changing off with lovely voice,
Sang a dirge. There you would have seen none of the Argives
Who did not weep, so stirring was the clear Muses' song.
Seventeen days for you, and also the nights alike,
Did we lament, both immortal gods and mortal men.
65 On the eighteenth we gave you to the fire and about you
Killed many fat sheep and cattle with crumpled horns.
You were burned in the clothes of the gods and with much oil

And with sweet honey. Many of the Achaian warriors
Marched around the fire in armor while you were being burned,
Foot soldiers and horsemen, and a great din arose.   70
But when the flame of Hephaistos had made an end of you,
At the dawn, Achilles, we gathered your white bones
In unmixed wine and in oil. And your mother gave
A golden two-handled jar. She said it was a gift
Of Dionysos, the work of highly renowned Hephaistos.   75
So in it, glorious Achilles, your white bones lie,
Mingled with those of dead Patroklos, Menoitios' son;
Apart are those of Antilochos, whom you honored
Above all your other companions after the dead Patroklos.
And then we, the sacred army of Argive spearmen, heaped   80
A great and excellent funeral mound up over them
On a strand jutting forward on the broad Hellespont,
So that it might be seen far over the ocean by men,
Both those who are born now and those who shall be hereafter.
And your mother asked the gods for beautiful prizes   85
And set them up for a contest amid the best of the Achaians.
Already you have been present at the burial of many men,
Of warriors; when, because a king has passed away,
The young men gird themselves and prepare for the prizes.
But you would have marveled in your heart most to see those,   90
The beautiful prizes that the goddess set up for you,
Thetis [1] of the silver foot. You were very dear to the gods.
So you did not lose your name even when you died, Achilles.
There shall be noble renown for you always among all men.
But what pleasure did I have, when I had wound up the war?   95
For Zeus planned woeful destruction for me on my return
At the hands of Aigisthos and my accursèd wife."
And so they said such things to one another.
The Runner, the slayer of Argos, came up close to them,
Leading the souls of the suitors subdued by Odysseus.   100
The two, marveling, went straight up when they saw them.
The soul of Agamemnon, son of Atreus, recognized
The dear son of Melaneos, renowned Amphimedon,
For he was a guest friend of his who dwelt in Ithaca.
The soul of the son of Atreus spoke out to him first: 105
"Amphimedon, what did you suffer to go under the gloomy
    earth,

1. A sea nymph and mother of Achilles.

All you chosen men of the same age? Not otherwise
Would someone pick out and gather the best men in a city.
Was it that Poseidon overcame you in your ships
110 By raising up oppressive winds and giant waves,
Or did hostile men ravage you upon the mainland
As you were cutting off their cattle and fine flocks of sheep,
Or as they were fighting on behalf of their city and women?
Tell me what I ask—I declare I am your guest friend.
115 Do you not remember when I came there to your house,
Urging Odysseus on to come along to Ilion
With godlike Menelaos upon the well-timbered ships?
An entire month we spent crossing the whole broad ocean
Since we could scarcely persuade Odysseus, the sacker of cities."
120 And then the soul of Amphimedon addressed him:
"Glorious son of Atreus, Zeus-nourished Agamemnon,
Lord of men, I do remember all the things you say,
And I shall tell you everything truthfully and well,
The evil end of our death, the way it came about.
125 We wooed the wife of Odysseus, who was gone so long;
She neither refused the hateful wedding nor carried it out,
Contriving for us death and black destiny;
And she devised in her mind this other deceit:
She set a great loom in the halls, and on it she wove
130 A large and delicate fabric. She told us at once:
'Young men, my suitors, since godlike Odysseus is dead,
Wait, though you are eager for this marriage of mine, till I finish
This robe, so that the yarn will not waste in vain,
The burial sheet of hero Laertes for the time
135 When the ruinous fate of long-sorrowful death seizes him,
Lest one of the Achaian women in the district blame me
If he who had won so much lay without covering.'
So she said, and the bold heart was persuaded within us.
Then every day she kept weaving there on the great loom,
140 And in the nights she undid it when she had the torches set up.
So three years she fooled the Achaians and persuaded them.
But when the fourth year came and the seasons came on
Of the waning months and many days came to an end,
Right then one of the women who perceived it clearly told it.
145 And we happened upon her undoing the shining fabric.
Then she finished it, though unwilling and under duress.

And when, having woven the great fabric and washed it,
She showed forth the robe that resembled the sun or the moon,
Just then some evil god led Odysseus from someplace
To the verge of the field where the swineherd had his home.   150
There, too, the beloved son of Odysseus had come
When he went from sandy Pylos in his black ship.
The two of them, contriving an evil death for the suitors,
Had arrived at the city of great renown. Odysseus
Was last, and Telemachos led the way ahead of them.   155
The swineherd brought the man, who wore vile clothes on his
    skin
And resembled a wretched beggar who was an old man
Walking with a staff. He had sorry clothes on his skin.
None of us could recognize that it was he
When he appeared suddenly, not even those who were older,   160
But we rebuked him with missiles and evil speeches.
Still, he held out all the while with enduring heart
When he was being beaten and rebuked in his own halls.
But when the purpose of aegis-bearing Zeus aroused him
He took up the beautiful weapons with Telemachos   165
And placed them in the chamber and locked the fastenings,
And resourcefully he gave the order to his wife
To set before the suitors the bow and the gray iron,
A contest and start of slaughter for us in our dread fate.
No one of us was able to stretch out the string   170
Of the mighty bow, for we were too weak by far.
But when the great bow came into Odysseus' hands,
Then all of us made a common outcry with speeches,
Not to give him the bow, however much he might say.
Telemachos alone urged him on and gave him the order.   175
Then godly Odysseus, who had endured much, took it in his
    hand,
Easily strung the bow and shot through the iron.
He went and stood on the threshold, poured the swift arrows out,
Peering round terribly, and hit King Antinoos.
And then on the others he let the groan-carrying darts fly,   180
Taking aim straight across. And they fell thick and fast.
It was known then that one of the gods was their helper for
    them.
For at once they went on through the house in their rage

And killed them one after another. A sad groaning
Rose as their heads were struck. The whole ground ran with
185   blood.
Agamemnon, this is the way we perished, we whose bodies
Are still lying uncared for now in the halls of Odysseus.
For the dear ones in the home of each man do not know it yet,
Those who, when they have washed the black gore from the
          wounds,
190   May lay us out weeping. For that is the prize of the dead."
Then the soul of the son of Atreus spoke out to him:
"Blessed son of Laertes, Odysseus of many wiles,
Truly you have won a wife of great excellence.
How good was the mind of blameless Penelope,
195   Daughter of Icarios, who remembered Odysseus well,
Her wedded husband! And so the fame of her excellence
Shall never die. The immortals shall make for men on the earth
A delightful song about constant Penelope.
Not so did the daughter of Tyndareus [2] devise her evil deeds,
Who killed her wedded husband; and a hateful song shall there
200   be
Among men, and she will bestow a harsh reputation
On womankind, even on one who is good in what she does."
And so they said such things to one another,
Standing in the halls of Hades under the depths of the earth.
205   The others, when they had gone out of the city, quickly reached
The fine, well-worked field of Laertes that Laertes had once
Acquired for himself when he had toiled very hard.
There his home was. And all around it a shed ran
In which the bondservants who did the tasks at his
          pleasure,
210   Took their meals and sat down and went to sleep.
In it there was an old Sicilian woman, who carefully
Attended to the old man in the field far from the city.
There Odysseus addressed a speech to his servants and his son:
"Come on inside of the well-built house now, and at once
215   Make a sacrifice of the best of the swine for dinner
And I shall test my own father out for myself,
Whether he recognizes me and perceives me with his eyes,
Or does not know me since I have been away for a long time."

2. Clytemnestra.

When he had said this, he gave the arms of war to the servants.
They went then swiftly into the house. But Odysseus   220
Went close to the fruitful vineyard to try him out.
As he entered the large orchard he did not find Dolios
Or any of the servants or their sons. They were gone off
Gathering wall-stones that would serve as a fence
For the vineyard. And the old man led the way for them.   225
He found his father alone in the well-laid vineyard,
Digging around a plant. He had a dirty tunic on,
A sorry patched one. And greaves of oxhide were bound
In patches on his calves to keep him from getting scratched.
He had gloves on his hands on account of brambles. On his head   230
He was wearing a goatskin cap, cherishing his grief.
When godly Odysseus, who had endured much, perceived the
       man
Worn down by age and with a great grief in his mind,
He stood under a stately pear tree and shed a tear,
And then he turned over in his mind and in his heart   235
Whether to kiss and embrace his father and tell the details
Of how he had come and arrived at his fatherland
Or should first ask him for details and test him out.
To him as he thought about it this seemed to be better:
To test him out at first with words of bantering.   240
With this in mind, Odysseus went directly to him.
The man was holding his head down and digging around the
       plant.
Standing beside him, his illustrious son spoke out:
"Old man, no lack of skill is yours as you tend
The orchard, but good care is yours. Nothing at all,   245
No plant, no fig tree, no vine, no wild olive tree,
No pear tree, no leek bed in the garden is without your care.
I shall tell you something else, and do not feel rage in your
       heart;
Your person is not well cared for, but along with woeful old age
You have a foul squalor and are wearing sorry clothes.   250
Not for idleness, surely, does your master not take care of you;
And nothing about your appearance conforms to the slave
In form or in stature. You look like a man who is king.
You look like such a man, who, when he has washed and eaten,
Should sleep softly. For this is the just way of old men.   255

Come, tell me this, and speak out truthfully:
Of whom among men are you slave? Whose orchard do you
    tend?
Tell me this really, so I may know it well,
If this place we reach is truly Ithaca, as this man
260 Has told me who met me just now when I was coming here.
He is not very clever, for he did not venture to tell
The details or to listen to my speech when I inquired
About my guest friend, whether he still lives and exists
Or is already dead and in the halls of Hades.
265 I shall speak out to you; understand and hear me well.
I once entertained a man in my dear fatherland
When he came to our place, and no other mortal yet
Among alien strangers came dearer to my house.
He declared his descent was from Ithaca, and he said
270 His father was Laertes, son of Arkesios.
I led him into my house and entertained him well,
Befriending him kindly, as there was much in my home,
And I provided him with the gifts of a guest, fitting ones;
First I gave him seven talents of well-wrought gold,
275 And I gave him a mixing bowl all of silver decked with flowers,
Twelve mantles of single fold, and as many coverlets,
And as many lovely robes, and as many tunics besides,
And in addition four shapely women who were versed
In excellent tasks, the ones he wished to pick out himself."
280 Then his father answered him, shedding a tear:
"Stranger, you have indeed come to the land you ask about;
But insolent and reckless are the men who possess her.
In vain you bestowed these gifts, if you gave countless ones.
But if you had found him alive in the land of Ithaca
He would have requited you well with gifts before sending you
285   back,
With good hospitality, which is right toward the man who
    begins it.
But come now, tell me this, and speak out truthfully:
How many years ago is it you entertained that man,
Your hapless guest, my son, if he ever existed,
That ill-fated man? Perhaps far from his friends and his
290   fatherland
The fish in the ocean have devoured him, or on the mainland
He has become the prey of wild beasts and birds. His mother

And father, we who had him, did not lay him out and mourn,
Nor did his richly dowered wife, the constant Penelope,
Wail for her husband on his bier and close his eyes,   295
As it is seemly to do. For that is the prize of the dead.
And tell me this really, so I may know it well:
What men are you from? Where are your city and parents?
Where indeed does the swift ship stand that brought you here
And your godlike companions? Or did you come as a passenger   300
On the ship of others who put you ashore and went away?"
Odysseus of many wiles addressed him in answer:
"All right, I shall tell you everything truthfully:
I am from Alybas, where I live in my famous halls.
I am the son of Lord Apheidas, the son of Polypemon.   305
My own name is Eperitos. But some god drove me astray
To come here from Sicania against my will.
My ship is moored yonder by the fields apart from the city,
But with regard to Odysseus, this is the fifth year
From the time he went away and left my fatherland,   310
That ill-fated man. Still, as he went, he had birds of good omen
On the right, in which I rejoiced as I sent him off.
And he rejoiced as he went. The hearts in us hoped yet
To exchange hospitality and give glorious gifts."
So he said, and a black cloud of grief covered the other.   315
He picked up the ashen dust in both of his hands
And heavily moaning poured it over his gray head.
The other's heart was aroused, and a piercing throb had already
Struck through his nostrils when he saw his dear father.
He leaped up, kissed, and embraced him, and spoke to him: 320
"Here I am, father, the very man you ask about;
I have come in the twentieth year to my fatherland.
But hold off from weeping and tearful lamentation.
I shall tell you right out; nevertheless, we must hurry.
I have slain the suitors within our own halls,   325
Punishing their heart-hurting injury and evil deeds."
And then Laertes answered and spoke out to him:
"If you are my son Odysseus who have arrived here,
Tell me now some very plain sign, so I may be convinced."
Odysseus of many wiles spoke to him in answer: 330
"First of all, take notice with your eyes of this scar
That a boar inflicted on me with shining tusk on Parnassos
When I had gone there. You and my queenly mother sent me

To my mother's dear father Autolycos, so I might get
335 Gifts that when he came here he promised me with a nod.
Come now, and in the well-laid vineyard I shall also tell you
The trees that you gave me once, and I asked you for each,
Myself as a child, following you through the yard. We went on
Through these very ones, and you named them and told me of
    each.
340 You gave me thirteen pear trees and ten apple trees
And forty fig trees. You named the vine rows the same way
To give me fifty of them. And throughout the grape season
Each was fruitful in turn. And there all sorts of clusters are
    on them
Whenever the seasons of Zeus weigh them down from above."
345 So he said. The man's knees and his own heart went slack
When he recognized the sure tokens Odysseus had shown him.
He threw his arms round his dear son and went faint for breath
As godly Odysseus, who had endured much, grasped him.
But when he caught his breath and the spirit was brought to
    his mind,
350 He answered him right away and addressed him with a speech:
"Father Zeus, you gods are still on tall Olympos, if truly
The suitors have paid for their reckless insolence.
But now I dreadfully fear in my mind that the Ithacans
Will soon all come against us here and send messengers
355 Everywhere to the cities of the Cephallenians."
Odysseus of many wiles answered him and spoke:
"Take courage, and do not give heed to this in your mind.
But let us go to the house that lies close to the orchard.
For there did I send Telemachos forth, and the oxherd
360 And the swineherd, to prepare a meal as.soon as they could."
As they said this the two went on to the lovely house.
There, when they had reached the well-situated home,
They found Telemachos, the oxherd, and the swineherd
Carving abundant meat and mixing the sparkling wine.
365 Meanwhile the Sicilian servant woman in his house
Washed Laertes and anointed him with olive oil,
And she put a lovely mantle round him. Then Athene stood
    near
And filled out the limbs of the shepherd of the people.
She made him taller than before and stouter to look upon.

He stepped out of the bathtub. His dear son was amazed at
    him;   370
As he saw him, the man looked like the immortal gods.
Then addressing him, he uttered wingèd words:
"My father, surely one of the ever-living gods
Has made you better to look on in form and stature."
Then sound-minded Laertes said to him in reply: 375
"Father Zeus and Athene and Apollo, would that I were just
    the way
As I was when I took Nerikos, the well-built citadel,
A headland on the shore, when I ruled the Cephallenians;
That way I might have been yesterday in our own halls,
Bearing armor on my shoulders, to stand by and ward off   380
The suitors. So in the halls I would have loosed the knees
Of many of them. In your mind you would have rejoiced."
And so such things did they say to one another.
But when the others had ceased from work and prepared dinner
They sat down one after another in seats and in armchairs,   385
Then they laid their hands on the meal. The old man Dolios
Came near, and with him were the sons of the old man,
Wearied from their tasks, since their mother had gone and
    called them,
The old Sicilian woman who fed them and carefully
Tended to that old man, since old age had taken hold of him.   390
And then, when they had seen Odysseus and noticed him
In their hearts, they stood in the halls amazed. And Odysseus
Addressed them with soothing speeches and spoke to them:
"Old man, sit down to eat; fully forget your wonder,
For we have waited a long time in the halls in desire   395
Of laying our hands on the bread, always expecting you."
So he said, and Dolios came straight to him, stretching forth
Both his hands. He took Odysseus' hand and kissed his wrist.
And speaking out to him, he uttered wingèd words:
"My friend, since you have returned to us who longed for that   400
But never thought to see it—the very gods themselves brought
    you—
Good health and great welcome! May the gods grant you
    wealth!
And tell me this truly, so I may know it well:
Does the prudent Penelope already clearly know

405 You have returned here, or shall we send her a messenger?"
Odysseus of many wiles addressed him in answer:
"Old man, she knows already. Why need you bother about
     this?"
So he said, and the other sat down again on the polished stool.
And the sons of Dolios around glorious Odysseus
Greeted him with speeches the same way and clasped his
410 hands.
They sat down one after another beside their father Dolios.
And so they busied themselves with a meal in the halls.
Now the messenger Rumor went everywhere fast through the
     town
Declaring the suitors' hateful death and destiny.
415 When all had heard it, they strayed in from every side
With murmur and groaning in front of Odysseus' halls.
They carried their corpses, each from his house and buried
     them.
They sent those from other cities, each one to his home,
Putting them upon swift ships for the fishermen to bring them.
Then they went in a body to the places of assembly, grieving in
420 heart.
And when they were gathered and had come together,
Eupeithes stood up among them and spoke to them,
As unforgettable grief lay on his mind for his son
Antinoos, the first one whom godly Odysseus had slain.
425 Shedding tears for him, he spoke out and made a speech:
"Friends, this man has planned a huge deed against the
     Achaians.
Some men he led away in ships, many noblemen,
And he lost the hollow ships, and he lost the men.
Others he killed when he came, the best Cephallenians by far.
430 Come now, before this man may get quickly to Pylos
Or to godly Elis where the Epeians rule;
Let us go. Or else hereafter we shall always be disgraced.
These deeds are a shame to learn about, even for future men;
Unless we avenge us on the murderers of our kinsmen and sons.
435 To my mind at least it would not then be sweet to live,
But I would die as soon as I could and be among the dead.
Come then, lest those men get a start on us crossing the sea."
So he said, shedding a tear. Pity seized all the Achaians.
Medon and the divine singer came up close to them

Out of the halls of Odysseus, since sleep had let them go.   440
They stood in their midst. Amazement seized every man.
Then Medon, who was sound in knowledge, spoke out to them:
"Listen to me now, Ithacans. Odysseus has not
Planned these deeds against the will of the deathless gods.
I myself saw an immortal god who stood close beside   445
Odysseus and resembled Mentor in every way.
Now the deathless god appeared in front of Odysseus
Encouraging him, and now he aroused the suitors
And rushed on through the hall. They fell down one upon the
        other."
So he said, and sallow fear got hold of all of them.   450
Then the old hero Halitherses spoke to them,
The son of Mastor; he alone saw both before and after.
With good intent he spoke out and addressed them:
"Hear me now, Ithacans, in what I am to say:
My friends, these deeds have come about through your
        wickedness.   455
You did not obey me or Mentor, shepherd of the people,
To make your sons cease from their stupidities.
They did a huge deed in their evil recklessness,
Wasting away the goods and dishonoring the wife
Of an excellent man. They thought he would come no more.   460
And now, so be it. Obey me in what I say,
And let us not go, so no one may find self-inflicted pain."
So he said, but they rushed on with a great war cry,
More than half of them, while the others stayed in a body
        there,
For his speech did not please their minds, but they were
        persuaded   465
By Eupeithes.[3] And then at once they ran on for their armor.
When they had put the glittering bronze round their skin
They gathered in a body before the town with a broad
        dancing-place.
Eupeithes was the leader for their foolishness.
He thought he would avenge his son's murder, but he was not   470
Destined to get back; there he was to meet his fate.
Then Athene spoke out to Zeus, the son of Cronos:
"Our father, son of Cronos, highest of all rulers,
Tell me when I ask, what plan of yours is concealed here?

3. The name means "Good Persuader."

475 Will you fashion further an evil war and dread battle,
Or will you establish friendship between both sides?"
And cloud-gathering Zeus addressed her in answer:
"My child, why do you ask me and question me about this?"
Why did you not think out this idea by yourself,
That Odysseus might indeed take vengeance on them when
480   he came?
Do as you wish, but I will tell you what seems fitting.
Since godly Odysseus has done vengeance on the suitors,
Let them solemnize an oath, that he may always reign.
And let us bring about oblivion for the murder
485 Of their sons and kinsmen. Let them love one another
As before, and let there be abundant wealth and peace."
When he said this, he aroused Athene, who was eager before.
She went down in a rush from the summits of Olympos.
And when the men had taken their fill of mind-honeying food,
Godly Odysseus, who had suffered much, began speaking to
490   them:
"Let someone go out and see lest they are coming close."
So he said, and the son of Dolios went out as he bid.
He went and stood on the threshold and saw them all close.
Right away he addressed wingèd words to Odysseus:
495 "Here they are nearby. Let us quickly arm ourselves!"
So he said. They rose up and got their armor on,
Four including Odysseus, and the six sons of Dolios,
And among them Laertes and Dolios put armor on,
Gray though they were, warriors by necessity.
500 And when they had put the glittering bronze round their skin,
They opened the doors and went out; Odysseus led.
Athene, daughter of Zeus, came up close to them,
Likening herself to Mentor in form and in voice.
Godly Odysseus, who had endured much, rejoiced to see her;
505 At once he spoke out to his dear son Telemachos:
"Telemachos, you will soon learn, now you have come yourself
To where men are fighting and the best ones are judged,
Not to disgrace the family of your fathers, who before
Were distinguished for strength and prowess on the whole
    earth."
510 Then sound-minded Telemachos said to him in answer:
"In my present spirit, dear father, you will see, if you wish,

That, as you say, I shall not at all disgrace your family."
So he said, and Laertes rejoiced and spoke a word:
"What a day is this for me, dear gods! I greatly rejoice
That my son and my grandson contend over excellence."   515
Bright-eyed Athene stood beside him and addressed him:
"Son of Arkesios, dearest by far of all my companions,
When you have prayed to the bright-eyed maid and to Father
    Zeus,
Brandish your long-shadowy spear at once and hurl it forth."
So she said, and Pallas Athene breathed great strength into him.   520
Then he prayed to the daughter of the mighty Zeus
And brandished his long-shadowy spear at once and shot it
    forth.
He hit Eupeithes through the bronze cheek piece of his helmet.
This did not keep the spear back; the bronze went right
    through.
He made a crash as he fell, and his armor clattered upon him.   525
Odysseus and his glorious son fell upon the fighters in the front
And struck at them with their swords and their two-edged
    spears.
Now they would have destroyed all and made them without
    return,
If Athene, the daughter of aegis-bearing Zeus, had not
Shouted with her voice and restrained the whole host: 530
"Ithacans, hold off from war, which is disastrous,
So you may separate without bloodshed as soon as you can."
So did Athene say. And sallow fear got hold of them.
As they were afraid, all their arms flew out of their hands
And fell on the ground, as the goddess uttered her voice.   535
They turned back toward the city, longing for life.
Godly Odysseus, who had endured much, shouted dreadfully.
He bunched himself up and swooped down like a high-flying
    eagle.
Then the son of Cronos shot a smoldering thunderbolt.
It fell before the bright-eyed daughter of the mighty father.   540
Then bright-eyed Athene spoke out to Odysseus:
"Zeus-born son of Laertes, Odysseus of many wiles,
Hold off and cease from the strife of impartial war,
Lest Zeus, the broad-seeing son of Cronos, in some way get
    angry."

545 So Athene said. He obeyed, and rejoiced in his heart.
Then Pallas Athene, daughter of aegis-bearing Zeus,
Established oaths for the future between both sides,
Likening herself to Mentor in form and in voice.

GLOSSARY

Achaians a collective appellation of the Greeks besieging Troy
Achilles the captain of the Myrmidons and the greatest hero of the Greeks at Troy
Aeolos lord of the winds
Agamemnon the leader of the Greeks at Troy; killed by Clytemnestra on his return home
Agelaos son of Damastor and a suitor of Penelope
Aiaia the legendary island home of Circe
Aietes the king of Colchis; father of Medea and brother of Circe
Aigisthos the cousin of Agamemnon and lover of Clytemnestra; after Agamemnon's murder, he became king of Mycenae
Ajax (1) son of Telamon; second to Achilles in prowess among the Greeks at Troy
  (2) son of Oileus
Alcinoos grandson of Poseidon; king of the Phaeacians at Scherie
Alcmene the wife of Amphitryon and mother of Heracles
Amphimedon a suitor of Penelope killed by Telemachos
Amphinomos a suitor of Penelope killed by Telemachos
Anticleia the daughter of Autolycos, wife of Laertes, and mother of Odysseus
Antilochos a son of Nestor killed at Troy
Antinoos son of Eupeithes; the ringleader and most insolent of Penelope's suitors
Antiphates king of the Lestrygonians
Antiphos one of Odysseus' crew eaten by the Cyclops
Aphrodite daughter of Zeus; the goddess of love
Apollo son of Zeus and brother of Artemis; the god of sun and light
Ares son of Zeus; the god of war
Arete the queen of the Phaeacians; wife of Alcinoos and mother of Nausicaa
Argos the general name for Agamemnon's kingdom
Artemis daughter of Zeus and sister of Apollo
Athene the goddess of the arts and special patron of Odysseus
Atlas the father of Calypso and the supporter of the pillars of heaven
Autolycos the grandfather of Odysseus

Cadmos founder of Thebes
Calypso a goddess living on Ogygia; daughter of Atlas; Odysseus stays with her for seven years
Charybdis a legendary whirlpool opposite Scylla

Cicones   Thracian allies of the Trojans raided by Odysseus
Circe   an enchantress living in Aiaia; daughter of the sun
Clytemnestra   wife and murderer of Agamemnon
Creon   a king of Thebes
Cronos   one of the older gods; the father of Zeus, Poseidon, Hera, Hades
Cyclopes   a lawless race of giants met by Odysseus

Danaans   like "Achaians," a general designation for the Greeks at Troy
Delos   an Aegean island sacred as the birthplace of Apollo and Artemis
Demodocos   the blind bard of the Phaeacians
Diocles   the son of Ortilochos, living at Pherai
Diomede   the ruler of Argos; a major Greek hero at Troy
Dodona   site of an ancient oracle of Zeus

Elpenor   one of Odysseus' crew; he falls off Circe's roof
Erebos   outer darkness for the dead
Erinyes   goddesses who fulfill curses and avenge crimes
Eumaeos   the faithful swineherd of Odysseus
Eupeithes   the father of Antinoos; killed by Laertes
Euryalos   a Phaeacian youth who taunts Odysseus
Eurycleia   the nurse of Odysseus and housekeeper in his palace
Eurylochos   the chief companion of Odysseus
Eurymachos   a suitor of Penelope's killed by Odysseus
Eurynome   a servant of Penelope's
Eurynomos   an Ithacan suitor of Penelope's

Hades   the god of the underworld
Halitherses   an Ithacan; son of Nestor and friend of Odysseus
Helen   wife of Menelaos; carried off by Paris to Troy
Hephaistos   son of Zeus and husband of Aphrodite; god of fire and the forge
Hera   queen of the gods; wife and sister of Zeus
Hermes   son of Zeus; messenger of the gods and guide of the dead
Hyperion   cognomen of the sun god

Ktesippos   from Samê; one of the suitors of Penelope

Icarios   the father of Penelope
Idomeneus   the grandson of Minos and king in Crete
Ilion   another name for Troy
Iros   nickname of Arnaios, the beggar at Ithaca

Laertes   the father of Odysseus and former king at Ithaca
Laodames   a Phaeacian; son of Alcinoos
Lestrygonians   a tribe of savage giants whose king was Lamos
Leto   the mother of Apollo and Artemis

Megapenthes   an illegitimate son of Menelaos
Melanthios   son of Dolios; the faithless goatherd of Odysseus
Menelaos   brother of Agamemnon and husband of Helen; co-commander of the Greeks at Troy

Mentes king of the Taphians, in whose guise Athene visits Telemachos
Mentor an Ithacan friend of Odysseus, in whose guise Athene guides
  Telemachos to Pylos
Minos legendary king of Crete and a ruler in the underworld
Mycenae the chief city of Homeric Greece and residence of Agamemnon
Myrmidons the followers of Achilles at Troy

Nausicaa Phaeacian princess, the daughter of Alcinoos and Arete
Nausithoos the colonizer of Scherie; son of Poseidon and father of
  Alcinoos
Neleus the founder of Pylos; son of Poseidon and father of Nestor
Nestor the aged king of Pylos and chief adviser for the Greeks at Troy
Nisos father of Amphinomos

Ogygia the legendary island home of Calypso
Oedipos a king of Thebes; son of Laios and Epicaste (in Homer)
Orestes son of Agamemnon; kills Clytemnestra and Aigisthos in aveng-
  ing his father's murder
Orion mighty hunter slain by Artemis; he appears as a constellation
Ortilochos a nobleman living at Pherai

Pallas an epithet of Athene
Patroclos the alter ego of Achilles at Troy; his death inspires Achilles
  to return to battle
Peiraios son of Klytios and companion of Telemachos
Peisander a suitor of Penelope's
Peisistratos Nestor's youngest son; Telemachos' companion on his
  journey to Sparta
Perimedes one of Odysseus' crew
Persephone the daughter of Zeus and Demeter; queen of the under-
  world
Pheidon king of the Thesprotians
Phemios son of Terpis ("Pleasure") and bard at Odysseus' palace
Philoitios the faithful herdsman of Odysseus
Phorcys a lesser sea divinity, the grandfather of the Cyclops
Polybos an Ithacan, the father of Eurymachos; also the name of a
  Phaeacian
Polyphemos a Cyclops, son of Poseidon
Poseidon son of Cronos and brother of Zeus; god of the sea, especially
  hostile toward Odysseus
Priam the aged king of Troy killed by the Greeks

Scylla a monster inhabiting a sea cave opposite Charybdis
Sirens two enchantresses luring sailors to destruction by their songs
Styx "Hateful" river of the underworld

Tiresias the blind seer of Thebes summoned by Odysseus on his visit
  to Hades
Theoclymenos a seer at Ithaca, friend of Telemachos
Theseus the great legendary hero and king of Athens

Thetis   a sea nymph and mother of Achilles

Tyndareus   from Sparta; father of Clytemnestra

Zeus   son of Cronos; king of the gods and specifically the god of the sky and of weather